BLOCKBUSTERS AND TRADE WARS

To David —

love
Peter
Brant

BLOCKBUSTERS

Peter S. Grant & Chris Wood

AND TRADE WARS

POPULAR CULTURE IN A GLOBALIZED WORLD

Douglas & McInytre
VANCOUVER/TORONTO

Douglas & McIntyre Ltd.
2323 Quebec Street, Suite 201
Vancouver, British Columbia
Canada v5T 4S7
www.douglas-mcintyre.com

National Library of Canada Cataloguing in Publication Data
Grant, Peter S., 1941–
    Blockbusters and trade wars: popular culture in a globalized world /
    by Peter S. Grant and Chris Wood.

    Includes index.
    ISBN 1-55365-009-3

    1. Popular culture—Economic aspects. 2. Globalization—Social aspects.
3. Cultural policy. 4. International relations and culture. I. Wood, Chris, 1953– II. Title.
HM621.G72 2004   306   C2003-910773-6

Editing by John Eerkes-Medrano
Jacket design by Peter Cocking
Text design by Peter Cocking
Jacket photograph by Alastair Bird
Printed and bound in Canada by Friesens
Printed on acid-free paper

We gratefully acknowledge the financial support of the Canada Council for the Arts, the British Columbia Arts Council, and the Government of Canada through the Book Publishing Industry Development Program (BPIDP) for our publishing activities.

CONTENTS

PREFACE

As we start a new millennium and notice the signs of globalization around us, there is a curious paradox. In the past few years, we have witnessed an unparalleled expansion in the distribution of books, television programs and other cultural products worldwide. On its face, this would seem to augur well for cultural diversity. There are seemingly more ideas, more pluralistic expression.

But behind this facade of apparent pluralism are disturbing signs. There is a greater concentration of sources of expression. Five huge record companies control more than 70 per cent of dollar volume in sound recordings. Hollywood dominates cinema film screens and floods local television with hard-to-resist drama. The concentration of media is growing apace around the world. It is harder and harder for "independent" producers to survive, whether in the United States or in any country where concentration is increasing. The distribution of cultural products is often in the hands of gatekeepers who reduce choice rather than expand it. In the book field, shorter shelf life and tightened supplier margins from big-box retail stores have increased the sales of bestsellers, led to publisher consolidation and hurt mid-list titles.

In the face of these problems, the public's perception is that nothing can be done. Globalization, aided by borderless technologies like satellite TV and the Internet, has seemingly rendered governments helpless. Quotas are largely considered ineffective or easy to avoid. And in any event, governments arguably cannot be involved in regulating cultural industries without compromising freedom of expression or breaching international trade obligations.

Are these perceptions well founded? Or are they misplaced?

As a Canadian lawyer practising in the area of communications law and cultural policy for the past thirty years, I have had occasion to study these issues in a very practical way. I have acted for broadcasters, satellite and cable TV operators, book publishers, music labels, magazine publishers, film and television producers, talent guilds and copyright collectives.

Canada provides an interesting case study. If globalization can be described as a process in which borders are eliminated and multinational companies can extend their reach across geographical boundaries, Canada has encountered this in the broadcasting field since the 1950s. The signals of U.S. television stations along the U.S.–Canadian border were freely available "off the air" to millions of Canadian homes in the 1950s and were permitted to be carried into homes of cable TV subscribers in communities across Canada in the 1970s. This had a profound effect on Canadian communications and cultural policy and forced Canada to confront, far earlier than most other countries, many of the issues now raised by satellite broadcasting and the global reach of the Internet.

Perhaps as a result, Canada has also had more direct experience in trade disputes in the cultural area than has any other country. Its attempts to carve out a space for its own cultural expression in the face of globalization have been challenged by its neighbour to the south on more than one occasion, and the lessons learned from these encounters provide an illuminating guide to the impact of trade law on culture.

In looking at these issues, I have focused on the field of popular culture—books, magazines, records, movies and broadcasting. This is not a book about arts policy or the performing arts, although the high arts share the same talent pool and often the same media as more mass-oriented expression. In American parlance, the companies that disseminate popular culture are typically categorized as being in the "entertainment" or "leisure" industries (along with gambling and sports). The word "culture" is typically relegated to areas like the ballet, symphonies and other branches of the performing arts, or applied to the area of "folk" or traditional arts and crafts.

But it is in the area of popular culture that globalization has made its most pervasive attack on local cultural expression and led to cries of U.S. dominance. It is also the area where the economic rewards are highest for the successful company, and where those companies are most likely to resort to trade law in order to maximize those rewards.

Two other preliminary points are worth raising.

First, this book is not focused on preserving cultures or on protecting a unique cultural identity. The idea of unique cultures being frozen in time, like flies in amber, has never been realistic. Indigenous cultures are constantly changing, not only in response to outside influences, but also because of internal changes. Modernization is not the same as globalization, and this book does not support suggestions that cultures must be saved harmless from change. In fact, the world of cultural expression is vastly enriched by the free flow of ideas across borders, even when those ideas challenge local cultures. The problem addressed in this book is how to provide space and choice for both domestic and foreign popular culture, not to prohibit the latter.

In the same vein, this book does not take the view of the cultural relativists that no cultural practice should be criticized. There is a huge difference between promoting diverse cultural expression and sanctioning cultural practices. When cultural practices offend human rights and fundamental freedoms, they may be rightfully condemned. But the focus here is on the world of ideas and on the need to make room for alternative expression in a world dominated by blockbusters.

To put a book of this size and scope together, I called on Chris Wood to help me in researching and writing it. Chris, a former senior bureau chief, national editor and business editor for the Canadian newsmagazine *Maclean's,* has wide experience in covering economic and trade issues. That, together with his sense of ironic good humour, kept us on track.

Although much of the book is based on my own experience and research, Chris and I supplemented this with extensive interviews and a survey of the burgeoning literature in this area. Singly or together, we have met with representatives of cultural industries in cities as disparate as Cape Town, Colombo, Paris, London, Frankfurt, Valencia,

Lucerne, Sydney and Rabat, as well as Toronto, Montreal, Vancouver, New York and Los Angeles.

Our research led us to inquire into what *The Economist* has described as the "curious economics" of cultural industries. Why and how do the products of popular culture succeed? Are they any different from ordinary commodities, and if so, how? Does the marketplace for popular culture automatically provide what people want to see or hear, or is it a distorted market? Are government measures that seek to ensure space and choice for underrepresented cultural products, particularly those created by their own nationals, justified? What impact does foreign-ownership policy have on the market for cultural products? How does competition policy affect this market? And, last but not least, what is the impact of trade law on the distribution of popular culture?

The result of our studies was instructive.

In particular, we discovered that there is a compelling economic case for keeping cultural products out of trade agreements that otherwise might preclude countries from maintaining space and choice for local cultural expression. Upon analysis, it becomes startlingly clear that markets for cultural products do *not* behave like those for widgets and that the imposition of trade liberalization rules designed for ordinary commodities would simply institutionalize the stark imbalances that characterize the world of popular culture.

We also learned that contrary to popular opinion, satellites and the Internet are not about to render governments ineffectual or powerless in acting to protect diversity of cultural expression. In fact, a number of structural measures, when properly applied, can be quite effective in maintaining a level of pluralism in cultural expression. This has proven to be true not only in countries around the world but even in the United States, where conventional wisdom disdains any regulatory involvement in programming.

In this book, we describe how the marketplace for popular culture works in practice and how governments around the world have tried to make room for local cultural expression in underrepresented genres. Some of the measures chosen by governments have been badly drafted or largely ineffective, or have had negative effects on freedom of expression. Also, the circumstances of each country differ, and measures that may be effective in one environment may be irrelevant in another.

In looking at all these examples, it is important to stress that we do not support structural measures for their own sake. We are opposed to censorship and to the imposition of prohibitory quotas that do not allow the best of foreign cultural products to be enjoyed by the citizens of every country. Local cultural expression can be impoverished if it is not open to foreign ideas. But it can equally be impoverished if it is dominated by the voices of another country.

In the end, it is possible to put together a "tool kit" of measures that government can implement to sustain or develop a broader range of popular cultural products, without undermining freedom of expression. The measures include support for public broadcasting, the imposition of reasonable scheduling or expenditure requirements on private broadcasters and other cultural gatekeepers, support for the creation of popular works through subsidies or tax incentives, the application of foreign-ownership rules in certain sectors, and the use of competition policy measures. As will be seen, most of these measures have weaknesses as well as strengths, and they need to be carefully drafted and implemented in order to be fair and effective. In addition, the cultural policy appropriate for one society may be quite different from that for another, just as every cultural product is unique.

To illustrate some of these points, we have focused on a particular cultural product: *Degrassi: The Next Generation,* a Canadian drama series for teenagers and young adults. Seen in Canada on the CTV network and around the world on a number of channels, including the ABC in Australia, France 2 in France and Noggin in the United States, the series deals with universal issues of growing up but is uniquely Canadian, taking a slant quite different from that of other programs in its genre. It is a popular program, outperforming most of the competition in its time slot. Yet *Degrassi* would not exist but for the tool kit of measures identified in this book. It is exactly the kind of alternative form of popular culture that would be silenced by the economics of the blockbuster if trade law were permitted to override cultural policy.

We are now in the midst of an international debate on the extent to which this tool kit of cultural policy measures should be affected by bilateral or regional trade agreements or by the multilateral trade regime of the World Trade Organization. UNESCO, having issued a "Universal Declaration on Cultural Diversity" on November 2, 2001, is now considering the development of a "New International Agreement on

Cultural Diversity," which would recognize the unique nature of cultural products and seek to permit government to take reasonable measures to support and enhance diversity of cultural expression without fear of trade retaliation.

That debate seems to pit many countries against positions taken by the United States government and the U.S. entertainment industry. But this is not an anti-American dialogue. In fact, as the following pages shall show, the same factors that create imbalances in the flow of popular culture around the world also impoverish diverse creative expression in the United States. The economics of the blockbuster and the prevalence of gatekeepers is just as problematic for pluralistic expression within the United States as it is outside it. We hope this book will contribute to a better understanding of the issues at stake and of what can be done to address those issues.

PETER S. GRANT
Toronto, 2003

CO-AUTHOR'S
NOTE

WHEN PETER GRANT suggested to me that there might be a book of mutual interest in the economics and public policy of culture, my curiosity was piqued. The economics (and, to a degree, the policy) of the "cultural industries" have scripted much of my professional existence.

I have spent thirty years observing how popular culture is made and sold, but always from the perspective of the fevered places where the stuff is assembled out of raw meat, flogged, sold or put down. In sum: the market.

My first permanent job was at a private radio station. I was a disc jockey. It paid barely above minimum wage. The entirely imaginary notoriety of appearing on the radio attracted an endless supply of potential replacements eager to subsidize a two-digit paycheque with boundless ego gratification. That was a first lesson in the Darwinism of the cultural trades. Lesson two was discovering how quickly compunction fades in the face of few hundred promotional singles begging for air. After the first half dozen, any song that failed to grab inside four bars got yanked before the fifth. Songs that opened on a drum roll didn't make it that far.

Later, with a friend, I launched a radio syndication business. It allowed radio stations to air knowledgeable programs about music without the expense of hiring someone who actually knew about music. Naturally enough, most preferred to go on playing long sweeps of soft favourites with no attempt to inform listeners about anything at all. The business succumbed to the creative destruction of the marketplace.

By 1980, I was earning my living as a freelance magazine writer. Editors (at least those with budgets) received far more proposals on any given day than they commissioned. What they paid, calculated against the time it took to research a topic thoroughly and produce a finished product, was normally laughably less than the minimum wage I had earned a decade earlier in radio. Most people who wrote for publication either did not make a living at it or made a poor one. But there were lots of magazines in Canada and the United States. If you were fast, met deadlines, managed to sell every snippet of research at least twice and had something the next ten guys didn't have, you could earn a living, and not a bad one.

In the mid-1980s, I went to work for Canada's *Maclean's* magazine. Here, each week brought a whole new series of Darwinian judgement days. There was never enough space, and Monday morning conferences squelched most story ideas in the first four bars. Each issue that reached the newsstand then fought for notice among a crushing multitude of other publications.

I have also written a couple of books, as well as a feature film screenplay. (The last has been under option a number of times, a fact that ranks it above 90 per cent of all other scripts while still deep in "no cigar" territory.)

An invitation to write about the market behaviour of broadcasting, popular music, magazines, books and film held immediate interest. It was a chance to put the economics of my own livelihood under a microscope.

The book Peter had in mind would illuminate the troubled intersection of economics and culture. The discussion promised to trace to its source the sour smell of falseness that always seemed to hang about the economic right's crabbed critique of cultural policies. In Canada, that critique has argued that if this country's cultural products have merit, the market will reward them. Not infrequently its advocates go further, asserting that popular Canadian "culture" is at best an artifice, a hot house flower that blooms only when force-fed on subsidies. The demeaning corollary, only relatively more rarely stated, is that Canadian creators—those, at any rate, who aren't in New York or California—are at best mediocre, coddled by "protectionist" policies.

I know the market. Let me tell you, it has never felt very protected, let alone coddled. But the disconnect is really between the critique and the evidence.

"Culture" is an elusive term. But each year hundreds of millions of purchases of Canadian books and magazines, of recordings by Canadian musicians and admissions to films, as well as hours of couch-time spent with Canadian TV, confirm that Canada has it—and that Canadians treasure it.

Yet it is also true that many publishers and music labels, television and film producers, in Canada and elsewhere, flirt with insolvency. Too many cultural nationalists like to blame this on the American imperium, a kind of culturo-corporate conspiracy seldom fully articulated but always represented as vastly powerful and, usually, malignant. This is as far removed from reality as are the Jeremiads of the right.

As Peter shared the fruits of many years' reflection and study, two things became clear. First: *why* the critiques of Canada's cultural marketplace fail to describe reality. And second, the alarming possibility that their misperceptions might soon become embedded in international law.

Bringing both insights to wider public view was an undertaking I readily embraced. Peter's wide-ranging curiosity and ready grace made the work an unexpected pleasure.

Whatever problems plague the market for popular Canadian culture, they have little to do with the products of that culture or their producers. They are not even peculiarly *Canadian*. They have everything to do with the unique economic behaviour of cultural products in general. That behaviour and its negative consequences are as evident in the United States as anywhere. The failure belongs to the market, not to the culture.

That is good to know. But the concern it raises should trouble not only cultural creators or those who work in, regulate or consult to the "industry" of culture. It should trouble us all, because culture, at the end of the day, belongs to each of us.

CHRIS WOOD

PART ONE

CULTURAL ECONOMICS

1

DISTINCT
VOICES

UGUST IN CANADA is the laziest month. Families who can, retreat from the city to cottage or campground. Politicians take to the barbecue circuit to mingle with the masses. Many industries cycle down into a state of somnolent semi-hibernation to give employees a chance to recharge their batteries on beaches or in the backyard. And in cities, suburbs and small towns across the country, classrooms fall silent.

Except here. On this sun-baked weekday morning in early August 2002, the kids of Degrassi Junior High are hard at work.

The school, mind you, is fictional. In real life, the bland brick-and-glass facade tucked into a treed corner of an industrial park in northeast Toronto conceals the studios, sound stages and discreet backlot of Epitome Pictures Inc., a television production company. Still, it is a safe bet that *Degrassi* is better known around the globe than any more authentic centre of learning in Canada.

Since it opened its doors in 1979 as the setting for the youthful conflicts, coming-of-age torments and weekly victories of an ethnically mixed batch of Canadian teenagers—first in *The Kids of Degrassi Street* (1979–86), then as *Degrassi Junior High* (1987–89) and later *Degrassi High* (1989–91)—the fictional middle school has been piped into living rooms in dozens of countries around the world. Across town at

CTV, one of the country's two private, English-language free-to-air networks, the latest incarnation of the long-running franchise, *Degrassi: The Next Generation,* is the highest-rated show among the most coveted viewers in its Wednesday evening time slot. In the United States, *Degrassi* is the year's highest-rated show on the kids-oriented Noggin cable specialty channel. The second-generation *Degrassi* gang is popular in Australia, Europe and Indonesia.

The series' compassionate but candid parables of coming-of-age in a complicated time have the knack of engaging audiences across cultural back fences very far removed from those of Degrassi Street. In Scandinavia, the original episodes were ratings winners among 1980s teens; now those fans have children of their own. Local broadcasters have built high hopes on them for the launch of *The Next Generation* later in 2002. In the People's Republic of China, Epitome president Linda Schuyler recalls, her mother's tour translator knew precisely two things about Canada: "Bethune! Degrassi!"

On this particular morning, current cast members "Ashley," "Paige," "Spinner" and "Fareeza" work through the morning's shooting schedule in one of Epitome's hallways—lined with school lockers to double as a *Degrassi* set. In a nearby classroom set equipped with folding tables arranged in a large open rectangle, the show's production staff holds a faculty meeting of sorts to discuss production glitches that might hinder the shooting of an upcoming episode.

Director Anais Granofsky leads the discussion. A regular player on the original *Kids of Degrassi,* Granofsky will make her series debut behind the camera on this episode. She cares deeply that everything go well.

One scene fills her with misgivings.

The episode finds *Degrassi* celebrating an International Day, a ritual familiar to any contemporary school-age urban Canadian—or the parent of one. It is intended to celebrate, mainly in the innocuous imagery of costumes and cuisine, the many faiths, nations, languages and colours represented in *Degrassi's* halls.

The goodwill turns sour when someone vandalizes the display that Fareeza has made, shattering a casserole and defacing the flag of her native country. Suspicion falls on Hazel, who has been taunting Fareeza for her conservative hijab head shawl. (A researcher off to Granofsky's right confirms the details of the garment that wardrobe needs to provide.) At this point in the script, Principal Raditch—dressed for the occasion in a Scottish kilt—calls both girls into his office.

It is here that Granofsky gets worried. How much authority can the actor playing the principal be expected to muster over bare knees? "I'm a little concerned it might be comical," she suggests.

"Are you saying Scottish people can't be serious?" Schuyler fires back.

"It was a red flag," insists the director, herself a confident bi-ethnic mix of Caucasian Canadian Jew and African-American.

Good-natured banter ensues about the authority quotient of men in skirts, the proper requirements of formal Scottish attire and the hazards of reverse political correctness. In the end, the knees stay bare. Scottish dignity will have to stand on its own.

Still, the question is hardly a frivolous one. *Degrassi* prides itself on living up to multiple mandates—and counts for its popularity on a form of multiple identity. *Degrassi*'s core audience is Canadian urban teens—a group as likely to have been born in Xuzhou or Mumbai as in Manitoba. The real and figurative streets of Canada's major cities— Toronto, Montreal, Calgary and Vancouver—are the most ethnically diverse on earth. They bring a new challenge to the central task of adolescents everywhere: forging an identity solid enough to carry them through adulthood.

Degrassi's mostly twentysomething writers are keenly aware of how easily the raw teenage sense of selfhood can be bruised. And how quickly that can trigger turnoff. Getting the note just right in many accents is critical to the popularity of the series, both in and beyond Canada.

A straight-on treatment of the facts of adolescent life is another quality the show takes pride in. *Degrassi* got its start on the CBC, Canada's public broadcaster, where Schuyler served an apprenticeship in children's educational programming. Although the show now is distributed mainly on commercial networks, it continues to deal with subjects other youth series find risky. An earlier *Next Generation* episode dealt with the embarrassment of a girl caught off guard by her first menstrual cycle, a moment dramatized onscreen with a visibly stained dress. Another concerned an adolescent boy's humiliation over an involuntary erection. Others have dealt with teen pregnancies, drinking, gender stereotyping and the temptation of drug use.

The trick in pushing the boundaries of acceptability lies in knowing how the lines shift around among *Degrassi*'s many audiences. "Some of them have trouble with some of the issues," Schuyler concedes over roast chicken and Greek salad in the studio commissary/ *Degrassi* cafeteria.

Flashpoints vary. "Canadians are more liberal than [viewers] practically anywhere else," Schuyler says. In Britain, broadcasters fret equally over portrayals of youthful sexuality and violence. Australians are relatively at ease with the sex—but not the violence. In the United States, violence ruffles very few feathers but depictions of dating across racial lines raise executive alarm. "If I responded to every distributor's concern," Schuyler says, "our kids would not be drinking, would not be driving without licences, would not be trying drugs, getting raped. They would not be doing any of these things that kids do."

"We might as well be producing a show for Disney," Schuyler sniffs.

And that is very clearly not what she has in mind. There is a grown-up subtext to her teen parables. When it came time to give a nationality to Fareeza, the girl whose gymnasium display is vandalized, Schuyler says, "It was very conscious that we chose Iraq"—a country likely to be at war with the land of Disney by the time the episode goes to air.

"But if you notice," Schuyler adds, "there was no reference to 9/11."

WELL-CRAFTED, elegantly produced and a proven hit with a lucrative young demographic, *Degrassi* would seem like a shoe-in for a spot on almost any broadcast schedule. Most certainly in Canada, where its values of candour, social tolerance and a respectful distance from the preoccupations of the superpower to the south all ring with the authenticity of a distinctly Canadian voice.

Relevance. Popularity. Quality. Surely this show has everything it needs to make it on its own in the marketplace.

But no.

Markets are not everywhere and always the same. Some are more perfect than others. And some are not perfect at all, producing results that confound not only expectations but the reasonable desires of their participants.

Such is the case with the products of popular culture, products whose value lies in their creative, expressive and symbolic content.

Left to the marketplace, *Degrassi* would simply not exist. Canadian teens and young adults might be watching a high school drama on Sunday nights, but that drama would be *Boston Public* or a remake of *Beverly Hills 90210*. Its stories might well portray the dilemmas of adolescence, but its lens would be that of another society with its own views on cultural differences, the balance of acceptable sex and violence and relations with a problematic world. The Canadian voice on those issues that *Degrassi* represents would not be heard.

This is not a presumptive assertion. It is the cold consequence of the mathematics of the market. In business, profit trumps popularity. And who can argue with that? What is seldom understood outside the executive offices of entertainment companies, however, is that profit does not necessarily follow popularity in lockstep. In the peculiar market of popular culture, the most popular offering is often not the most profitable one. And in the case of adolescent drama series for television, not even being the number one hit in its time slot with a sought-after age group would be enough to get *Degrassi* on the air in its own country.

This is, of course, hugely counterintuitive. There have never been more television channels than there are today. There have never been more books. The entire world seems overwhelmed by creative expression of every tone, note, persuasion and bent. The post-industrial experience, some argue, is almost nothing but idea and emotion: the "information society," "knowledge workers," "the creative class." Certainly for the professional person in a developed country—the most likely reader of this book—among the greatest challenges of daily life is simply keeping up with the flood tide of expressions vying for attention and response: e-mail, proliferating media in every form (especially electronic), advertising spreading insatiably to every available surface.

How, in all of this, can there be *any* creative idea that is denied an opportunity to assault us?

Yet that is precisely the paradox which concerns us. Amid this apparent plenty of media and message, the spiritual and intellectual nourishment that comes only from a true variety of cultural diet is increasingly neglected. Behind the walls of best sellers and multiplex screens exhibiting the latest blockbuster once every quarter-hour, other voices, in their rich and necessary diversity, are obscured and at risk of fading into the silence and dark.

More and more movies, books and music pass through fewer and fewer hands on their way from creator to consumer, as corporate conglomerates increasingly dominate the world's commercial culture. This relative handful of conglomerates and the even more ubiquitous calculus of maximum return quite rationally seek to eliminate all but the most highly profitable of creative expressions from circulation. Mere value to an audience or even merely modest profits do not measure up against maximizing value to shareholders.

A MATH LESSON from *Degrassi* illustrates how the peculiar economics of popular culture defy intuition.

The show's popularity—in economic terms, consumer demand for it—is not in question. In Canada in 2002–2003, viewers aged 12–34 chose *Degrassi* over all other programs on the air in its time slot. Among girls aged 12–17, an astonishing one in four of all viewers were tuned to *Degrassi* on those nights. The show's national reach was greater than that of any other Canadian drama series.

But in the labyrinth of bottlenecks and surprise off-screen gatekeepers that characterize markets for culture, audiences do not decide what television programs to buy and put on the air. Broadcasters do.

Now consider the arithmetic facing CTV's acquisition executives as they chose what program rights to buy for broadcast.

For the right to air two episodes of *Degrassi*—sixty minutes of programming—Epitome's price to CTV was C$252,000. In 2002, that was about US$165,000.

Alternatively, CTV could buy Canadian rights to one of many dramas already produced for U.S. audiences, heavily promoted on U.S. channels widely seen in Canada—and available for US$50,000.

What explains the threefold difference?

Certainly not the sums spent to produce the programs. Epitome spends the equivalent of US$750,000 to create an hour of its teen drama—low by North American standards. In the United States, television series producers typically lavish US$2 million on a one-hour drama —and frequently spend more.

There are evident reasons for the difference. In general, creators of cultural wares in English-speaking Canada can hope to amortize their costs across a potential audience of, at best, about 23 million people; in French Canada, barely 7 million. U.S. creators have a potential audience of 300 million people.

That is reflected in what networks pay for broadcast rights in each country. U.S. networks typically pay US$1.4 million for an hour of series drama—eight and a half times what CTV pays for *Degrassi.*

That alone might give U.S. shows an advantage, if enough of the extra money ends up "on the screen." It could instead go to stars whose performance might, or might not, reflect the extra "rent" they collect. There is no shortage of expensive flops to make the case that big budgets do not necessarily overcome a lame script or limp acting.

Yet such are the looking-glass economics of popular culture that whatever its quality, when this expensively produced U.S. program arrives on a buyer's desk in Canada—or anywhere else after its first sale—its price will be a small fraction of its original cost.

Later in the book we will return to the peculiar ways that creative goods behave in the marketplace. As we will see, taken together they confound every assumption on which market fundamentalists rely. These effects are not U.S.-specific. Nor do they depend on the merit— or otherwise—of any particular film, book or CD. They are true of all symbolic goods and producers.

It is enough to note here one of the most important of these peculiarities, well explained by *The Wall Street Journal.* "Intellectual-property based businesses," Alan Murray observed in the bible of capitalism, "behave differently from others. Their costs are concentrated upfront—in artistic creation, or research and development. The costs of actually 'making' the product—discs of the hottest new recording, for instance—are minimal."

This point is critical. For creators of popular culture, it means that once the first copy of any work is paid for, more copies—to say nothing of exhibiting an existing copy for broadcast—cost next to nothing. Or, to put it another way: once any television program's production cost is recovered, additional rights can be sold for any price above zero—*and still make a profit.*

Armed with this peculiar advantage among others, international media vendors put before program buyers offers that they frequently cannot refuse. If it were simply a matter of price, says Stephen Stohn, Schuyler's husband and business partner, "no rational broadcaster could afford to pay the full cost of *Degrassi,* even if it were drawing three times as much audience."

How then does *Degrassi* get made at all? In part, because CTV pays three times for the Canadian show what it would for a U.S. import. Its motive for doing this is clearly not commercial; it arises from conditions attached to CTV's broadcast licence. Advances on export sales, investor equity and Epitome's own risk capital cover another two-fifths. The rest is financed through funds raised from mandated levies on cable and satellite TV distributors to support Canadian drama, tax credits and government subsidies.

Quality makes *Degrassi* popular. But in the paradoxical market for works of the creative imagination, popularity alone did not make it possible. What did that was policy: a tool-kit of measures Canada has enacted to level the stage and secure its citizens' rights to tell their own stories—whether in words, music or moving images.

SUCH PERVERSE EFFECTS are not limited to Canada. They are artifacts of all creative products in every country. Accumulating and mutually reinforcing each other over time, they produce a marketplace of expression in which the megaphone of the blockbuster increasingly drowns out the whispers of the independent, the alternative, the local and the marginal.

This is not an academic or theoretical concern. "Culture" is what makes us who we are, as individuals and as societies. The products of cultural creators—songs, stories told in print or on a screen—provide the templates of our lives. Free access to the fullest variety of expression is not a social luxury. It is the very substance of freedom.

More than that, cultural expression is the essence of how we imagine our way into the future. Circumstances change. We adapt or perish—one and all. And neither societies nor individuals adapt without a capacity for self-discovery, an ability to orient themselves to the forces around them. That is the irreplaceable function of culture: to exchange our visions of ourselves and of how we fit with others, to help us each navigate towards our complex hopes, dreams and destinies.

But the making of culture is also an industry. Its business is transacted in markets. This is not a matter of choice, either. The most potent expressions of culture, because they touch the greatest numbers of people, are those of mass-market books, popular recorded music, commercial movies and television. These forms of popular culture are products of commercial enterprises. Their production shares features with other large industrial undertakings: a need for substantial physical and financial resources, the requirement for many specialized material and human inputs, the capacity for mass-produced units of sale that reach mass audiences.

And yet, what is sought and bought by the individual members of those audiences is not really a product in the physical sense at all. It is an experience. The object of a consumer's desire is not a stack of paper between cardboard covers marked up with ink, even less a shiny plastic disc or strip of celluloid an inch and a half wide and a mile long. What we value is the ephemeral transfer of an imagined life from the author's mind to our own, the few minutes of emotion provoked by a song, or the hour and a half we spend in another world conjured up by coloured light moving across a screen.

Beyond these paradoxes are deeper currents at work in the contemporary world. "Culture" is increasingly viewed as both a field of economic competition and a vector of power. In the post-industrial regions of the globe, it is an engine of great wealth. In other regions, where modernity is either a still-distant goal or even actively resisted, many authorities denounce the creative expressions of "developed" nations as moral time bombs, threatening to replace proud traditions with a plastic monoculture of consumerism.

As advocates of global economic liberalization seek to bring every nation into the ambit of trade agreements, others fear an erosion of identity and seek shelter behind the bulwarks of culture. "Peoples and nations are attempting to answer the most basic question humans can face: Who are we?" Samuel P. Huntington writes in *The Clash of Civilizations: Remaking the World Order.* "And they are answering that question in the traditional way . . . by reference to the things that mean most to them . . . ancestry, religion, language, history, values, customs and institutions. They identify with cultural groups: tribes, ethnic groups, religious communities, nations, and, at the broadest level, civilizations."

"Previously isolated peoples are being brought together voluntarily and involuntarily by the increasing integration of markets . . . and remarkable advances in telecommunications," says Diana Ayton-Shenker in an analysis for the United Nations of human rights and cultural diversity. "The resulting confluence of peoples and cultures is an increasingly global, multicultural world brimming with tension, confusion, and conflict in the process of adjustment to pluralism."

These conflicts of interest and perception have come together on a global stage, where diplomatic and commercial actors are playing out a drama whose implications for the diversity of popular culture are immense and whose denouement is far from clear. Canada is not alone in recognizing that markets left to the law of the jungle do not necessarily serve audiences well. To the contrary: virtually every other country with a functioning market economy—including the United States of America—has taken steps to secure better order in those markets and happier outcomes for their creators and citizens. Those measures have been resoundingly successful. In many countries, a vibrant diversity of local and foreign creative expressions compete for time, attention, and discretionary spending. But those measures are now under attack.

Global trade negotiations, captive to misplaced faith in the undifferentiated equivalence of conventional and cultural products, have placed at risk the tool kit of measures that dozens of the world's countries have used successfully to secure their citizens' rights to have their own voices heard.

That story is too easily portrayed as casting the United States against other countries. What is true is that U.S. administrations have long forcefully advocated a view of culture that is strongly in the interest of that country's big corporations—even as it has been at variance with the evidence of the marketplace, with America's own experience and even, frequently, with its actions. That view asserts that culture is nothing more than entertainment, as one American critic defines it: "the act of diverting, amusing, or causing someone's time to pass agreeably." Products of cultural expression, in this view, simply serve consumer demand for diversion, amusement and time-passing. In themselves they are no more meaningful than a ham sandwich or a fishing rod. Hence, they may be treated in trade law and international commitments just as ham, bread or fishing rods are treated.

This equation of creative expressions of the ephemeral interplay of self and society with ham and cheese is simple-minded on its face. It is also not what the empirical evidence of the market confirms or the actions of successive generations of American industry and U.S. governments reflect. Even so, it has a strong currency in the arguments advanced for extending the conventions of "liberalized" economic theory, as expressed in global trade agreements, to the expressions of popular culture.

IT IS THIS DUAL NATURE of *culture as idea* and *culture as commerce*, this Janus face of art and industry, that renders our subject so challenging.

Like that dilemma of subatomic physics—you can discern the electron's charge, or where it is, but *not both at the same time*—commercial culture eludes both full and precise definition. Policy-makers who assume it can be analyzed like any other commodity are as confounded by the irrepressible unpredictability of audiences as investors seeking to plot the payback curve of art. This is the paradox we hope, in the balance of this book, to begin to understand and resolve.

Chapter 2 begins at the root of the problem by examining where popular culture comes from in the first instance, and why cultural production and decision-making tend to cluster in only a few centres. Chapter 3 looks closely at the "curious economics" of the production and distribution of popular culture to understand why the marketplace for popular culture is quite different from that for ordinary commodities. Chapter 4 examines two of the most important anomalies of popular culture, namely, the unpredictability of demand and the question of why advertising and promotion are so necessary to achieve success. Chapter 5 then explores the disproportionate advantage of size in the field of popular culture, and how this has led to an increasing tyranny of market concentration in distribution. This discussion sheds instructive light on the nature of the problem we face: how the rise of a "blockbuster" mentality and an illusory plenty in popular media can coexist with the reality of cultural malnourishment in a world where gatekeepers control shelf space.

At the centre of this paradox is the inescapable fact that commercial culture is both industry and art. The nature of its products as "goods" is at war with their nature as "stories," which contain value only when infused with meaning by an audience's emotional, psychological, religious, social and political state of mind. Songs are not hammers. Cultural goods are not widgets. Chapter 6 explores this interplay of national context and economic exchange in the global trade in popular culture to unravel how price discrimination leads to trade domination.

Part Two of the book examines in closer detail the policy tools that have historically been used to provide choice and space for underrepresented cultural expression. We canvass the effectiveness of each in light of the experience of their application in Canada and other markets. Chapter 7 examines the problem of identifying the nationality of a product of popular culture, and the ways in which various countries have approached the matter. Chapter 8 explores the record and potential of public broadcasting for promoting cultural diversity. Chapter 9 looks at where content scheduling quotas succeed—and where they fail. Chapter 10 investigates whether regulations that mandate private-sector spending on underrepresented programming can promote diversity. Chapter 11 examines the impact of foreign-ownership policy. Chapter 12 looks into the application of competition law and policy as possible levers to restrain the cultural tyranny of conglomerates and gatekeepers. Chapter 13 presents the evidence for and against the use of direct public subsidies in preserving market space for the human story in all its richness. Finally, Chapter 14 addresses a number of criticisms that are sometimes levelled against these policy tools.

Part Three looks forward to the future. Chapter 15 examines whether the tool kit of measures that have been effective until now is doomed to irrelevance, as many critics contend, by "borderless technologies" like satellite broadcasting and the Internet. Chapter 16 examines the impact of existing and prospective international trade agreements on popular culture. In particular, it explores how some disciplines currently being advocated may imperil the capacity of national governments to deploy effective cultural policies. Chapter 17 puts forward the outline of a new international instrument that might protect the ability of governments to deliver what is surely any regime's most fundamental obligation: to preserve its citizens' freedom and capacity to be who they are. Finally, Chapter 18 returns to the problem confronting programs like *Degrassi* and the urgency of giving such creative expression room to grow.

But this has all been by way of overture. Let us get on to the soul of the story.

2

CREATIVE
CLUSTERS

M ORE THAN twenty-five years ago, in July 1976, one of us was visiting the Inuit community of Pangnirtung, on Baffin Island, just below the Arctic Circle. At the local lodge he encountered the least expected of fellow travellers: a film crew working for Eon Productions Ltd.

A documentary for *National Geographic*, perhaps?

No. The crew had just finished shooting the climax of the opening sequence in the tenth James Bond film, *The Spy Who Loved Me,* starring Roger Moore and financed by United Artists.

In this famous sequence, Bond appears to be skiing high in the Alps, chased by a horde of sharpshooting skiers. All appears hopeless as Bond skis along the top of a mountain plateau. But the mountain runs out. Bond skis off a steep cliff into mid-air. He begins falling. There are fully twenty seconds of soundless free fall, during which Bond's skis come off. Suddenly he sprouts a parachute covered with a colourful Union Jack. A close-up shows Bond gently descending, a weary but bemused smile on his face. The opening credits begin to roll over Carly Simon's rendition of "Nobody Does It Better," possibly the best-known of all the Bond themes.

It is an astounding sequence, still ranked among the ten best action stunts ever captured on film. To achieve it, the producers needed a mountain with a long ledge ending in a sharp cliff and a sheer drop of over a mile. One of the few mountains fitting this description is Asgard Peak in Auyuittuq National Park on Baffin Island, just north of Pangnirtung. Stuntman Rick Sylvester received $30,000 to do the stunt, out of a total budget for the film of US$13.7 million. He and the film crew had waited ten days for the wind to die down. When the weather cleared briefly, they shot the footage in a single take with no rehearsal.

The 35 mm film had been airlifted to Los Angeles for processing. The crew stood by in the lodge, waiting for a phone call to tell them whether the shot had been successful or if they would need to go back and do it again. The good news came late in the day. Every camera but one had lost sight of Sylvester shortly after he plunged off the ledge. However, a single second-unit camera had managed to film the whole plunge.

The next day, saying goodbye to Sylvester and the crew, the writer toured the community of Pangnirtung. It is a small place, with barely a thousand inhabitants and only a few hundred buildings, huddled between an icy fjord and a mountain range. One of the buildings is home to a unique centre of cultural production, now called the Uqqurmiut Centre for Arts & Crafts.

Inuit art, sometimes still referred to as Eskimo art, is world famous for its striking soapstone carvings of traditional people, polar bears, walruses, drum dancers and shamans. It is also known for its distinctive prints and drawings and small craft items, displayed in art galleries around the world. The community of Pangnirtung is home to a surprising number of internationally recognized Inuit carvers, graphic artists and tapestry weavers.

Printmaking is a Pangnirtung specialty. Every year the Uqqurmiut Centre publishes a series of limited-edition prints. The designs are captivating and ever-changing. How they come to be is almost equally intriguing as a reflection of Inuit society. Annually, every adult and child in Pangnirtung is invited to submit a design on traditional subjects. They receive a nominal sum for each drawing. Hundreds are submitted. A committee selects a dozen of the most compelling drawings and uses them as the basis for a series of finished images. Limited editions of hand-reproduced prints are sold in galleries round the world; the images also appear in a mass-produced annual calendar.

During the filming that July, Pangnirtung witnessed the production of popular culture from opposite ends of a very wide spectrum. At one end were its own talented printmakers, at the other was the visiting Hollywood-financed film crew—but both groups could be said to be part of the "cultural industries."

Making paper images of Inuit life and legend might seem very far from being an industry. But to succeed, it requires sophisticated production techniques, a financing structure that imposes quality control on the selection of subject matter and a distribution system to market and sell the resulting cultural products worldwide. The same is true for the most expensive form of popular culture, the blockbuster feature film, of which the Bond series is the exemplar. The difference is in degree, not in kind.

But clearly, cultural industries are not evenly distributed around the globe. We start our inquiry into the economics of popular culture, then, by asking why this is so. Why do cultural industries tend to locate in certain places and not in others? Why, in particular, is Hollywood so dominant in the creation of blockbuster movies, and not some other city, like Seattle? Why is a certain sector of the music industry located in Nashville and not Peoria? Why do book publishers congregate not only in particular cities, but on particular streets in cities?

POPULAR CULTURE, it must be remembered, is a team sport. True, some stages of the modern manufacture of cultural products remain comparatively solitary. The initial creator, whether of prints, books, songs or screenplays, may work alone. But bringing his or her product to its eventual audience requires the input of numerous other specialists and considerable sums of money, in addition to the cash value of whatever time the creator has invested.

Take the oldest and most basic mass-produced cultural good: the book. Once written, it is generally edited by someone skilled in a craft quite different from that of original composition. Whether it is to appear in hardcover or paperback, someone with an eye for visual effect must design the front and back covers; designers devote some thought as well to the appearance of the text. Typesetting is no longer the specialized occupation it was in the days of printers' devils, but even computer-set type profits from a proofreader. Printing and binding are industrial processes that are mainly automated, but the machines that do the work cost millions of dollars and their owners rely on enormous print runs to justify the investment. Once printed, books must be distributed and (authors hope) promoted, tasks that demand further specialized skills.

Much the same process applies to creating a sound recording, with the additional complication that the composer's work must be brought off the page and transformed into actual music. Occasionally since the advent of digital recording, a musician bypasses this necessity by operating a computer to render files that can be transferred directly to a compact disc. But this is the exception. More often it involves actual musicians with warm bodies and real instruments making melodies in a performance hall or recording studio. If the work is choral or symphonic, these performers and instruments may number in the hundreds. Even a studio recording by a nominally solo artist frequently entails the work of a dozen or more sidemen and session musicians. A specialized sound engineer and producer are also part of the team that creates the finished "master"—the equivalent of the author's manuscript. The packaging, mass dubbing, distribution and promotion of a commercially released CD all roughly parallel the requirements of book publishing.

Magazines, because they involve so many contributors, fall closer to the complexity of sound recordings than to books, with the additional challenge of meeting recurring and often very tightly timed production deadlines.

Movies and television increase by at least another order of magnitude the team effort and capital needed to make a finished cultural product. A good sound-recording studio can be contained in a closet, and many an album has been laid down in a musician's basement. Filmed drama or comedies that aspire to commercial release consume vastly greater resources. The staff list for the *Degrassi* series—modest by North American standards—runs to more than seventy people. A mid-sized feature film may have a cast and production crew—not counting extras, outside suppliers and studio overhead—of several hundred.

They include the handful familiar to most moviegoers or couch potatoes: stars and supporting actors, writers and directors. Others belong to crafts that figure further down the credit list: directors of photography, art and set decorators, casting supervisors, props masters, makeup artists and costume designers. Some have curious titles:

grips (in charge of camera dollies and anything else that moves on a set) and gaffers (in charge of lighting and whatever plugs in). Then there are trades that few associate primarily with show business at all: carpenters who construct sets and the painters who paint them, electricians, teamsters who drive the vehicles that carry cast and equipment to and from every unionized location shoot, caterers who keep the commissary stocked. Then there are some whose very existence is unknown outside the business. Continuity supervisors make sure the outfit Julia Roberts wears as she enters a motel from the outside matches what she wears inside, in a scene filmed days later. Stand-ins take the place of higher-paid actors when a scene is being blocked out for the purposes of lighting and camera angles. Wranglers keep track of the whereabouts of all the rest of a sprawling production crew.

Then there are the people who may contribute only briefly, but significantly, to a production: day-players on television series, animal handlers, providers of vintage automobiles to period pieces, stuntmen and stuntwomen, voice coaches, special-effects creators. Still others begin their role only when principal photography ends: film editors, composers, post-production supervisors.

For a film or television show to romance an audience and meet its timetable and budget (at least as important to the producers backing it), every one of those many people must perform to at least a minimal standard of competence. To lift a show above the noise, a significant number must perform at a level well above the merely competent. It will not suffice for only the star to sizzle, the director to know her craft or the script to be well constructed. All the parts must work well on their own and, ideally, even better together.

Prints and books are by far the cheapest cultural good to produce; filmed entertainment is by far the most expensive. Books, requiring fewer inputs, are also the easiest to produce to a competitive competence. Scripted film or television drama (even more than comedy) is correspondingly the hardest to "get right."

Access to the many and varied skills required for these team efforts implies a corollary condition: that each specialist enjoys enough work to stay in business and keep in practice. If lighting designers cannot make at least a minimal living, they will eventually be forced to find other work. If they cannot work often enough, their skills will atrophy or at least fail to develop. Their contribution to whatever production they do work on will likely fail to achieve the necessary minimal standard, pulling down the collective result—however skillful the other contributions to the common effort may be.

These multiple skills also cost money—frequently exorbitant amounts of it. Taken together, the subjective requirement for hot talent and the concomitant need for cold cash have a major bearing on where cultural industries locate.

Economists like Michael Porter—who pioneered the notion of "cluster theory"—have articulated the market mechanisms that encourage industries to coalesce in certain places. They would call the locally concentrated critical mass of available work and available crew a "thick market." In thick markets, there is enough regular work to support many providers of each specialty, whether they be book editors, sound engineers or set dressers. As a result, when producers undertake a new project, they have a choice of suitably skilled workers to select from.

Thick markets of specialized suppliers tend to have a wealth of relevant "back and forth linkages"—a broad supply of many specialties. Hence producers of complex creative goods such as filmed entertainment can find not only *all* of the varied specialists they require for a given project—set dressers, grips and gaffers—but also a *choice* of suppliers of any given specialty.

A related mechanism in the formation of industrial clusters further illuminates why many creators congregate in particular places to produce the complex products of commercial culture. This is the effect first noted by the classical economist Alfred Marshall more than a century ago. He suggested that industrial districts arise in part because of "knowledge spillover." Although Marshall was never able to model the phenomenon in mathematical terms, he believed propinquity encouraged an informal but economically significant exchange of trade information. As he put it: "The mysteries of the trade become no mysteries but are, as it were, in the air." A non-economist might think of it as the propensity for people in the same business to talk shop in social situations or the value of networking. Cheekier analysts have identified it as "that constant and necessary industry database known as gossip."

The spillover effect goes beyond the direct participants in creative enterprise. It embraces those satellite activities that, while not strictly necessary to the production of cultural goods, nonetheless support, serve or exploit the producers. They include managers and agents who represent authors, actors, musicians and sometimes other in-demand craft specialists; concert promoters and impresarios; contract publicists who hire on to individual productions or concert tours; book, music and film reviewers; trade journalists and the publications that employ them; celebrity scribes and paparazzi photographers. For this demimonde, proximity is the key to access, and access next to godliness.

The requirement for a sophisticated production infrastructure and the impact of knowledge spillover go far to explain why cultural industries tend to agglomerate in only a few centres. But another factor also contributes powerfully to this result, one unique to the field of cultural industries: the "A-list" effect.

The phenomenon was first observed in the field of performing arts, where it is also referred to as the superstar effect. The emergence of a small number of supernova performers, it is theorized, has less to do with their talent than with other factors. Most consumers have difficulty remembering more than two or three names in any specific performing genre, but thanks to recording media they can select those few from a global talent pool. The social benefits derived from discussing well-known artists with friends may exceed the solitary pleasure of appreciating a less-known performer even if she is more talented. All these factors lead demand to concentrate on a few select artists (the A-list) in each field of popular culture. Thus, very small differences in innate ability may result in very large differences in popularity and incomes.

OVER THE DECADES, various cities have been centres of critical mass and cluster economies for different forms of popular culture. Vienna at the end of the nineteenth century was such a centre for classical music and opera. London of the same era was a centre of staged entertainment and book publishing. By the mid-twentieth century, New York had eclipsed London on both counts, and it remains today the English-speaking capital of the musical stage and America's epicentre of publishing and television news media. In its somewhat smaller universe of country music, there is only one Nashville.

But no production capital of any contemporary cultural genre comes close to rivalling the dominance that Los Angeles exerts over moviemaking. Los Angeles County (which embraces Hollywood and

Burbank as well as the eponymous city) is the undisputed nine-hun-
dred-pound gorilla, the original King Kong (it invented the metaphor)
of filmed entertainment. Vienna in its day served Europe. London
served the Empire. Nashville serves North America. L.A.'s celluloid fantasies light up the entire planet. "To be on the same playing field with
everyone else," Canadian actor Eugene Levy tells aspiring thespians,
"you have to do it in L.A., because that's just where it happens."

Although the numbers go up and down, American movies have typically commanded 80 per cent (and often much more) of world big-
screen revenue; U.S. television fiction programs a 70 per cent share.
Seventy per cent of the filming happens in Los Angeles, ten times the
amount done in the next-largest U.S. centre of New York City and *six
times* the *combined* production of the next four English-language
countries with film industries—Canada, the United Kingdom, Australia and New Zealand.

Why does Hollywood rule the field of blockbuster films? The answer, like movies themselves, turns out to involve a little bit of light,
some more luck and a lot of money.

The first moving pictures, like the first audio recordings, came from
the prolific laboratory of Thomas Alva Edison. Viewers peeped into a
darkened box to watch a few seconds of moving images with limited
plot. One snippet showed a mustachioed gent taking a pinch of snuff
and sneezing, another a ballerina twirling once. Nonetheless crowds
flocked to Edison's first "kinetoscope" parlour, opened in 1894.

A kinetoscope could entertain only one person at a time. Auguste
and Louis Lumiere soon overcame that hurdle. The French brothers
exhibited the first projection film in 1895. Within a decade, theatres
across Europe and North America were showing newsreels and short
movies. But lawsuits among competing holders of patents for various
aspects of film production hampered the nascent industry's development. The deadlock broke in 1908, when major holders pooled their
patent rights—and promptly began buying up film distributors in an
attempt to take control of the entire cinematic value chain.

Until then, the critical advances in film had all taken place on the
U.S. east coast or in Europe. But the Motion Picture Patents Co.'s
predatory attitude produced an unintended consequence. It sent
many talented early moviemakers fleeing to California, as far as possible from the company's reach.

That was not the only reason to locate in southern California. The bright, dry weather was good for exterior shooting, and unions had yet to organize local film labour. On such attributes early producers laid the foundations of modern Hollywood. William Fox created 20th Century–Fox; Carl Laemmle founded Universal; Marcus Loew assembled Metro-Goldwyn-Mayer (MGM) and Adolph Zukor became the controlling figure at Paramount.

The introduction of talking pictures, followed by the Great Depression, badly shook the studios. The original moguls were forced to turn to eastern bankers to finance the conversion to sound. In return, the financiers demanded a brutal industry restructuring that left five companies in control of Hollywood: Warner Brothers, RKO, 20th Century–Fox, Paramount and MGM.

It may have hurt, but it also ushered in a golden age of studio profitability. In-house writers, full-time crews and contract players sustained a continuous production line of comedies, dramas and musical spectaculars. Subsidiary distributors fed their output to captive chains of movie theatres. "Stars" had glamour but no freedom: multi-year contracts obliged them to make whatever movies the studios dictated with little liberty to demand higher pay. The handful of theatres the studios did not own had no more leeway: coercive block booking obliged them to exhibit anything the studio sent them, the turkeys along with the hits. Studios could, and did, manipulate every transaction from the conception of a film to the final credit-fade onscreen for maximum return.

It was a picture too perfect to escape challenge for long. In 1938, exhibitor complaints against block booking prompted the U.S. Department of Justice to initiate an anti-trust investigation. Sparring continued for a decade, distracted by war. But in 1948, the U.S. Supreme Court finally heard the case. Its ruling, which came to be known as the Paramount Decree after the lead defendant, ordered the studios to give up ownership of exhibitors and foreswear block booking. Impressively, the decree would hold for five decades.

But like the Great Depression's earlier blow, the Paramount Decree proved a lesser shock than did a concurrent revolution in technology. Once it had been talkies. At mid-century it was television. "The public," as Richard Caves puts it, "could now enjoy B-movie entertainment at home, at no marginal cost and in the company of a six-pack and an undershirt."

Television triggered a transformation in Hollywood far more sweeping than the reorganization of the 1930s. The studios' in-house production model of permanent stars, writers and crews dissolved. Within a decade "the Majors," as they continued to be called, reduced their ongoing activity to the three functions that would most reliably preserve their earnings: financing and distributing new movies, and managing the rights to their libraries of existing ones.

The actual making of films atomized into a freewheeling business of one-off deals. Entrepreneurial producers secured scripts, packaged "talent," hired crews from the pool of newly independent (and frequently unemployed) craft specialists and brought them all together— often on sound stages rented from the majors—just long enough to complete a production. The new model sharply increased the value of personal contacts. Work as an actor or screenwriter or lowly third grip relied more than ever on wide informal networks of personal acquaintance, keeping a close ear to the grapevine and "being there" at the right moment.

But none of this posed a challenge to Hollywood's title as the capital of big-budget moviemaking or as the production centre for the emerging new medium of series television. Indeed, quite the opposite happened.

Martin Dale has described the neural system by which major studios "green light" a project in these terms:

> The Majors directly employ 15,000 people in their film divisions and provide work for another 150,000, but commissioning rests in the hands of the studio chiefs. The "genius of the system" is the wider editorial apparatus that exists in Hollywood. There is constant dialogue between the senior studio executives, the top agents, the leading producers and the star talent which determines which projects feel "right" or not. This is a community of around 200 top "players" ...
>
> "The business is all about relationships with talent," says one agent. "You learn to quickly form an opinion—is someone still 'in the business' or not. People can disappear overnight" ... The top 200 players are divided into a series of fiefdoms which coalesce around each studio and the main agencies. But each fiefdom has feelers which stretch throughout the movie colony. There is constant feedback ...

As a result, "cluster" dynamics, "knowledge spillover" and the A-list effect have all continued to reinforce Hollywood's unique critical mass. So long as the "green light" (financing for particular projects) stayed in Hollywood, then the A-list talent would also hover there, hoping for a positive nod and hiring agents to push for the next deal. The heart of the producers' task is to marry talent and financing, so producers too must go where the green lights are.

In a classic feedback mechanism, the converse also applied. As long as the talent and agents bringing proposals stayed in Hollywood, then the green-light mechanism also had to stay there, so as not to miss out on the next blockbuster package. The networking involved in the new Hollywood was omnipresent and inexorable. To be part of the network, one had to "be there."

The result is that despite the institutional collapse of the studio system in the 1950s, the locus of decision-making never strayed from Los Angeles. The strict corporate camps of the studios may have blurred into the looser affiliations noted above. But, if anything, Hollywood's primacy only increased.

A measure of the forces at work is the insignificance of the changes that occurred when foreign owners bought some Hollywood studios. Even when Japan's Sony bought Columbia, Australia's Murdoch bought Fox, and Canada's Seagram and later France's Vivendi bought Universal, the decision-makers for their film projects stayed firmly in Hollywood. They had no choice; that was where the A-list talent was. As expanding budgets raised the sums at risk and production packages predominated, the pressure to make decisions in Hollywood only increased.

The dominance of Hollywood is not due solely to the cluster effect. A number of other factors also contribute: the majors' control of theatrical distribution, the barriers to entry arising from the unique risk–reward ratio of popular culture and the advantages that arise from wielding price discrimination in different markets. Each of these factors will be explored in later chapters.

What is not in question is that once Hollywood achieved critical mass, it was never eclipsed. It remains the undisputed centre of production and distribution of the blockbuster film. According to figures from the Motion Picture Association of America (MPAA), which represents major studios, 543 movies were made in the United States in

2002. Of those, MPAA members released 220. Significantly, that number included virtually all of the 50 titles that managed to gross more than $20 million in domestic (which, for the MPAA, includes Canadian) box-office receipts that year. Total box-office in 2002 was a record US$9.5 billion.

IF THESE DYNAMICS are real and independent of any magic potency in the southern California water or genetic pool for talent, they should also be observable in other countries.

As, indeed, they are.

Two world wars and an economic depression shattered Europe's moviemaking infrastructure, along with much else. But eventually Europe did rebuild. In the 1950s and 1960s, Rome and Paris became centres of production for directors like Francois Truffaut, Jean-Luc Godard and Federico Fellini, who cast A-list stars like Sophia Loren, Marcello Mastroianni and Catherine Deneuve in movies that drew significant foreign audiences. In the same era, Italy pioneered a production form later to be harshly criticized in Hollywood as the "runaway"—standing in for the American frontier in a series of "spaghetti Westerns." Britain sustained a critical mass of production centred in London.

In the past quarter-century, a handful of additional film and television production clusters have developed. A few emerged organically, mainly where large domestic audiences speaking languages other than English constitute markets that Hollywood is ill-placed to satisfy. Active production centres in India and Hong Kong are examples. By 2000, the almost-800 films made annually in India surpassed the number shot in the United States. Hong Kong makes fewer—133 in 2000—but exports them to audiences in the rest of southeast Asia, Taiwan and South Korea. Japan exports few feature films, but its animated productions are widely viewed abroad. Lesser known is Nigeria as a production centre for direct-to-video feature-length movies that circulate widely in the rest of Africa.

Where large linguistically and culturally distinct domestic audiences have not existed, governments and filmmakers have still sought to create conditions in which film and TV production might coalesce into a critical mass. Screenwriters, directors and actors in many countries, including Canada, Britain and Australia—and, for that matter, in

U.S. states such as North Carolina and Texas—have wished to make films on their own physical as well as cultural turf. Policy-makers are lured by the millions of dollars and thousands of jobs that keep the movie-making machine turning over. In Europe, Latin America and the non-U.S. anglosphere, substantial efforts and significant public resources have been invested in various attempts to trigger self-sustaining creative clusters.

That Hollywood remains Hollywood should not be taken as proof that those efforts have failed. The undertaking is a complex one—as is any attempt to assess its success.

To begin with, the critical mass necessary to support a viable cultural industry clearly depends on the product in mind. For some products, like blockbuster films, a large industrial infrastructure may be necessary. But for others, like the production of Inuit prints, sound recordings, or the publishing of books, it is a different story. Authors of literary fiction can live anywhere (although their agents must stay close to the "green lights" at publishing houses). High-quality recording studios can be found in most major cities (and, indeed, in many smaller ones).

Audiovisual products uniquely require an especially elaborate infrastructure. But even there, opportunities may exist to diversify centres of production. To begin with, the talent required to produce films has much in common with that for television drama. Measures to support the accretion of a critical mass in television production may thus also have a positive impact on film.

Moreover, certain categories of audiovisual production can support distinct clusters: documentaries, for instance, or animation. A critical mass of schools, talent, production facilities and access to financing can create a self-sustaining industry in these sub-genres even where large-scale dramatic features may be out of reach.

The Canadian experience here is particularly telling. In the past two decades, government policy has succeeded in creating audiovisual production clusters in three Canadian cities: Toronto, Vancouver and Montreal.

Prior to 1984, independent film and television production essentially did not exist in Canada. State-owned corporations (the Canadian Broadcasting Corporation, the National Film Board and the Canadian Film Development Corporation) dominated the very limited amount of dramatic production. A brief foray into tax-incentive financing for feature films had ended disastrously in the late 1970s. But in the mid-1980s, the government introduced a carrot (a federal subsidy for independent Canadian drama) and a stick (a regulatory requirement that private broadcasters air new Canadian drama). With this combination, an industry gradually came into being.

Over the next fifteen years, thousands of hours of drama were created. A critical mass of audiovisual infrastructure emerged to produce the new programming. And as that programming steadily improved in quality, a fortuitous event occurred. The Canadian dollar declined relative to the U.S. dollar, until by the mid-1990s there was a 35 per cent differential. (In 2003, the Canadian dollar strengthened and reduced the differential to only 25 per cent.)

The result was that Canada suddenly became not only a centre for its own dramatic production but a lure for foreign-location shooting. The major Hollywood studios commissioned and financed productions in Canada for the same reason that Italy had once been a popular location to make spaghetti Westerns: the combination of skilled crews and (comparatively) low costs.

By the mid-1990s, Toronto, Vancouver and Montreal could each claim to have achieved the critical mass of many specialists necessary to modern filmmaking. A trade digest of production service companies and talent agencies in Vancouver runs to 432 glossy pages, covering everything from animatronics to wrap-party venues. The producers, cast, day-players, writers, publicists and suppliers who make *Degrassi* are among more than 46,000 people who work in filmed entertainment production in Toronto (compared with 60,000 in New York).

As moviemaking entered its second new century, Vancouver and Toronto were internationally significant producers of filmed entertainment. In a study by Roger Martin, dean of management at the University of Toronto, that city was identified as the world's second-largest exporter of television programming. Between 1998 and 2000, according to a 2002 report to California's state legislators, Vancouver and Toronto together "produced more MOWS [movies of the week] than the U.S. [and] captured nearly half of all MOWS shot worldwide."

The combined value of audiovisual production in Canada reached C$5.1 billion in 2002, consisting of $3.3 billion in Canadian production and $1.8 billion in foreign-location shooting. Included in the latter total was the 2003 Academy Award winner, *Chicago,* filmed in Toronto.

It is worth putting those numbers in perspective. The combined value of production in all three Canadian centres about equals that of New York City—and was less than one tenth of Hollywood's output. But it was a remarkable achievement nonetheless.

Moreover, it was one for which the tool kit of cultural policies deployed by a succession of Canadian governments could take substantial credit. Researchers who studied Toronto alongside fourteen other media centres in Europe, North America and southeast Asia concluded: "This unusually comprehensive policy framework, enacted by senior levels of government in Canada out of a long-standing concern to promote home-grown culture, has almost single-handedly nurtured the development of Toronto's entertainment, media and publishing cluster."

BY THE TURN of the century, the original city of celluloid dreams had begun to take note of its rivals' success. Even though production spending and employment in Hollywood continued to climb, craft unions in particular seethed at the notion that work that might have been done there was instead going to Toronto and Vancouver. A succession of studies and reports sought to document what many in Los Angeles viewed as predatory Canadian subsidies designed to lure "runaway" productions north. The most exhaustive of those attempts— including the 2002 study done for California—failed to find any evidence that the state was at risk of slipping from the pinnacle of the A-list of filmmaking locations.

Unnoticed in Los Angeles was a fact that to Canadian film and television creators was especially ironic. At the same time that California's unions bemoaned the loss of "runaway" productions, their northern counterparts were experiencing a precipitous decline in the shooting of scripts actually written in or about Canada. Meanwhile the roster of allegedly runaway features and MOWs all had one thing in common. Most creative inputs (the "above the line" talent that includes screenwriters and directors as well as stars) and all of the money still came from only one city—and it was neither Toronto nor Vancouver. For anyone hoping to make a film for $15 million or more (entry level for a commercial feature with a "name" star), only one road led to a green light: Hollywood Boulevard.

The studios may be shooting more projects in lower-cost foreign locations than before. But deciding which films get made is still done where it has always been, where the A-list talent and top film executives who are able to approve such projects live.

This may be entirely acceptable if you are an American filmmaker. But for creators from other countries, the implications are daunting.

Credit where it is due: Hollywood has long been a magnet for the best and the brightest of the world's filmmaking talent. Spokesmen like Motion Picture Association of America chief executive Jack Valenti are fond of citing this fact in adopting the language of cultural diversity. As an industry based on ideas and entertainment, Valenti and others claim, Hollywood moviemaking is open to the "best" from every culture.

But this claim is disingenuous. The real Hollywood vision is, rather, to see other countries as farm teams feeding talent to the majors. The talented foreign creators brought to Hollywood rarely make films about their own countries or backgrounds. Rather, they are hired to make the movies that Hollywood's decision-makers believe will do well—first in U.S. theatres and second as products for export. There is a big difference. Simply put, filmmakers who work on Hollywood's dime make Hollywood's movies (and it would take a dedicated filmmaker abroad to resist the dollars Hollywood can offer).

That being said, there is a bright side to the Canadian experience. Despite reverses and disappointments, Canada has shown that once a critical mass of skills, service companies and domestic financing is created, local television drama that speaks to a country's stories and experiences *can* be made successfully. And while it may not be possible to make successful big-ticket films without Hollywood's affirmative nod, it is entirely possible to make successful smaller films that have cultural specificity.

THIS CHAPTER OPENED with the contrasts generated when a Hollywood-financed production spent tens of thousands of dollars to film a twenty-second action sequence near Pangnirtung on Baffin Island. Twenty-five years later, a more interesting intersection between the film industry and the world of the Inuit took place just west of there.

It happened over the summer of 1999, in the tiny community of Igloolik. Director Zacharias Kunuk and an all-Inuit cast shot the first feature film ever produced in their own language. Called *Atanarjuat (The Fast Runner)*, the film was a three-hour epic based on Inuit legend, shot in digital video in the High Arctic, then converted to 35 mm film in Vancouver. The story, shown with English subtitles, featured the same themes of nature, shamans and magic that populate the world of Inuit art exemplified in the Pangnirtung prints.

This time, the whole production was conceived, created and produced in the North. Financed in part by the National Film Board of Canada and in part by anticipated licence fees from Canadian pay-television services, the "green lights" for the film came not from Hollywood but from within Canada. The budget for the film was $1.9 million. And because the production used digital video instead of film, there was no need to send the rushes south for processing, as was necessary with *The Spy Who Loved Me*.

Atanarjuat met the same challenge all small-budget films do: its distribution to theatres around the world was problematic. But wherever it did reach the screen, critics raved. The Inuit epic won the Camera d'Or for best first feature at the Cannes film festival in 2001. "Not merely an interesting document from a far-off place," said *The New York Times*, "it is a masterpiece."

It is a masterpiece, however, that proves less about what it is right with Hollywood than about what is necessary in the tool kit of public cultural policy. This will become more evident in the chapters ahead.

3

CURIOUS
ECONOMICS

IN ANY STUDY of this type there is some spinach—a portion of the
meal distinguished more by its nutrition than by its flavour or texture. This is it.

In coming to understand how markets determine what we watch,
read and listen to, we must focus on a handful of quite specific and
unique economic characteristics of those products. The following
chapters will show how those characteristics play out in the limelight
and backstage of movies, television, recordings and books. There will
be sizzle and steak to come. But those courses will be easier to follow
and enjoy if we first acquire a concise familiarity with each of these
characteristics in the abstract. That is the purpose of this chapter. It is
brief and concentrated, and, as Popeye found, it will fortify us for the
adventures to come.

The last chapter discussed how intangible inspiration, skill and
hard money affect the decisions regarding where cultural products are
made. It noted that the creation of film, television programs, books,
magazines and sound recordings tends to concentrate in centres that
attract a critical mass of talent and support. Their production exhibits
"cluster effects" enhanced by "knowledge spillover" and an "A-list factor" that gives a few individuals disproportionate clout.

We turn now to the question of how such products, once made, behave in the marketplace. What attributes mark their distribution and

sale? Do books and movies, music recordings and television shows be-have in accordance with the same laws of market influence and outcome as other commodities? Or do the interests of vendor and consumer play out differently for cultural products than for more tangible and inter-changeable goods—a car, a cup of coffee or a box of detergent?

Some might consider these questions extraneous. Of course there is a difference between culture and other products, they say. Films, books and music express ideas and tell stories; they inform and enter-tain. Ordinary commodities, like cars or detergent, are by contrast essentially utilitarian. They perform a useful function but do not con-tribute to intellectual discourse.

It is obvious that cultural products do provide something quite different from ordinary commodities. Popular books, music and mov-ing images give voice and expression to our souls, psyche and identity. Not even all the advances of psychometry and behavioural genetics have yet produced reliable means to measure these values—let alone render them into monetary units of exchange. It is understandable therefore that economists find them difficult to discuss and are in-clined to dismiss as irrelevant public policy that wishes to focus on the value of the ideas embedded in cultural products.

Yet, clearly, cultural products are also bought and sold. They re-spond to forces of supply, demand and competition. There is, inar-guably, a true and vital marketplace of cultural products.

So an essential question remains. Do cultural products perform in the same way as ordinary commodities in the marketplace? Or do they have some unique attributes that call for a different approach to regu-lation or public policy than might be appropriate for ordinary goods and services?

At a time when the field of economics has ascended to a place of primacy as the standard for judging public policy, these are crucial questions. This is all the more true given that an uncompromisingly economic paradigm frames the ongoing effort by the multinational companies in the entertainment business to seek rules that would bring international commerce in cultural products under the ambit of trade agreements. (We will have much more to say on this subject in Part Three).

The economics of the arts have been much studied. A number of treatises and some academic journals are devoted to the subject. But oddly enough, until recently, comparatively little expert attention has been directed at the economics of *popular* culture. A major contribution appeared in 2000, with the publication of Richard Caves's monumental work, *Creative Industries*, the first comprehensive attempt to analyze how creative activities are organized and why deals and contracts among their participants are structured as they are. More recent studies have further advanced understanding of what *The Economist* has called "the curious economics of the business."

This chapter lays out in concise terms the key economic attributes of cultural products. It provides a conceptual framework for understanding how the market for popular culture is different from that for conventional merchandise. The three chapters that follow trace the activity of these attributes in the real world of domestic and global cultural production and distribution. They will show how the concepts work in practice.

To assist in this analysis, Table 3.1 identifies a number of key differences in attributes that distinguish cultural products from ordinary commodities. Some of these differences apply only to certain cultural commodities. Or they may apply with greater or lesser force, depending on the product. Equally, a handful of non-cultural products—toys, pharmaceuticals and software—share one or two of these differences from other more conventional goods. Still, most of these differences are generally true for the great majority of cultural products. Collectively, they provide a framework for the analysis to follow, and they amply demonstrate that in fact as well as presumption, cultural products are significantly different from widgets.

TABLE 3.1: *Why Cultural Products Are Not Like Ordinary Commodities*

Attribute	Ordinary Commodity (e.g., Car, Detergent)	Cultural Good or Service (e.g., Book, CD, TV Broadcast)
Nature of Product	Serves utilitarian purpose	Communicates ideas—information or entertainment
Nature of Production Process	Assembly line; each unit requires significant resources	Expensive one-time process; creates intellectual property that then can be cheaply stored, duplicated and delivered

Marginal Cost of Unit of Product	Significant	Insignificant
Predictability of Demand	Demand largely predictable month after month	Difficult to estimate demand in advance of incurring cost
Substitutability	Large degree of substitutability with competing brands	Limited substitutability; product is perceived as unique; copyright law protects monopoly on each title
Time Line of Demand	Demand for product continues indefinitely until next product cycle (measured in years)	Demand falls off sharply after introduction of the product and when next product replaces it (measured in weeks or months)
Who Determines Demand	Ultimate consumer	Ultimate consumer in the case of books and movies within the choices made by gatekeepers; advertiser in the case of magazines and commercial broadcasting; cable or satellite gatekeeper for niche broadcast channels
Setting the Price	Non-discriminatory; arbitrage precludes market differentiation	Within markets is often set at a conventional "going rate"; between markets is discriminatory (by market, nature of use, and time line of use); copyright law permits unlimited subdivision of markets
Pricing Latitude	Dependent on competitive forces of demand and supply; constrained by significant marginal cost and non-discriminatory pricing	Marginal cost is insignificant, and pricing of cultural products can be highly discriminatory between markets
Nature of Consumption	Each unit of product is consumed and is not available to others	Original intellectual property is not consumed but can be made endlessly available; "public good" attributes
Time Line of Advertising	Continual advertising over many years to reinforce brand	Intense advertising at time of introduction of product before it is displaced by next product

NATURE OF PRODUCT

The first attribute to note is the most apparent—namely, that the basic nature of a cultural product like a book or a film is to communicate ideas and emotions, whereas an ordinary product serves a utilitarian purpose. Of course, even ordinary products like cars or soap frequently attempt to convey emotional overtones in marketing and branding. There are also commodities that are not, strictly speaking, utilitarian—gourmet food, lingerie and perfume come to mind. But even these products serve their purpose in their material form, be it a slice of foie gras or frilly lace. In general, the value of a cultural product is mostly in its symbolic or representational content, not its physical form or utilitarian attributes. It is, in that sense, a product that is *experienced* (or an "experience good"), rather than one that is conventionally consumed or employed for some subsidiary purpose (such as a hand tool or an appliance).

Because they work with ideas and emotions, the creators of cultural products are frequently driven by motives that are not purely profit-seeking. This "art for art's sake" principle may result in works that satisfy the creators' own aesthetic choices but do not attract popular demand. It is also one of the reasons for a persistent, universal and in conventional economic terms inexplicable oversupply of creative products, far exceeding demand. Later, we will see how this leaves consumers to struggle in the cultural marketplace with a "too much information" effect.

NATURE OF PRODUCTION PROCESS

This difference between cultural products and ordinary commodities is critical. Cultural products typically involve an expensive, time-consuming but one-time process of creation, in which almost all of the cost is incurred to make the first or master copy. That process is often a "one off" effort by a team of workers brought together specifically for that project. The film industry in particular involves the creation of expensive prototypes that require huge initial expenditures. But whether the product is a feature film, a television program or a sound recording, the process creates intellectual property embodied in the master copy (nowadays sometimes reduced to a digital bit-stream) that can be cheaply stored, duplicated and delivered. The master copy is never consumed. At the same time, that large initial production cost cannot be avoided. As economists would say, it has been "sunk"—regardless of whether buyers emerge for the product or not.

By contrast, an ordinary commodity like a car or a box of soap is produced in many copies on an assembly line. Significant capital-intensive resources are required to produce each unit, and each copy consumes a more or less significant amount of new raw material (less in the case of a box of soap, more in that of a BMW). Correspondingly, however, producers of conventional goods can cut their losses and cease making a product for which a market fails to appear.

MARGINAL COST OF ADDITIONAL UNITS

Once the master copy of a cultural product is created, making additional copies incurs an insignificant marginal cost. A copy of a $100 million feature film can be produced on VHS or DVD for less than a dollar. The manufacturing cost of a hardcover book, which may have taken a year or more for a creative team to write, edit and design, is less than three dollars for an additional unit. For mass-market paperbacks, magazines or sound recordings, the marginal cost of an additional unit is typically less than twenty-five cents.

Conventional commodities—such as the player for that DVD or VHS recording—require additional raw materials and frequently complex pre-manufactured sub-components. They need sophisticated continuous capacity for production, assembly and packaging. As a result, the marginal cost of each additional unit of a conventional product is significant. (Pharmaceuticals and software are two non-cultural products that share the distinctions of high initial "sunk cost" in development and minimal "marginal cost" of producing subsequent units for sale.)

NATURE OF CONSUMPTION

When an ordinary commodity is sold, it is consumed and is no longer available to anyone else. A loaf of bread sold to one person cannot be sold to another as well.

In contrast, a cultural product has value not for what it is, but for the experience it conveys. The mere conveyance does not consume the original source of that experience—the master copy. It can be endlessly conveyed at insignificant marginal cost to any number of additional consumers. In that regard, intellectual property is often described as a "non-rival" good, in the sense that its use by one person (or firm) in no way limits its use by another.

PREDICTABILITY OF DEMAND ("NOBODY KNOWS")

Most ordinary commodities operate in a market in which demand is to some extent predictable. In many cases, the need for the same product keeps recurring as older units are consumed. At the same time, having consumed a product once, consumers know what to expect and, if it was satisfactory, can be confident in ordering it again. Repeat consumption also makes it possible to contribute further to predictable demand by advertising a brand continually over time.

By contrast, each cultural work is unique. Each consumer can judge the work's merits only in the consumption (watching the movie, reading the book). As a result, the demand for any proposed cultural product is extremely difficult to predict in advance of incurring the cost of its creation. One of the most-quoted aphorisms describing Hollywood, coined by screenwriter William Goldman in *Adventures in the Screen Trade*, reminds the unwary that "nobody knows anything."

The risk factor in launching new works of popular culture is impossible to overestimate. Simply put, the great majority of cultural products do not succeed: few people buy the CD or watch the movie, and the investment in the creation of the intellectual property is not recouped. Adding to the risk is the blunt fact that research and pre-testing are notoriously ineffective in the realm of popular culture. Until audiences actually experience a creative product, it simply cannot be evaluated. In advance of the actual release of the title, *nobody knows*.

This was dramatically confirmed in a study published in 1994 on the selection of television drama series by the U.S. commercial networks. Despite the use of a number of indicia (for example, well-known talent, track record of the creators, focus groups) in deciding which pilot series to select for the season's schedules, none of those indicia had any statistical ability to predict which series would actually succeed.

In discussing this matter, a distinction must be drawn between demand for a particular title—typically unpredictable—and aggregate demand for all cultural products of a particular kind, which is fairly

stable. Thus, analysts studying the movie industry, the recording industry or the publishing sector can often develop accurate predictions
for total box-office admissions or overall unit sales. Similarly, the average number of hours devoted to television viewing has remained surprisingly constant. What is harder to predict in advance of release is
which title will be wildly successful in obtaining sales or viewers and
which will fail.

NO SUBSTITUTES

Ordinary commodities operate in markets that have a large degree of
substitutability among competing products. Because those products
fulfill a utilitarian function, different vendors can compete head-to-
head with different brands that perform essentially the same function.
Patent laws aside, it is very difficult to protect an ordinary commodity
from the entry of a competitor, whether a new player in the market or
the launch of a store brand.

In contrast, cultural products are infinitely variable. Each movie or
book title or sound recording—even by the same artist or creative
team—is perceived as unique. Copyright law protects this uniqueness
by prohibiting the unauthorized distribution or sale of copies of a particular title, effectively reserving the market for that title to its exclusive owner. Even within a subject-matter niche, like books for children,
individual titles are distinct and unique, as parents familiar with the
appeal of Harry Potter can attest if they have ever tried to foist an alternative title on their children.

This monopoly quality of each artist and unique work may be
thought of as the "no substitutes" rule. It explains why some artists
make such large "rents," as economists would have it, and others
starve. If you are Brad Pitt or Celine Dion or Oliver Stone, *no one else is.*
Similarly, if you have written *The Handmaid's Tale* or *"G" is for
Gumshoe*, these are the only versions of those stories that exist. If audiences develop a taste for the "cultural good" you uniquely create, you
are the monopoly supplier of that good and able to demand a monopo-
list's premium for making it available.

The distinctiveness of cultural products also means that the demand for each title is to a large extent independent of the demand for
other titles. Someone who has just purchased a pair of running shoes is
unlikely to purchase another pair until the first pair has worn out.

Someone who purchases a romance novel is very likely to purchase a second romance novel and a third.

One of the features contributing to the uniqueness of cultural products is the fact that they are often culturally specific—with references rooted in a particular society or country. This adds to their diversity. It also results in those titles being more likely to be popular and successful when they are marketed in the society to which they refer. However, those same titles then typically suffer from a "cultural discount" when marketed in other countries where the cultural references do not have as much resonance.

DECAY TIME OF DEMAND

The demand for many ordinary commodities continues indefinitely. For staple products like flour, sugar or beer, it may continue forever. For manufactured products like cars, demand continues at least until the next product cycle, which is typically measured in years.

The products of popular culture behave quite differently. Each title has its brief moment in the sun. Then within weeks or at most months, the consumer moves on to the next entertainment or informational experience. Certain cultural products like magazines and romance paperbacks have this decay factor built right into their business plan: at the end of the month, unsold copies of the current issue are ruthlessly removed and replaced by the new issue, with a new cover and all-new features. The decay time for news and sports programs is even more dramatic; there is little or no market for a day-old news program or a sports event that is not "live."

There are some exceptions: the demand for some cultural products can extend beyond their first appearance. Movies in theatres can have an afterlife in home video and television, giving rise to the value of film libraries. Books that turn out to be bestsellers or classics may stay in inventory and form part of a publisher's backlist. But for almost all cultural products, demand falls off sharply soon after their first introduction. For most, it drops almost to zero. Toys are an exception on the other side of the equation: they are a conventional tangible product that also frequently suffers rapid "decay time" in the marketplace. On the other hand, toys may also be considered simply another variety of cultural product.

WHO DETERMINES DEMAND

It's said that the customer is always right. In most marketplaces for conventional commodities, the consumer is the active agent of the choice to buy. From the car lot to the coffee shop, the customer is king.

Consumer sovereignty is a good deal more restricted when it comes to cultural products. The marketplace for popular culture is largely dominated by "gatekeepers," "chokepoints" and "tastemakers," who decide (nominally on the consumers' behalf) which products get shelf space and which will be excluded from audience consideration. To give the most oft-cited example, commercial television broadcasters choose what programs will appear on their schedules; radio stations select a fraction of the available recorded music to air. But since they are focused on selling advertising, their choices tend to reflect only the preferences of the demographic desired by advertisers, not the preferences of all viewers. Moreover, as we shall see, the pursuit of profit margin over audience size (two quite different elements in a broadcaster's calculation) can easily produce the anomaly of a less popular program airing in place of a more-popular one. Maximizing profit may also preclude programming that serves a public interest in, for example, educational programs for children or a fully informed citizenry.

Similarly, cable or satellite television companies that decide what specialty or pay channels are available for purchase and how they are packaged may have other agendas in mind besides maximizing the number of viewers of a particular channel.

Gatekeepers are just as omnipresent in determining the contents of bookstores, cinemas and the racks of magazines and paperbacks in mom-and-pop variety stores. Since there are always far more titles available for exhibition or display than there are shelves (or screens or airtime) to display them, some pre-selection is almost unavoidable. But gatekeepers at best make imperfect proxies for consumer demand, and they often reflect conflicting interests.

PRICING

One of the most compelling differences between cultural products and other commodities is the latitude for "price discrimination"—the ability to set prices differently for different markets, independently of the cost incurred. In most ordinary commodities, the significant marginal cost of producing each additional unit effectively sets a minimum floor for the price of the product. With open competition, prices for equivalent brands will tend to settle out at that marginal cost. Since one commodity can substitute for another, arbitrage will take place if major price differentials appear between different markets.

But these constraints are ineffective against cultural products. Suppliers cannot price their creative products at marginal cost, since that is close to zero. Pricing on that basis would never recover the one-time cost of the master copy. To recover that cost and maximize return, the owners of the rights to the product carefully segregate their markets and price their products on a highly discriminatory basis between each market.

Within particular markets, retail prices for cultural products often settle into a uniform "conventional" price per unit that reflects neither the cost nor the demand for a particular title but rather what is seen in the industry as the "going rate" for all movie tickets, hardcover fiction titles, music CDs and the like. The going rate far exceeds the marginal cost of each unit (given the need to recover the initial cost) and reflects a variety of factors, including the overall price elasticity of demand for cultural products of that kind in the market. Given the unpredictability of demand for particular titles, this approach serves the interest of all the players by giving all products with shelf space a similar price point and, it is hoped, an equal chance at success. In a market of this kind, the return to the distributor and eventually to the creator varies not with the price but with the volume of sales.

When markets and buyers can be differentiated, however, a more discriminatory pricing approach is used. In doing so, distributors benefit from the fact that copyright law permits owners of the content of a cultural product to control its lawful distribution. The rights conveyed not only allow the owner to prevent the unauthorized duplication or public performance of the work, but also facilitate something even more useful: the unlimited subdivision of markets for the product. In setting different prices for the same cultural product in markets subdivided by time, geography and medium, vendors are able to capture the highest return possible from each market.

The benefit of what is called the "orderly marketplace" is best seen in the film industry. For a typical Hollywood feature film, the first market "window" is its appearance in North American cinemas, where it may play for anything from one week to (rarely) a year. The second window for a North American feature is its release to DVD or video cassette rental and sale. Here a film will typically be available for six months to as long as a year. The third conventional window is exhibition on pay-TV—in the United States, HBO or Showtime. This window again usually runs for about six months. The fourth window is network television. After that, the film moves to a fifth exhibition window in domestic television syndication (station-by-station release) or cable networks. All of these windows have different prices attached to them.

For each class of exhibitor, release to foreign markets is regarded as a separate window from domestic release. Some windows may also run concurrently. Foreign-cinema release may overlap domestic video, for instance. As the theatrical window draws to a close, some movies may appear on airplane screens or as in-room hotel entertainment. Completing the run through all the windows in every territory can take as long as seven or eight years from the date of a film's first release.

Economic logic underpins the orderly marketplace. The idea is to extract the absolute maximum "consumer surplus" (what each consumer is willing to pay for the experience of enjoying the product) from every class of audience before making it available to the next. Thus, the first window is designed to capture viewers prepared to pay the highest price to see the film to fullest advantage on a big screen with industrial-strength sound. The subsequent rental-video window captures consumers who are unwilling to pay for the cinema experience but ready to pay a moderate premium to watch the film at their convenience. A third pay-TV window targets consumers prepared to part with less again, but still something, in order to watch a film uninterrupted by commercials. Those willing only to watch for free will eventually see the film on conventional off-air TV (and pay for it by sitting through the commercials).

At each window, both the price paid by each viewer and the amount that flows back to the owner of the film declines. Someone who spends $12 on a cinema ticket to the latest feature may put as much as $6 into a distributor's pocket. When a family of four rents a video for $5 and watches it together, the return to the distributor may be only 20 to 30 cents per viewer. When the same film is broadcast over the air to a million people, the broadcast licence may pay only pennies—or fractions of pennies—per viewer.

The phenomenon of price discrimination also pervades the sale of cultural products across borders. Those sales can involve the export of physical copies of the work (for which the marginal cost per unit is very low) or the grant of intellectual property rights to the work (for which the marginal cost is zero). In either case, the price charged for the same title can differ markedly between countries.

As Chapter 6 shows more directly, this is particularly relevant for the sale of television movies and drama series to television broadcasters around the world. The prices charged for broadcast rights in various countries bear no relationship whatever to the original cost of the program. Rights to programs costing US\$2 million or more to make in the United States are typically sold to U.S. broadcasters for upwards of US\$1.4 million and to broadcasters in other countries for prices ranging from US\$1,000 to US\$150,000. The prices are also highly discriminatory between different countries.

Executives in the commercial television industry take such price discrimination for granted and often fail to realize how unusual the practice is. With ordinary commodities like cars or packaged goods, price discrimination between territories is almost impossible to maintain (apart from recovering transportation costs) because of arbitrage and anti-dumping rules. With cultural products, transportation costs are minimal, while price discrimination between markets is protected by copyright law and is inherent in the exploitation of the work. As we shall see, however, the effect of this discrimination is to undermine the application of normal economic theory to the sector.

The low marginal cost and price discrimination that distinguish the export of cultural products also undermine a principle applied in international trade economics, namely, the theory of comparative advantage. This theory, first developed by British economist David Ricardo in the nineteenth century, states that each country should specialize in those industries in which it is relatively efficient. It should export part of that production and take in exchange (or buy with the proceeds) goods in whose production it is, for whatever reason, at a comparative disadvantage. Because specialization and free exchange among nations yield higher real incomes for the participants, the theory provides a strong argument for free trade, even if some countries have to abandon certain sectors because they are at a comparative disadvantage.

But as Chapter 16 will explain, the theory encounters some major problems with cultural products. How does one measure a country's comparative advantage when the products it produces have a marginal cost close to zero? And how does one compare products when they are not substitutable, when the symbolic content (intellectual property) that provides the value in each copy is unique? Moreover, the language and ideas of each product can have cultural specificity, increasing demand in certain societies and lowering it in others.

TAKEN TOGETHER, the attributes identified above amply demonstrate the "curious economics" of the business of popular culture. But they also support two critical observations about the products of that business.

The first is that *most cultural products fail to achieve commercial success, and it is virtually impossible to predict ahead of time which products those will be.* This makes the cultural business exceptionally risky. That risk is further heightened by the brief opportunity that cultural products have to prove themselves before they are discarded in favour of the next new thing.

The second observation, however, is the converse of the first. *If they are successful, cultural products can produce a much higher reward than any ordinary commodities can.* Once the cost of the first or master copy has been recovered, the marginal costs of selling additional copies are tiny. Once the first cost is amortized, virtually all the revenue from the sale of additional copies or from the exploitation of a work in additional markets is profit.

These two principles combine to set up a risk–reward dynamic that is addressed more fully in the next two chapters. That dynamic is one of the qualities that makes the cultural industries so alluring. It certainly contributes to the astounding number of new titles that annually buck the unfavourable odds in seeking exposure to audiences.

But a third observation is also worth noting at this point: *cultural products that are attractive to consumers in a large geographical market have a lower risk and a much greater potential reward than do those that are produced for a smaller market.* The reason is that with the larger market, there are a greater number of potential customers over which to amortize the fixed costs of the master copy, after which the product can go into profit. If a product is culturally specific to consumers in a small country or society, however, and its cost is comparable to that of a product produced for a larger market, it is much more difficult to reach a break-even point even if the product is quite popular in the smaller market, simply because there are fewer potential consumers that may be interested in the product. This can be called the "small country" problem, since it is endemic to the cultural industries in smaller countries around the world. The problem becomes even more difficult when the title is culturally specific to a smaller society within a country: for example, titles with references specific to French Canadians. Language differences contribute to cultural specificity but are only one of the differences distinguishing one society from another and reflected in the extraordinary diversity of cultural products around the world.

The risk–reward dynamic leads most companies in the cultural industries to attempt one or more of a number of strategies of risk reduction. As later chapters will show, all too often the net effect of those strategies is to constrain the choices available to consumers.

With these differences between cultural products and ordinary commodities in mind, it is now possible to apply economic theory to the field of popular culture.

A first observation economists would make is that many of the attributes we have discussed show cultural products to be, to a greater or lesser degree, what they would call *public goods*. The term "public good" is often misunderstood. The label is typically applied to the provision of services like national defence, education, roads, and health and welfare programs. Looking at this list, people often mistakenly assume that the words "public good" simply refer to goods or services provided by the government, or products that are somehow suffused with a public interest.

To economists, however, public good has a very technical meaning. It refers to a good whose production cost is independent of the number of people who consume it. Public goods also have two distinct aspects: "non-excludability" (that is, non-payers cannot be excluded from the benefits of the good or service) and "non-rivalrous consumption" (one person's consumption of the product does not reduce its availability to another consumer). The latter aspect is also referred to as the "joint consumption" characteristic.

Most cultural products qualify as public goods within these definitions. A good example might be the creation and dissemination of a live television program, like *The Oprah Winfrey Show*. The cost of creating the program is fixed, as is the cost of transmitting it. One viewer's "consumption" of the show does not reduce its availability to another viewer.

Some cultural products—like broadcasting generally and free-to-air television programs specifically—are pure public goods. Other cultural products combine some elements of privateness and some elements of publicness. The *content* of films, books, magazines and sound recordings is a public good; but the content is delivered to customers in the *form* of a physical copy that constitutes a private good. Still, given the high fixed first-copy costs and low marginal costs of these products, their predominant attribute is that of a public good.

This "public good"–ness of cultural products—to say nothing of the numerous other ways in which their behaviour deviates from that of conventional products—is a problem for economists. By and large, economists base their understanding of markets on several assumptions. One of those is that market transactions involve only goods of a purely "private" nature. Another is that consumers have perfect information about the range of products they are choosing from. Economists further assume the presence of many competing vendors in markets that present no significant barriers to entry by new players (where there are constant returns to scale). Lastly, they assume that this environment generates a wide choice of readily substitutable competing goods.

In these circumstances, free competition will theoretically produce a market equilibrium at which the price of any good is equal to its marginal cost and social welfare is maximized. This is what economists call an "efficient" market, since theoretically no other price could improve on the market outcome without making someone worse off.

THE TROUBLE with applying this theory to cultural goods is that these goods fail to support a single one of its underlying assumptions.

First, they are public goods, not private goods. Accordingly, market prices are highly discriminatory and far exceed marginal cost.

Second, consumers cannot choose among cultural products on the basis of perfect information. Because these are "experience" goods, consumers must purchase the good before they can fully evaluate it. Moreover, the decision to give shelf space to certain products is often made not by consumers themselves but by a gatekeeper, who is an imperfect proxy for consumer sovereignty.

Third, because of high fixed costs, cultural industries in fact operate under conditions of sharply increasing returns to scale. As Chapter 5 will show, larger firms in the business of distributing cultural products possess significant advantages that present nearly insurmountable barriers to the entry of new competitors.

Finally, cultural goods are not substitutes for each other. Hence, even if there were no barriers to the entry of new suppliers (and there are), perfect competition between alternative suppliers would not exist.

Given this vast gulf between assumption and reality, it is obvious that markets for cultural products cannot be relied on to generate "efficient" outcomes even within the limited perspective of economists. Given all the peculiarities of cultural products, economists examining these markets would describe them as inherently prone to market failure. By that, they do not mean the failure of a particular cultural product to be successful. As we have seen, the fate of any particular product is unpredictable at best. Rather, economists are referring to the failure of the market as a whole to do what markets are presumed to do best, that is, to lead to the best possible outcome for the greatest possible number of participants. Or, as economists would say, to maximize social welfare.

This realization has long underpinned the regulation of broadcasting. Virtually every country regulates entry to its market by broadcasters and imposes public-service obligations on them to ensure a socially balanced mix of diverse programming. But the same symptoms of market failure are increasingly being recognized in other sectors. Existing models for the production and distribution of books, films and sound recordings all face criticism for failing to provide the full range of choice that consumers and citizens may want.

These unique attributes also render the hallowed trade theory of "comparative advantage" inapplicable to cultural products. However valid the theory of comparative advantage may be for ordinary commodities, it breaks down entirely in serving the interests of nations in regard to cultural products. As Chapters 6 and 16 will show, unrestrained globalization in cultural trade would not yield higher real incomes for all, let alone a wider choice of expressions. Instead, it would simply institutionalize the dominance of a few and prevent governments from taking effective measures to ensure opportunity (success can never be guaranteed), space and choice for a diversity of their own citizens' cultural expression.

Little in this analysis is likely to surprise those who responded to the question at the outset of this chapter with the intuitive reply that "*Of course* there is a difference between culture and other products." To many people intimately involved in the creation of cultural goods, it is self-evident that cultural products are different from widgets. Cultural goods embody ideas and stories. They wield a symbolic influence that goes far beyond the narrow marketplace of commodities to influence such subjective areas as social cohesion, national identity and cultural sovereignty.

Here, economists typically lapse into the language of "merit goods" and "social goods" and the indeterminate "externalities" of cultural products. They refer to the benefits to society that arise from the creation, production and distribution of these products, but that are not and cannot be measured by their market price.

In the face of such externalities many economic analysts throw up their hands in tactical surrender, admitting their inability to deal with those values. Yet most choose simply to roll on past this defeat, declaring in effect that such values, since they cannot be measured, are too trivial to impede the strategic sweep of their vision. One critic, writing in the *Yale Journal of International Law,* provides an example. Analyzing "culture and other 'non-economic' concerns," he concedes that "in many markets, the price of A/Vs [audiovisual products: films and television programs] may not fully reflect the value of cultural integrity. Recognizing this incongruence is crucial because welfare maximization occurs only when prices fully reflect all the costs and benefits of an action to the society as a whole." But a moment later, he counters that "culture, the cultural content of A/Vs, and the interaction between the two are so difficult to measure that ... regulations ... based on the national origin of A/Vs provide only dubious cultural benefits."

The tendency to belittle cultural benefits because they are hard to measure is a common theme in the writings of economists who wander into the subject to take potshots at cultural policy. Perhaps this is understandable. They may find it frustrating to discover that their conventional economic theories cannot be made to apply to a sector that does not behave like the marketplaces they hypothesize.

But just because economists lack instruments to assign monetary value to cultural or social merits does not make them less vital—or less worth defending. Social benefits not mediated by markets may indeed be hard to measure. But that does not mean they can simply be defined out of existence. Tools capable of mitigating the market failure and ensuring shelf space for diverse cultural expression are of more than dubious benefit. As later chapters will show, the returns from well-made and flexibly applied regulation can be both demonstrable and significant.

With these preliminary observations in mind, we turn next to a closer look at the economics of popular culture in action—on the pages, screens and sound systems of the global marketplace.

4

WHY
HITS
ARE
FLUKES

T HE SCENE OPENS on an aerial panorama. Beneath a black and empty sky, neon citadels of hope and heartbreak glitter on Las Vegas's fabled Strip. Soon, there will be a corpse.

It is the opening sequence of the highest-rated dramatic series playing on American television—*c.s.i.: Crime Scene Investigation.* The slick and stylish weekly whodunit airs on the CBS television network on Thursday nights. It is the first show in a decade to put a serious dent in rival network NBC's vise-like grip on that evening's audience. In its second season, a spinoff series—*c.s.i.: Miami*—has just launched. By the time the production exhausts its value in repeat broadcasts and syndication in the United States and elsewhere, it is likely to return to its owners a jackpot worth more than a billion dollars.

One of those owners is the CBS network itself, a unit of giant New York–based Viacom Inc. The other is less known and very much smaller: Alliance Atlantis Communications Inc. of Toronto. Viacom's annual revenues are around US$20 billion, from its television networks (of which CBS is only one—it also owns several cable channels), the Paramount movie studio, theme parks, a publishing wing and other units. Alliance Atlantis brings in less than C$960 million a year. The two will split the hundreds of millions of dollars *c.s.i.* is likely to earn over its lifetime on a fifty-fifty basis.

The Canadian company is there because CBS asked it to be.

Why would a deep-pocketed U.S. giant hand over half of a huge hit to a Canadian company one thirtieth its size?

Part of the answer lies in a factor explored in Chapter 2—the power of place. By 2000, Alliance Atlantis had been a presence in the capital of filmed entertainment for more than a decade. As a separate entity, Alliance had produced a landmark Canadian–American series called *Due South* for CBS. The series did well during its brief run and better than the show that eventually replaced it. For its part, Atlantis produced a chain of well-crafted MOWs (movies of the week) for the U.S. network, culminating in a hit mini-series based on the life of Joan of Arc. By the time the two merged in 1998, the combined entity had earned a place on the A-list of TV production outfits.

"The weekly series business is an exclusive club," says Peter Sussman, head of the merged company's television division. "It's a big boys business and you can't be in it unless you can show big boyness." And Alliance Atlantis has proven its stature. "We have become as high as you can get in the game of TV movies and miniseries in Hollywood," Sussman notes. By 2000, "CBS's view of us [was that] we probably had the brains and resources and wherewithal and the financial strength to stick it out for two hundred episodes of the series."

But that still doesn't explain why a $20 billion-a-year giant felt compelled to allow half of a mega-hit to be owned by a comparative pipsqueak—albeit a respected one.

The answer lies in the attribute that makes commercial culture less a conventional business than a scaled-up version of a Vegas crapshoot. Every time a network launches a new series, a publisher launches a new book or a music company unveils a new CD, its chances are no more certain than those of the dice on the green felt table. *Nobody knows* whether it will turn up a gold-plated hit or a ten-ton turkey— only that the chances of the turkey are far better than the odds of the hit.

Even without marquee stars, a thirteen-episode season of a contemporary television drama can quickly run up $50 million in production costs. The CBS executive who invited Alliance Atlantis to cover half of that was simply acting like any reasonable bookie ahead of an upcoming Super Bowl. He was laying off his bet.

"Shows don't come with labels saying 'Hit,'" Sussman notes. "It is still a very risky business—risky for us, risky for the studios, risky for the networks. Everybody is looking for partnerships."

This chapter explores how the game is played. It will survey the enormous prizes that keep punters coming back to the table and examine the strategies high rollers employ to shave the odds in their favour. And it will show how those strategies not only muscle aside smaller players but mock the claim that in picking winners, consumers are sovereign.

THE ODDS working against any new work of popular culture are difficult to overstate. One Hollywood movie boss reports that his studio gets ten thousand proposals for movies in any given year. Fewer than a hundred are accepted for "development"—being worked up into a camera-ready script. Of those, the studio makes only a dozen into actual movies.

Every year, producers pitch some three thousand dramatic series ideas to U.S. network executives. Between August and November, the six networks commission writers to turn about three hundred of those into scripts. Starting just before Christmas, that number is further winnowed down, as the networks order perhaps fifty of those to be filmed as pilots—with a handful more being shot in part. Of those, perhaps two dozen will eventually be given an airing. Half may survive into a second season. *Two* might hope to qualify as bona fide hits.

Consider the fate of the show initially scheduled to appear just before *c.s.i.* on Thursday nights. Although it was also new, *The Fugitive* had several apparent advantages over the Vegas-set show that followed it. It was a remake of a series that had been successful in the 1960s. It employed a concept that had sustained a successful movie. And it was supported by considerably more promotion. Despite all that, it bombed, becoming one more soon-forgotten failed bet.

At every stage of this process, money flows like water. The price of making a single pilot—which may or may not air, and then may or may not win a series spot—can reach US$6 million. Small wonder gaming turns up frequently as a metaphor for the business of popular culture. *New York Times* film critic Elvis Mitchell described the decision to release a contemporary movie as akin to "betting the mortgage on a roulette spin in Vegas."

A colleague of Peter Sussman's, Victor Loewy, CEO of Alliance Atlantis's film distribution business, says of sending movies out to theatres: "You know every time you buy a lotto ticket. We opened *Spy Kids II* yesterday [in Canada]. Two million dollars of prints and advertising has gone out of our pockets and we haven't got a clue how it's going to perform. We don't know." (As it turned out, *Spy Kids II* earned US$86 million in North American box-office, too little, after exhibitors took their 50 per cent cut to recoup its estimated $68 million production and launch costs.)

Larry Gerbrandt, a senior analyst with Kagan World Media, a Hollywood research firm, notes: "The exciting thing about the movie business is the same thing that's exciting about investing in Broadway plays. You never know when you're going to invest in the next *Titanic* or the next *Cats*. And the rewards on those are so extraordinary. It's better than hitting the Powerball lottery."

The lottery is not limited to television or movies. For nearly two years, MCA Records paid a mounting tab in expectation that Irish teenager Carly Hennessy would break out among young music fans the way pop sensation Britney Spears had. It was not an unreasonable expectation. The comely and personable Ms. Hennessy had toured Europe in the musical *Les Miserables* before the age of ten and released a Christmas album in her home country. When she turned up in Los Angeles in 1999, MCA signed her to a six-album contract with a $100,000 advance and an apartment in Marina Del Rey paid for by the label. For the next twenty-four months, it shelled out for recording studios, producers and promotional junkets until by the time Hennessy released her first CD in late 2001, MCA had sunk US$2.2 million into its preparation. After three months, the disc had sold all of 378 copies—each representing a little under $5,000 of MCA's investment. Finally the label cut Ms. Hennessy loose.

Not that Carly was in bad company. Record executives estimate that fewer than 5 per cent of CDs released ever become profitable. To break into the black in the United States, a major-label CD needs to sell more than 500,000 copies. In 2001, just 112 of 6,455 albums released— *1.7 per cent*—reached that mark.

In the *nobody knows* casino, the difference between books and music, magazines and movies, is essentially the difference between bingo and roulette: there really isn't any, except that the tickets are paper instead of plastic. In the United States in 2000, more than 870 new magazine titles joined 4,600 already jostling for shelf space. And

65 per cent of the copies of *all* titles delivered to newsstands ended up in shredders. Canadian book publishers release approximately ten thousand new hardcover and paperback titles each year, U.S. publishers about eight times that number. Only a small fraction of the titles in either country sell even five thousand copies.

Viewed this way, what mainly distinguishes books from music and both from filmed entertainment is the size of the bankroll required to step up to the table. Books represent the quarter slots of the culture casino, music CDs the five-dollar blackjack tables. Effects-laden "event" movies with top-flight A-list stars are the equivalent of Vegas's invitation-only, $25,000-minimum high-roller stakes.

Even at the middle of the high end, the bets are impressive. "At least once a month," writes British author Martin Dale in *The Movie Game,* "a Major [studio] releases a new $50 million film ... knowing that within the first week it may gross anywhere between zero and $100 million."

In fact, the real money at risk is greater than even those figures imply. Substantial as it is, the production budget represents only the cost of the master of the finished film—the so-called "negative cost." Prints that will be distributed to theatres and advertising to support the release (collectively, "P&A" costs), typically add a further 60 to 100 per cent of the negative cost. By 2002, average Hollywood production budgets of the major studios had soared to $58.8 million. P&A brought the total sum being gambled on a merely average studio movie that year to almost $90 million.

"Box-office gross" conceals more hazards. Depending on how long a movie runs, theatres retain 30 to 70 per cent of ticket receipts. A Hollywood rule of thumb is that a film must gross *at least twice* its cost before it begins to earn a profit. Once P&A is thrown in, that $50 million movie must therefore earn $200 million at the box-office to have a prayer of breaking even.

Even that calculation leaves no room for the creative accounting that film distributors famously deploy (discussed in more detail in Chapter 5). Most money stays in the hands of the film's distributor and is never credited to the production, sustaining another Hollywood aphorism: "There *is* no back end."

The *nobody knows* principle is no more unique to Hollywood than it is to movies. It is the general reality of cultural goods everywhere.

Dale details several examples of fortunes put at risk by non-U.S. movie producers—and how their bets played out:

➤ Through pre-sales and its own funds, Britain's Carolco raised $106 million for its 1995 *Cutthroat Island;* the film earned back less than $20 million worldwide and Carolco went bankrupt.

➤ A consortium of Argos Films in France, Germany's Road Movies and Australia's Village Roadshow invested $27.5 million to make 1991's *Until the End of the World;* it did under $1 million in U.S. box-office and by Dale's count, under $10 million in the rest of the world.

➤ By contrast, 1994's *Four Weddings and a Funeral,* made for under $5 million, netted $67 million in after-cost profits for its primary investor, Anglo-Dutch PolyGram.

Echoing the pattern of A-list actors and the rest, fewer than 5 per cent of movies earn about 80 per cent of the industry's profit, according to economist Arthur de Vany. Notes S. Abraham Ravid, of the Rutgers University Business School: "The distribution of returns is ... composed of many films that flop and some that are phenomenal hits, rather than the many 'average' films a normal distribution would imply." Of 150 or so films released by major studios in North America in any given year, Martin Dale reports in *The Movie Game,* "under ten films gross over $100 million, another ten films gross over $50 million. The last fifty films (a third of the total) have meagre grosses."

Harold Vogel, in his analysis *Flickering Images: The Business of Hollywood,* describes "the virtual dichotomization of the theatrical market into a relative handful of hits and a mass of also-rans ... in which four out of perhaps a dozen major releases generated as much as 80 per cent of total revenues." Elsewhere Vogel estimates that up to 70 per cent of all major films released lose money.

And those odds are for the minority of films fortunate enough to get a chance on the large screen. A larger number do not even get that far. A telling 2002 study by Frank Rusco, of the U.S. General Accounting Office, and University of Calgary economist W. David Walls discovered that even among movies shot by studios or large independent production companies in North America, more than one in five *were never released* to theatres. Of films made by small independents, *80 per cent* were never released.

In Great Britain, the proportion of films left to languish in the vault rose steadily during the late 1990s, passing 50 per cent in 1998. By mid-

July 2002, close to 60 per cent of all films made in Britain during 2000 had not yet been released to theatres.

Although many films without theatrical release did eventually earn some money from video and other "secondary" sales, those that first appeared on the big screen "earned over 97.7 per cent of all income from secondary markets," Rusco and Walls note.

IF THE ODDS against winning make pop culture resemble Las Vegas on a grand scale, so does the jackpot that awaits the lucky few. It can be enormous. As this book was being written in 2003, the most outsized winner of the past season was moviedom's *My Big Fat Greek Wedding*. Made for less than $5 million, the modest story of more or less just what the title suggests, one immigrant daughter's very ethnic wedding to a non-Greek beau, had earned a North American box-office of over $200 million since its release. (It also won its Canadian-born creator and star a prime spot on CBS's schedule for a spinoff sitcom, although the show was later cancelled.)

The even more spectacular box-office grosses posted by big-budget "event" films may or may not represent equivalent multiples of their higher production costs. Still, the 2002 summer hit *Spider-Man* was expected to make a material difference to the bottom line of its corporate parent Sony, after it earned $675 million worldwide within six weeks of its May release. Sony spent $139 million (plus P&A) to make the special-effects-laden blockbuster. The summer of 2002 comedy chart-topper, *Austin Powers in Goldmember,* made for $63 million (plus P&A), brought in $212 million in two months.

The all-time record-holder remains 1997's *Titanic.* One of the most expensive bets ever played in the culture casino, it cost more than $200 million to launch. But it had earned, by late 2002, a staggering $1.8 billion in worldwide box-office.

A close runner-up, however, is *Gone With the Wind.* Made in 1939 for the then considerable sum of $3.9 million, it has earned $1.15 billion for a succession of rights holders over the decades since.

Gone With the Wind benefited, as do all such winners, from the unique economic attributes of cultural products identified in the previous chapter. Once the sunk costs of the initial copy were recovered, the returns from its exploitation in subsequent copies, in foreign territories or new technologies (the DVD version of *Gone With the Wind,* for instance), went straight to the bottom line. Meanwhile, because the intellectual property is not itself consumed, no matter how many millions of people have already seen it, *Gone With the Wind* can be enjoyed by an almost infinite number of additional millions of paying viewers in the future.

And the potential pot seems close to bottomless. Audiences in developed countries spend more and more each year not only on movies but on all classes of entertainment. According to the Motion Picture Association of America (MPAA), Canadian and U.S. moviegoers have spent more money on cinema admissions every year for a decade, reaching US$9.5 billion in 2002. In Canada, while after-tax income for the average household barely increased between 1982 and 1999 (growing just 4 per cent over seventeen years), spending on "event admission"—a category that includes sporting events as well as music concerts and movies—went up by 47 per cent. Indulging at home increased even more, with households spending a staggering 253 per cent more for entertainment delivered over television in 1999 than in 1983. In Britain, film admissions in 2002 were the highest they had been in three decades.

"Entertainment," says Sam Christensen, a Hollywood consultant to film stars, "is the modern term we apply to story-telling. That human need—to tell, hear and repeat stories—goes back to our beginning. We need entertainment as we need food and shelter."

THE PRIZE is unparalleled. But so is the risk. How to reduce risk?

Perhaps the simplest strategy is to bet only on perceived winners. In the culture casino, this happens in two ways: favouring only A-list stars, and attempting to clone past winners. Evidence suggests the results may be somewhat Pyrrhic in producing fewer outright flops but also fewer big hits. At the same time, the strategy has perverse effects—reducing audience exposure to a wider variety of talent, especially the new and the niche, and raising nearly insurmountable barriers against the entry of any player who lacks big-money backing.

The phenomenon is a general one. In mid-2002, novelist Alice Thomas Ellis lamented the way Britain's publishers increasingly piled incentives on established writers at the expense of the undiscovered. "Vast sums are lavished on already-rooted and blooming authors," Ellis wrote, "leaving nothing to nourish potential seedlings."

Earlier that year, David Kirkpatrick reported in *The New York Times* that two important book distributors in the United States had merged. Publishers Group West, he wrote, had previously handled "little-known publishers [that] sell eccentric books." It was acquired by Advanced Marketing Services, a company that "typically sells enormous quantities of relatively few books," with three quarters of its output sold through discount warehouses like Costco and Sam's Club. "The warehouses," Kirkpatrick noted, "usually carry only a few hundred books but . . . can send sales of those books soaring." The new company would create "a powerful new gatekeeper" between readers and authors, he predicted.

As commercial producers of culture—publishers, record labels, film and TV studios—merge into ever-larger entities, the focus on only the most profitable artists and projects has tightened sharply. Nowhere is the trend more apparent than in recorded music. When Universal Music acquired PolyGram N.V. for $10.4 billion in 1998 to create the world's biggest record company, among its first acts was to shed some two hundred artists. Other labels have also sharply cut back on all but their highest-grossing acts.

Those who did not make the cut were by no means all as unheard-of as Ms. Hennessy. Rod Stewart and David Bowie have each sold millions of records; at the start of 2002, both were without labels. Virgin Records (a unit of EMI Group, the last large stand-alone music company) even paid Mariah Carey $28 million to tear up her multi-album contract with the company.

Jazz saxophonist Branford Marsalis was a producer for Columbia Records until 2002. "Given the parameters that exist today," Marsalis believes, "you could take somebody like Bruce Springsteen and there's no way he could get a contract on a major label. Stevie Wonder wouldn't be acceptable. Talent is secondary, even tertiary. The only way the president can keep his job is by delivering hits, not by delivering good music."

Still, it is in filmed entertainment where the biggest risks lie—and the magnetism of the A-list is irresistible. "The great lie of the movie business," says film journalist Michael Cieply, "is 'the material is everything.' The material is actually nothing. What really drives the entire business is star power."

New York Times film critic Elvis Mitchell advances an explanation: "There's so much about the business that is ruled by fear. [The thinking is] 'If Tom Cruise is in the movie, well it's going to be a hit. And if it's not a hit with Tom Cruise in it, well it's not our fault because the last five Tom Cruise movies were hits.'" Or, as yet another film journalist, Richard Natale, observes: "A bad movie with Bruce Willis will make more money than a bad movie without Bruce Willis."

The thinking is not wrong. In his survey of the economic literature and of movie profits, S. Abraham Ravid discovered that the presence of a star did little to improve the chances that a particular film would be a hit. On the other hand, "such stars may provide 'a floor' to the revenues of a film," thereby reducing the risk that the executive who produced it would be associated with a flop.

The impulse to rely exclusively on A-list stars has trickled down from big-budget studio movies to smaller-budget ventures, dismaying indie filmmakers like Allison Anders. The maker of *Mi Vida Loca* (1994) and *Things Behind the Sun* (2002) says that potential investors in even small films increasingly demand a 'name' cast before they will advance funds. "Now you really have to have huge stars," she laments, "I mean *huge,* for a $2 million movie."

British film distributor Michael Ryan agrees: "It used to be possible for smaller companies to go out and finance a film out of pre-sales. Now it's just not possible unless you've got a Stallone, a Schwarzenegger, a Willis, a Sharon Stone—and even then it takes a long time."

If the absence of a star can kill an otherwise promising project, the presence of one can breathe life into the most unlikely material. In 2003, Australian-born Hollywood A-list actor Mel Gibson completed a film based on Biblical accounts of the last twelve hours of Jesus's life— with the cast speaking their lines in Latin and the Aramaic language spoken two thousand years ago.

The A-list halo goes beyond the Actors' Guild to a handful of other "above-the-line" creators. Most television writers in Hollywood labour to survive the ruthless process of elimination that whittles down several thousand pitches to a handful of pilots and even fewer series that will be greenlit for any given broadcast season. A handful, says Peter Sussman, "can come in to make a pitch where the network will say, 'We'll buy it . . . What's it about?' David Kelly or Steve Bochco are the ones that are visible."

A correspondingly small group of A-list directors and producers carry similar free passes to the most senior ears at major studios.

Again, the effect is to raise the bar for new candidates. "The decisive role of talent focuses power in the hands of the Majors and agents," writes Martin Dale in *The Movie Game*. "The studios try to lock in talent by 'first look' deals, by which they put up overhead and development spending in return for first right of refusal. This makes it very difficult for outsiders to break into the business . . . The problem is access, which usually depends on personal contacts and/or an established indie reputation."

As Allison Anders and Michael Ryan observe, however, acquiring the credits necessary to establish that reputation—absent access to stars—increasingly presents aspiring filmmakers with a Catch-22.

A variant on turning repeatedly to the same A-list stars is to turn repeatedly to the same properties—cloning previous successes through sequels, prequels or "franchise" extensions.

This is hardly new. Shakespeare mined the history of the Tudor kings for a string of stage hits. There have been innumerable serialized book characters since Arthur Conan Doyle brought us the continuing adventures of Sherlock Holmes. The most famous version of *The Maltese Falcon*—the one starring Humphrey Bogart—was in fact the third film based on Dashiell Hammett's novel. Perhaps the most successfully cloned character in film history is James Bond. Agent 007 has appeared in more than twenty films to date, with yet another in development, and has spawned any number of knock-offs, including copious allusions in the *Austin Powers* series (itself in its third clone as of this writing). Other film franchises include the *Friday the 13th* series (ten and counting), *Halloween* (eight), *The Muppets* (six) and *Dirty Harry* (five).

Even so, sequels and prequels, with their perceived low risk, command an ever-greater share of studio investment. The summer and fall of 2002 were dominated by a brood of clones. To name only some: the *Goldmember* installment in the Austin Powers series, *Men in Black II*, *Red Dragon* (prequel to the earlier *Hannibal* and *Silence of the Lambs*), *Spy Kids II*, *Stuart Little 2* and *Star Wars: Episode 2*. Other 2002 films cloned earlier television properties to the big screen: *Scooby-Doo*, *The Powerpuff Girls* and *Hey Arnold! The Movie*.

Clones also occupy growing screen time on television. CBS and Alliance Atlantis's second-season extension of *Crime Scene Investigation* to *C.S.I.: Miami* is but one example. The venerable *Law & Order* police procedural has been replicated in two offspring series. As of this writing, CBS has plans to revive the 1960s scripted comedy *The Beverly Hillbillies* in a "reality-TV" format; Fox has a similar scheme to bring back the same era's *Green Acres* as a "reality" show.

Whatever their creative merit, every clone absorbs money and screen time that might otherwise bring audiences a new voice or different perspective on the world.

And still, *nobody knows.* The low-risk promise of cloning winners or leaning on star power is not always borne out in the delivery. Sitcoms built around alumni of the long-running *Seinfeld*—Jason Alexander, Julia Louis-Dreyfus and Michael Richards—all stiffed.

An even more spectacular flame-out awaited a bizarre attempt to graft the appeal of television personality Rosie O'Donnell to the 125-year-old homemakers' magazine *McCall's.* The strategy copied the successful transfer of Martha Stewart and Oprah Winfrey's television identities to branded periodicals. *McCall's* owners Gruner+Jahr (a unit of German media giant Bertelsmann) renamed their fading publication *Rosie* in early 2001. The identity graft failed when O'Donnell abruptly quit her talk show and took to publicly declaring herself "a big-mouthed fat lesbian" and "uber-bitch."

O'Donnell's assertions were especially hurtful to G+J in the light of another highly popular odds-shaving strategy: playing to Main Street, U.S.A. "Playing in Peoria" may not matter to Canadian, Indian or German creators who consciously settle for a purely domestic audience, or to fringe musicians content to play the rave circuit. But for any creators who aspire to consequential "international" sales or the audiences that pay off big-budget cinematic bets, their work must first prove popular in middle America.

"Everything revolves around the U.S.: the earth, the sun and everything else," says Victor Loewy, Alliance Atlantis's executive in charge of acquiring film rights. "Any film that doesn't get acclaimed in the United States, there's not a hope in hell to make it anywhere else except its own territory."

Indeed, in the scales of corporate judgement playing in Peoria may trump even star power. Director and screenwriter Kevin Smith recalled for a PBS broadcast in 2002 his experience trying to find a home for *Dogma,* a 1999 film in which a descendant of Christ is called to defend humanity from renegade angels.

We had a cast which included Ben Affleck and Matt Damon follow-ing *Good Will Hunting* winning a writer Oscar [and making] $125 mil-lion. Universal watched it and passed. MGM watched it and passed. Columbia watched it and passed. Everyone loved the movie and said "Absolutely it's marketable with this cast, but we can't do it." All of them didn't want to get involved because it was raising the ire of a re-ligious group called the Catholic League.

Although this book's focus is mainly on the cultural products of en-tertainment—movies, scripted television, books and music—the ac-tions of Time Warner's CNN in the wake of the 9/11 terror attacks are illuminating on this point. The Atlanta-based news network prided it-self on the number of its non-American correspondents, promoting the added authority they brought to coverage of world attitudes. But an In-dian-born producer who worked at CNN at the time recalled how a panel of American editors with no foreign experience vetted every cor-respondent's report before allowing it on the air. Reports deemed to de-mand too much knowledge of foreign affairs for U.S. viewers, or any that included "actuality" regarded as insufficiently "America-friendly," even items destined only for CNN's international broadcasts and never to be seen in Peoria were killed or sent back to be reworked.

In this way, the limited horizon of Main Street, U.S.A. becomes the lens and filter for whatever the wider world might wish to say to itself through the story-telling language of popular culture.

In fact, even Peoria may be too wide a lens for some corporate ven-dors of culture. In pursuit of the most profitable audience "sweet spots," media giants are increasingly abandoning consumers who are perceived to generate only fractionally smaller returns. In doing this, their choices simply affirm the priorities of music executives for whom only platinum-selling artists are of interest.

In 2002, ABC came close to cancelling *Nightline,* whose audience it deemed undesirably old, as the pricetag of poaching rival network CBS's youth-oriented *Late Show with David Letterman.* In an extensive survey for *The New York Times* of the disappearance from television of independent producers, journalist Bernard Weinraub wrote:

By all accounts some of the shows [earlier independents] made—*Soap, All In the Family, Benson, Maude, Golden Girls*—would not pass muster today. The lead characters would not fit snugly into the prized youth market: they are too old, too ethnic, too female. "Try doing a show today like *Golden Girls* about three older women," said one top network executive. "Good luck!"

Each of these strategies may serve to reduce risk in the *nobody knows* casino of popular culture. But each also strips away a little more of culture's variety. With each clone, each recourse to the same short A-list, each new pander to the narrow interests of youth or Middle America, supposedly "sovereign" audiences are deprived of more diverse choices—and of the opportunity to either acclaim or reject them.

Would the large cohort of North American baby boomers slipping past their fiftieth birthday warm to a comedy about three of their generation approaching their own golden years? Who knows? We are unlikely ever to find out.

RISK-CONTAINMENT STRATEGIES do not end with eliminating the chancy. In a variety of ways, big publishers, major record labels and the conglomerated Hollywood film and television studios have learned that popularity can simply be fabricated.

There is no question that contemporary markets have the capacity to present an apparent cornucopia of choice. Book superstores such as Canada's Chapters-Indigo chain, and Borders and Barnes & Noble in the United States, place great emphasis on their wide selection of titles—typically as many as 150,000 in a single store, compared with 30,000 to 50,000 in the smaller independent outlets they have largely replaced.

Some observers equate this apparent enormity of selection with effective "consumer sovereignty." American commentator Nick Gillespie, writing in *Reason Online,* for instance, finds evidence of "a massive and prolonged increase in art, music, literature, video, and other forms of creative expression" in the 3,500 radio and 670 TV stations that have come on-air in the United States since 1970, the 10,000 video titles available at the average rental outlet, the 139 independent American films released in 1997 (compared with 100 a decade earlier) and the 1.3 million books in print in the United States (compared with 83,000 in 1950). Topping off his inventory of abundance are some 2 billion pages of information on the World Wide Web.

But this apparent "more" turns out to deliver less than at first it promises. Where is the greater choice if those 3,500 radio stations are owned by a mere handful of corporations that increasingly program their chains as one? As a cruise around the television dial in any contemporary North American home will quickly demonstrate, many "different" stations may well be broadcasting the same program at any given hour of the day.

But even where the *variety* is real, effective *choice* may be another matter. Merchandising theorists have begun to challenge the wisdom of packaged-good makers who fragment consumer brands into multiple, narrowly differentiated products. Faced with a vast array of marginally distinct mustards or toothpaste, they point out, busy consumers too often simply pick at random—or turn away.

The vast numbers Gillespie celebrates do not diminish this wall-of-mustard problem. To the contrary, they only amplify it. Given the infinite variety of cultural experience, it would be easier to taste all the mustards than to reach an informed opinion about any more than a minute fraction of the books on the shelves at Borders.

The *too much information* problem presents creators and consumers with reciprocal challenges. For the audience, the problem is to find the one product on the overflowing shelves—which CD, which book or video—that will most perfectly satisfy their mood, interests and desires at the present moment. For creators, the challenge is to cut through the cacophony and capture the attention of those individuals who will most appreciate their work.

In this battle for attention, big players deploy decisive advantages, effectively undermining consumer preference. The strategies, used in every cultural sector, include dominating shelf space, practising barrage advertising to overwhelm "word of mouth" with "buzz" and co-opting opinion leaders.

Book publishers illustrate the first strategy most visibly. Go to your local book superstore and examine the layout. You will quickly discover the designated "best sellers" arrayed most prominently across the most visible in-store real estate. Often entire walls are papered in face-out copies of the latest heavily promoted title. A consumer who enters her local Chapters or Borders without a specific work in mind must pass in front of the serried ranks of best sellers before she gets to the aisles where the other 149,950 titles are stocked, spine out.

This of course is no accident, nor is the arrangement usually up to the staff of the particular outlet. In fact, the practice closely mimics the way in which supermarkets have for years charged packaged-good makers for shelf footage. Major publishers offer chains substantial inducements in exchange for favourable displays. These inducements may take the form of extra-deep discounts in wholesale prices or straight-up cash: so much for the end of an aisle, so much to be near the checkout, so much for a wall in the main foyer or for a window display, so much for "face-out" rather than "spine-out" shelving on a regular aisle.

The aggressive promotion of best sellers in warehouse chains and book superstores has driven the North American sales of top-moving titles from hundreds of thousands of copies to several millions in the last fifteen years. Overall book sales have risen only modestly over the same period, however—implying *a decline* in the total sales of other titles.

Promotional placement is of course available to any publisher who wishes to pay for it. In practice, it is the privilege of deep-pocketed corporate houses. Not for the first time, "the rich get richer, and the poor get poorer," as editor Michael Korda wrote, in a history of the book business titled *Making the List*.

The film-industry equivalent of buying shelf space is the "wide opening." Its pioneer was Lew Wasserman, a titan who ran Hollywood's most powerful talent agency, MCA, before taking over Universal Studios. It was in the latter role that he created what is now widely regarded as the prototype of the blockbuster: 1975's *Jaws* (wags have observed more than once that Wasserman understood sharks). Until then, most movies were launched in what were termed "rolling openings," screening first in a few major cities and appearing later in a circuit of smaller centres. Wasserman opened *Jaws* on 460 screens, taking an enormous bite of the day's box-office.

The wide opening is now axiomatic for big-budget releases—and involves far more screens. By 1995, virtually all of the 150 or so movies released by major studios in the United States and Canada opened on more than 800 screens. By the turn of the century, 2,000- to 3,000-screen openings were commonplace. In 2001, *Harry Potter and the Sorcerer's Stone* opened in the United States on a breathtaking 8,200 screens—nearly a quarter of all the theatres in America. On its opening weekend in Canada that year, *Goldmember* managed to seat an even more astonishing 52 per cent of all cinema admissions.

Opening wide accomplishes a number of things.

The first is to maximize the effect of marketing. The most common way to promote a film is on television. The medium lends itself to movie trailers but is also the most expensive type of advertising. Opening wide gives the best chance of seating everyone drawn by the advertising to want to see a particular movie. (In France, interestingly, regulations actually prohibit the use of TV advertising to promote movies in theatres, significantly lessening the blockbuster effect and giving smaller movies a better chance at finding audiences without having to mount comparable massive ad campaigns.)

Big opening-weekend box-office also has a secondary effect akin to that created when a book appears on a best-seller list or a CD hits *Billboard*'s Top 40 chart. It catalyzes a follow-the-leader response. Richard Caves calls it "herd behaviour." In *Creative Industries,* he writes: "Herd behaviour might arise from people's ignorance, or cost of informing themselves, about their benefit from some consumption choice. [In the case of "experience goods"] the consumer cannot ascertain the actual value without making the purchase . . . Better than deciding on just her own hunch, the consumer looks to see what everybody else is doing."

In truth, in the one-on-one nature of appreciating music, a movie or a novel, what the herd likes says little about what may please an individual. But with a surfeit of choices to consider, box-office data "feels like information," as critic Elvis Mitchell puts it. "It becomes a way to sell the picture. 'America's Number One Comedy.' Or the biggest hit in a month with a vowel in it. Or the biggest hit on Friday the 13th in 1999. All these kind of meaningless sobriquets that are basically ways of saying, 'if this movie attracts a lot of people then it must be worthy of our attention.'"

A second advantage arises from the way exhibitors and distributors split box-office receipts. At the start of a run, as much as 90 per cent (though more typically 70 per cent) of box-office goes to the distributor. By attracting as many viewers as possible to a movie's first weekend, opening "wide" puts more money in studio hands.

There is a third advantage. Big openings help drive a film's subsequent returns, in two critical ways. Studios use box-office statistics as a selling point in promoting a film later in its run; we'll return to that below. Box-office also influences how much a film will earn in secondary "windows" of exhibition such as video and television, as Chapter 5 will show.

There is yet a fourth merit to the big, splashy opening. With enough advertising, a studio can dress up a turkey as an eagle long enough to fill seats for a weekend and begin to recoup its investment before bad reviews take hold. "It's a pre-bought hit," explains Lucy Fisher, a former executive for MGM, 20th Century–Fox, Warner Brothers and Sony before establishing her own Red Wagon Productions. "You spent so much money that you got people to come the first weekend, even though they didn't like it and they won't tell their friends."

Or as Kagan World Media's Larry Gerbrandt says: "The studios have gotten so good at cutting the trailers, marketing the films, creating that 'buzz'—it's not word-of-mouth but it's that 'want-to-see' buzz—that they can put butts in the seat on opening weekend." Promotion, in other words, can trump the judgement of those who have actually experienced a movie's good- or badness.

But the wide opening is available only to the biggest of the big. Every additional copy of a film adds about US$1,000 to the "prints" portion of a distributor's P&A investment. For a blockbuster, the combined bill can easily top $100 million (although, as Chapter 5 will show, that tab is effectively lightened when the studio or its parent also owns a network).

And again the strategy draws the oxygen of attention away from other creative candidates. "It's the most brilliant thing they ever did, to report box office to the public," fumes Allison Anders. "It used to be it was only reported to the trades. Nobody cared. Now the local anchorwoman's going, 'Oh, I haven't seen any of those on the top five. I better get out and see those.' I think that indies have really . . . suffered."

Films promoted with wide openings "now earn over 95 per cent of all theatrical revenues," reports Martin Dale. Since that dominance carries over into subsequent earnings, "wide release patterns are an additional 'barrier to entry' and make the film business very ruthless." *Jaws*, indeed!

ANOTHER WAY audiences can sort wheat from chaff among the flurry of cultural products vying for attention is to seek third-party advice. Typically this comes through reviews—of books, CDs or filmed entertainment. Most reviewers, it should be said, appear to approach their task with sincerity and attempt to give candid, if necessarily subjective, appraisals. But here again, rational actions may lead to skewed outcomes.

Reviewers who know that certain movies are going to benefit from big promotional campaigns reasonably anticipate that their own audiences will be most interested in those titles. So it happens, as it did during the writing of this chapter, that on one single day the same three films received front-page attention in the entertainment sections of *The Wall Street Journal, The New York Times, The Globe and Mail, The National Post* and *The Vancouver Sun.*

Many people today are more likely to consult television than a newspaper for reviews. This is particularly true for filmed entertainment. Television networks in recent years have obliged with a plethora of "newsmagazine" shows that focus on entertainment and entertainers. Virtually all are owned and produced by the same networks that produce the shows they "review" and share corporate ties to the studios whose movies they report on. It is far from clear in these broadcasts where the function of review bleeds into that of promotion.

For readers, book clubs offer another source of advice about the nearly two hundred new books that appear in an average week in Canada—or the 1,500 that come out in the United States. Although their appeal has waned over the years, more than 4 million Americans still subscribe to one or another of the five biggest clubs in that country. The original Book-of-the-Month club, launched in 1926, was an independent enterprise. Today, Book-of-the-Month is owned in part by Time Warner, which also owns Little, Brown and Time-Life Books, and in part by Germany's Bertelsmann, owner of the Random House, Knopf, Vintage and Doubleday imprints.

NOTHING IS LIKELY to alter the fundamental uncertainty of *nobody knows*. Punters will continue to overlook long odds in hopeful pursuit of huge winnings at the casino of popular culture.

We have discovered ways to pare those odds, however. Cloning the winners, cozying up to A-list players and spending heavily, whether to dominate the field by "opening wide" and owning shelf space, or to occupy the "mental real estate" of audiences, can all materially shift the favour of Lady Luck. But those strategies take more than "big boyness." They conspicuously advantage a handful of giant conglomerates most capable of sustaining a high volume of plays, huge investments and an integrated exploitation of the statistically rare win.

As we shall see.

5

WHY
BIG
IS
BEST

ALLAN GREGG has had only a glancing acquaintance with failure. A charming polymath with a taste for aromatic cigars and rock-and-roll bar acts, the salesman's son from Edmonton, Alberta, has been a senior adviser to Canadian prime minister Brian Mulroney, a sought-after market researcher, a successful entrepreneur and host of a public television program. His singular encounter with professional disaster came when he made the mistake of setting up in business against the combined weight of the media behemoths known generically simply as "the Majors."

At the time—the late 1990s—it seemed like a good idea.

During the previous decade, Gregg had picked up a certain familiarity with the workings of the music industry. He gained his knowledge of managing rock bands—most notably a group called The Tragically Hip—the way other successful men own hobby farms: as a recreational sideline with at least the theoretical possibility of a profit. From that vantage point, Gregg saw one independent music label after another disappear in a rolling wave of industry consolidation. He thought he spied opportunity.

As the music multinationals fattened on the acquisition of mid-size labels like Motown, A&M, Virgin and Island Records, still smaller companies that remained independent continued to rely on them to distribute releases to radio stations and retail stores. In Gregg's view, the Majors were certain to give priority to their own brands—relegating the remaining small fry to distant second-class status. "Our view was that there would be an opportunity for an independent domestic distribution channel," he says.

In 1999, Gregg and a handful of partners persuaded investors to sink c$15 million into the creation of the first Canadian-owned "full service" music label in half a century. The new Song Corp. would sign acts, oversee recordings, distribute CDs to retail and promotional outlets across the country and publish the associated sheet music. To accomplish the mission, Gregg and partners quickly built up Song's staff to 83 employees—60 of them dedicated to the labour-intensive business of promoting and distributing music. "Our marketing pitch was, 'Look, we can do what the multinationals do, but unlike the multinationals, you will be a priority for us, you won't be the last in line.'"

But faults began to appear in that premise almost immediately. First, the independent labels Song expected to flock to its service kept their distance. Hyper-concerned about cash flow, they were skeptical of the new venture's staying power. "Being a lower priority and being paid was way more important to them than being a high priority and maybe not getting paid," Gregg eventually had to concede.

"And on the second front, far from wanting to cast off the independent product, the multinationals fought harder than ever to maintain it."

It quickly became clear that the Majors were unafraid of using their dominance in order to preserve it. When Song came close to signing one small label for Canadian distribution—the two had already exchanged letters of intent to consummate the deal—the Major that had been handling its product in the United States intervened, offering the small company what Gregg calls "a carrot and stick" proposition. "They said [to the independent label], 'Look, we will reduce our distribution rate if you stay with us on a North American basis. And if you don't stay with us, *we are kicking you out of the United States.*"

One of the independents for which Song Corp. held Canadian rights was Dutch label Road Runner Records. And for a year the relationship seemed to work well for both partners. Road Runner's heavy-metal rock acts sold about c$2 million worth of CDs in Canada, enough to earn the Dutch company substantially more in royalties than the US$200,000 Song had advanced when the contract was signed. As the arrangement was expiring, Song offered an advance of US$275,000 if Road Runner would renew.

It was then that Gregg received a call from a Road Runner executive in Holland. He said, "I've got an offer from Universal for US$3 million over three years. I'm sorry, but you're going to have to match that if you are going to keep the relationship."

Universal's offer implied sales more than three times what history suggested was likely. But the advance was non-refundable: even if the expected sales did not materialize, Road Runner would keep the funds. Recalls Gregg: "I said, 'Look, we're doing the math here and we can't see any way in the world we would ever recoup that advance. Do they know something we don't?'

"He said, 'No.'

"I said, 'Well, doesn't that worry you?'

"He said, 'No, I need the money.'"

Within months of losing the Road Runner contract, Song declared bankruptcy. Its problems extended beyond the loss of the Dutch deal. Gregg and his partners had spent heavily on upscale offices and promotion in expectation of revenues that never materialized from its flawed business plan. Still, Gregg says now, the loss to Universal signalled the beginning of the end.

Was the Universal bid predatory? Economists would probably disagree. But the real lesson is in the value of having critical mass and a large pocketbook.

The story of Britain's FilmFour—an offshoot of that country's independent television broadcaster, Channel 4—reflects a parallel experience of entering the ring against the Majors.

Launched in 1982, Channel 4 created its film subsidiary to make low-budget films of the sort identified in North America with arthouse cinemas. Its first production to gain attention was the mordantly funny *My Beautiful Laundrette*. In the early 1990s, the company had two more breakout hits with *Four Weddings and a Funeral* and *Trainspotting*. The latter, a gritty depiction of heroin addiction made for £1.7 million, grossed £12.3 million at home and another $US16.5 million in North America.

Emboldened, FilmFour set out to conquer Hollywood—or at least the Hollywood model of big-budget, wide-appeal movies. In 1999, the company signed a co-production deal with Warner Brothers. The partnership's first release was a romantic thriller set in Second World War France. *Charlotte Gray* cost US$25 million to make and grossed $668,000 in its North American run. Next out of the gate was the even more expensive dark comedy *Death to Smoochy*. It cost US$50 million to produce with star Danny DeVito—but still grossed only US$8 million in North America. More flops followed. After losing £28 million in 2001, FilmFour was forced to give up its Hollywood dream and withdraw from feature production. Later, in 2003, FilmFour re-emerged with new plans, but the budget to support its slate of proposed pictures had been cut by two thirds.

Like Song Corp., FilmFour discovered that shallow pockets almost always doom the little guy to finishing last in any attempt to break the Majors' hammerlock on the economics of commercial culture.

AS WE SAW in the last chapter, it is impossible to command an audience's appetite for any work of culture. They either like it or they don't. And *nobody knows* which it will be.

Big-company "suits" have not shown any better judgement of what will be successful than have indie mavericks. "There are lots of examples of studio moviemakers being given total artistic freedom and driving the ship onto the rocks with an enthusiasm that takes your breath away," says Sony chairman Howard Stringer. At the same time, each new movie season throws up another example of an unforeseen title becoming a popular blockbuster.

Given that random outcome, the little guy would appear at the very least to have an even shot. If anything, you'd think that the Majors' high overhead might even convey a slight edge to the outsider.

So why have the same six big Hollywood studios lasted for seventy-five years and few, if any, new players emerged? Why are the music industry and the book industry dominated by only a few giant companies? Is there something in the air of the cultural marketplace that rewards size?

The answer, in brief, is yes. Only, the explanation is not so much in the air as in the mathematics. Most books, most music CDs, most television programs and most movies do not succeed—whether the word is considered in artistic or economic terms. And when the odds are long against a win on any given play, single plays are a losing strategy.

Or as Larry Gerbrandt puts it: "If you have to live and die one film at a time, you're probably going to die."

But the converse is also true. When most single plays fail, the only winning strategy is to enter often. But that strategy is available only to players of significant size. For those who can afford to stay at the table, it works. "One *c.s.i.* pays for a lot of failures," says Les Moonves, president of CBS, which rejects as many as fifty series for every one it makes into a pilot.

Movie studios play out the same strategy, on much bigger bets. The major studios each spend up to $500 million a year simply to "develop" scripts from which to choose only the most promising. They then turn ten to twenty of those scripts into movies on budgets (for production and launch) of up to $250 million a pop. Then they pray that *one*, at least, becomes a hit—although *nobody knows* which one it will be.

To stay in the game, writes Martin Dale, "a company must have annual resources of around $1 billion and a five-year plan involving close to $5 billion. These high stakes explain why the Majors' position is virtually impregnable."

Contrast this with FilmFour's bet-the-farm style of play. "FilmFour had to close down because it invested in a couple of larger-budget films that didn't pay off and it didn't have any money left," notes David Hancock, a lead analyst at British film market research and publishing firm Screen Digest. "One flop, and your company's gone bust."

"The thing about the Majors," Hancock continues, "is that because of rolling credit lines and guaranteed income through videos and TV and stuff, they can do this on a permanent basis. They have slates of twenty-five, thirty films a year." Sheer scale, in other words, allows the Majors to stay in the game—without going broke—until their dice get hot.

A slate of titles and A-list stars—accompanied by fat advertising budgets—carries other advantages. One of those is the edge it gives the Majors in securing the best exhibition dates in cinemas.

Film exhibitors may debate whether any particular title will be a blockbuster. Indeed they quite reasonably anticipate that most will not. But a few will. So, how to choose between an unknown title from a Major and an unknown title from an independent? The latter did well at a distant film festival but has no advertising budget. The Major's film may be a dog but comes with enough advertising to ensure it "opens" big, even if it later sinks into well-deserved oblivion. The Major also has fifteen or twenty more films in the pipeline, of which at least one may be that elusive hit. The indie is a one-shot.

The outcome is not rocket science: a rational exhibitor will give her best play dates to the big boys.

But in fact even the most boffo box-office seldom returns enough to cover a movie's production cost, let alone the P&A investment of launching it. So why do studios keep making and launching motion pictures?

The answer is that cinema exhibition represents only the warm-up round of a much larger game. Payoffs—and they are many—come elsewhere.

The objective of play is to wring the greatest profit possible from products whose appeal, animated by the imagination, is easily trans-ferred from one medium to another. As Chapter 3 showed, almost all the cost of creative goods is spent in making the first copy. Thereafter, the marginal cost of reproducing that original is close to zero. This gives owners wide discrimination to price copies to greatest effect. Copyright law, in turn, maximizes that effect by abetting the subdivi-sion of markets into temporal windows and territories of exploitation. The game then is to play out a property across as many windows and territories as possible, extracting maximum return from each.

To do this, it is helpful if you happen to own or control a significant number of windows or territories. In fact, all these dynamics are most effectively exploited by organizations with sufficient scale to play the game of *nobody knows* over many rounds and across both time and space.

THE LAST TWO DECADES have witnessed an unparalleled reign of corporate cannibalism among producers and distributors of popular culture. In country after country, one company after another has been absorbed into its neighbour. By the turn of the century, the global mar-ketplaces of publishing, recorded music, film production and broadcast-ing had all increasingly come under the control of giant corporations.

Scale is not the only respect in which the biggest and most multi-national of these conglomerates tower over the rest of the creative universe. As significant as their size is their multi-faceted presence in many realms of culture. This is what allows the Majors to squeeze the maximum return from each rare winning play.

The most diversified (as of this writing: Time Warner, Viacom, Vivendi-Universal, and Walt Disney Co.) operate simultaneously in virtually every arena. They create audiovisual entertainment for both the large and small screens, and distribute it at both wholesale and retail levels. They operate free-to-air, cable or satellite television systems. They publish books and periodicals. They produce and distribute recorded music. And they provide Internet service, content or both, and manage theme parks or resorts that further exploit brands and copyright properties rooted in their creative enterprises.

The Majors have their roots in Hollywood's pre–Second World War studio system; indeed, the gilded names of many original studios live on in today's media conglomerates. But the companies as they presently exist coalesced only in the last two decades of the twentieth century.

Newspaper tycoon Rupert Murdoch set the avalanche rolling with his 1985 acquisition of 20th Century–Fox, a venerable moviemaker, financier and distributor. Acquiring Fox gave the Australian print baron a U.S. base. He extended his foothold by assembling independent U.S. television stations into the brashly down-market and stridently chauvinistic Fox Channel and then launching a cable news service under the same brand. By the turn of the century, Murdoch's News Corp. had become a major presence in broadcast, cable and satellite television in Asia, Britain and Italy as well.

In 1989, Japanese electronics maker Sony Corp. also reached across the Pacific. It bought Columbia TriStar, a producer and distributor of big-budget Hollywood movies that also owned a highly valued music label. That same year, U.S. publisher Time Inc. merged with another of the original big names of moviemaking, Warner Communications, to form Time Warner Inc. In 1995, Time Warner absorbed Turner Broadcasting Systems, which owned several powerful cable channels, including CNN and a valuable library of MGM movie titles.

The merger mania escalated in the second half of the 1990s:

➤ Viacom Inc., previously a television syndication and cable system operator, acquired first the international Blockbuster chain of video rental outlets and then Paramount, another old Hollywood studio. In 1999, Viacom merged again, this time with Columbia Broadcasting System (CBS), to bring its reach to network television.

➤ Disney, long a force in family entertainment through animation, feature films and theme parks, bought into broadcasting with the 1995 purchase of American Broadcasting Corp. (ABC).

➤ Canadian beverage giant Seagrams Inc. acquired Universal Studios (in 1995) and then Anglo-Dutch music giant PolyGram (in 1998) before itself being bought by French industrial conglomerate Vivendi.

➤ Germany's privately held broadcast and print goliath Bertelsmann moved into U.S. publishing, buying the extensive imprints of New York–based Random House in 1998.

➤ Finally, as the high-tech bubble peaked in early 2000, Internet provider America Online (AOL) parlayed its inflated market cap into a merger with Time Warner. The deal created what was for a time the world's fourth-most-valuable corporation, worth an estimated US$350 billion before its stock plunged in 2001. But even as that valuation fell, AOL Time Warner—its name reverting to Time Warner in 2003— remained the most powerful single player in the marketplace of commercial culture.

Although none of the groupings is static, the long-term trend towards the concentration of ownership seems irreversible. Indeed, while Vivendi-Universal, for instance, was on the verge of disposing of its non-American publishing divisions as this book was being written, the proposed €1.25 billion divestment raised eyebrows in France. If it proceeded, the deal stood to give buyer Lagardere SCA control of more than three quarters of the French market in educational and reference books.

"Less than ten corporations, most based in the U.S.A., own most of the world's media industries," observes Daya Kishan Thussu, a communications critic on the faculty of the University of North London. "With integration from content origination through to delivery mechanisms, a few conglomerates will control all major aspects of mass media: newspapers, magazines, books, radio, broadcast television, cable systems and programming, movies, music recordings, video cassettes and on-line services."

Even a cursory survey of the Majors' range of assets and activities is awe-inspiring.

In Time Warner's library are 5,700 Warner Brothers and MGM feature films, 32,000 television episodes and 13,500 animated titles—to which Warner's production slate continues to add. To deliver video entertainment to American homes, the conglomerate owns a broadcast network (wb), a cable distribution system and a clutch of high-profile cable channels including Home Box Office (hbo), tbs Superstation (formerly Turner Broadcasting), cnn and the Cartoon Network. Several of those are also carried on cable or by satellite to audiences in dozens of other countries. On the Internet side, America Online is the leading service provider in the United States and a branded presence in Canada, Europe and elsewhere. Warner Music Group is the world's second-largest music company, deriving half its revenue from non-U.S. sales; its labels include Elektra and Atlantic. In addition to its eponymous international newsweekly, Time Inc. produces about three dozen major titles, including *Sports Illustrated, People, Business 2.0* and *Entertainment Weekly*. Another division boasts best-selling book titles.

Viacom's film library is nearly as deep. It owns 2,500 feature films inherited from Paramount, whose production history goes back to 1912. They include such blockbusters as *The Godfather* and *Titanic*. It also owns thousands of episodes of such small-screen properties as *Frasier, Cheers* and *Star Trek*. Its channels for delivering that content range from film distributor United International Pictures to cable brands mtv and Nickelodeon (carried in more than 80 and 100 countries, respectively) and more than 6,000 Blockbuster video-rental outlets in two dozen-countries. In the United States, Viacom's broadcast interests embrace both the august cbs television network and the much newer Infinity radio network, which owns more than 163 stations. Three dozen book imprints clustered under the Simon & Schuster name release 2,400 new titles a year, including many properties aimed at children spun off from Viacom's mtv.

As this was being written, Vivendi-Universal still owned the world's biggest music company. Its Universal and PolyGram units distributed fully one third of *all* cds sold in the United States in the first half of 2002. Universal also held the world's second-largest film library. Delivery channels included America's usa Network, a 23 per cent interest in Britain's BSkyB and half of France's Canal+, as well as free-to-air television, cable, cinemas and video distributors in a dozen more countries. In Europe, Vivendi provides Internet connections and content to millions of subscribers in France, Britain, Italy and Germany. Even after divesting itself of France's biggest book publisher (assuming that sale won regulatory approval), it would retain the Houghton Mifflin stable of U.S. publishing imprints. Through Universal, the company also owns theme parks in the United States, Japan and Spain.

Theme parks exploiting a formidable cast of copyright characters are a big part of the Walt Disney Co. empire as well. But the world's second-biggest media conglomerate after Time Warner also embraces a major U.S. television network in ABC and minority stakes in several European broadcasters. Its cable channels—many viewed internationally—include the Disney Channel, ESPN and—in a joint venture with the Hearst Corporation and NBC—A&E (Arts and Entertainment), the History Channel and the Biography Channel. Its Disney, Buena Vista, Miramax and Touchstone film production and distribution brands all have subsidiaries in television and home video—and again operate internationally. Content from all those finds its way into print through Walt Disney Book Publishing and more than twenty magazine titles, and onto CDs on half a dozen music labels. In partnership with Microsoft, Disney launched an Internet portal presence in late 2002.

Sony Corp. is best known for the electronics that generate nearly two thirds of the Japanese company's revenue. But its cultural holdings are substantial nonetheless. Its Columbia TriStar division owns a library of 3,500 feature films augmented by a steady stream of new productions (it made the 2002 blockbuster *Spider-Man*). The company owns an international film distributor and 900 cinema screens around the world. Through Columbia TriStar Television, it holds rights to a further 40,000 small-screen episodes as well as ongoing properties such as the perennial game show *Wheel of Fortune*. Sony Entertainment Television is one of more than 25 international cable and satellite channels it owns. The Columbia record label is also an international presence, with acts like Bruce Springsteen, Michael Jackson and Mariah Carey in its stable.

Murdoch's News Corp., as already noted, has a foot in Hollywood film and television production through 20th Century–Fox, as well as U.S. broadcast and cable channels also under the Fox name. Its Sky and Star TV services give it cable, satellite or broadcasting presences in Europe and Asia; in 2003, it sought to add the U.S. direct-to-home satellite service, DirecTV. In print, the company owns more than 160 newspapers in 16 countries, including London's venerable *The Times* and the household franchise *TV Guide*. Through its HarperCollins publishing group, it produces more than 40 book imprints ranging from C.S. Lewis's classic Narnia tales to page-turners by mystery magus John Grisham.

Books are also the cornerstone for the seventh international Major, Germany's closely held Bertelsmann. At the annual Frankfurt Book Fair—the Cannes of the book world—its Random House umbrella of more than 30 imprints stakes out an entire block of display space in the fair's largest exhibition hall. Illuminated panels tout Random's catalogue of 20 Nobel and 48 Pulitzer laureates, among them V.S. Naipaul, Toni Morrison and Günter Grass. Bertelsmann's Gruner+Jahr is Europe's largest magazine publisher, with more than 80 titles there and in North America. The company is also Europe's biggest film producer and owns television and radio outlets in ten countries. Its BMG music group embraces more than 200 record labels, including RCA and Arista. For good measure, the company also owns the world's second-largest manufacturer of CDs, Sonopress.

AGGLOMERATION PROCEEDS APACE, albeit on a comparatively smaller scale, in national and regional markets. In a list of the world's top fifty media corporations, entities like Japan's NHK, Germany's ARD, Brazil's Globo empire, Britain's BBC and Italy's RAI all place high, with revenues in the billions of dollars and operations in two or more forms of communication each (broadcasting, TV or film production, print, music recording or the Internet). In the past decade, Britain's Virgin Group has joined Italian music company BETA to create a pan-European satellite television outlet called Superchannel (before selling it to American NBC). German publishing house Springer Verlag extended into satellite television.

In Canada, film and television production houses Alliance and Atlantis merged in 1999. The combined firm subsequently absorbed a handful of smaller independents such as Salter Street Films (which produced the subversive 2002 hit *Bowling for Columbine*) and owns and operates more than a dozen Canadian specialty channels. CanWest Global Communications, a regional television broadcaster, extended its reach from coast to coast, acquired a Toronto-based production house and then bought up the country's largest chain of metropolitan daily newspapers in 2000. In the same year, Quebecor Inc., a printing company that owned a number of French-language newspapers and magazines, acquired a significant stake in Vidéotron, the third-largest cable company in Canada, as well as TVA, the largest private French-language TV network in Canada, and some specialty channels. Not to be outdone, BCE Inc., having previously acquired control of Bell ExpressVu, the Canadian direct-to-home (DTH) satellite company, bought CTV Inc., the owner of the largest Canadian English-language private TV network and more than a dozen specialty channels. It next bought 40 per cent of TQS, the second private French-language network, and then merged its broadcast properties with the publisher of *The Globe and Mail*.

In Italy, the phenomenon took on political overtones when tycoon Silvio Berlusconi, who already owned the country's largest publisher and biggest advertising agency, took control of its three private television networks and a clutch of production companies. Lavish positive coverage by his networks was widely credited for Berlusconi's success in two subsequent campaigns to lead Italy's government.

It is imperative to note, however, that many, if not all, of these regional powerhouses exist both as beneficiaries of the tool kit of public policy and as the consequence of market forces in their regional and national economies. A dozen organizations on the top-fifty list are *public* broadcasters, operating under national mandates and supported by a variety of statutory licence fees or taxes. Among them are NHK, ARD and the BBC, respectively ranked in tenth, eleventh and twelfth place among media giants. Brazil's Globo, Canada's CanWest, and the American USA Networks and Clear Channel all profit from policies designed to ensure that critical gateways for expression remain in the hands of citizens of those countries. Without such measures, many regional and national companies would inevitably find themselves targeted for acquisition by multinationals hungry for market share and global penetration.

IN THE CASINO of popular culture, corporate executives and economic theorists widely regard such rampant agglomeration as essential to extract the maximum value from each rare gold-plated hit. There are three fundamental strategies for accomplishing this.

The first, already discussed, is to divide all possible audiences for any popular work into discrete "windows" or "territories" and then sell the work separately to each one. This is what economists of culture-as-entertainment call "the orderly marketplace."

The second is to replicate the core value that audiences find in a winning work (usually a fictional character or world: Mickey Mouse, Harry Potter or the universe of the Smurfs) in as many different forms across as many different media as technology permits.

The third is to keep on reselling whatever proves popular for as long as audiences show an appetite for it. In film and television, this is known as the asset value of libraries. In books and music, it is the value of the "backlist."

All three strategies rely on the intangible value at the heart of all cultural goods. That appeal does not reside in their material form—the paper of the book, the plastic of the CD or the celluloid of the film print. Instead, it lies in *the individual audience member's experience* of that work. Recall the low marginal cost of creating copies of those works. In material terms, duplicating a work of popular culture for additional "consumption" costs anything from a few dollars for a hardcover book to a fraction of a penny for a television episode delivered digitally to a television audience of millions of viewers.

This feature of cultural economics places in the hands of copyright owners a commercial lever of extraordinary might: *the power to price.* If creating additional copies of the latest hit by Eminem or Tom Hanks costs next to nothing, then the commercially profitable price for that copy can be set at anything from near zero to whatever the market will bear.

In the event, unsurprisingly, the price more often settles at the latter point than the former.

At the same time, one audience's enjoyment of a work does not exhaust its appeal or availability ("utility," to economists) for other audiences. In this, as we noted earlier, cultural products more closely resemble "public goods" like national defence than either conventional tangible goods or services like an individual massage or corporate audit.

The strategies of the orderly marketplace, cross-exploitation and "evergreen libraries"—perennially popular titles—are designed to take the greatest advantage of these distinctive economic properties. To maximize the advantage takes not only scale but also a presence in as many sectors and markets as is corporately possible.

THE ORIGINS of the first strategy—the orderly marketplace—lie in the evolution of copyright for printed books. Conventionally, these rights were sold on the basis of geographic territories. Buyer A acquired the right to publish a work in Britain. Buyer B might acquire the right to publish the same work in the United States, and buyer C the rights to Germany or France. This form of assignment continues to apply to published works wherever copyright rules are respected (in the developed world and most major developing countries, if not in some less-developed regions).

The global marketplace for recorded music and filmed entertainment follows a similar geographic approach to dividing the world into distinct, discrete territories. (We will return to a more detailed examination of this subject in the next chapter.)

But there is another way to subdivide the market for the most "experiential" of cultural goods: visual entertainment. That is, into *temporal* instead of *geographic* parts—the exhibition of the same work in the same territory but at different times and by different means. These temporal assignments are known in the industry as "windows" of exhibition (although the term is also sometimes given to sequential exhibition in different geographic territories). And they are choreographed with exquisite care.

The sequence of the orderly marketplace for feature films was described in detail in Chapter 3. Television shows and films produced either directly to video or as movies-of-the-week follow more truncated paths.

Each window contributes something to a product's eventual total payout. The domestic theatrical window typically accounts for between a fifth and a quarter of what a film will earn during its life. Its foreign theatrical and domestic video windows each return roughly another fifth to a quarter of that lifetime return. Foreign video, which follows theatrical release, contributes about 14 per cent. Domestic and foreign television windows collectively will contribute another 20 to 25 per cent to the eventual total.

This system goes far to explain why so many films continue to be produced, despite the appallingly small number that return their cost at the box-office. For most, the box-office window is regarded as little more than a "loss leader"; the real returns come later. Says *Screen Digest* analyst David Hancock, "You might not make any money on the film in the cinemas. But you have the rights to the film based on seven years. And you will in the long term make your money back, if you have the patience to wait four or five years."

On its face, the window system would appear to treat each film on equal terms. But that is not the case in practice. In several ways, the big international Majors (and their various regional or national emulators) squeeze out a disproportionate amount of the system's juice.

They are, for one thing, better capitalized and hence better placed to wait out the early loss-accruing years of a film's life cycle. To sell a film through every available window in every territory and monitor the payment due for each exhibition is not a trivial task. The Majors are able to amortize that management cost over multiple properties.

Second, while very few films recoup their cost in cinema release, a film's performance at the North American box-office bears a heavy influence on what it will earn in subsequent windows. Some influence is informal: a film with big "domestic" box-office will command a higher price in "foreign" distribution because of the implied evidence of its popularity with audiences. Some is formal: contracts between film distributors and pay-TV broadcasters typically set the price the latter pay per viewer in mathematical relation to a film's box-office earnings. The result is the same in either case. Films that benefit from a wide release, heavy P&A spending and consequent "big opening" go on to take the lion's share of revenue in later windows.

Sony Corp. USA chairman Howard Stringer puts it this way. "If you don't spend a lot of money on marketing, you don't generate big box-office. People will start saying, 'Well, if you didn't have a big opening weekend you weren't a success.' And if I'm not a success, I can't sell it to television or cable and I threaten my video sale and DVD sales and so forth. So there is a sort of spiral pressure."

Indeed, academic researchers Frank Rusco and W. David Walls found that a film without a box-office record stands virtually no chance of earning any significant subsequent revenue. "Films [that] had box-office earnings," they reported, "earned over 97.7 per cent of all income from secondary markets." At the dawn of the twenty-first century, 90 per cent of all box-office earnings (and hence of all secondary revenues) went to films distributed by the Majors.

Volume allows the Majors to keep playing the *nobody knows* lotto long enough to score the occasional hit. Volume plus access to secondary windows lets them recoup at least some of what they lose on the intervening flops. Broadcast rights to movies are sold in bundles, usually of ten or more titles. Typically, the bundle contains one or two certified hits, some mediocre films—and a certain proportion of outright dogs. As one distributor familiar with the system puts it: "For television we make a big package where we take a locomotive film and then we attach all kinds of [expletive] and then we just sell it." For those with the requisite clout and breadth of product, it's a way to make even dogs pay their way.

Further advantage lies in the Majors' vertical integration: owning many of the windows themselves. In addition to a particular film, a conglomerate may own the distributor that sells rights to it, the cinema chain that exhibits it in the first window, the video store that rents it in the second, the pay-TV service that shows it in the third and the television network and cable channel that broadcast it in the fourth and fifth. "Each corporate filter between the consumer and the end producer will take a cut of revenues," says Martin Dale in *The Movie Game*.

"Viacom is as good an example as any of vertical integration," observes Kagan's Larry Gerbrandt. "Paramount produces the movie. [Viacom CEO] Sumner Redstone's National Amusements is one of the largest exhibitors in the country. They also own Blockbuster, so the movies go from Sumner Redstone's theatres to Blockbuster stores. After that it goes to Showtime, [Viacom's] pay window. Then CBS is a network window. After that it could go into syndication on the CBS TV stations. So in theory a Paramount film can play on virtually every one of its windows on a Viacom property. And in each case, they can maximize the revenue that is generated."

Or as News Corp. president Peter Chernin put it in a 1998 statement: "If you look at the entire chain of entities—studios, networks, stations, cable channels, cable operations, international distribution—you want to be as strong in as many of those as you can. That way, regardless of where the profits move to, you're in a position to gain."

A SECOND STRATEGY by which the Majors appropriate an ever-increasing share of the public's cultural spending relies less on vertical integration than horizontal connections. In deference to a particularly dazzling display of its effectiveness in late 2001, this might be thought of as the "All *Harry Potter,* all the time" strategy. Its essence is to leverage the emotional appeal of a core property (in this case, the engaging boy hero of a series of fantasy novels by British writer J.K. Rowling) across as many different forms of exploitation as possible.

Consider the many ways in which Time Warner brought Harry to U.S. audiences in the autumn of 2001. At the centre of the marketing offensive was a movie that Warner Brothers produced, *Harry Potter and the Philosopher's Stone* (*Harry Potter and the Sorcerer's Stone* in the United States). Its Moviefone affiliate promoted and sold tickets to 3,672 theatres unspooling the movie on 8,200 screens (roughly one quarter of all screens in America on the film's opening weekend). AOL's online portal, which serves one in two American Internet subscribers, peppered its pages with Potter promotions and links to related sites; AOL's 137 million members were also directed to sites selling Harry merchandise. Time Warner magazines like *People, Time, Entertainment Weekly* and *Sports Illustrated* carried ads, contests and editorial content about the film. More ads appeared on Time Warner's cable system, which serves about one in five American homes, and on those four top-ten cable channels that its Turner Broadcasting subsidiary owns. Warner Music Group produced and sold CDs of the film's soundtrack. With Harry's ubiquity assured, Time Warner turned exclusive worldwide rights to promote the film and its sequel into yet another asset, selling those to Coca-Cola for US$150 million.

Such tactics are not the exclusive preserve of the majors. Canada's Epitome Pictures licenses its *Degrassi* characters for promotional campaigns by Kraft Foods and Procter & Gamble, among others. Atlantis Alliance does promotional deals for Canadian movie releases with the Burger King chain. Britain's HIT entertainment earned nearly 40 per cent of its €294 million revenue in 2002 from sales of merchandise based on its animated Bob the Builder and Thomas the Tank characters.

But two factors skew the potential returns in favor of the giants. First, as with managing a film property's sequential deployment through the many-paned windows of exhibition, managing the merchandising and promotion of copyright characters is no trivial task. A single popular character like Winnie the Pooh may appear on thousands of items churned out by hundreds of manufacturers in dozens of territories under widely varying contract conditions. Monitoring them all requires the dedicated attention of specialized staff. The demand on a small company's management time can easily overwhelm the potential return.

Second, it is the Majors that own most of the best-known and easily exploitable names. Winnie, like Mickey, Spidey and the Roadrunner, is a company animal.

SUCH HOUSEHOLD NAMES in fact are emblematic of the third leg to the Majors' structural dominance, one that rests atop the overflowing libraries of past hits. It is no accident that Bertelsmann's Random House boasts of its catalogue of perennially popular Nobel Prize winners or Time Warner of its archived collection of Warner Brothers cartoons. John Steinbeck and Bugs Bunny are among the two giants' most valuable assets. They are properties whose costs are long since paid off and whose revenues now are almost pure profit.

Not every film, book or musical recording is worth reissuing. But evergreen popularity makes some names—Frank Sinatra, Raymond Chandler, *It's a Wonderful Life*—the cultural-goods equivalent of the proverbial licence to print money. Not only do such names continue to attract new generations of audience, but—especially in the case of music and video—each new generation of technology affords a new opportunity to sell them another time to consumers who may already own them. Thus the advent of CDs allowed Capitol Records to reissue dozens of existing Sinatra tracks to fans who were replacing their collections of vinyl. Similarly, the DVD breathed wonderful new commercial life into Capra's classic.

A library is an ace in the hole for even such a "mini-Major" as Alliance Atlantis. The company owns limited rights in its own country and in Britain to some seven thousand titles, including some that distribution executive Victor Loewy calls "absolute pearls": *Terminator, Rambo* and *Pulp Fiction*. "A solid library is a gold mine that can tide you over the bad years," he explains. "Video was first, then DVD and pay-per-view and HDTV. Every time that happens, you just drag out those titles and put them out again. This is what keeps us going. It generated C$150 million for us [in 2001]. Just the library, *$150 million.* It's a lot of money."

Assets in the Majors' vaults are valued at much higher figures. In 1992, Turner Broadcasting valued its 1,500 MGM titles at US$1.2 billion; they earn Time Warner a conservatively estimated minimum of US$70 million to $80 million a year. According to Martin Dale, the collective asset value of the big studios' film inventory grew from US$840 million in 1973 to US$5 billion in 1988, and has continued to soar since. In the judgement of one KPMG study, the worth of film libraries multiplied by 15 to 20 times in the two decades after 1980, and that of television libraries by factors of 30 to 50 times. "On this basis," Dale asserts, "the combined annual library earnings for the Majors is probably well in excess of [US]$1 billion worldwide."

"Films that I made 25 years ago, [like] *Midnight Express*," says former Sony studio executive Peter Guber, "[I'm] still getting checks from the re-release to a new DVD. *Sleepy Hollow* is making money in some airliner, at some hotel, in some television station in Paraguay and Venezuela and someplace in eastern Europe." For United Artists, a studio brought to its knees by the colossal 1980 flop *Heaven's Gate*, the collected adventures of James Bond have amounted, quite literally, to a licence to live.

A rich library conveys benefits beyond cash flow. In a game that demands the risk of enormous sums of capital (a minimum of US$100 million to $150 million upfront for a big-budget spectacle), library assets offer a fulcrum for financial leverage. Says film journalist Michael Cieply: "Very big bankers suddenly realized there was enormous value in libraries [and] they could loan money against it because they could project out the impact of cable and video and say, 'Hey, we can resell every movie that's ever been made.'" It is a form of collateral that cannot possibly be matched by the uncertain future prospects of a single movie venture.

DRIVING ALL THESE MACHINATIONS are powerful works of the imaginations of individual creators. The Majors' wealth rests on J.K. Rowling giving imaginative existence to the Hogwarts School of Magic, on Mel Blanc demanding to know "What's up, doc?" or James Cameron framing that swooping shot of Leonardo DiCaprio embracing Kate Winslet on *Titanic's* towering bow.

This is worth recalling before we note one last way the Hydra-headed conglomerates of culture beef up their bottom lines. It is not, properly speaking, a strategy for maximizing returns from successful plays on the wheel. Instead it is a way to keep as much of that return as possible from flowing back to the creators.

What has sometimes been called "studio accounting" has been a *bête noire* of generations of artists, especially in music and filmed entertainment. Its features are particularly egregious in the recording contracts offered to aspiring musical artists. Typically, those contracts provide an advance against future record sales. From that sum, artists are required to meet the expenses of recording—studio rental, the cost of hiring session musicians and sound engineers. Should their recording sell, that advance is charged against their share of any profits. And so, they discover, are many ancillary costs: catering for promotional events, the hire of a limousine to carry them to press interviews, the price of extra "promotional" copies of CDs added to a retailer's order. If a first CD loses money, those losses are carried forward and charged against the profits of any subsequent ones. If, despite this flurry of deductions and offsets, a certain CD does eventually earn a net return due the artist, a portion will be held back to cover the possibility that the *next* record will again lose money.

A recent U.S. case study showed that a four-piece rock band with a gold record (sales of more than 500,000 albums, a status achieved by only 128 out of more than 30,000 records released in 2002) would end up with only about US$40,000 for each performer.

In addition, few standard recording contracts contain any penalty to discourage labels from simply underreporting royalties owed to artists they have signed.

Recording companies insist that such terms are necessary to the economics of *nobody knows*. Given the tiny proportion of recording acts that strike gold- or platinum-level sales, executives insist that more generous provisions would threaten the labels' viability.

Not surprisingly, that contention, and the terms of recording contracts, are subjects of sharp debate and frequent lawsuits. In 2001, a coalition of American recording artists, including such stars as Madonna, Sheryl Crow and the Eagles' Don Henley, launched a campaign to lobby for legislation to require more equitable contracts. At the time of this writing, the campaign continued with no legislation in sight. At least one advocate, Courtney Love, had settled her differences in a private agreement with her label, Vivendi's Universal Music Group.

With costs vastly higher and recoupment often delayed for years, the opportunity to intercept revenue from filmed entertainment before it reaches creators is even greater. A famous story illustrates the

Hollywood maxim that "There is no back end." In 1939, Mae West signed one of the first contracts purporting to commit a portion (25 per cent) of the net profits earned by *My Little Chickadee* to the buxom star. West died in 1981. Four years later, an audit uncovered the fact that Universal Studios had not yet paid her a single cent.

AS THEY HAVE SWEPT UP an ever-growing share of the commercial sales of popular culture in the last decade, and possessing so many advantages of scale and scope, the Majors ought to be afloat in profits. Curiously, this has not recently been the case.

Time Warner, the group's most gargantuan member, posted a loss of US$98.7 billion in 2002, the deepest red ink in U.S. history. The next-largest, Viacom, while profitable, earned only $685 million on its $23 billion in sales, a net margin of less than 3 per cent and a return on equity just above 1 per cent. Disney did better, posting a profit of $1.1 billion on revenues of $24.6 billion—a return on equity of 4.8 per cent.

Among non-American Majors, only Sony reported scraping into the black in the same period, earning ¥9.3 billion on revenues of ¥7 trillion—a barely perceptible margin of 0.22 per cent and a return on equity little better at 0.66 per cent. Vivendi's scramble to unload assets was driven by the need to reduce debt and return to profitability after losing $997 million on its $57.4 billion in revenue. Murdoch's News Corp. posted a whopping $6.5 billion loss on $15.2 billion in revenue. (Bertelsmann does not report results, but it too was trying to unload assets in 2003.)

Results have been no more heartening on a sectoral basis. Few of the developed world's book publishers have ever been money-spinners. But music labels have also seen sales drop in recent years. And even television networks, from Britain's Channel 4 and France's Canal+ to Canada's Global, have experienced tough times. In 2001, only two of six U.S. networks reported year-end results in the black.

Theories abound. One holds that as show business became more tightly bound up with corporate agendas, judgements became dulled by "too much biz and not enough show," in the words of one movie veteran. Argues Martin Dale: "The Majors are now run in an MBA technocratic management style which tries to transform the art of making movies into a science. This has tended to result in a climate of fear, creative sclerosis and what Jeffrey Katzenberg has described as 'an invisible wall between power and talent.'"

The notion finds wide support in Hollywood. Says producer Lucy Fisher (*Gladiator*) of pitching movie proposals to contemporary studio executives: "The people you're having to convince now are less apt to have a capacity for actually loving a movie. The fact that something is 'good' might not even be on the scale of reasons to make a movie."

"The movies that get made [are] those that appeal to the marketing and distribution team," agrees Peter Bart, editor of industry bible *Variety*. "The green-light process consists of maybe thirty or forty people. There's one group to discuss the marketing tie-ins: how much will McDonald's or Burger King put up? There's one group to discuss merchandising, toy companies and so forth. Someone else is there to discuss foreign co-financiers. Everyone is discussing the business aspects of the film. It's unusual for someone actually to talk about the script, the cast, the package—whether the whole damn thing makes any sense."

But bad movies are not the same thing as bad business. A more plausible theory notes that the "negative costs" of filmmaking—the direct costs of production—have been rising faster than average returns for two decades. Observes Harold Vogel, in a discussion of Hollywood economics in the 2000 anthology *The Public Life of the Arts in America:* "Costs of production have, since 1980, been rising at compound annual rates of well over twice the inflation rate and ... marketing costs over this span more than quadrupled. The return on revenues (operating margins) meanwhile, have fallen by at least one third."

A popular focus of blame is on risk-averse executives who try to protect their careers (as discussed in Chapter 4) by engaging A-list talent at any price.

"There's a temptation," concedes Sony USA chairman Howard Stringer, "to throw money at stars who can open a picture as a kind of a failsafe." The temptation leads film financiers to return repeatedly to the same short list of the most recognized stars. Often, Stringer adds, the first question asked in considering a new project is: "Can Tom Cruise do it? Can Tom Hanks? Mel Gibson?"

"If you're trying to make a risk into a sure thing," says *New York Times* film critic Elvis Mitchell, "you're going to make the same thing, often with the same people, over and over and over again."

British commentator Danny Leigh, writing in *The Guardian* in 2002, complained of the same "bunkum that packing a movie with stars will lead, inevitably, to full cinemas" infecting decisions for U.K.

films. The result, he added, has been "the stuffing of [British films] with all-too-familiar faces ... endlessly revolving before us like the last dozen suitcases at an airport baggage claim."

Such thinking also induces studios to meet almost any price that such "bankable" talent demands—raising their rents vertiginously. Arnold Schwarzenegger's appearance in *Batman and Robin* earned him roughly $1 million per onscreen minute.

Huge paydays for the chosen bite deeply into profits, even on a hit film. Nicolas Cage commanded $20 million for his starring role in the art film *Captain Corelli's Mandolin*—more than a third of its production budget and nearly as much as its total gross ($25 million) at the North American box office. According to executives at 20th Century–Fox and DreamWorks, which put up $100 million to make 2002's *Minority Report*, star Tom Cruise and director Steven Spielberg are likely to collect more than 35 cents of every dollar the film makes— including revenue from secondary windows like DVD and video sales. An estimated 40 per cent of gross revenue from *Men in Black II* is reported to be owed to its stars Tommy Lee Jones and Will Smith, its director Barry Sonnenfeld and its producers, which again include Spielberg. (It can be assumed Messieurs Cruise, Spielberg, Jones and Smith are savvy enough, and have good enough accountants, not to be fooled by the sort of bookkeeping fancy footwork that kept Mae West out of the profits from *My Little Chickadee* until her death.)

Meanwhile, the tight focus on the A-list tends to exclude even the most highly talented unknowns from opportunity. "I can remember a studio—not mine—running away from Russell Crowe," Stringer recalls, "because 'Nobody's ever heard of Russell Crowe.' Well, nobody's ever heard of *anybody*. Nobody'd heard of Peter O'Toole until *Lawrence of Arabia*."

The escalating earnings of top stars and a few offscreen specialists like Spielberg has carried a steep price for the rest of the motley crew involved in filmmaking. The more producers spend to engage the names their backers insist on seeing in lights, the less is left over for other expenses, including "below the line" workers. "Hollywood's top 200 [individuals] earn over a third of all salaries," notes Martin Dale, whereas "the average wage rate for film and TV [is] well below [that of] other sectors such as mining, aerospace, finance, computers and engineering."

What is true for film has also been true for television. "We're paying a third lead in a show the same amount of money we paid a series lead three years ago," complained one television producer in 2002.

"The industry has failed to produce quality network programming at prices that reflect the current economic environment," Walt Disney Co. president Robert Iger confided. "The general cost of doing business has risen above what the marketplace can afford."

There is evidence that the phenomenon of superstar rents rising to irrecoverable heights goes well beyond Hollywood and the film world. Although professional sports is not a field under study here, the complaint is widely voiced among proprietors of those franchises.

A similar effect has bedevilled some book publishers who have advanced huge sums to celebrity authors. With a big advance on the line, the publishers have spent heavily on promotion and printed tens of thousands of copies to meet the wave of demand the advertising was meant to whip up. When the title encounters anemic sales, those costs are irrecoverable; the publisher is left to eat the loss. Richard Caves catalogues several examples in *Creative Industries:* 70 per cent of the print run of then-U.S. president Bill Clinton's 1996 volume *Between Hope and History,* Caves notes, languished unsold on shelves (although his wife's biography, *Living History,* became a huge best seller in 2003). O.J. Simpson prosecutor Marcia Clark earned back only about half the $4.5 million that Viking advanced for her 1997 memoir, *Without a Doubt.* Simpson defence attorney Johnnie Cochran did no better for his publisher Ballantine, selling fewer than half the copies printed of his *Journey to Justice.*

Caves and others have also observed that the acquisition of publishers by big corporations paradoxically only encouraged such folly. Where small independent houses, perennially short of cash, carefully estimated likely sales before offering relatively miserly advances, the deep pockets of conglomerate backers encouraged auction markets for hotly anticipated celebrity properties.

Meanwhile, the conglomerate focus on cross-exploitation of properties has withered interest in authors whose appeal seems likely to be limited to the printed page. A growing number of literary agents simply refuse to take on clients whose books seem like poor candidates for adaptation to other media. "One needs every single outlet," says British agent Jilly Cooper, "film, telly, everything you can get your hands on."

Adds another U.K. literary agent, Luigi Bonomi: "If a potential client is not interested or willing to do television or newspaper work, you have to ask yourself, 'Is it worth taking them on?'"

Danuta Kean, contributing editor at *The Bookseller,* a British book trade periodical, sees danger in that. "The loss of the literary specialist entails serious cultural risks," she argues, "as agents, their heads more in media bars than manuscripts, restrict what is published in print to whatever looks good on screens large and small. The impact on readers will be calamitous."

That not to say the A-list is static. It's plainly not. Names are added and names drop off all the time.

American book publishing circles were nonplussed in 2002 when titles by such normally reliable best-selling authors as Tom Clancy (*Red Rabbit*), Michael Crichton (*Prey*) and Stephen King (*From a Buick 8*), all underperformed. In Hollywood, Holly Hunter, firmly in the "A" league in 1993 with a best-actress Oscar for *The Piano,* found herself a decade later well down the alphabet. (Winona Ryder, nominated that same year for a supporting role in *The Age of Innocence,* had slipped even further, thanks to her conviction on a shoplifting charge.) By contrast, Russell Crowe, once beneath studio consideration for a lead role, by 2003 was as prime an A-grade name as there was.

Similarly, the Majors have a long history of recognizing the brightest foreign and independent filmmakers and offering them jobs. Crowe, for one, is an Australian. Warner Brothers plucked director Alfonso Cuaron, whose irreverent US$2 million comedy *Y Tu Mama También (And Your Mother Too!)* was an unexpected art-house hit, from Mexico to direct the third mega-budget installment of *Harry Potter.* Taiwanese director Ang Lee's independent 1994 romantic comedy *Eat Drink Man Woman,* shot in Chinese, earned him a chance to direct *Sense and Sensibility* two years later for Columbia. And after his *Crouching Tiger, Hidden Dragon* overcame subtitles to wow North American audiences in 2000, Universal tapped Lee to direct its 2003 comic-book spinoff *The Hulk.* The Hollywood A-list contains so many Canadian names (James Cameron, Jim Carrey, Mike Myers ... and on) that some analysts in Canada blame the shortage of home-grown film hits partly on the exodus of top talent.

As noted earlier, however, this phenomenon does not result in the Majors making blockbuster movies in the accents of diversity. Warner hired Cuaron to make *Harry III*, not *Tu Mama II*. Lee's *Hulk* is tilted more to Peoria than to Taipei. Another A-list Aussie, Mel Gibson, has shed his native identity (and accent) so thoroughly that he can slip with ease into the role of an American Revolutionary War idealist in *The Patriot* or a midwestern corn farmer in *Signs.*

"You come to Hollywood, you're part of this multinational culture factory," says Australian-raised director Phillip Noyce (*Sliver, Clear and Present Danger*). "You take a best-selling author, add a guaranteed movie star that brings a first-weekend gross, add $30 million, and it comes out the other end. It's all so predictable. But with time, you grow to be alienated from your own culture."

The Majors, in short, may harness the world's talent. But they make Hollywood's movies.

TWO MORE derivative dynamics induce additional feedback forces within this system. The first is a steady acceleration of play accompanied by rising stakes in every sector of the cultural casino. The second is the Majors' overt use of clout to expropriate ever more of the game.

We noted earlier the growing concentration of book sales: fewer titles by fewer authors selling far greater numbers of copies through fewer corporate outlets. With that concentration has come an increasingly sharp and inequitable division of returns: much greater rewards for the handful of A-list authors, shrinking profile and reward for the rest of the field.

Less apparent to the average reader is the speeding up of the entire cycle. The rise in velocity takes hold even before some books are printed. "There's more information being passed around faster on Web sites and e-mail," notes Gillian Blake, an editor in the New York offices of Scribner. "Agents submit to so many places, often to every house and every imprint within those houses, that a novel gets a certain buzz before it's even sold." The result, Blake adds, is that editors feel pressured to put up a pre-emptively high offer merely to keep a potentially hot property out of competitors' hands.

On the shelf, however, many titles have less time to find an audience. Equipped with sophisticated inventory-control software, chains like Canada's Chapters-Indigo, or Borders and Barnes & Noble in the United States, closely monitor which volumes fly off the shelves and which move more slowly. The latter are quickly culled and sent back to publishers. Even popular titles seem to enjoy less leeway than they did previously. Barnes & Noble in 2001 announced that it had begun to remove books from its in-house best-sellers list after twelve months—regardless of their actual sales performance. Many publishers have also begun to cull the number of titles they retain in print on their backlists. Seeking to reduce the cost of warehousing inventory, they maintain only those titles with the strongest sales.

A comparable acceleration is at work in recorded music. Tension in that sector has been compounded by a slide in overall sales that is widely blamed on the popularity of file-sharing pirated tracks. In June 2000, *The New York Times* reported that albums released that year by Eminem, Britney Spears and 'N Sync "had the three fastest debuts in the history of recorded music." Eighteen months later, after two years in which music sales fell by more than 13 per cent in the United States, *The Wall Street Journal* noted that music labels planned "to hit shoppers with an unusual blitz of A-list releases. Practically all at once, everyone from U2 to Eminem to Whitney Houston will be arriving in stores, along with a barrage of marketing tactics."

In television the dynamic is again reflected in two dimensions, with bigger bets and faster turns of the wheel. Networks are both spending more money than ever on the most promising new shows and cancelling them faster if they fail to connect with audiences. In 2002, Fox committed an unprecedented US$6 million to a pilot for the series *Fastlane*. Months earlier, NBC cancelled *Battery Park*, a police drama series, after just four episodes; ABC euthanized a hospital drama, *Wonderland*, after only two.

The time pressure to perform is no less extreme, and the bets even bigger, on the big screen. The average cost of a Hollywood-studio movie jumped by more than 50 percent between 1995 and 2000, reaching US$82 million (negative costs plus launch costs). But over the same period, the number of films whose ticket sales plunged after their first week also escalated. An example is *Pearl Harbor*. The $153 million, effects-laden historical drama earned more than half its North American gross in its first two weekends in theatres. "Basically by Friday night at midnight when the fax machine purrs and you have the numbers," says producer Lucy Fisher, "you know whether your movie is over or not and whether the two years or five years you spent working on [it] were basically for naught."

"A picture like [*One Flew Over the*] *Cuckoo's Nest* could play for week after week with only maybe a 7 per cent drop," noted actor-producer Michael Douglas in a 2001 interview with the U.S. Public Broadcasting Service. "Now there's no time for a movie to breathe because by the next weekend there's three, four, five other pictures coming in, each maybe who's spent an average of $25 million for their marketing. So you don't have a chance to find your legs."

Some pictures don't even get in the cinema door. In September 2000, Lions Gate/TVA Films bought distribution rights to *The Weight of Water*, a mystery based on a best-selling novel, starring Sean Penn and Elizabeth Hurley. Then the film sat on a shelf. Explained Lions Gate vice-president of distribution John Baine: "There are only two windows per year when you can release a small art movie. Early fall and early spring. You don't want to be out in late fall against the Oscar contenders, or in summer against the blockbusters." After missing those windows for two years, *Weight of Water* "began to feel stale," Baine noted. In early 2003, it was finally released—on video.

THERE ARE MORE CHANNELS of television available to more viewers in more countries on Earth than ever before. In many countries, more books are being published and printed than ever before. Technology has brought the price of recording music and reproducing it on a CD within reach of anyone with a few thousand dollars and a personal computer. Hundreds of movies are made each year in several dozen countries.

Yet, *made* is not the same as *seen, read* or *heard*. Nor does the mere multiplication of channels guarantee that the programming they carry is diverse. The appearance of plenty thus conceals a deeper poverty.

"The many channels and choices are more apparent to the public than the narrow range of voices," observes Danny Schechter, executive editor of Mediachannel.org, a Web site of media criticism. "The power concentrated in this maze has, over time, replaced democracy with its own self-referencing mediocracy."

"The cartel's rise," worries Mark Crispin Miller in *The Nation*, "has made extremely rare the sort of marvellous exception that has always popped up unexpectedly, to startle and revivify the culture."

"Global hype of manufactured blockbusters and superstars can, and does, replace diversity, quality and new talent," agrees Nicholas

Johnson, a law professor at the University of Iowa and a former member of the U.S. Federal Communications Commission.

That view is not limited to the left of the political spectrum.

"It's sad," concedes Ted Turner, CNN's outspoken founder as well as a Time Warner shareholder and director. "We're losing so much diversity of thought."

Worries Frank Blethen, the publisher and CEO of the Seattle Times Co.: "Concentration of ownership is all about money and power. The bigness of chains and the singular financial focus of public companies drive out all values and objectives that are not short-term and financial. Values such as diversity are mutually exclusive with the faceless investors and their money managers' relentless quest for short-term profits and higher stock prices."

This paradox should not in fact surprise us. It is telling that all these voices raising concern for the diversity of expression come from within the United States, where the raw chemistry of the marketplace has freest rein to determine which cultural products rise above the noise and which are subsumed beneath it. For, in fact, these perverse outcomes are not anomalies of the market. They are perfectly natural outcomes of it.

Recall from Chapter 3 that the mythic perfection of the market's "invisible hand" is predicated on several assumptions about the nature of goods—none of which holds true for creative products. Virtually every one of the differences identified there between conventional and creative goods serves to strengthen the market hand of the conglomerates.

An overabundance of creative works unknowable in advance of purchase obliges consumers to rely on other guidance—taste-makers, gatekeepers, A-list names and box-office—in making a selection. Money effectively buys all four.

Scale allows conglomerates to weather many losses in the *nobody knows* lottery. Only they can afford to keep playing until the odds finally deliver that elusive blockbuster hit.

When it eventually comes, money, scale and the "public" qualities of creative goods align to favour conglomerates yet again. Only they are equipped to exploit a property across multiple windows of exhibition, channels of delivery, media and territories to extract its maximum value.

Playing the incremental odds and percentages, however, conglomerates rationally lavish their efforts to drive ever-greater audiences to those few blockbusters. Their priorities have no reason to include the new, the experimental, the alternative, the exotic, the local or the niche—the works that explore new ways forward for humanity, the "R&D of the soul." Without the tool kit of policies that exist in most nations of the world, voices we need to hear would speak only to empty rooms until, one by one, they fell silent.

Silence would fall not because some black-hat villain willed it so, but simply because that is the way the curious economics of culture work. The next chapter will show how those same forces play out in the global arena.

6

GLOBAL
VISIONS

TWO SCENES from Africa.

The first takes place on the stage of an elegantly restored Edwardian granite-and-sandstone edifice in central Cape Town. A Canadian actor is at the podium. R.H. Thomson is in the South African capital to address a conference of cultural activists. He begins by describing his recent overnight journey on British Airways Flight 48 from London's Heathrow to the city at Africa's southern tip. More exactly, he describes the in-flight entertainment BA offered under the general title *The Best of the World.*

It began, Thomson recalls, with a news compilation assembled by Atlanta-based CNN. That was followed by a film and television episodes. "On this screen Tom Cruise was saving the world. On that screen, Spider-Man was saving the world. As we travelled over culture after culture, over language after language, they were all silent. Inside the plane it was all violent crime dramas, all one and a half cultures. It was all British or American."

The other scene takes place on the ground, some thirty thousand feet below the speeding jet. Again it is night, this time at a refugee camp in Kakuma, Kenya. The camp's seventy thousand displaced and impoverished residents live in mud huts. They share rations of gruel that sometimes afford less than half the minimum daily calories called for by United Nations guidelines, and there is one latrine for every 150 people.

But on this occasion, they have also received a contribution from the world capital of entertainment. An organization called Film Aid has come to the camp, as it does three times a week. The organization has the backing of actor Tom Hanks and studio mogul Harvey Weinstein, among others. It wields a budget of US$800,000, underwritten largely by the U.S. State Department.

The aid equipment it unloads from a new white truck consists of a large silver movie screen and a projector. Tonight, Hollywood's donation to the refugees' well-being is a couple of hours' escape into the Technicolor fantasy world of *The Wizard of Oz*.

DO THESE SCENES reflect a phenomenon that is good or bad?

To many, the near-ubiquity of made-in-America entertainment is a kind of cultural imperialism that smothers indigenous viewpoints under a consumerist dogma captured by the idea of McWorld. To others, it is simply the exercise of personal freedom by "citizens in each country who decide what movies they want to see, what TV programs they want to watch," as Motion Picture Association of America (MPAA) chief executive Jack Valenti asserts.

A South African lawyer who attended the conference that Thomson addressed in Cape Town and who occasionally does work for Valenti's MPAA expressed what might be a middle view. "We are absolutely swamped with American content," sighed Adeera Bodasing. "It's all right up to a point. But after a while you want something else."

In fact, it is a mischaracterization to argue that the world's burgeoning trade in popular culture is an American monochrome. As we will see, that is far from the truth. What *is* true is that the unique economics of those goods operate in the same paradoxical way in the international marketplace as they do in domestic markets—resulting often in the same perverse outcomes.

The most dramatic distortions arise from the peculiarities of cost and price that creative goods display. Chapter 3 showed how almost all the cost of a cultural product is sunk into the first copy, whose reproduction or exhibition incurs only nominal marginal cost. It mentioned that this practice permits almost limitless flexibility (discrimination) in pricing. The pages ahead will show how this circumstance results in many cultural goods—not only those from the United States—being exported to foreign audiences at prices that bear no relation either to the cost of production or to that of producing a comparable substitute in the receiving market. Yet such pricing is immune from the conventional remedies against international dumping.

The other certainty about international trade in music, books and filmed entertainment is the immensity of the reward. Set aside for the present the hard-to-quantify dimension of cultural influence—even though that consideration is explicit in many nations' policies on the subject, including those of the United States, Canada and France. The dollars alone command attention.

In 1997, the most recent year for which United Nations estimates are available, the international trade in cultural goods (exclusive of domestic sales) was worth US$213.7 billion—a greater than fourfold increase since 1980. That figure is equivalent to purchases worth nearly US$45 by every man, woman and child on Earth. If it were the gross domestic product of a nation, that nation would be the world's twentieth-largest economy. If it were the sales of a single company, that company would eclipse the largest existing pan-national corporation, Exxon Mobil, with $210 billion in revenue. And the figure has surely continued to grow since 1997.

Driving its growth are both rising consumer wealth—most notably in Asia—and technology. Two decades of development in digital and satellite transmission and widespread government deregulation have fuelled a frenetic increase in the number of television channels available in most countries. In many countries, channel choice expanded from as few as one or two public broadcasters in 1980 to dozens of private providers today. An explosion in television set ownership nearly doubled the number of receivers in the Americas between 1980 and 1996, and increased the number of sets in Asian homes by a staggering *six times*. Rising incomes also translate into more discretionary spending on music CDs, VCRs, books and magazines.

Consumers discovered the Internet in the 1990s, adding an entirely new dimension to cultural trade. It quickly reached out to most corners of the world, to the point that Chinese is expected to overtake English as the most-used language online in the first decade of this century.

This effusion of media and vast expansion of trade in creative products signal a new era in our sense of what culture is.

Not that long ago, most culture was strictly a local affair. Creative goods and cultural practices (forerunners of what trade economists today call "services") tended to be regionally distinct. Culture was generally "exported" only as a by-product of conquering armies. Occasionally it was also "imported" along with exotic new technologies. Europe acquired gunpowder in the Middle Ages, for instance, and aboriginal North Americans acquired horses in the sixteenth century. In both cases, the acquisitions irreversibly altered the course of regional cultures.

Technologies able to capture cultural experience in portable form— first in printed books and much later in photographs, music and moving images—made possible their wider dissemination and commercial exchange.

The initial flow, borne on a wave of colonial expansion, was mainly from Europe outward to the rest of the world. For the first three centuries after Christopher Columbus, cultural "trade" was essentially a one-way system, gushing forms and ideas from the creative centres of Britain, France, Spain and Germany to their "possessions" in the Americas and later Africa, the subcontinent and East Asia. As late as the early nineteenth century, most books read in North America were written in Europe. The first feature film shown in the United States was made in France. Profits from the imported 1912 silent epic *La Reine Elizabeth* funded the establishment of Famous Players Film Co., later to become Paramount Pictures.

In the twentieth century, the flow changed. Especially after the Second World War, the United States eclipsed Europe as the primary source of almost every kind of cultural product. From blue jeans and baseball caps to Marilyn Monroe and Madonna, American images, ideas, fashions and musical beats found audiences from Samoa to Smolensk.

At the dawn of the twenty-first century, the exchange of cultural products has become a much more multilateral affair. Globally in 1998, according to UNESCO, 12 of the world's nearly 200 countries produced 80 per cent of its cultural exports, and 13 were responsible for the same proportion of imports. In terms of the number of films, although not in total production cost, the world's largest producer of films is no longer Hollywood. It is Mumbai (formerly Bombay), a.k.a. Bollywood.

India's history of filmmaking is a long one. The first feature was made there barely a year after *La Reine Elizabeth:* 1913's *Raja Har-ishchandra* portrayed the life of a mythological Indian king. By the late 1990s, Bollywood was turning out as many as a thousand titles a year—twice as many as Hollywood. Many of these films find international audiences, giving India a positive balance of trade on films that is almost unique beyond the United States. Bollywood's trademark musical spectacles often emphasize themes of "the poor-pure-and-just vs. the rich-urban-and-unjust" that are widely popular in Africa. Up to 62 per cent of movies shown in some East African and Central Asian countries come from India, not America. A British cable channel launched in 1999 is dedicated entirely to Indian fare, and Britain hosts an annual Bollywood film festival. *Ramayan,* an Indian TV series, has been dubbed into English, Mandarin, Cantonese and Sinhalese, along with other languages, and aired in the United Kingdom, the United States, Africa, Sri Lanka, Malaysia and Indonesia, among other places.

"Our films have reached half the world," boasts director Mira Nair. "The Middle East, all of Africa, all of Russia, the Far East and the Indian diaspora everywhere—the half of the world that Hollywood has not yet recognized."

Much of Bollywood's output finds its primary overseas audience in Indian emigré communities. But that may be changing. "India, given its competence in English ... and its marketable film-based popular culture," argues Daya Kishan Thussu in *Electronic Empires,* "is well placed to become the first southern nation to achieve a significant presence in the U.S.-dominated global media market." Harbingers of that future may be such films as *We Stand United (Hum Saath Saath Hain),* which in 1999 became the first Indian movie to break into *Variety's* top-twenty weekend box-office earners, and Nair's 2001 film *Monsoon Wedding,* which earned US$14 million in North America and £1.5 million in Britain. A 2002 film by Canadian director Deepa Mehta brought an ironic gaze to the intertwined themes of India's cinematic and social conventions on the one hand and its broad diaspora on the other, with a film titled *Bollywood/Hollywood.*

India is only one of a dozen significant non-American players in the international market for cultural products. Iranian films are seen widely in the Arabic world. Roughly 40 per cent of films screened in francophone Africa come from France, rather than North America.

Both China (with Hong Kong) and the Philippines also make more films annually than does the United States, according to UNESCO. Many of those, especially Hong Kong's martial-arts action movies, find large audiences in Africa, Latin America and the rest of Asia. Nearly 40 per cent of the titles screened in Pakistan are from Hong Kong (whose "Canto-pop" music recording stars also have large regional followings). Thailand, which made nearly two hundred films a year in the 1990s, had a regional hit with 1999's *Nang Nak.*

East Asia's cultural reach is growing. "Our biggest market right now is the U.S.," asserts Joshua Lau, founder of Hong Kong's YesAsia. The company specializes in selling Asian culture, from Korean videos and Canto-pop CDs to Japanese *anime* comics, to customers located outside the region. "Many Asian movies have a U.S. version," Lau notes. "There are more than 10 million Asians living in the U.S. [and] we have 10 to 20 per cent non-Asian customers." The last figure, he adds, is growing steadily.

Japan has been uniquely successful in establishing a wide international audience for the distinct aesthetic sensibility of its animated films, comic books and television shows. *Anime* works have found passionate audiences in Europe and the United States, where seventy-five Japanese TV shows and movies were released in 2001—ten times the number screened a decade earlier. In September 2002, the Virgin megastore at Times Square in New York City anchored an *anime* festival featuring fourteen titles. The same month a section-front review in *The Wall Street Journal* described director Hayao Miyazaki's dubbed-into-English animated feature *Spirited Away* (distributed by Disney in North America) as "a masterpiece . . . that's as funny as it is brilliant, beautiful and deep."

Japan is also responsible for one of the very few cultural properties that may have a credible claim to rival Mickey Mouse's hold on young imaginations worldwide (Winnie the Pooh might be another): a rotund white cartoon feline with a trademark strawberry hair barrette. The globally recognized Hello Kitty appears in books, magazines and videos and adorns more than twelve thousand products, ranging from individually wrapped prunes to skateboards, microwaves and even vibrators. Sanrio, the company that owns "Kitty-chan," sold US$929 million worth of what it calls "social communication gifts" built on the copyright character in 2001.

If Bollywood musicals, Hong Kong kung fu action flicks and Japanese *anime* have each impressed their own style on world audiences, other countries have found success in niche markets or with more generic fare.

Brazilian television giant TV Globo, for instance, exports its *telenovela* serials to more than 140 countries. One series, *Escrava Isaura (Slave Girl Isaura)*, proved a massive hit in countries as disparate as Russia, France, Italy and China (where more than 450 million viewers followed the show). TV Globo's *telenovelas* have been so popular in Portugal and among Latino audiences in the United States that in both countries they have inspired accusations of "reverse media imperialism."

Mexico has similarly exported its TV soaps to Spanish-speaking audiences abroad, including those in the United States, and to a few non-Spanish markets like China. But a film industry that in the 1940s and 1950s churned out dozens of westerns, romantic dramas and art-house works for international Spanish audiences has long been in eclipse. That may be starting to change with a new generation of brashly commercial directors like Alfonso Cuaron: *Y Tu Mama También* earned US$13.6 million in North America and €1.2 million in Spain.

As the world's favourite "second" language, English provides at least as great an advantage to countries like Canada and Australia as it does to India. Britain also remains one of the world's biggest exporters of books, music, periodicals and filmed entertainment. In all three cases, filmed and (more often) television productions are also frequently dubbed into other languages for non-English audiences.

According to various and somewhat disputed accountings, either Canada or the United Kingdom is the world's next-largest exporter of TV shows after the United States. A report to the California legislature in 2002 attributed to Canada nearly half of all movies-of-the-week shot in English in 1999–2000. Canadian government statistics claim "exports of cultural goods and services" worth C$2.35 billion in 2000—an increase of 47 per cent in a four-year period. Toronto's Alliance Atlantis and Vancouver studio Lions Gate routinely earn more than half their production income from sales outside of Canada. In addition to the *Degrassi* series, crime dramas like *Cold Squad* and *Da Vinci's Inquest* can be found on TV schedules in many countries, as can animated productions like *Babar, Reboot* and *Angela Anaconda* and reality-based productions like *Weird Homes.* French-language TV productions from

Quebec air regularly in France and francophone Africa. A smaller handful of Canadian feature films have also found foreign success: in early 1999, sci-fi thriller *CUBE* was the number two box-office draw in French cinemas.

More established as international properties are Canadian writers and musical performers. Artists like Shania Twain, Celine Dion, Diana Krall and rockers Nickelback have large followings in the United States and beyond North America. Three of the six novelists shortlisted for the 2002 Man Booker Prize, awarded in Britain, were Canadian.

A study of British television in 2000 asserted meanwhile that "the U.K. is second only behind the U.S. in international programme sales." The world news service of the venerable BBC is the only global competitor to American CNN. The public broadcaster's children's, nature and documentary output is also widely seen on almost every continent. Long-running British soap opera *Coronation Street* and such dramatic series as *The Bill* air in many countries. Producers have also had success exporting formats for game and reality programs that can be reproduced with a local flavour in receiving countries; examples include *Who Wants to Be a Millionaire* and *Teen Idol* (produced in the United States as *American Idol* and in Canada as *Canadian Idol*).

British novelists and pop music stars are longstanding staples of international sales racks. A number of U.K.-based periodicals are among the select few internationally distributed publications with large readerships beyond their own national diasporas. And despite the financial travails of its leading film producers (woes widely shared everywhere except Hollywood—and to a degree even there), Britain continues to make movies that find both critical and popular success beyond its shores. Art-house film *Billy Elliott* and the Warner-funded blockbuster *Harry Potter* franchise are just two recent examples.

The next leading non-American, English-language cultural exporter is Australia. Foreign sales of that country's film and television productions were worth A$175 million in 1999–2000. Eight of the seventy most popular shows airing on television in the United Kingdom in one recent survey were produced Down Under (the rest were British-made). In addition to producing scripted series like *Home and Away* and *Neighbours,* Aussie producers have, like their British peers, sold game and other show formats to broadcasters in foreign countries. A handful of Australian authors (Patrick White, Thomas Keneally and Tim Winton, who joined the 2002 Man Booker shortlist), movies (*Babe, Crocodile Dundee, Moulin Rouge*) and musicians have also gained international audiences.

In other languages, other publishing nations also have strong markets. China and Taiwan print substantial volumes of material for Chinese-reading diasporas around the world. Germany, until recently the world's largest producer of published titles, continues to sell the printed word to roughly 100 million German-speakers in Europe and beyond. France similarly serves French readers in Canada and Africa.

ALL THIS EVIDENCE of brisk multilateral trade in the products of many thriving popular cultures cannot mask an overarching reality. In most if not yet quite all of the world and every cultural sector, but especially in the emotionally potent media of television and filmed entertainment, the 900-pound gorilla of cultural trade wears an unmistakable red-white-and-blue top hat.

"Eighty per cent of all the movies and television programs anyone, anywhere might see were either made in the United States or were financed by American studios and production companies," Richard Pells wrote in 1998. The figure has changed little since—perhaps dropping a bit for television, but if anything climbing for feature films. While *Variety* and other Hollywood trade papers have complained lately of falling sales for American TV shows in Europe, UNESCO reported in 2002 that "85 per cent of the films shown around the world originate in Hollywood." Some indicators of Hollywood's global reach:

➤ In 1995, with film production in Britain at a twenty-year high, 83 per cent of all the movies screened in Britain were American.

➤ Two years later, *The Economist* reported that American films were garnering "an astonishing 95 per cent" of cinema box-office in Britain.

➤ The same magazine reported: "In the European Union the United States claimed 70 per cent overall of the film market in 1996, up from 56 per cent in 1987."

➤ 88 of the 100 top-grossing films worldwide in 1998 were American; 7 more were American co-productions with other countries, for a total of 95 of the top 100.

➤ A 1999 report by an industry group advising the Irish government on film and television policy wrote: "U.S. films command some

80 per cent of world market share in theatrical film and some 70 per cent market share in television fiction."

> UNESCO's *World Culture Report 2000* listed the U.S. share of the film market in thirty nations; in only three was it less than 50 per cent. In eight, including Hungary, the Netherlands, Mexico, Brazil and Portugal, it was more than 90 per cent.

> In Ecuador, which makes an average of only four films a year, 99.5 per cent of imported movies are American. Other examples of U.S. film market share (with the country's own average yearly film output in parentheses): Costa Rica, 95.9 per cent (two films); Australia, 72 per cent (18 films); Syria, 86.1 per cent (two films).

> Four of the ten most popular films screened in France in 2001 were made in that country—but 50 per cent of the cinema tickets sold were for American movies.

> Even in India, the home of Bollywood, 70 per cent of imported movies come from the United States.

> A report to the California legislature that surveyed moviemaking in the United States, Britain, Canada and Australia concluded: "In 1999, U.S. film starts represented 82 per cent of the four-country total, about the same as in 1994."

> Of the nine most-watched international television channels in 1998, U.S. corporations owned eight (in declining order by viewers: MTV, ESPN, CNN, NBC, Discovery, CNBC, TNT and Cartoon Network). Ninth-ranked BBC World had half as many subscribers (60 million households) as the least-watched American channel (Cartoon Net, with 125 million). Time Warner alone owned three of the top eight.

> Viacom's MTV boasts that it is "the most widely distributed network in the world," reaching more than 314 million households in 83 countries in 1999. Its biggest audience is in Asia, followed by Europe and North America. Although MTV regional programs air in Russian, Mandarin, Portuguese, Spanish, German and other languages, music performed in English is the most often heard.

> By 2002, two U.S. channels aimed solely at children—Viacom's Nickelodeon and Disney Kids—each had more than 300 million subscribing households worldwide.

> In English Canada: 80 per cent of prime-time television and 95 per cent of feature films watched are American; all of English Canada's most popular TV dramas in the fall of 2001 were American-produced.

> According to a 2001 report by the Council of Europe Cultural Ob-
servatory, television "fiction of North American origin amounts to
more than half of programming on German, French and Spanish channels, with a peak of a little more than two-thirds on Italian schedules."

> 62 per cent of television programs aired in Latin America and
the Caribbean originate in the United States. The figure is higher than
70 per cent in Brazil, Mexico and Argentina, despite those countries'
own active production industries.

Other countries may make movies. But, as *The Economist* remarked
in a survey of cultural industries in 1998, "American films are the only
ones that reach every market in the world." If the U.S. share of global
screen time falls short of complete monoculture, Daya Kishan Thussu
and others do not overstate the case in describing it as a "hegemony."

The American presence in most other media is less overwhelming
but still locally significant.

Music may be the most diverse form of popular cultural expression.
From Morocco and Egypt to sub-Saharan Africa, across the Muslim
crescent, among India's polyglot populations and east to Oceania,
north across Central Asia, China and the expanses of Russia, from the
Canadian Arctic to Tierra del Fuego, local performers record an astonishing variety of styles and musical dialects. Algerian *rai,* Caribbean
ska and the *kwela* dance music of South Africa's townships and their
counterparts around the globe all reflect vigorous local identities. Domestic recordings constitute 96 per cent of India's audio CD and tape
cassette market, 81 per cent of Egypt's and about 75 per cent of Brazil's.

Some of those recordings travel. Many flow through channels created to serve ethnic diasporas. Punjabi CDs find their way to specialty
outlets serving Sikh communities in Toronto and Vancouver. Cassettes
in Arabic from the Persian Gulf are sold in Muslim boroughs of London and Chicago. Vietnamese videos from Saigon appear in New Or-
leans. "World" music has also emerged as a category of its own in many
markets, with shelves set aside for it alongside space devoted to Pop,
Rock, and Urban genres.

Still, of the recordings that enter what might be called the legitimate market (the one in which copyright is generally respected and
mostly paid for), more than 70 per cent of the dollar volume is represented by one or another of the international music Majors. Of those,
only one is not a member of the cultural conglomerates club identified

in Chapter 5: Britain's EMI Music Group (and it has recently flirted with several paid-up Majors, including Time Warner). As we have seen, the ascendant trend is to focus promotion and resources on only a diminishing few top-selling artists—implying an increasingly impoverished range of "diversity" in global music catalogues.

Radio also remains an overwhelmingly local or at most national-scale enterprise in most of the world. Correspondingly, broadcasts often serve up the music of diverse audiences. Even so, within the limits of a common language—or even sometimes across them—something close to hegemony again emerges. About 65 per cent of music played on Canadian private radio stations is foreign—most of it American—and the proportion might well be higher without the country's local-content broadcast quota. Strikingly, French-language radio in Canada has also demonstrated a tendency, in the absence of quotas, to play an overwhelming majority of foreign (and English) music. One of the writers, vacationing in Spanish-speaking Costa Rica, was struck by the extent of North American English-language music encountered on that country's radio waves—from James Taylor to Shania Twain.

The experience of a recent South African initiative is telling. Organizations representing musicians and sympathetic regulators hoped to assert a "performance copyright" in recorded music, obliging broadcasters to make payments to artists reflecting the value of music they aired. The initiative was derailed when closer study showed that 90 per cent of the money collected would be owed to non–South Africans, most of them living in much richer countries in the northern hemisphere.

Print culture also remains comparatively diverse across geographies, languages and identities. Outside of countries that have low literacy levels or very struggling economies, many national, regional and even quite local periodicals flourish. A visit to a coffee shop in almost any city in the developed world will turn up half a dozen or more advertising-supported journals that are frequently distributed free of charge. Countries like Mexico, Brazil, Taiwan, China, India and the Philippines all support strong local periodical markets.

Books are published in large numbers and many languages on every continent. A visit to the annual Frankfurt Book Fair, the world's largest gathering of the book publishing trade, drives home the point. In 2002, some 6,700 exhibitors from 100 countries promoted no fewer than 400,000 individual titles—ranging from the latest American thriller to kid's books from New Zealand—in eight large halls in the heart of the city. Figures from the International Publishers Association and UNESCO reinforce the point. Through the late 1990s, Denmark, Mexico, Thailand, Iran and Argentina all published more than 12,000 new book titles a year; Turkey, Sri Lanka, Vietnam, Finland and Colombia each produced between 4,000 and 8,000 titles; even economically hard-pressed Uzbekistan and tiny Cyprus issued 1,000 new books apiece. China published 100,000 titles.

Yet here too the picture is not uniform. African nations, apart from Egypt and South Africa, produce a paltry number of books. The number of titles translated annually into Arabic, a language spoken by 280 million people in twenty-two countries, is fewer than the number translated into Greek, spoken by only 10 million people.

At the same time, a small handful of countries and even fewer languages dominate *international* book sales. Of the world's top ten exporters of books in 1995, eight were western. Two—the United States and Britain—together had sales ($US3.7 billion) greater than the next six combined. Books in only two languages—English and German— sold more than all others in the top-ten group. And much of what is published in the three most-exported languages—English, German and French—is released by one or another of the Majors (in the latter two languages by units of either Bertelsmann or Vivendi).

Among titles regarded as "international"—whether periodicals or best-selling fiction—English rules, and with it the Majors. Notes Daya Kishan Thussu: "Of the ten most translated authors of fiction in the world (whose books have been translated into twenty-five or more languages), as many as nine originally wrote in English." The exception is Jules Verne, who wrote in French. While Colombia's Gabriel García Márquez, Trinidad-born V.S. Naipaul and Indian native Salman Rushdie, to name three, have all won large and appreciative international followings, it is striking that the latter two write in English and live in Britain.

"The U.S.–U.K. 'duopoly,'" Thussu asserts, "dominate global newspaper and magazine markets as well." Of the eight most widely circulated international newspapers and magazines in 1998, seven were American, led by *Reader's Digest, National Geographic,* and *Time.* The lone exception was *Elle,* owned by Vivendi's Hachette. Among the six leading international business journals, four were American, the remaining two British. "At the beginning of the twenty-first century," Thussu concludes, "the West continues to set the international cultural agenda."

THE EXPLANATION for both American domination in filmed entertainment and the more limited hegemony the Majors enjoy in other cultural goods can be found once again in the unique economics of cultural products.

The performance of any foreign cultural product in a particular marketplace is determined essentially by two variables: its cultural relevance to the audience there, and its price. Without the appreciation for a cultural experience, local audiences will generally ignore it at any price; consider the non-success of Sumo wrestling anywhere outside Japan. Where "foreign" cultural goods hold appeal for "local" audiences, however, that appeal alone does not determine success.

As Chapters 4 and 5 demonstrated, audience "sovereignty" is imperfect and easily manipulated. In practice, as we shall see in the pages ahead, price often trumps popularity in determining what content businesses offer to their audiences. Nowhere is that effect more powerfully felt than in the high-cost, high-value sector of filmed entertainment.

To deal first with the variable of cultural relevance, recall once again that the "experience goods" of commercial art are different from widgets. A hammer drives a nail equally well in any language. A wool blanket keeps you equally warm on the Russian steppes or the pampas of Patagonia. The same is not true for a novel, a recorded song or an episode of television. What is merely risqué in Alabama may be deeply offensive in Azerbaijan. Rushdie's *The Satanic Verses* wowed some westerners but enraged many Muslims.

Economists recognize that some cultural goods travel better than others across these differences of value and perception. They call the effect "cultural discount." Stuart McFadyen and others describe it this way:

> A particular television program (or other cultural good) rooted in one culture, and thus attractive in the home market where viewers share a common knowledge and way of life, will have diminished

appeal elsewhere as viewers find it difficult to identify with the style, values, beliefs, history, myths, institutions, physical environment, and behavioral patterns.

The reverse effect might be called a "cultural premium." Richard Caves articulates that idea in his book *Creative Industries:* "Creative goods are consumed in cultural contexts that vary from country to country. The good inevitably bears marks of the cultural ambience in which it was created. It therefore tends to appeal more to consumers steeped in the same or similar cultural ambience."

Cultural discount or premium does not require an international border or even language difference for effect. In 2001, Canada's Alliance Atlantis released with considerable fanfare a film called *Men With Brooms.* A "dramedy" starring Leslie Nielsen, it was set in the world of competitive curling. In smaller cities and rural towns across English Canada, where the curling rink is the centre of social life in winter and local bonspiels have started players on their way to the Olympics, *Men With Brooms* outdrew even heavily hyped Hollywood blockbusters. In Canada's big cities, where half the population comes from cultures in which the sport is unknown, the movie was less successful. Similarly, a Canadian TV drama like *Black Harbour,* set in Nova Scotia, garnered far higher ratings in the Maritimes than elsewhere in Canada. *North of 60* had incredible ratings north of the latitude for which it was named, but did far less well below the Arctic Circle.

Occasionally, "cultural discount" is alchemized into the desirably exotic. *Monsoon Wedding* and *Crouching Tiger, Hidden Dragon* both found audiences in North America despite the films' Asian roots. Citing the example of *Billy Elliott,* Jeongmee Kim, a researcher at the University of Nottingham's Institute of Film Studies, observed: "Although cultural discount is viewed as a disadvantage in trading a film, [it] can be used to promote the film, focussing on the national and cultural origin of the film."

In the global trade in creative goods, the effect of cultural discount on filmed entertainment is very different from its effect on such genres as news and sports.

News broadcasts rely for relevance on covering events of direct significance to their audience, placing a high premium on geographic and community specificity. Similarly, sports appeal largely to fans with strong partisan loyalties to local, state/provincial or national teams. In Canada, even though the vast majority of households have direct off-air or cable access to local and network news broadcasts from the United States, 92 per cent of viewers instead watch domestic news. Similarly, *Hockey Night in Canada* remains one of the country's highest-rated programs, whereas the annual broadcast of the American football Super Bowl championship draws sharply lower audiences north of the Canada–U.S. border than south of it.

The same high cultural discount can be discerned in global audiences for international news channels. Daya Kishan Thussu notes that while both CNN International and BBC World have cumulative audiences running to many millions of households, in no foreign market is either watched regularly in more than a very small percentage of homes. In the United Kingdom, "the combined *daily* audience for the main prime-time news broadcasts of the two dominant British terrestrial broadcasters alone is greater than the total *monthly pan-European* reach of CNN" (emphasis added).

The discount may be large on comedy as well. Humour, it is said, is "the angry art." People in different places tend to be angry at different things. "Whereas drama is eternal and universal," observes screenwriter Robert McKee, who lectures widely on the craft of storytelling, "comedy is topical. It has to be about what is going on in society now. In order to understand the jokes, you have to understand the social reference. If you don't know the social institution, you don't get the joke." Hence, "comedy doesn't travel well."

Exceptions to that rule are broad physical comedy or slapstick—the stuff of Charlie Chaplin's silent-era classics and the enduringly popular exertions of Bugs Bunny, Sylvester and Tweetie Bird or the Roadrunner. Animated entertainment has another advantage over cultural discount: it is comparatively cheap and easy to dub without incurring the disconcerting effect of dialogue that doesn't match the movement of live actors' lips.

Documentaries about science, technology, nature, art or history (especially those without an onscreen presenter) are also easy to dub into other languages. In most instances, they also deal with subjects that travel well. Their low cultural discount helps explain the foreign success of channels such as *Discovery* and *National Geographic*.

Similar factors explain the lower discounts that apply across different cultures to certain genres of non-animated filmed fiction. Futuristic science fiction or fantasy settings in which a degree of cultural remoteness from the present is part of the inherent appeal also incur comparatively minor discounts. Witness the success of the *Star Trek* television and *Star Wars* movie series. Sex also speaks in any language, which goes far to explain the global appeal of *Baywatch*.

So too do explosions, physical conflict and acrobatic violence, reasons frequently cited for the wide attraction to effects-laden, action-adventure extravaganzas like *Spider-Man*, the *Terminator* series or 2002's *XXX*.

"American movies," says Richard Pells, advancing a popular rationale for Hollywood's conquest of world cinema, "seemed less verbal and more cinematic. They were driven by their narratives, by action and spectacle that required no dubbing or subtitles, and by actors who did not need to use words to convey their deepest emotions." Much the same case could be made for the popularity of Hong Kong's martial arts and kung fu epics.

Other genres may not travel well in their initial production but still find a form of cloned life as licensed formats. *Who Wants to Be a Millionaire, Teen* (or *American*) *Idol* and *Big Brother* all originated in Europe and were reproduced with domesticated content for audiences in the United States. *Fear Factor* was based on Japanese antecedents. *Survivor* originated in the United Kingdom but has been "localized" for audiences in the United States and Asia. The BBC game show *Do the Right Thing* started life in Brazil as *Voce Decide*. Australia's Becker Group has licensed its *Battle of the Sexes* around the world. Sony Television did the same with *Wheel of Fortune*. In all these cases, the formats transcended cultural differences only after "foreign" content or personalities were replaced with "local" ones.

Who Wants to Be a Millionaire, licensed in more than fifty countries, offers a particularly telling example of cultural discount and premium. A version featuring a Canadian host with "Canadianized" questions drew ratings in Canada three times higher than a merely "North Americanized" version broadcast from New York.

Where some products encounter a cultural discount, the ease with which others hold wide appeal by virtue of extravagant spectacle, localization or dubbing can be described as a kind of cultural transparency.

WHERE LITTLE DIFFERENCE of "style, values, beliefs, history, myths, institutions, environment [or] behaviour" exists, what then decides a cultural product's success or failure?

The answer is often, in a word, money.

As noted in Chapter 2, a single talented author working alone can write a dazzling manuscript. The financial requirements for recording a musician's brilliant performance—or even a group's—are hardly much greater. But the cost of putting comparable quality "up on the screen" is of another order of magnitude entirely. In the case of a movie made for the Majors, close to US$60 million is spent on just an average film. Designated blockbusters frequently enjoy budgets of twice to more than three times that figure.

By contrast, production budgets in Canada seldom rise above C$2 million (US$1.3 million) and in India or Italy rarely go over US$3 million. British films and American "indies" seldom have more than US$6 million to put on the screen. Even at the top end of the range, those amounts represent barely a tenth of what a Major invests in a merely run-of-the-mill production. The entire budget of the most expensive non-U.S. venture would fall short of the sum needed to hire a single actor with stature considered sufficient to "open" a Hollywood movie.

Prints, advertising ("P&A") and clout with exhibitors on the scale required to force a new movie into the awareness of jaded audiences is likewise beyond reach of any but the Majors. "The majors control distribution operations in over forty countries," says *Screen Digest* analyst David Hancock. "They have the infrastructure to make a film an 'event' movie. No one else does." At US$31 million, the average Motion Picture Association–member investment in P&A alone is ten times the production budget of most independent films.

Put another way, the enormous price tag incurred by either an A-list star or splashy special effects—let alone both—ensures that even a poor rival to Sony's *Spider-Man,* Vivendi's *Minority Report* or Time Warner's *Harry Potter* remains beyond reach for those outside Hollywood. "We're the only country that can really afford them," says Sony Corp. of America CEO Howard Stringer. "When countries like France and Italy do very narrowly focused provincial subjects, they can create art, but they can't create a large audience."

For television, the resource gap between American producers and those elsewhere is less dramatic but still significant. Recall that the

Canadian producers of *Degrassi* are able to budget the equivalent of US$750,000 for each screen hour of their serial teen drama. (This is high; many Canadian drama series, including those in the French language produced for the market in Quebec, must work with lower budgets.) Budgets for independent British productions of all types average under US$200,000 a screen hour. Compare those amounts to the minimum of US$2 million and often $3 million or more lavished on an hour of American television serial drama.

Supporting the American program's much richer budgets are the amounts U.S. advertisers are prepared to pay for the opportunity they provide to reach that country's huge and wealthy television audience. All else being equal, an audience of 300 million people can clearly "afford" to spend more on creating an hour of entertainment than can one of 60 million (in Britain's case) or 30 million (in Canada's). On a strictly dollars-on-the-screen basis, it is not difficult therefore to see why U.S. TV productions, like U.S. films, may be able to boast higher "quality" than those of other countries.

But a more invidious consequence of cultural economics is revealed when we examine the way films and television shows are sold on the international market. It is not solely that the cost of American productions can be amortized across that country's much larger population.

Chapters 3 and 5 pointed out that what is being sold is not the material good itself—a master video tape or film spool—but the right to exploit a given title by exhibiting or broadcasting it in a certain territorial or temporal "window." Such geographic rights are almost universally sold by national territory, although in some cases they are sold on a regional basis often rooted in the "footprint" of satellite transmission.

What is more significant is the almost limitless discretion that vendors have to set any price they like for those rights. That discretion applies irrespective of their country of origin and flows again from the economics of cultural products. Almost all the cost is sunk into the first copy; the marginal cost of creating or transmitting additional copies is minimal. Like related public goods, cultural products are enjoyed but not consumed when one audience enjoys them. They remain available for enjoyment by limitless subsequent audiences.

What that means to the vendors of a show like *The West Wing, ER,* or *C.S.I.: Crime Scene Investigation,* or for that matter *Degrassi, The Bill* or *Home and Away,* is that they are free to set a different price in every territory in which they sell the program. In practice, the price is usually some function of the number of television sets in the territory (the available audience), the wealth of its residents (their ability to pay) and the number of broadcasters bidding for the program (its auction value). The goal, however, is always the same: to achieve the highest price the market will bear that is below the cost to broadcasters of making or buying an equivalent program from domestic producers.

The effect of this goal is apparent in Table 6.1, which compares the average prices received for U.S. TV movies and one-hour drama series in a sample of the world's markets. The prices listed—drawn from a survey conducted by an industry trade magazine—are for the same hypothetical program in every territory.

TABLE 6.1: *Price Discrimination in the Global TV Market*

	Two-Hour TV Movie	One-Hour TV Drama
Cost of Production and Average U.S. Network Licence Fee		
Original Cost	$4 million	$2 million
U.S. Broadcast Fee	$3 million	$1.4 million
Price Charged by U.S. Distributor to Foreign Broadcaster for National Rights		
Australia	$30,000	$15,000
Austria	20,000	15,000
Belgium	25,000	15,000
Brazil	20,000	10,000
Canada	100,000	50,000
Czech Republic	15,000	10,000
France	100,000	60,000
Germany	200,000	75,000
Hungary	15,000	10,000
Italy	100,000	50,000

Japan	40,000	25,000
Mexico	15,000	10,000
Netherlands	40,000	25,000
Poland	30,000	25,000
Scandinavia	35,000	25,000
Spain	60,000	35,000
United Kingdom	100,000	75,000

Note: Figures are average prices paid in 2003 in U.S. dollars by terrestrial free-to-air broadcasters in the named territories for first-run U.S. TV movies and TV dramas, as reported by *Variety International,* March 24–30, 2003. Prices for U.S. sitcoms, documentaries and children's programming are significantly lower.

What do these prices show?

First and most obviously, they demonstrate that the prices charged for broadcast rights in various countries bear no relationship whatever to the original cost of the program. Rights to programs costing $2 million to make in the United States are sold abroad for prices ranging from $10,000 to $75,000.

Second, the grid shows that prices are highly discriminatory between countries, even when population and income are taken into account. Mexican broadcasters pay an average licence fee of US$15,000 for the right to show a U.S.-distributed movie of the week to 102 million potential viewers. To air the same show to 31 million people, Canadian broadcasters pay US$100,000—a twentyfold difference in per capita terms. Britons (GDP per capita: US$23,200) must pay five times for a one-hour American TV drama what Belgians (GDP per capita: US$26,900) pay, and three times more than either Australians (US$25,800) or Japanese, who are both more numerous (127 million to 60 million) and richer (GDP per capita: US$25,800) than the Brits.

Unmistakable in Table 6.1 is the stark cost difference between an imported hour of television drama and a locally produced one. Recall that *Degrassi,* for instance, costs its Canadian makers about US$750,000 an hour to produce. A Canadian broadcaster could fill that same hour with American programming for as little as US$50,000, although prices range much higher for top-rated shows.

The difference becomes even more dramatic in other countries. To undercut the price of a U.S. import, a producer in the Czech Republic, for instance, would need to sell an hour-long program for less than $10,000. "The Danes and the Dutch," Richard Pells acknowledges in *Not Like Us,* "had to spend more money for one minute of original drama produced in Copenhagen or Amsterdam than for an hour-long episode of *Dallas* or *Miami Vice.*"

The pattern is repeated across every other program genre. A half-hour American sitcom can be had in Brazil for $5,000, in Austria for $4,000 and in Hong Kong for $1,000. Broadcast rights to a movie-of-the-week originally made in Canada or the United States for a budget of $4 million to $5 million can be acquired in Britain for $100,000, in Poland for $30,000 and in Mexico for $15,000.

These numbers illustrate more strongly than any other single piece of evidence the "curious economics of the business" noted in Chapter 2. The international market for TV programs is built on the remarkable fact that U.S. distributors will make money *no matter how low the price* they charge for a particular program. The marginal cost of supplying the program to the foreign market is close to zero—the cost of making a tape of the program and shipping it to the foreign broadcaster. No matter how cheaply a local broadcaster can buy or make an indigenous drama, distributors of U.S. shows can undercut that cost.

It is this feature above all that makes the television program marketplace unlike any conventional market.

THE FULL PERVERSITY of such freedom to price-to-market becomes clear when one considers the implication for broadcasters' profits. "If you make a TV show or film that a lot of people want to watch, you will do very well," the Motion Picture Association of America's chief executive, Jack Valenti, asserts at every opportunity. "If you make a TV program or film that few people want to watch, you will not do well." In fact, discriminatory pricing turns this evident truism on its head. Contradicting Valenti, it ensures that for many broadcasters, even less-popular imported programs can be more profitable than more-popular domestic ones.

This paradox is not difficult to understand. Profit is a function of margin: revenue less cost. If cost is sufficiently low, lower revenue can generate more profit than higher revenue, if the latter is earned only at a significantly higher cost. In the case of broadcasting, a domestic program may generate a bigger audience than an imported one, without attracting enough additional revenue to justify its very much higher cost. By contrast, an imported show that attracts a smaller audience will still pay out a generous profit against its comparatively fractional acquisition cost.

The dynamic is well demonstrated in Britain. Daya Kishan Thussu records that in a sample week in mid-year 1997, the "top forty programs in terms of audience size . . . were all home produced." Yet when David Graham & Associates subsequently analyzed where British broadcasters realized their greatest profits, in a study for the British Department for Culture, Media and Sport, they encountered a revealing fact. By comparing audience, advertising revenue and program cost, they estimated which programs returned most to the broadcasters' bottom line. Predictably, long-running soap operas like *Coronation Street* or *EastEnders* were the most profitable. But after those were accounted for, acquired foreign programs, despite attracting smaller audiences than independent U.K. productions, were routinely more profitable for the broadcasters who aired them.

In the case of Britain's most-watched commercial service, ITV, David Graham & Associates estimated that acquired (imported) programming returned £270 million in net profit—compared with £163 million for the better-watched programs purchased from independent U.K. producers. The difference was even greater for other commercial off-air channels. For second-ranked network Channel 4, "acquired programming generates 80 per cent (£159 million) of overall positive contribution," the study reported; British productions generated only £25 million. For the country's newest and smallest off-air broadcaster, Channel 5, an estimated £98 million profit from acquired programs—especially movies—made up for actual losses in virtually every other program category (with the exception of repeats).

Significantly, Graham and his associates noted that acquired programs from all sources cost the broadcasters on average about £18,000 a screen hour. Independent U.K. programs cost an average of

£110,000—a sixfold difference. In a direct comparison of what Channel 4 paid for British and U.S. programs in 1997, the study found that U.K.-made fare cost about £56,000 an hour, American programming about £16,000.

British producers who try to drive down costs to compete simply end up handicapping the quality of their productions at every stage. It is not only that low budgets cannot run to top stars or splashy special effects. Even preparation for shooting suffers. As just one unhappy consequence, critic Andrew O'Hagan wrote in *The Daily Telegraph* that "almost every British film made today is four or five drafts short of being good enough."

The pattern is familiar in every other broadcasting nation. Observes an analysis of trade in audiovisual programs (television and film) completed for the Australian government in 2002: "Imports are charging onto local screens, mainly from the U.S.A.... There's no doubt that imports are financially attractive—especially in an environment where the commercial networks have been under increasing shareholder pressure to contain costs ... Broadcasters can buy overseas programs for much less than the cost of producing a local drama."

To many critics of Hollywood, this looks like dumping—selling a product for export at a price below what is charged for it in the home market. In theory, such dumping violates Article vi of the 1947 General Agreement on Tariffs and Trade (GATT), later subsumed into the agreements that created the World Trade Organization (WTO). But the charge depends on a critical distinction.

The accusation of dumping can be applied only to goods, not to services. A book or DVD that changes hands on its sale may be a "good" within the meaning of GATT. But when the copyright in a film or television program is merely licensed for exhibition or broadcast in another country, nothing changes hands. The transaction is deemed to be a "service"—and hence immune from both GATT and accusations of dumping.

The distinction is a fine one, however, and the merits of the argument on either side are debatable. They will be examined more closely in Chapter 16, which will consider in more detail how GATT, the WTO and the General Agreement on Trade in Services (GATS) treat cultural products.

WHAT IS INDISPUTABLE is that the combination of all these factors—cultural transparency, big budgets and onscreen production
value, and infinitely flexible price—has given films and television programs produced in the United States an unassailable advantage in
global markets. Although the trade in creative products in general may
be multilateral and some other countries are significant participants,
no other nation enjoys the scale or uniformly favourable balance of
trade that the United States does.

"The U.S. movie industry alone has a surplus balance of trade with
every single country in the world," Jack Valenti testified to the U.S. Sen-
ate in February 2002. "No other American enterprise can make that
statement."

And significantly for other countries doing business with the
United States, nothing else earns that country more money than its
creative products do.

While American films dominate cinema screens in Europe, Canada, South America and much of Asia, movies from the rest of the world
are almost invisible in the United States. Of 30,000 American movie
theatres, only 250 regularly show foreign films. According to Martin
Dale, foreign films' share of screen time in U.S. theatres has fallen from
5 per cent in the 1960s to about 0.5 per cent at the turn of the century.

In 1997, UNESCO estimates, 388 million Europeans watched some
480 Hollywood films. Only 53 million Americans saw European films.
"U.S. dominance in the cinema field is an old story," Nils Klevjer Aas
noted in a report for the Council of Europe's Cultural Observatory in
2001. "This hegemony has only deepened. The balance of trade with
the United States is deeply in disfavour of the European audiovisual industries—and the deficit is rising, from a little more than $2 billion
USD in 1988 to more than $7 billion in 1999."

An Australian analysis in 2002 estimated that country's annual
deficit to the United States on films and television at a record A$500
million (US$280 million).

Note David Graham and his associates about Britain: "Although the
U.K. is second only behind the U.S. in the international programme
sales market, it continues to operate a balance of trade deficit—heavily
influenced by the purchase of the U.K. rights to U.S. films." Britain's
most successful film ever, *Four Weddings and a Funeral,* earned less

than half as much at the box-office even on its own turf as Hollywood's *Jurassic Park*, which played at the same time in British theatres.

Although India produces more movies than does the United States, exports them widely and, almost singly in the world apart from the United States, enjoys a positive balance of trade in filmed entertainment, American foreign sales of movie rights in 1993 were worth *750 times* as much as Indian sales.

A Canadian estimate is that exhibition fees for Hollywood movies take some c$200 million a year out of this country. In 2000, Statistics Canada estimated, Canadian broadcasters spent another us$300 million on American television program rights.

Filmed entertainment—feature films and television—lead the positive American trade balance on creative products. The export of books and music recordings contributed additional millions to a surplus in cultural trade that was worth us$28.23 billion in 2001, according to an analysis for the U.S. International Intellectual Property Alliance (iipa).

Trade in cultural products, in fact, is one of the very few areas in which the United States as a nation makes money in global trade. Overall, the United States in 2001 ran a deficit in merchandise trade of between us$411 billion and $426 billion (the difference depending on what basis is used for the accounting). That deficit was partly offset by a surplus on trade in services of $80 billion. The largest single contributor to that surplus was the sale to foreign buyers of $89 billion worth of "copyright products." The category includes software such as Microsoft's Windows operating system, which runs on more than 90 per cent of the world's personal computers, as well leisure and business applications and video games, in addition to music, books, movies and television shows.

The same study for the iipa underscored the contribution that foreign sales of cultural products make to the wider American economy. "Export statistics may grossly underestimate the true value," the study noted. "A single master version of a film print [may be] valued at a few hundred dollars in U.S. export statistics. From that master version however, copies or exhibition rights may generate millions of dollars in sales." Fuelled by exports, it reminded readers, U.S. employment in filmed entertainment grew between 1977 and 2001 three times as fast as the American economy as a whole.

Domination of the world's cinema and television screens, in other words, is not just a matter of cultural pride to the United States. Its contribution to the superpower's economy is of strategic importance.

THESE FIGURES underscore two other significant themes.

The first is the potential of cultural creators to contribute greatly to a country's wealth—quite apart from its artistic vigour or its social and emotional understanding of itself and its identity.

The second is the significance that American business and government leaders attach to preserving that country's enormously profitable hegemony in global cultural exchange.

Both themes will be revisited in Part Three, when we come to grips with the critical challenge facing other countries in the arena of international trade liberalization. In negotiations progressing under the General Agreement on Trade in Services (GATS), the United States leads a campaign to embed the perverse market economics of cultural goods within the protection of international trade law. Chapter 16 will show how successive American administrations have come to the muscular defence of the Majors in seeking to preserve and extend their advantages. Chapter 17 will examine alternatives to the GATS regime.

The chapters immediately ahead first examine the variety of ways in which public authorities have sought to mitigate the least desirable outcomes that flow naturally from the economic peculiarities of creative goods. Some of those measures have been widely adopted and yet have failed to achieve their goals. Others have been widely criticized— yet are clearly effective.

PART TWO
THE CULTURAL TOOL KIT

7

THE
NATIONALITY
OF
CULTURE

T HE BRIDGE ON THE RIVER KWAI is a classic of filmmaking. Its portrayal of human dignity, redemptive honour and heroism in the face of brutality continues to resonate with audiences nearly half a century after it was filmed in 1957.

But to whom does credit go for this high point of cinema culture?

To Hollywood? Columbia Pictures was the lead financier for its US$3 million production budget, and American William Holden starred as commando Major Shears. Major elements of the screenplay were written by U.S. citizens, and Holden was the highest-paid actor in the film, with an unprecedented profit position.

To the United Kingdom? Briton David Lean directed the film. Sam Spiegel's London-based company, Horizon Pictures, produced the film and contributed to its financing. British actor Alec Guinness starred as the captive Colonel Nicholson. It is his character who inspires his fellow prisoners of war (most of whom were also played by British actors) to complete the rail span of the movie's title and who ultimately destroys it. And it was a company from Sheffield, England, that constructed the bridge used for the filming.

Or to Sri Lanka? Most of the movie was actually shot at Kitulgala, near Colombo, rather than in the Burma of its setting. The actors who played Siamese girls in the film were in fact from Ceylon (now Sri

Lanka), as were most of the extras who appeared as Japanese soldiers. To this day, almost fifty years later, the location for the movie continues to be noted as a tourist attraction in Sri Lanka guidebooks.

Or even perhaps to France? The film was based on a novel (*Le pont de la rivière Kwai*), by Frenchman Pierre Boule. (Boule also received an Oscar for the screenplay, although in fact he did not write it. It had been written principally by Carl Foreman and Michael Wilson, two Hollywood writers who were blacklisted during the McCarthy era and who only later received the award.)

Many other movies similarly resist typing for their national DNA.

Take another war story made four decades after *Kwai*. *The English Patient* opens on a scene of a mortally wounded soldier lying in a field hospital. But he is not English. He is in fact a Canadian soldier, a citizen of the same country as Michael Ondaatje, who wrote the novel on which the movie is based. Except that Ondaatje, as it happens, was also born in Colombo (coincidentally, in the same year—1943—in which *The Bridge on the River Kwai* is set). Again a primary supporting role is played by an American, Willem Dafoe, and an American studio, Miramax, put up the bulk of its US$40 million budget. Yet Britons Ralph Fiennes and Anthony Minghella respectively starred in and directed the work. A Frenchwoman, Juliette Binoche, plays another primary supporting character. And the film was shot mostly in Italy and Tunisia.

MUCH THE SAME DECONSTRUCTION can be worked on many other products of popular culture. Culture itself defies straightforward national attribution, a fact for which anyone who enjoys a little salsa on their French fries or chutney with their lamb chop must be grateful. Identity is ambiguous. This has less light-hearted implications for many ethnic minorities living amid assertive national majorities. It is even popular in some right-wing circles in North America to denounce the very idea of multiculturalism as subversive, a dubious mark of divided loyalties, insincere citizenship and, at the extreme, a kind of racism.

But nationality remains one of the most useful as well as most convenient perspectives from which to grasp the threat to diversity in the marketplace of popular culture. National governments, moreover, are the primary actors able to mount a response to the perverse outcomes of cultural economics. And almost without exception those responses are framed in policies that draw distinctions among creators, vendors or products of culture based on their national "identity."

Most nations, for instance, are party to the General Agreement on Tariffs and Trade (GATT). The agreement establishes a general obligation on member nations to treat "like" goods from other countries no less favourably than their own. But Article IV also gives them the right to exercise screen quotas for "films of national origin." And as later chapters will show, many countries have also enacted content quotas for locally produced television programs. They and others may provide awards, subsidies or tax incentives available only to "national" cultural products.

But what exactly is a "film of national origin"?

Should national origin by determined by the citizenship of the creators? Should it be based on the locus of the financing or ownership of the copyright to a work? On the physical location of the film set or recording studio? Or should it rely on the most subjective test of all, the subject matter? To the extent that cultural products involve creative inputs from citizens or companies belonging to more than one country, the problem becomes thornier.

GATT offers little help: nowhere in the agreement is "national origin" defined. And although the World Trade Organization (WTO) started a process in 1994 that is intended to harmonize rules of origin, nine years later it has yet to bear fruit. Each GATT nation is still left to decide for itself what the phrase means.

The citizenship of those who create culture offers clear merit as a reference point for identity. First, it is transparent: a passport equals identity. Second, it can be invoked to support a diverse range of indigenous expression without prescribing (or *pro*scribing) any particular expression. If every country supported creative work by its nationals without regard for what they created, the result would surely enrich humanity even if their works did not always explicitly reflect national geography.

But citizenship alone is not without complications.

In 2002, for example, controversy arose as to which books written in English could compete for the prestigious Man Booker Prize, commonly known as "the Booker." As the rules then stood, novelist citizens of Canada, India, Australia, Nigeria, Jamaica and Tuvalu—and indeed of any of four dozen or so other Commonwealth countries—could all be considered for the literary award. But not novelists from the United

States, no matter how impeccably Anglo-Saxon their family stock might be. A report that the limitation might be lifted in 2004 to make Americans eligible for the prize ignited a furor. The prize panel's 2002 chairperson, Lisa Jardine, hotly denied the report. Opening the competition to Americans, she said, would make the Booker "as British an institution as English muffins in American supermarkets."

In the end a Spanish-born Canadian, Yann Martel, took the British prize for a book inspired by a Brazilian that featured an Indian boy adrift on the ocean with a tiger from Bengal and an African zebra. Martel had shared the short list for the prized British institution with two other Canadians, one of whom was born in India whereas the other—in an irony that apparently escaped Jardine—was born in the United States.

Compound identities are particularly familiar, if not always comfortable, to Canadians. Among seventeen developed countries surveyed by the Organization for Economic Co-operation and Development (OECD), only Australia has more residents (as a percentage of population) born somewhere else. Nearly one in five working Canadians is an immigrant. The country's biggest province is home to another fifth of Canadians who possess a pronounced sense of their separate francophone identity. Many aboriginal Canadians—a smaller but much older minority—find identity in one of dozens of "First Nations." Little wonder questions of identity are abiding preoccupations for many Canadian artists, wherever they were born. Filmmaker Atom Egoyan, born in Egypt, raised in Victoria and resident in Toronto, is shadowed as closely by his Armenian background as Vancouver-born author Joy Nozomi Kogawa by her Japanese one or singer Susan Aglukark by her Inuit heritage.

Identity and citizenship get more confused again when cultural creators move from one country to another. The most time-honoured route for this migration is to the United States, and the paradigmatic example is again Canada.

Generations of Canadian actors, from Mary Pickford to Mike Myers, have found success in Hollywood at the apparent expense of any significant attachment to—or public identification with—their homeland. "It is a general rule," observed Kevin Myers (no relation to Mike) in Britain's *The Sunday Telegraph*, "that actors and filmmakers arriving in Hollywood keep their nationality—unless, that is, they are

Canadian. Thus Mary Pickford, Walter Huston, Donald Sutherland, Michael J. Fox, William Shatner, Norman Jewison, David Cronenberg and Dan Aykroyd have in the popular perception become American, and Christopher Plummer, British. It is as if, in the very act of becoming famous, a Canadian ceases to be Canadian, unless she is Margaret Atwood, who is as unshakably Canadian as a moose."

Once creators enter the U.S. industry and market, they typically can no longer look to their country of origin for financial or other support. There is some argument for this. Many who "make it" in America need no further career support (an A-list property like Mike Myers commands more money for a single picture than many Canadian cultural-support agencies give out in a year). And if a country is to support its nationals on public funds, it is not unreasonable to want them to succeed at home.

That said, disqualification based on expatriate residency may also trigger unintended consequences. Should young Canadian musicians struggling to get a foot in the door of their industry's continental capital in Nashville be penalized for their ambition by being stripped of support at home? If a successful Hollywood emigré like Leslie Neilsen comes home to make a distinctly indigenous movie like *Men With Brooms* (in which the Yukon-born actor starred), should the production pay for his contribution by forgoing "national" treatment?

Canada may encounter these problems more than most countries do. But mass mobility and global markets catalyzed by two centuries of technological innovation have blurred the bright dividing lines of identity for everyone everywhere. "Canada's problems," remarks philosopher Andrew Potter in a discussion of multiculturalism, "are the world's problems."

James Shapiro, reviewing *the dictionary of global culture,* a self-consciously post-modern attempt to escape the western canon in identifying the world's most significant intellects, makes the point nicely:

What does it mean to call Flannery O'Connor and Richard Wright "American" writers at the outset of entries while describing Amy Tan as "Chinese-American" and Philip Roth as "Jewish American"? . . . Why call J.R.R. Tolkien an "English writer" and Israel Zangwill a "Jewish" one if Tolkien was born in South Africa and Zangwill was a native Englishman?

Some critics use examples like these to deride the very idea of using a creator's citizenship as any sort of guide to whether a book, recording or film should be treated as "national" for the purpose of policy. Instead they suggest that subject, not author, should determine a work's "nationality."

But this proves problematic as well. Do Ernest Hemingway's stories collected in *The Snows of Kilimanjaro* truly represent the voice of Tanzania? Does *Tears of the Sun,* a recent Stars-and-Stripes-waving guts-and-guns vehicle for Bruce Willis, authentically express a Nigerian point of view? Should Canadians value Yann Martel the less because Pi was not cast adrift in Hudson Bay?

A much greater risk lies in this. Subject matter in popular culture is, to state the obvious, *subjective.* That makes it difficult to judge by transparent standards: think Olympic ice-dancing. More dangerous still, policies that set out to confer or withhold state favour based on the subject matter of a work enter a slippery slope that risks delivering the unwary into the sterility of "official" culture, if not the cells of censorship.

ONE ESCAPE from the Scylla and Charybdis hazards of censorship and content-analysis is to declare the entire enterprise a lost cause. As Michiko Kakutani wrote of the Booker controversy:

> In the brave new world of the 21st Century, where the fates of countries and individuals are increasingly intertwined, nationalist literatures... are becoming obsolete. It's a global phenomenon that includes the wholesale trading of narrative styles and ideas across continents and national borders.

Some would argue that Kakutani's "internationalism" is not new at all, that it is in fact the secret of how American—specifically, Hollywood—culture has come to achieve global hegemony.

In this view, the United States attracts the brightest talents the rest of the world has to offer. Those creators then shape the form, colour, texture and attitude of what America exports back to the rest of the world in books, music, TV programs and especially film. What overly sensitive citizens of other countries take to be cultural imperialism is, in this light, only their own reflection—seen through a made-in-the-U.S.A. mirror.

"The United States was, and continues to be, as much a consumer of foreign intellectual and artistic influences as it has been a shaper of the world's entertainment and tastes," asserts Richard Pells. "As a nation of immigrants from the nineteenth to the twenty-first centuries, and as a haven in the 1930s and 1940s for refugee scholars and artists, the United States has been a recipient as much as an exporter of global culture." Hollywood in particular, he argues, from Charlie Chaplin and Mary Pickford, through Alfred Hitchcock and Roman Polanski, to Arnold Schwarzenegger and Ang Lee, "has functioned as an international community, drawing on the talents of actors, directors, writers, cinematographers, editors, and costume and set designers from all over the world."

"In effect," says Pells, "Americans have specialized in selling the dreams, fears, and folklore of other people back to them."

This view is not exclusive to Americans. The simultaneous release in the summer of 2000 of German director Wolfgang Petersen's *The Perfect Storm* and countryman Roland Emmerich's *The Patriot* (which starred Australian Mel Gibson) prompted one German newspaper to headline: "Thanks to Germany: Hollywood imports patriotism and war." *The Economist* embraced Pells's perspective in a 1998 report on resistance to American culture. "One reason for Hollywood's success," the British newsmagazine wrote, "is that from the earliest days it was open to foreign talent and foreign money. And now, two of the most powerful studios, Columbia TriStar and Fox, are owned by foreign media conglomerates."

Some regard this development as promising. Sony's American chairman and CEO Howard Stringer, for one, points to Ang Lee's surprise subtitled hit *Crouching Tiger, Hidden Dragon* as evidence that "for the first time, you're seeing the studios reach out to foreign countries to develop local theatre, local movies, in a way that broadens their appeal." But even Stringer admits that "*Crouching Tiger* is the exception rather than the rule." More often, he concedes, "the difficulty of thinking about a large audience is that the quality of your films is likely to suffer. You're into the lowest common denominator. And we see a lot of it."

Moreover, the idea that Hollywood—or the United States more generally—is merely a sort of central service facility polishing other country's "dreams, fears and folklore" into finished products that are shipped back sensibility and insight intact is clearly nonsense. At the very least the American mirror changes the message in highly material ways. Before Columbia Pictures agreed to finance *The Bridge on the River Kwai*, the studio insisted that the story's escaped prisoner of war be American. Any Teutonic DNA lurking in *The Perfect Storm* was well watered down.

The pioneer of this trend has long been the Walt Disney Co. The empire of the Mouse has for decades "re-told" stories from numerous non-American cultures in its globally popular animated features. But whether that retelling represents the exchange of a range of authentic cultural expressions or merely the ongoing export of middle-class, middle-brow, middle-American conventions in a variety of colourful ethnic costumes is another matter.

Shu-Ling Berggreen, an associate professor of journalism and mass communication at the University of Colorado in Denver, with Katalin Lustyik, analyzed Disney's versions of two folk tales, one nineteenth-century children's story and a revered historical event, from four different world cultures. They were curious to see how faithfully Disney's *Mulan, Aladdin, The Little Mermaid* and *Pocahontas* preserved the text, subtext and texture of their originals. Their conclusion, in brief, was "not very."

"Disneyfication focuses on synchronization, one-dimensionality and uniformity, disregarding cultural origins and original story lines," Berggreen and Lustyik noted in an unpublished 2002 paper. In one illustration of Disney's trampling on cultural authenticity, the two point to the "orgy of hugging displayed" at the end of *Mulan*, in which the heroine of the title spontaneously embraces the Chinese emperor. "Hugging, especially between male and female in public, is not customary among Chinese," they observe, "and hugging between a civilian and an emperor was forbidden." A not-so-subtle racism also runs throughout all four movies, they assert: "Disney's good characters look clean and white, for example Aladdin modeled on Tom Cruise, and speak perfect American English. Bad characters [are] dirty and dark . . . have beards, big noses and speak with thick foreign accents."

Does it matter? In a particularly telling passage, the two American academics note that audiences in a variety of cultures exposed to Disney's products "get upset with the distortion of myths, literature and historical events that they are familiar with, but not with those introduced to them for the first time." In other words, viewers may be outraged with the "Disneyfication" of their own folklore, but they take the Mouse kingdom's version of someone else's for good reporting. "As a forty-five-year-old Chinese puts it: 'I am glad I saw *Pocahontas*. I didn't know anything about Indian culture before and I'm happy the English did not trash the Indians as they did with other colonies.'"

This, to put it mildly, is hardly encouraging if globalized, export-led retellings are to be the future of local, distinct and diverse cultural histories everywhere.

As the Majors seek to maximize their profit from ever-pricier blockbusters, even the authentically American is becoming attenuated. "The more Hollywood becomes preoccupied by the global market," noted *The Economist* in its 1998 report, "the more it produces generic blockbusters made to play as well in Pisa as Peoria. There is nothing particularly American about boats crashing into icebergs or asteroids that threaten to obliterate human life."

Concedes Lucy Fisher, the Hollywood producer of the Russell Crowe epic *Gladiator:* "The global audience is as important as the domestic audience now, which is good and bad. The good is that there's more people to see a movie. The bad is there's more formulas that people are trying to apply, like action, so they can appeal to or appease the foreign markets."

IF THE PURSUIT of profit gives American creators incentive to generalize their work's identity, the demand that faces producers in other countries comes closer in magnitude to Wolfgang Peterson's cinematic tidal wave. Very few audiences outside the United States are big or rich enough to support more than bare-bones budgets for demanding genres like feature film or series television drama. Producers have long looked past their own borders for extra funds. But several factors have combined in recent years to turn the search into a life-or-death imperative.

Broadcast deregulation in many countries in the 1980s and 1990s spawned a proliferation of new television channels. But it also fragmented audiences. That left many channels with fewer viewers and diminished resources. At the same time, public broadcasters, similarly motivated by pro-market sentiment, cut back fully funded in-house production units and opted instead to buy programs from independent outsiders. But neither cash-strapped private broadcasters nor penny-pinching public ones have been willing to fully cover the cost of the shows they sought to buy. To make up the difference, independent TV producers increasingly must make additional sales to broadcasters beyond their borders.

Filmmakers have faced much the same perfect storm in business conditions. In many countries, public agencies created to support indigenous cinema experienced budget cuts. They sought to make the most from reduced funds while at the same time prodding filmmakers to rely less on subsidies and appeal more to audiences. Many found an answer to all three objectives in requiring foreign distribution or overseas broadcast licences as a pre-condition of public financing.

And whatever Richard Pells or *The Economist* may choose to believe, the idealized middlebrow American looms large in any producer's pursuit of an audience large enough to fund her aspirations.

"Producers from Toronto to Toulouse to Tokyo are working overtime, feverishly racking their brains to make the viewer in Toledo, Ohio, comfortable," Canadian documentary producer John Kastner wrote. The price of Toledo's comfort has often been the same specific detail he counts on to give his documentaries relevance at home. "If I altered the story, played down the Canadian reality," he fretted about one experience, "I might 'make the sale,' which in turn would have covered most of the production costs. But in this case [a series about paroled sex offenders] that difference is the crux of the story."

"In order to create Canadian films and documentaries we have had to destroy them," laments Canadian producer Martyn Burke. "If you go to New York and say, 'I've got this great idea. It involves Kenora, Ontario,' they're going to look at you blankly and say, 'If you can add Peoria as well as Kenora then we'll be happy.' Are we going to do anything that's Canadian, or is it going to be this kind of nowhere-land?"

The effect is most powerful in regard to film and television, but not limited to those forms. Canadian musicians pitching their talents to Nashville have long known to drop references to Minnedosa or Kapuskasing from their repertoire—or at least change them to Muskogee and Kalamazoo. Even some Canadian book publishers confide that they are reluctant to accept book proposals or manuscripts not written with U.S. readers primarily in mind.

In fairness, however, the tradeoff of "identity" for "making the sale" is not limited to making a work America-friendly. A panel discussion associated with the annual 2002 Prix Jutra awards—Quebec's version of the Oscars—had to be rescheduled to accommodate an unexpectedly large turnout to debate the sensitive topic, *Tourner en anglais: trahison culturelle ou nécessité?* ("Shooting in English: necessity or cultural treason?"). The dialectic underscored what will be no great novelty to Canadian readers: that many francophone creators regard "Canadian" and "Québécois" as meaning two entirely different things in terms of their cinema.

In a similar vein, European filmmakers have been scorned for co-productions that mingle creative inputs from several countries in order to raise larger budgets and reach wider audiences. Critics deride the generic screen identities that result as bland "Euro-pudding."

A similarly pejorative vagueness of identity attaches to films shot in one place but portraying another. The Burma of *River Kwai*, as noted, was really Ceylon (now Sri Lanka). The city in the 2003 hit *Chicago* was in fact Toronto. Vancouver is such a celluloid chameleon that a local magazine once published a map of "Hollywood's Vancouver" in which various neighbourhoods were identified by places they had "played" on screen, from Hong Kong to Quantico, Virginia (home of the FBI, as portrayed in *The X-Files*).

IN SHORT, solving the "identity" problem by declaring that identity doesn't matter in the modern world is no solution at all. Identity *does* matter. These illustrations point not to its irrelevance, only its vulnerability. They provide further evidence of the relentless erosion of diversity that the perverse economics of culture make inevitable in the absence of public policy to counter them.

Yet, for every country that has decided to defend the indigenous expression of its cultural identity, there must be some test to qualify which expressions "belong" to that country—which expressions are "national" for policy purposes. There must be some way to determine whether a particular film, television program, book or sound recording qualifies.

Granted, identity is a fuzzy concept. No test can define it with perfect precision. But that does not mean policy is incapable of devising a test that will do so within a perfectly acceptable degree of *im*precision. Some of the muddle may be dispelled by making a critical distinction between "cultural" and "industrial" definitions of creative identity.

Cultural definitions of identity seek their coordinates in the full sweep of a community's history, images, archetypes, beliefs and heroes. Does a mukluk on the screen make a movie "Inuit"? Does a character dining on poutine make a novel authentically "Québécois"? Do either of these props make those works "Canadian"?

Industrial definitions of identity serve a different, narrower and more verifiable function. They seek out objective reference points in the location of technical, creative or financial inputs and may be entirely silent on subjective markers of identity.

By this measure, *The English Patient* (ironically enough itself an exploration of the problem of identity) may rate as culturally Canadian but not industrially so. Arguably *River Kwai* could be seen through an "industrial" lens as either American (where the money came from) or Ceylonese (where it was shot), and through a "cultural" lens as British (or at least European).

Governments have leveraged this distinction to devise a variety of policy instruments. Their complexity varies with the products they are designed to address. Books are easier to assess than is recorded music. Both pose simpler questions than filmed entertainment.

In practice, these tests tend to reflect both cultural and industrial scales in differing degrees. For many jurisdictions, the priority is economic: creating conditions conducive to clusters of production. Others, especially small jurisdictions, may accept that as a low-likelihood outcome and instead seek only to preserve room on the cultural shelf for works that reflect local "dreams, fears and folklore." Given the multiple factors that are candidates for consideration, most tests favour "points" systems that assign different weights to each of a menu of variables.

It is striking that one test for determining the nationality of a cultural product is virtually never used. That is the one suggested for this very purpose in the 1994 *WTO Agreement on Rules of Origin*. That agreement sets out a process intended to harmonize the different rules that WTO member nations use to determine a product's nationality or "origin." The general principle is that the "origin of a particular good" should be "either the country where the good has been wholly obtained or, when more than one country is concerned in the production of the good, the country where *the last substantial transformation* has been carried out" (emphasis added).

The problem with this test arises from the distinction encountered in Chapter 3 between the original first copy of a creative work and a retail or exhibition copy of the same work. Creation of the intellectual property embedded in the "master" copy may take place in one country and copies of the work may be made separately in another one, using locally supplied paper, ink, film or plastic. Many books "published" in North America are in fact printed and bound in Hong Kong or Taiwan. And it is a little-known fact that many if not most release prints for Hollywood films exhibited in theatres in the United States and Canada are not made in the United States but at low-cost processing labs in Canada that specialize in that business.

Most cinema films are imported as release prints. Seldom after it has been copied for release does the master ever again leave the studio's vault. In this context, the words "films of national origin" could be interpreted to assert that for trade purposes most films made in Hollywood are really Canadian, simply because the release prints were duplicated there—a plainly nonsensical reading from any cultural perspective.

In other words, of all possible tests for establishing what is a "national" creative product, the one employed in international trade law turns out to be *least* useful, because it relies on the culturally irrelevant locus of making copies of the original. The significance of this absurdity will become more apparent when we examine the GATT and WTO trade regimes more closely in Chapter 16.

Clearly the only meaningful question relates to the origin of the master or original copy of a creative work.

But as we have seen, there are a variety of ways to seek answers to this question. How far should the test turn on the citizenship of the creators who made the work? What weight should be given to the location where it was made? What of the corporation that financed it and owns the master: should the location of its head office count? How about the citizenship of its controlling shareholders? And should the test concern itself with the most subjective measure of all, whether the cultural product is actually "about" the country in question?

The weight given each of these questions may push the conclusion in a different direction.

The remainder of this chapter will not catalogue every cultural identity test on the books of every jurisdiction, but it will look at examples from several of the most active markets for popular culture. Most but not all examples occur in the sectors where diversity is under greatest stress: film and television.

Some of these markets are national. Australia, Canada and South Africa each have stand-alone criteria for determining the domestic status of various genres of cultural product. Others are supranational: the European Union and the (not entirely congruent) Council of Europe have differing standards that apply to film and television under the auspices of various agreements, directives and programs. Europe's supranational standards for cultural "identity" coexist with national tests. The following pages will also examine a sampling of the latter from Spain, Britain, Italy, Germany, Norway and France. Collectively, these tests illustrate a range of possible responses to diverse policy priorities.

Although the U.S. federal government does not employ any tests to determine the national origin of cultural products, some other American jurisdictions do. Several states subsidize film production; they understandably limit support to productions that hire local crews.

The question also arises in establishing who is eligible for those coveted golden statuettes awarded annually by the Academy of Motion Picture Arts and Sciences. The rules for the Oscars require that only one film from each country may compete for the "best foreign-language film" award. Candidates must be produced outside the United States and be nominated by a committee from the submitting country that includes film craftspeople. Furthermore: "the submitting country must certify that creative talent of that country exercised artistic control of the film." Yet, despite that explicit requirement, not even the Academy has always been certain which films "belonged" to which foreign country. Some Britons were affronted, for example, when the Academy rejected that country's 2003 nominee for best foreign-language film. *The Warrior,* by London-born director Asif Kapadia, features Hindi dialogue and was shot in the Indian state of Rajasthan. Reflected its (French) producer, Bertrand Faivre: "They just looked at it and said it doesn't look like an English movie the way we think an English movie should be, and that's it."

Keeping that in mind, let's examine how a number of countries distinguish national cultural products from foreign products.

AUSTRALIA

The Australian Broadcasting Authority (ABA) in 1999 revised an earlier standard for assessing "Australian content" and compliance with minimum domestic-content quotas in that country. The primary test of the new standard required an "Australian program" to be "produced under the creative control of Australians."

It established a number of criteria for determining whether a program had been produced under Australian control:

➤ the producer is Australian, *and*
➤ *either* the director *or* the writer is Australian, *and*
➤ at least "50 per cent of the leading actors or on-screen presenters" are Australian, *and*
➤ the program is produced and post-produced in Australia.

Specific genres must meet additional requirements. In the case of drama, at least 75 per cent of supporting cast members must be Australian. And for animated programs, at least three Australians must be included among the production designer, character designer, supervising layout artist, supervising storyboard artist and key background artist. An "Australian" person is taken to mean either a citizen or permanent resident. Under an agreement between Australia and New Zealand, however, the ABA accepts programs that have been determined by similarly structured tests to be "produced under the creative control of New Zealanders" as equivalent to "Australian" programs for the purpose of minimum content quotas.

CANADA

Standards for assessing the "Canadian" status of film and television programs have undergone a number of changes since Canadian content rules for television were first introduced in 1961. The current criteria, adopted in 1999, were largely based on rules established by the Canadian Radio-television and Telecommunications Commission (CRTC) in 1984, but are now under further review by the federal Department of Canadian Heritage.

Pending the conclusion of that review, Canadian films and television programs remain subject to three different systems for assessing their nationality. One is administered by the CRTC to ensure that broadcasters satisfy its requirements for Canadian content. Another is administered by the Department of Heritage's Canadian Audio-Visual Certification Office (CAVCO) for the purpose of certifying works eligible for a federal film and video production tax credit. Telefilm Canada—recently integrated into the Canadian Television Fund, an agency supported in part by government funding and in part by a levy on cable and direct-to-home (DTH) satellite distributors—uses the CAVCO test with additional requirements.

To be certified as "Canadian" by the CRTC, a television program has to meet requirements in three areas.

Producer: The "central decision-maker of a production from beginning to end" must be a Canadian. Individuals or corporations must be prepared to demonstrate their effective control of a production by "submitting, upon request, ownership documents, contracts or affidavits [and] an independent legal opinion confirming that financial and creative control of the production is Canadian." Foreigners may receive "vanity credits" as executive producers only if they limit their production role to that of an observer, and only if the Canadian producer is paid more than the aggregate compensation of all credited foreign producers.

Points: Productions in most genres are required to accumulate at least six points, awarded on a weighted basis for Canadians performing identified functions, as follows:

- director: 2 points
- screenwriter: 2 points
- lead performer (or lead voice): 1 point
- second lead (or voice): 1 point
- production designer: 1 point
- director of photography: 1 point
- music composer: 1 point
- picture editor: 1 point

In addition, at least one of the director or screenwriter, and at least one of the two lead performers, must be Canadian (with exemptions granted only on application for "compelling reasons").

Expenditures: At least 75 per cent of a production's budget (less some identified expenses, including compensation for Canadian creative personnel) must be paid to Canadians. Likewise, at least 75 per cent of post-production and lab costs (not including paying the picture editor) has to be paid "for services provided in Canada by Canadians or Canadian companies."

The CRTC also recognizes as "Canadian" any program that is certified so by CAVCO or Telefilm Canada. That is made easier by the fact that CAVCO's test essentially mirrors the "points" portion of the CRTC system. To earn certification for the federal tax credit, a production needs to earn six points—the same number that qualifies for "Canadian" standing with the CRTC.

Telefilm Canada also uses the same basic test—awarding points on the same basis as CAVCO and the CRTC—but sets the bar higher for certification as "Canadian." The agency administers separate investment funds for television and feature film with the same broadly cultural goal—to "present a distinctly Canadian point of view."

The Telefilm Canada feature-film fund, according to its published guidelines, is intended to support fictional movie dramas "with significant Canadian creative elements, including Canadian stories, themes, talent and technicians, and which reflect Canadian society and cultural diversity." To meet that standard, a film must accumulate at least eight out of ten possible CAVCO points, "not disguise its Canadian location" and be "under Canadian ownership and ... financial, distribution and creative control."

The Canadian Television Fund (CTF) is explicitly directed at "cultural programming ... It does not support 'industrial' or 'foreign service' productions or those that cede control to foreign entities." The agency's guidelines amplify that theme: "These productions speak to Canadians about themselves, their culture, their issues, their concerns and their stories. These productions reflect the lives of Canadians across the country and reveal Canadians and their society to the viewer." To that end, television productions need to score a perfect ten out of ten possible CAVCO/CRTC points. Again, the standard requires that "underlying rights are owned ... by Canadians." To meet the requirement for CTF support, however, a production also needs to be "visibly" Canadian. That is: "shot and set primarily in Canada" and "speaks to Canadians about, and reflects, Canadian themes and subject matter."

Yet another standard applies to projects conducted under any of the dozens of co-production treaties Canada has signed with other countries. Typically, signatories to those agreements each grant "national" recognition to joint ventures involving filmmakers from both. To secure "Canadian" status, a treaty-sanctioned co-production does not need to pass a points test or demonstrate visibly Canadian elements of theme or imagery. The primary issue is citizenship—corporate and individual. A Canadian participant is required to be "a Canadian-owned company under the effective control of Canadians" and to own rights to the finished work in Canada. In addition, "the producer, the crew, and the personnel exercising control over the creative, financial and technical aspects of the Canadian share of the project must be Canadian citizens or permanent residents," according to a Telefilm bulletin on the subject.

The Canadian rules are complicated and not free from criticism. In a report issued in mid-2003, a Canadian parliamentary committee noted that the rules had "become so complex that they defy easy description or explanation. They are contradictory, produce absurd results and do not make creative sense." But efforts were underway as this book was being completed to simplify the rules and make them more rational.

SOUTH AFRICA

Broadcasting in South Africa has been subject to continuous study, reform and restructuring aimed broadly at expanding services and opening the industry to wider access by the country's eleven language groups. In February 2002, the Independent Communications Authority of South Africa (ICASA) issued a position paper on South African content on television and radio. It set broad goals for an impending new public policy to encourage "national" content:

> South African television and radio need to reflect and engage with the life experiences, cultures, languages, aspirations and artistic expressions that are distinctly South African ... South African music and television programmes need to be produced by a wide range of South Africans, for South African audiences, in languages of their choice.

The position paper committed ICASA to establish a definition of "South African" music, but did not elaborate a standard.

It did, however, do so for television drama. Echoing the phrasing in the Australia standard, that standard defined "South African drama" as "programming which consists of South African television content and in which South Africans have exercised direction over the creative and administrative aspects of pre-production, production and post-production." The test for determining whether South Africans had exercised that direction, like the Canadian and Australian systems, is based substantially on the citizenship of individuals holding key production roles. Specifically, it requires that

- the director and/or the writer of a program be South African, *and*
- not less than 50 per cent of the leading actors in a program be South African, *and*
- not less than 75 per cent of "the major supporting cast" be South African, *and*
- not less than 50 per cent of the crew be South African.

EUROPE

Beyond the broadest of abstractions the idea of a unitary Europe corresponds poorly to reality, certainly not to the complex layers of national, sub-national and supranational jurisdictions that constitute the continent's legal architecture. Multiple region-wide forums, treaties, agreements and initiatives, embracing different sets of national participants, coexist. The European Council and Council of Europe are—bewilderingly to the non-European—different and distinct entities, as are the European Commission, the European Union and the Parliament of Europe. Within the fifteen nations of the European Union proper, subsidiary jurisdictions—German *Lander;* French *departments;* municipal governments everywhere—exercise various degrees of authority. In some cases, "national" groups—Britain's Scots and Welsh, Belgium's Flemish and Walloon language communities, Spain's Basques—have measures of political autonomy.

It is beyond the scope of this discussion to undertake an encyclopedic review of how all of these groups attempt to come to grips with the national character of every possible artifact of commercial cultural expression. We will limit it instead to a variety of treatments of the most complex, commercially valuable and coveted forms of expression: feature film and series drama for television. Some of these are under pan-European aegis; others are national.

An early initiative of the European Community was a 1963 directive intended to ensure the free circulation within the community of any film "having the nationality of a member state." The directive remains in force forty years later.

To be considered "national" to a member state, a film must satisfy a number of requirements:

➤ The original version must be recorded in the language of a member state (or one of the languages of a state like Belgium, which has more than one).

➤ The director and "authors" of the film must be nationals of a member state or "belong to its cultural domain." The writers of a film's screenplay, adaptation from another work, dialogue and musical score are considered to be "authors." The director may be from a non-member state if the other four are all from a member state.

➤ The producer is a national or resident of a member state; or, if the producer is a company, it is incorporated and does business mainly within the community, or "its activity is effectively and permanently linked to the economy of a member state."

➤ Studio shooting is done within the European Community, and no more than 30 per cent of exteriors are shot on location outside it.

As with the measures adopted in Australia, Canada and South Africa, the European directive identifies a work's nationality largely with the nationality of its key creators. But it also includes some consideration of where the production is located—one way to capture the member states' interest in where its budget might be spent.

The determination of who belongs to the "cultural domain" of any European state is necessarily subjective. Each state nominates a competent authority to make the determination within its jurisdiction. In the Netherlands, according to a comprehensive 2000 review by the European Audiovisual Observatory (a project of the Council of Europe):

> A person is considered as belonging to the Dutch cultural domain where he has close links to Dutch culture, based on language or any other element. A foreigner established in the Netherlands for a long time or a person who once had Dutch nationality and lives in a foreign country will be considered as having close links to Dutch culture.

A second directive emanated from the European Community in 1989, directed at opening Europe's television program market to freer internal trade while at the same time preventing its domination by imported (that is, mainly American) broadcast fare. Known as the "Television Without Frontiers" directive, it required member states to ensure "where practicable" that broadcasters devote a majority of air time (excluding news, sports, game shows and advertising) to "European works." The directive was subsequently embraced by and extended to additional European countries, not members of the European Union (EU), that agreed to the 1989 European Convention on Transfrontier Television, a pact designed primarily to protect the principle of freedom of speech among signatories that included several former Soviet-bloc nations and the Vatican. Yet other European nations, members of neither the EU nor the convention, have since also enrolled in the "Television Without Frontiers" open market.

The "Television Without Frontiers" directive places no specific requirement on either the language or the shooting locale of works eligible to qualify as European. The works must, however, "originate" in and be "mainly" made by creators who reside in a state that is party to the initiative. The state where a work originates need not be the same one that its creators live in. But work *and* creator must be resident in the same *category* of party state. That is, both must come from states that are members of the EU, *or* from non-EU parties to the Convention, *or* from European states that are members of neither. A work originating in an EU state, created by residents of a non-EU state, does not qualify. Similarly, the production of a qualifying "European" work must be "supervised and actually controlled" by a person or company established in one or more states of the same *category* of party-state as the one where it originates.

A flip side of the directive's extra-EU reach is that it did not come into force automatically in every EU (or indeed non-EU) state. It had to be implemented by each national legislature. Some of those chambers articulated additional tests for works to qualify as European.

France, for instance, instituted a points system similar to Canada's. The point total required for qualification varies by genre. For feature films, fourteen points must be accumulated by engaging EU-state nationals in key roles, according to the following scale:

➤ director: 3 points
➤ scriptwriter: 2 points
➤ other "authors": 1 point
➤ first lead performer: 3 points
➤ second lead performer: 2 points
➤ at least 50 per cent of other performers: 1 point

- cameraman: 1 point
- sound engineer: 1 point
- editor: 1 point
- art director: 1 point
- European lab or studio: 2 points

As these continent-wide standards evolved after 1963, most European nations also instituted various forms of support for films that portray, in Richard Pells's words, *their* "dreams, fears and folklore." Or, as Telefilm Canada would have it, productions that speak to their citizens "about themselves, their culture, their issues, their concerns and their stories." Those measures, however, needed means to distinguish "their" films from other people's. As the European Audiovisual Observatory noted in its 2000 survey: "Public support to the film industry . . . depends in each country on the nationality of a film. The concept of nationality of a film is thus regarded as the link between a film and the culture and/or the economy of a country."

Every country went at the task a little differently. The results bear intriguing witness to differing perspectives on the proper balance point along the spectrum between "industrial" and "cultural." Here is how some work.

BRITAIN

Britain amended its former system for assessing the "Britishness" of movies in 1999. Its present system is almost entirely divorced from notions of culture and even of identifying a film's nationality with its key creative individuals. Instead, it focuses strongly on the location of production in the United Kingdom.

A "British" film may be in any language. Britain considers its "authors" to be the production entity that made it rather than the people holding key production roles like director or writer. "Production undertakings" based anywhere in the EU qualify as "national" for the purposes of British film identity.

What *is* critical to Britain's determination of nationality is money. At least 70 per cent of a film's production budget must be spent in the United Kingdom. In a revealing detail, however, the labour component of a production's budget, for the purposes of calculating U.K. spending, may *exclude* the amount paid to any one individual who is *not* a citizen of either the EU or the Commonwealth. The provision allows U.K. productions to hire Hollywood A-list stars whose top-price salaries are exempt from the U.K. spending provision. A related exemption allows productions to qualify as "British" with a somewhat higher local spending ceiling (75 per cent of budget) if they want to deduct *two* salaries for non-EU, non-Commonwealth individuals, at least one of whom must be an actor. This second option extends potential "British" status to a film with both an American star and an American director.

NETHERLANDS

The Dutch take an almost diametrically opposite tack to the British. Films judged "Dutch" for the purposes of the 1963 EU directive on European film may be made by any EU producer or production company and shot anywhere in the EU. They must, however, be shot in the Dutch language. They must also be directed, written, adapted for the screen and scored by "authors" who are either Dutch nationals or who "belong to the Dutch cultural domain." Moreover, the majority of the cast and senior production crew, including lead actors, production manager, director of photography, sound engineer, art director, costume designer and film editor, must likewise be either Dutch nationals or belong to the Netherlands' "cultural domain."

NORWAY

The requirements for certification as a "Norwegian" film are less demanding in the letter, although in practice they may sharply limit the number of productions that get over the bar.

There are no requirements regarding a "Norwegian" film's "authors," nor any regarding its crew, cast or location of shooting. The film's producer must be an "independent" Norwegian entity, but that designation may include a foreign company registered in Norway whose local branch is headed by a Norwegian citizen or a foreigner living in the country—so long as the company is not commercially or financially linked with a broadcaster.

The one critical test that Norway does impose has to do with language. To qualify as Norwegian, a movie must be shot in either the Norwegian language or Sami, the language of the aboriginal people more familiar to non-Norse as the reindeer-herding Lapps.

FRANCE

As befits a country long identified with staunch defence of the purity of its language, France has some of the most detailed provisions for determining the nationality of its films—and places great weight on the use of French. The country provides automatic financial support for 25 per cent of the production costs of films of "French original expression" and may grant additional selective funding to such projects.

A film meets the test for "original expression" in French when its original version is shot entirely or principally in French or in a regional language used in France. The emphasis is on the language in which the film is shot: features dubbed into French, or made in another language by French actors, do not qualify. Exceptions may be made only for filmed versions of operas written in some other language (which may be shot in the language of the original libretto), documentaries shot in a language dictated by their subject and animated works.

Producers and a film's "authors" may be from any EU member state. A "French" film may be shot anywhere in the EU, but only with the "collaboration" of a studio established in France. The film must also accumulate a minimum number of points—depending on genre—awarded for each qualifying individual in identified creative roles. To qualify for points, individuals must either be French nationals, French residents, or nationals of another state that is either an EU member, party to the 1989 European Convention on Transfrontier Television, or has a coproduction agreement with the EU.

To receive a funding subsidy, however, "French" productions must also meet a substantially more complicated test that breaks the production's 'French' content down into seven categories. Separate scores to a potential total of 100 points are awarded for the nationality of the production company, the language of shooting, the "authors" (director, author of a work adapted to the screen, screenwriter, dialogue writer), performers, technicians, non-technical crew, and the location of shooting and post-production work. A film qualifies for support at 25 points, with the amount rising to the maximum provided for when it scores 80 points.

GERMANY

Hewing closer to the British line than the French, Germany in 1993 dumped the notion of "German" film from its statutory lexicon in favour of the more neutral locution "film eligible for financial support." Still, its requirements continue to contain strong cultural elements in addition to more economic tests. Compared with the French, Dutch and Norwegian criteria, however, language is a secondary consideration.

If a film's producer is an individual, he or she must live in Germany. But a production company may be incorporated anywhere in the EU or even within the wider European Economic Area. Shooting must take place in Germany, and up to 30 per cent of exterior shooting (by duration of the shooting schedule rather than screen time) may be done in another country where the script demands it. (This maximum may be exceeded under certain circumstances.)

Germany places no requirement on production crews. It does, however, require that a film's director either be a German citizen (of any language), be a national of an EU state or one party to the European Economic Area, or belong to the "German cultural domain." The latter category includes citizens of German-speaking countries or regions like Austria and Alemannic Switzerland, or individual German speakers from other countries who are "active on the German cultural scene." Although a film need not be shot originally in German, it must be released in a German version, and its first exhibition must take place either in Germany or at a film festival where it is identified as representing Germany.

SPAIN

Films eligible for financial support in Spain must be shot there in either Spanish or one of the nation's other official languages. The production company must either be Spanish or one owned elsewhere in the EU but based in Spain. Raw film must be developed in Spanish laboratories. At least three quarters of a film's "authors" (director, author of an adapted work, screenwriter, dialogue writer and score composer) and of its principal crew must be either Spanish or nationals of another EU state.

ITALY

In contrast to the straightforward Spanish regime, Italy allows a production to demonstrate bona fides as a film "of national production" qualifying for public funds through any combination of a choice of proofs, not all of which need be satisfied. Among the proofs are these:

> ➤ The director is an Italian national.
> ➤ The author (or the majority of authors, in the case of a collaboration) of an underlying story is Italian.
> ➤ The scriptwriter (or the majority of scripwriters, in the case of a collaboration) is Italian.
> ➤ The composer of the score is Italian.
> ➤ The majority of the exteriors are shot in Italy.
> ➤ Studio shooting is done in Italy.
> ➤ The majority of the lead actors are Italian.
> ➤ Three quarters of the supporting actors are Italian.
> ➤ The director of photography, editor, art director or costume designer is Italian.
> ➤ The other crew are Italian.
> ➤ The production has collaborated with Italian service companies.

Feature films "of national cultural interest" qualify for higher levels of support. To achieve that status, a production must satisfy further requirements, including the highly subjective one of "having sufficient artistic and cultural qualities." The film's production company must be Italian (that is, be majority owned by Italians and registered in Italy). The film must be shot or dubbed into Italian. The director, screenwriter and author of any underlying work must all be Italian. And either the composer of its score or all four of the director of photography, editor, art director and costume designer must be Italian.

TWO GENERAL PRINCIPLES can be distilled from this survey.

The first is that each country has different priorities in framing its cultural policy. Reasonable people can differ on the definition of what is local, and there is wide scope for diversity. This includes employing a looser test for the application of local content rules and a tighter one to determine eligibility for subsidies. Hence it is for each country to determine for itself what constitutes a cultural product of "national origin."

The second principle is that while a variety of tests may be used, when it comes to the core determination of what is "national," most countries focus on the individuals or companies wielding artistic control, *not on the subject matter* of the film, book or sound recording. That is: they focus on the nationality of the *author,* not the *thought.*

Strict market theorists attack the latter principle as thinly veiled, old-fashioned commercial protectionism. Their case is this: state intervention in the market for popular culture is justified only for those so-called "merit" goods that produce beneficial "externalities" unaccounted for in their transaction price. Governments are justified in supporting a more cohesive society but not in aiding productions that simply create local jobs. In this light, policy tests for "identity" should ignore the locus of production or authorship of a work in favour of determining whether its *content* contributes to a heightened sense of cultural identity.

In fact, as this survey illustrates, many countries do require a level of cultural specificity before they will provide public subsidies to a program. However, countries generally avoid such tests when setting local content rules for private television.

There are a number of good reasons why they do so.

First is the risk, already noted, of entering a slippery slope inclined towards censorship and state-prescribed thought.

Second, even if the hazards of a "command culture" can be avoided, the infinite variety of cultural expression simply defies litmus testing. Consider that hardy staple, the crime drama. Many countries make them. In America: *NYPD Blue, Law & Order, C.S.I., Boomtown*. Canada has its *Da Vinci's Inquest, Cold Squad,* and *Omerta*; Britain its *Inspector Morse* and *The Bill*. Germany has *Polizeiruf 110* and *Alarm für Cobra 11;* Australia, *Blue Heelers*. All these could be called "cop shows." All contain universal themes of transgression and justice. But they are neither indistinguishable nor interchangeable. Each reflects the particular ideas and contributions of individuals of different national origins. Each *feels* different. For a government agency to require each program to fill out a scorecard for cultural specificity on each script before it qualified as local content would be Kafkaesque in its futility and irrelevance.

Third is the cold fact that inspiration alone does not bring popular cultural expression to the marketplace. As Chapter 2 showed, cultural industries require an infrastructure, a critical mass of activity, in order to grow and thrive. These exist only on a steady diet of projects in progress. Similarly, as noted in Chapter 4, individual producers who try to live and die one project at a time are fated to die. Publishers who publish literary fiction may also need to publish cookbooks in order to survive (Simon & Schuster was built on profits from cross-word puzzle books).

For all these reasons, it is entirely reasonable for a country to recognize "industrial" as well as "cultural" criteria of production for the purposes of cultural policy. At the heart of the matter is a delicate balance: making it possible for citizens to make and distribute popular culture rooted in their own experience, without dictating what they choose to create. The capacity to express must not derogate from freedom of expression.

That said, some kinds of programs export more easily than others. There are at least two reasons why it may be appropriate to direct fewer scarce public dollars to such programs. One: public subsidy is far less likely to make the critical difference that triggers their production. Two: the more such programs approximate some generalized "international" cultural identity, the more egregiously will any state subsidy appear to offend the principle of market neutrality in international trade.

A sophisticated cultural policy, in sum, recognizes that a range and continuity of creative production is as important as single works of brilliance. It seeks a balance between products that are so culturally specific that their cost must be entirely borne at home and others no less important for the continued vitality of their cultural capacity but that may need less support from the state.

THE FOREGOING EXAMPLES make clear the many possible ways to interpret creative "nationality." Some countries place their policy emphasis on the commercial aspect of popular culture, others on the cultural. But in the end, there must be a degree of symbiosis between the two. There can surely be little objection to a country that wishes to see its people able to express their experience creatively with their feet still on their own soil. Achieving that, however, entails a responsibility not only to ensure that creators have the capacity to express themselves in the media of popular culture, but also that national audiences have the opportunity to hear, view or read their work.

In general, larger countries with stable, ongoing creative industries (such as Britain and Germany) are least specific in relying on language or subjective markers as the basis of public support. They favour tests of economic presence or significant involvement by their nationals in the production enterprise.

Smaller countries, which are less likely to sustain ongoing clusters of activity in the capital-intensive business of filmed entertainment

(Norway, the Netherlands), set a lower standard for economic presence. They put greater weight on the visible or audible reflection of cultural values onscreen.

Perhaps reflecting a position between these extremes, Canada and France do a little of both.

We can also now reach a conclusion about *The Bridge on the River Kwai*. By most of the tests described above, it would be considered a British film, not a Hollywood or a Sri Lankan one. The key role of creative decision-making was firmly in the hands of a British director, David Lean. And most countries would conclude that the presence of a British-based production company and the predominance of speaking roles performed by British actors would outweigh the influence of all other contributions—even William Holden's.

The "national"—and indeed "cultural"—values embedded in commercial creative goods can indeed be put to systematic and reasonably transparent tests. The chapters that follow will show how various jurisdictions have built on the capacity to distinguish "national" works in order to support their creation.

8

PUBLIC
BROADCASTING

F EW TELEVISION PROGRAMS have a stronger claim to possess a "national" identity than the Canuck-to-the-core Canadian production *This Hour Has 22 Minutes*. Reflecting the high cultural discount on comedy and current events, its appeal travels no farther afield than its home broadcast signal. Yet, within Canada, its sketch characters and regular features have become cultural icons.

The weekly half-hour of topical satire finds its material in the latest developments in Canadian politics, society and business. National politicians live in dread of a no-win encounter with fearlessly rude housewife-journalist Marg Delahunty (Mary Walsh). Accosting hapless victims on U.S. streets, the feature "Talking to Americans" spins comic gold from the widely shared Canadian resentment of how little the neighbours know (or care) about them, eliciting gullible responses to such fictional events as the completion of Canada's national igloo. Even the show's name is a Canadian inside joke. It refers to an earlier, equally popular but altogether serious newsmagazine program called *This Hour Has Seven Days*.

The publicly owned Canadian Broadcasting Corporation (CBC) cancelled that hard-hitting series after its second season for being *too* edgy. Its no-holds-barred satiric successor is one of the longest-running and most popular shows on the CBC schedule, although funding problems briefly jeopardized its prospects for a renewal in 2003.

Together, both the original and later *This Hour* exemplify much of the virtue and susceptibility attributed, not only in Canada, to public broadcasting.

MOST OF THIS BOOK deals with the economic behaviour of cultural products in the marketplace. In most countries besides the United States, however, broadcasting—and in particular television broadcasting—began as a *public* rather than a *private* enterprise. And in every country including the United States, at least some measure of responsibility to the public interest has been explicitly invoked in the course of asserting the state's right to regulate what was widely if unscientifically referred to as the "airwaves." In most of the world still, even where other media are unregulated and private broadcasting flourishes, the latter is often held to account for obligations of public service. Most private television broadcasters also share their audience with broadcasters owned or supported by the state.

This has been so since not long after the first radio stations signed on the air in the 1920s.

From the outset, national authorities recognized the immense significance of the new technologies of first audio and later audio-visual broadcasting. The capacity of radio and television to shape and inform citizens' awareness of their material circumstances, social environment and ultimately political choices was almost immediately evident. That alone compelled governments to take an interest in how the broadcast media evolved.

So did a technical consideration. It quickly became clear that there were more would-be broadcasters than there were available frequencies. Some independent referee was needed to allocate frequencies among broadcasters. That role fell naturally to government. When free-to-air television in the limited "very-high frequency" (VHF) band appeared after the Second World War, the same issue resurfaced.

Australian commentator Terry Flew and others have called this the "social contract" at the heart of traditional broadcasting. "Requirements on the broadcasters to meet social and cultural policy objectives (e.g., local content) are offered," Flew notes, "in exchange for exclusive access to the airwaves and the ability to earn monopoly profits." The idea retained its force even as monopoly became oligopoly, since there were still far fewer available frequencies than companies wishing to use them.

But in North America and other developed regions, cable networks able to deliver far more television channels than were available free-to-air began to erode "spectrum scarcity" as early as the 1970s. They were followed in the 1980s by satellites capable of delivering even larger arrays of channels directly to home receivers over wide terrestrial footprints with little regard for national frontiers. By the beginning of the twenty-first century, all three vectors of delivery—free-to-air, cable and satellite—witnessed a further vast expansion of their capacity as broadcast signals were converted from analog to digital modes. In Europe, fewer than fifty television channels in 1989 blossomed to some 1,500 by 2002. The Internet held the prospect—if not yet the reality—of essentially unlimited "spectrum."

For those full of faith in the perfection of markets, the burgeoning number of possible channels has obviated any further need for either government regulation of audiovisual media or of "public service" broadcasting. Professor Peter Humphreys, of the University of Manchester, put the case this way: "The removal of technical and regulatory restraints on market entry, it was argued, would result in a medium increasingly resembling the press, characterized by multiple and diverse products and the rule of consumer sovereignty."

But it is a view at odds both with cultural economics and with widely valued "externalities" that markets fail to capture. As we have seen, the power to price, promote and control the menu of choice tends to trump "consumer sovereignty" in the marketplace. And commercial motivations are not always parallel to national, political and public interests, the desire for sectarian or ethnic self-expression or the independent values of pluralism and cultural diversity.

Regulators often attract criticism for constraining either free markets or free opinions. Technological innovation continues to alter the array of forces in the field. The balance of this chapter surveys how various jurisdictions have accommodated competing concerns in the structure of public service broadcasting. It also illustrates the range of pressures to which those systems are subject, as well as some responses.

Although there is wide variety in how the task is best accomplished, there is broad agreement among public broadcasters in the developed democracies about what their job is. Wherever they exist, public broadcasters operate under some form of government mandate to operate in the public interest. In a chapter devoted to these agencies in his 1996 book *Mass Media and Media Policy in Western Europe,* Peter Humphreys identified the classic elements of that mandate:

> ➤ comprehensiveness of access, "supplying educational and informational as well as entertainment programmes ... to the whole population";
> ➤ pluralism in "diverse programming to respect cultural, religious and political beliefs, [and] to cater to cultural variety";
> ➤ "catering for national identity and community";
> ➤ non-commercialism, with broadly based public funding; and critically,
> ➤ "independence from vested interests and government."

Public broadcasting executives from many nations have formed a self-described "virtual organization" to exchange and share concerns. Its membership embraces agencies in Algeria, Poland, Bosnia-Herzegovina, Macao, Israel, Sweden, Canada and France, among many other places. The organization's Web site displays a set of principles that broadly echo those of Humphreys:

> ➤ to serve the varied needs, tastes and interests of mass and minority audiences, while upholding the integrity of diverse cultures and languages;
> ➤ to provide quality programming for children and adults that informs, educates, entertains and advances social equity;
> ➤ to maintain editorial integrity and operational independence from political, ideological and economic intervention;
> ➤ to enrich and strengthen the cultural, social and economic fabrics of the communities we serve;
> ➤ to deepen national and international mutual understanding of peoples and their social, ecological, economic, political, cultural and technological environments;
> ➤ to use new and existing technologies to extend the range and effectiveness of their services;
> ➤ [to] treat audiences as citizens rather than solely as consumers.

Of all these goals, it is the last that captures most succinctly the idea at the heart of public broadcasting: audiences are citizens before they are consumers.

Implicit in that idea is the conviction that the needs of the one are different from the needs of the other, and that a broadcasting universe operated purely to satisfy commercial ends will fail the first in pandering to the second.

Bernd Holznagel, a professor of administrative law at the Institute for Information, Telecommunications and Media Law in Münster, Germany, expands on the idea of "market failure in commercial broadcasting":

> Contrary to what is generally the case in the market economy, the programme output of commercial broadcasters is not primarily determined by consumer interest. What comes first for commercial broadcasters are the wishes of the advertising industry . . . The programme-related interests of minorities . . . have a chance of being taken into account only if they promise particularly high earnings. [Moreover] quality programmes in the fields of culture, education and information are merit goods . . . characterized by the fact that consumers would in general only be willing to pay an amount which would be insufficient to cover production costs . . . The consequence would be permanent shortage.

Ideologues of the right—and certainly many private broadcasters— contest the idea that commercial interest is incompatible with meeting the needs of consumers as citizens. But public broadcasters operating under a wide variety of architectures can plausibly claim to meet the higher aspirations they set themselves.

PERHAPS NONE has a better claim than the venerable British Broadcasting Corporation (BBC). Known to its millions of domestic listeners and viewers over the years, on the whole affectionately, as either "Auntie" or "The Beeb," the BBC's role dates back to 1922. In that year, Britain's postmaster general brought together executives from the country's major radio manufacturers and organized them into something called the British Broadcasting Company. Its mandate was to generate broadcasts in the public interest that, not incidentally, would also give customers a reason to buy radios. Although created under government patronage, the new company's board and management was to operate at arm's length from the ministry of the day. Broadcasts themselves were also to be divorced from all commercial association. There was to be no advertising on the air. Funding would come from licence fees charged annually to the owners of radio sets.

Five years later, those principles were enshrined in a royal charter establishing the rechristened British Broadcasting Corporation. They remain essentially unchanged in the twenty-first century.

The BBC has grown in that time from a tentative new venture to a globe-straddling brand with annual revenue the size of Iceland's. Licence fees, which in 2002 cost each British household that owned a television set £112, generate an annual income of almost £3.2 billion. Fully half the hours Britons spend in front of the tube are devoted to one or another of the Beeb's six national channels. Two of those are over-the-air: the general-interest BBC1 and the more rarified BBC2. In addition, the corporation has launched two new analog and two more digital channels delivered by cable and satellite since 2000—targeting arts-and-music viewers (BBC4), pre-schoolers (CBeebies), pre-teens (CBBC), and the prized young-adult segment of 25-to-34-year-olds. According to a study for the OECD, the corporation's annual spending on original television programs is greater than the *total amount* invested in film in the rest of the European Union. BBC radio has also expanded over the years, and now broadcasts five domestic services with nationwide coverage.

The BBC World Service broadcasts over radio in English and forty-three other languages. Bolstered by a separate subsidy from the Foreign Office, it provides audiences in many places with their most reliable window on events beyond and often within their own countries—as well as giving the British perspective on events a planetary reach that most nations can only envy. BBC World, an advertising-supported all-news channel, reaches some 230 million households globally, approaching the international reach of ESPN and posing the only serious rivalry to Time Warner's Atlanta-based CNN International. The service is a huge vendor of individual programs and series as well. BBC's *Teletubbies* series raked in international sales of US$1.9 billion; its franchised *Weakest Link* format has garnered millions more. Meanwhile, the corporation has taken partners in Canada and other countries to repackage its vast library of children's, science and documentary programs into a variety of specialty cable channels.

Across the eight decades since its founding, the BBC can justly claim to have served as well as a groundbreaker and standard-setter for private commercial broadcasting. Within two years of the Beeb's 1927 charter, its engineers began experimenting with television. Scheduled television broadcasts began in London in 1936—three years ahead of the National Broadcasting Company's inaugural schedule in New York (and fourteen years before the CBC brought television to Canada).

Both the British and American TV services were interrupted by the Second World War, resuming thereafter. BBC TV went back on the air in mid-1946. Within a decade, the monopoly public-service model began to relax, although the public *interest* remained a prominent priority. Britain's first independent commercial television channels received licences in 1954 and went to air the following year. Private commercial radio was sharply expanded in the 1970s. More private competition in television appeared in 1984 with the licensing of Channel 4. Since then, dozens more free-to-air, cable, satellite, analog and digital, basic, pay and specialty television signals have joined the increasingly crowded dial.

Significantly, however, consequential public-service obligations were attached to the licensing of each of the BBC's early private competitors. ITV, the first to be licensed, was structured as a regional service with statutory public-service obligations. Regulators closely scrutinized and approved its programming plans. Channel 4 was mandated to serve social and ethnic minority groups and to invest in innovative and risky programming.

The public television service, meanwhile, not only survived the competition, it arguably set the pace. A 1999 study of twenty public-service broadcasters (PSBS) by the international McKinsey Group relied heavily on the example of the BBC in concluding that the most successful public services "have maintained their influence on the overall development of television by inducing their commercial competitors to offer equally distinctive programs. In effect, PSBS can and do act as regulators of the television industry as a whole."

Or, as a former managing director of Britain's independent Channel 4 acknowledged to McKinsey: "The BBC keeps us all honest."

Indeed, the Beeb remains so strong against its plethora of competitors that some complain it has become too successful. "It's as though there's this one great shark and the rest of us are being kicked about by the currents that its tail creates," Jon Snow, a news anchor on privately owned Channel 4, told *The Guardian*'s Stuart Jeffries. "It's very difficult to match its clout. It has created a completely unfair competitive environment."

Other critics call into question the fairness of funding the BBC through a licence fee that falls equally on all, regardless of their means or fondness for its programming. A survey in 1999 found that Britons who judged the BBC a fair value for their money barely outnumbered those who thought it not: 45 per cent to 42 per cent. The government-appointed panel that commissioned the survey also noted that some-one who earns Britain's minimum wage needs to work for almost a week in order to pay the licence fee.

Corporation executives make no apology. "The people who complain aren't our viewers, they're our competitors," noted Rupert Gavin, CEO of BBC Worldwide, its international sales arm. "We have no interest to be a ghettoized high-brow broadcaster." BBC director general Greg Dyke has wryly observed that his is "an unusual job. You get criticized for winning."

And after dodging the 1980s Thatcherite zeal for privatization (the Iron Lady's attention having perhaps been diverted by the private ITV network, which carried the decade's most merciless satire, *Spitting Image*), the BBC seems secure in its licence-fee-supported status. "The prospect of the U.K. without the BBC funded by the licence fee is any-where between improbable to impossible," British culture secretary Tessa Jowell asserted in early 2002. "The BBC is one of the most loved and trusted U.K. institutions."

That trust was severely challenged in August 2003, when the BBC's critical reporting of the British government's justification for the war in Iraq became the subject of a judicial inquiry triggered by the suicide of Dr. David Kelly, the BBC's main source for its story. But the inquiry underlined as never before the importance that the country placed on having a BBC that was credible and trustworthy.

It is a trust still rooted in the intangible. No structural device ensures the BBC is responsive to its audiences in the way that ratings, advertising revenue and stock prices are purported to do for commercial broadcasters. Licence fees provide a stable and substantial income irrespective of the popularity of its schedule. Its director general answers to a board insulated by its royal charter from egregious political interference, although the BBC chair and director general do have to appear annually before the DCMS select committee of the British House of Commons to account for the BBC's performance. Apart from this, such outside direction as it receives has typically come once every couple of decades from Royal Commissions established to consult the British public at arm's length from the Beeb's management.

Yet the model's durability and appeal is undeniable. In 2002, BBC1 re-established itself as the United Kingdom's most-watched channel, overtaking ITV in audience ratings for the first time since the 1950s.

IT IS ALMOST an article of American faith that markets are the only reliable barometer of how the public sees its interest. Thomas Paine's dictum that "government even in its best state is but a necessary evil" carries the authority of received wisdom. "Culture" as a merit, apart from the book value of a copyright, holds about as much substance for American legislators as do psychic auras. Those convictions have shaped American broadcast policy from its beginning.

While Britain's government marshalled early broadcasters behind the public-service mandate of the BBC, the U.S. Congress as much as possible left the nascent industry to seek the straightest route to a positive bottom line. When conflicts over frequency allocation (as well as an international treaty assigning bandwidth among nations) finally forced Congress to act, it rebuffed a campaign to have a quarter of available channels set aside for public use. Instead, America's elected representatives in 1934 turned the entire subject of broadcasting over to the newly created Federal Communications Commission (FCC). That autumn, the new commission held unpublicized hearings heavily dominated by a new industry lobby called the National Association of Broadcasters. Afterward it reported "that commercial broadcasting was doing a superior job of meeting the public interest and that non-profit broadcasting was unnecessary."

It was the last time any branch of the U.S. government would formally deliberate the fundamental structure of the American broadcasting industry. Commercially oriented programs supported by advertising (or, much later, subscriptions) became and have remained the overwhelmingly dominant way Americans experience radio and television.

Nonetheless, a handful of non-profit and community radio stations did survive. And in 1938 the FCC allocated a remote reach of the high-frequency spectrum, then regarded as having no commercial value, to non-profit broadcasters. By 1945, with private broadcasters beginning to eye the "FM" (frequency modulation) band for its revenue potential, the FCC withdrew that exclusivity but still reserved twenty FM channels for non-commercial use. And in 1952, when the regulator undertook its first systematic national allocation of television channels, it reserved some across the United States for educational use. The following year, America's first non-commercial television station, KUHT-TV, began broadcasting from the campus of Houston University.

In the heady decade of the 1960s, with such progressive causes as civil rights flowering in Washington, a new campaign for some form of U.S. public broadcasting emerged. In 1962, for the first time ever, the U.S. Congress approved limited public funding for educational television. Five years later, the Public Broadcasting Act authorized the creation of a Corporation for Public Broadcasting with an initial budget of US$5 million—about half the amount President Lyndon Johnson had sought.

The new agency enlisted existing non-profit television stations in the establishment of two operating subsidiaries. The Public Broadcasting System (PBS) was launched in 1969 with a mandate to develop and distribute non-commercial TV programming. Its first major undertaking, a children's show called *Sesame Street*, began airing the same year. In 1970, the Corporation for Public Broadcasting launched National Public Radio (NPR) in partnership with ninety existing non-commercial stations.

It is likely that only a very small minority of Americans have ever heard of the Corporation for Public Broadcasting. They are more likely to be familiar with PBS and NPR. But those entities are themselves both diffuse organizations controlled by their members—344 public television stations and 607 non-commercial radio outlets. Neither PBS nor NPR tries to coordinate a national schedule along the lines of commercial networks like ABC, NBC, CBS or Fox—or even of CBC or BBC radio. Apart from a handful of high-profile programs like the nightly PBS *News Hour with Jim Lehrer* and NPR's popular weekly *Prairie Home Companion* and daily *All Things Considered*, the two operate mainly as clearing houses. Scheduling is left to the preference—or whim—of local managers.

The bottom-up structure goes deeper than programming. Both NPR and PBS are owned by their member-stations; neither owns its own outlets. Universities or colleges hold most NPR station licences. Of the 171 television licences that underlie the PBS network, non-profit community groups hold about half, and colleges and universities hold another third. Twenty state authorities provide public television within their borders. Seven other licences are held by local or municipal agencies.

Similarly, only a fraction of the "public" funds that underwrite either PBS or NPR reach them by way of federal taxpayers. The Congressional appropriation for the Corporation for Public Broadcasting has risen over the decades, reaching US$365 million in 2003. The corporation remains the largest single source of funds for both NPR and PBS. But both raise the majority of their budgets from other sources: state and private foundation grants, corporate sponsorships and periodic fund-raising drives directed at viewers and listeners. In all, tax streams contributed less than a third of the total $1.2 billion spent on U.S. public television and $600 million that went to public radio in 2000.

Judging the systems' accomplishments in their three decades of existence is difficult—and may depend on a choice of which end of the telescope to examine. PBS boasts that in one recent ratings sweep (October 2001), more than 73 per cent of American television-owning families watched at least some public television. Public TV's prime-time rating in that period was 1.7. That meant more people were watching it than were tuned to any of TBS (Turner Broadcasting, mainly a movie channel, with a 1.4 prime time rating), Nickelodeon (1.2), CNN (1.1), A&E or Discovery (both at 0.9). Twenty million Americans a week listen to NPR radio stations. The Muppet menagerie of *Sesame Street* has entered the iconography of modern childhood alongside Pooh and Mickey. A few other programs, like NPR's *Prairie Home Companion*, have also found foreign audiences.

And both services can with some justice claim to set a high standard for excellence and innovation. "NPR," according to its Web site, "has won every major award in journalism for news and cultural programming in America." PBS's site notes that it "was the first [in the United States] to distribute television programs by satellite, and the first to use closed captioning."

But those boasts offer frail reeds against the promotional onslaught of American mainstream commercial broadcasting. Public television's 1.7 rating in October 2001 amounts to an average family watching it for eight hours during the month—about as much as many families watch commercial television in an average *day*. Overall, public radio and television in the United States garner about 2 per cent of the total broadcast audience.

That picture is rife with irony. Audiences for U.S. public broadcasting—whether PBS documentaries or NPR's classical and jazz music—tend to be from the wealthier, better-educated American "elites" least in need of public subsidy. While American-way conservatives regularly decry the statist overtones of a publicly subsidized broadcasting system, the structure of both NPR and PBS is far more in keeping with the Founding Fathers' concern for citizen autonomy at the grassroots than are the integrated media empires of the culture conglomerates.

"In short," Robert McChesney notes, "public broadcasting [in the United States] was set up to ensure that it was feeble, dependent and marginal." Nonetheless, "surveys show it to be one of the most highly regarded public expenditures. The Republicans abandoned their efforts to 'zero out' federal support to public broadcasting in the mid-1990s when they realized that it was a decidedly unpopular move across the political spectrum."

Even where market theology is most nearly universally embraced, it appears that a majority of citizens believe there are some cultural values it fails to deliver.

CANADA'S PATH to nationhood has long found its footing somewhere between the rock of British heritage and the hard place of American geography. So it was with broadcasting.

The country has a pride of early accomplishments in the field. The most dramatic demonstration of radio's early potential occurred in December 1901, in a drafty tower on a treeless hill outside St. John's, Newfoundland. There Guglielmo Marconi strained to catch the three clicks of a Morse code "S" in his rudimentary earphones, confirming that a signal transmitted from Poldhu in Cornwall had crossed the Atlantic Ocean. In 1920, Marconi's Montreal laboratory became the second in the world to begin regular voice transmissions, one month after Westinghouse researchers in Pittsburgh initiated the medium by broadcasting the result of that year's presidential election.

Within a decade a "radio craze" (foreshadowing the much later dot-com frenzy surrounding the Internet) spawned a chaotic scramble by commercial, political and religious interests to launch broadcasting stations. At the same time, signals from powerful transmitters based in the United States and owned by that country's nascent commercial broadcasters began flooding Canadian airwaves, setting off political and cultural alarms that resonate to this day. In 1928, the Canadian government assigned a royal commission to sort out the mess. As one newspaper put it: "The question to be decided is whether the Canadian people are to have Canadian independence in radio broadcasting or to become dependent upon sources in the United States."

Reflecting the competing pulls of the British and American models, the Aird Commission heard submissions both from advocates of public broadcasting and from the American National Association of Broadcasters. Its report in 1929 recommended that Canada follow the British lead and establish a publicly owned monopoly national broadcaster, supported by both radio licence fees and limited advertising.

For a variety of reasons, this never happened. Canadian commercial broadcasters exerted pressure against the public model. In the wake of the stock market crash that coincided with the Aird Commission's report, a government strapped by the Great Depression had few resources to spare for creating a transcontinental broad-casting system. And the first stab at giving institutional form to the envisaged service was deeply flawed. Nevertheless, by 1936, Conservative prime minister R.B. Bennett finally settled on a more workable structure for a Canadian Broadcasting Corporation (CBC). The new CBC would be managed at arm's length from government, funded partly by parliamentary appropriation from general tax revenues and partly by a licence fee on radio receivers. Bennett left room for private commercial broadcasters but made them subject to CBC regulation.

Apart from the licence fees, which were dropped in 1953, the CBC and the essence of Canada's mixed public–private broadcast landscape have endured into the twenty-first century. The CBC radio network became part of the national fabric with its coverage of Canadians at war between 1939 and 1945. In 1952 the corporation, in partnership with private investors, brought television to Canada. In the same decade its Quebec-based French-language service, La Société Radio-Canada, became a powerful catalyst in that province's transformative Quiet Revolution.

When private television emerged to compete with the CBC in the 1960s, it did not receive commercial carte blanche. As happened in Britain, Canadian regulators imposed expectations of public service—including significant domestic content in broadcasts—as requirements of the private stations' newly minted licences. Those requirements, as will be made clear in the chapters that follow, have remained critical elements of Canadian cultural policy quite apart from the role of the country's public broadcaster. (Authority to regulate other broadcasters was taken away from the CBC in 1958 and invested in a separate regulatory agency, now the Canadian Radio-television and Telecommunications Commission, better known as the CRTC. In addition to licensing broadcast, cable and satellite undertakings, the CRTC regulates telecommunications in Canada.)

Yet even as the CBC celebrated the fiftieth anniversary of its introduction of television, it remained plagued by many of the same tensions that afflicted its creation. CBC Radio, which now sustains two non-commercial national services in both English and French, holds on to broad public support, especially in the more remote and rural regions less well served by commercial stations. But CBC Television has struggled to retain its share of Canadian audiences against commercial rivals.

Two English-language and two French-language private commercial television chains now compete for viewers' time and attention along with several more regional quasi-chains and, in larger cities, local independent stations. In English Canada, the CBC's all-news specialty service CBC Newsworld strains for audience share against CNN, BBC and a service owned by the private Canadian CTV chain. In French Canada, its RDI news service competes with Le Canal Nouvelles, operated by the private network TVA, owned by Quebecor Inc. In most time periods and markets, CBC Television trails its private competitors badly.

Still, much that critics and audiences embrace as the best in distinctly Canadian television programming continues to originate with the CBC. Those productions include serial dramas like the widely exported *Da Vinci's Inquest* and specials with purely domestic appeal, such as the epic mini-series *Canada: A People's History,* as well as the impudent and long-running *This Hour Has 22 Minutes.* In Quebec, where the majority French-speaking audience sustains a higher culture premium for homegrown productions, Radio-Canada does better. Its drama and local variety and talk shows are regularly among the province's most-watched programs.

The CBC provides its radio service without commercials, but continues to sell advertising on television. The bulk of its budget, however, comes from annual appropriations from national tax revenue. The appropriation, currently about C$1 billion a year, renders the corporation's nominally arm's-length management vulnerable to the shifting tides of parliamentary sentiment.

The support of the public at large has proven fairly durable, however. Support for the principle of funding a national broadcaster from public taxes runs about as high in Canada as in Britain. One poll conducted in 2002 for the admittedly pro-CBC advocacy group Friends of Canadian Broadcasting found that 41 per cent of Canadians thought the public broadcaster should get more money; 9 per cent thought funding should be cut. A separate study in the same period funded in part by CanWest Global Communications (one of the CBC's private competitors) found that nearly twice as many Canadians would maintain or increase the CBC subsidy (60 per cent) as would reduce or eliminate it (35 per cent). And a parliamentary committee report in mid-2003 provided strong support for the CBC, recommending increased and stable multi-year funding for the corporation.

Meanwhile, the public side of Canada's "mixed" approach to broadcasting has continued to evolve independently of the CBC. Five provinces support their own educational television services, and one—Ontario—does so in both English and French. Licences awarded to three non-denominational religious services, the same number of multi-ethnic channels and a network aimed at aboriginal viewers also carry substantial public-service mandates.

ELSEWHERE OUTSIDE the United States, public broadcasting has far more often been the norm than the exception. In most nations, broadcasting began on lines akin to the British model before drifting closer to the Canadian style of a mixed environment of public and private ownership. That pattern was particularly evident in television, the technology for which—especially in its early years—required substantial investment.

Beginning in the 1980s, a florescence of pro-market thinking and the appearance of cable, satellite and digital technologies able to carry many new channels sharply accelerated the emergence of new commercial channels. These often challenged the dominance of public broadcasters but rarely replaced them. Indeed, in France, Germany and Italy, the courts have ruled that each state's constitution obliges it to ensure that public-service broadcasters provide "a balanced and pluralistic" range of programs.

The following sections sketch the wide range of public broadcasting models that now operate in some leading nations. For them we are heavily indebted to the work of Peter Humphreys in *Mass Media and Media Policy in Western Europe* and of Carole Tongue in "Public Service Broadcasting: A Study of 8 OECD Countries." In particular, we have drawn the approximate licence fees charged in each country where they apply from Tongue's survey.

FRANCE

While a succession of regimes ruled France for the first few decades after the Second World War, the national broadcaster—then known as Radiodiffusion–Télévision de France (RTF)—operated under more-or-less overt political control as the official "Voice of France." Opposition leaders were not infrequently excluded from newscasts or suffered from "malicious editing." After a change in government, reforms undertaken in 1974 broke up the public broadcaster's centralized bureaucracy and split its on-air service into three channels. Fresh reforms in the early 1980s attempted to distance the renamed Office de Radiodiffusion–Télévision de France (ORTF) from the national government. Finally in 1987, responding to pro-market arguments in an atmosphere of expanding spectrum, a right-ist government privatized the largest public chain, TF1. TF1 quickly crushed its main commercial competitor, Le Cinq, and emerged as the country's most powerful private network.

France has also launched a number of culturally oriented satellite channels, either alone or as joint ventures with other French-speaking nations, as with TV-5, or, notably in the ARTE cultural service, with its leading partner in the European Union, Germany.

A single regulator, the Conseil Supérieur de l'Audiovisuel, governs both private and public television in France. It allocates frequencies and licences and is charged with ensuring that the two remaining public channels, France 2 and France 3, meet guidelines for public service set out in an act of the French parliament. Those guidelines are consistent with the common mandates for public broadcasting laid out earlier: "to provide information, cultural enrichment, entertainment and diversity in programming." The public television channels are also expected to encourage innovation and to meet detailed quotas for airing national productions.

French viewers, like those in Britain and many other European nations, support the ORTF through a licence fee on television ownership (roughly C$200 a year per household in 2002). France 2 and France 3 also sell advertising, however, and routinely receive additional funding from the government's general revenues.

Even after additional restructuring in the 1980s, Peter Humphreys asserts in *Mass Media and Media Policy in Western Europe,* France's *dirigiste* political culture has not entirely faded: "There remained distinct traces of surreptitious politicisation about the system."

ITALY

Neither transparency nor political independence—nor indeed, even much strict legality—appear ever to have characterized the Italian television scene. For the first two decades of its existence, Italian public broadcaster Radiotelevisione Italiana (RAI) was under the indirect control of the country's dominant Christian Democratic Party. Reforms in the 1970s somewhat loosened the Christian Democrats' grip but mainly by passing control of two of RAI's three channels to its rivals, the Socialist and Communist Parties. "In effect," notes Peter Humphreys, "the Italian viewer could choose the ideological flavour of the news and current affairs programmes that s/he watched."

At the same time, a loophole in national regulations allowed a largely unregulated commercial television industry to establish itself, initially in the form of local stations that quickly formed national networks. In the 1980s, the three largest of those networks came under the control of a single entrepreneur, Silvio Berlusconi.

In 1997, new reforms placed broadcasting and telecommunications under one regulator with separate sub-commissions for each. Advised by a National Users Council of "experts in a wide range of fields from law to education" and a National Viewers Council representing the wider public, the broadcast commission of the Istituzione dell' Autorità per le Garanzie nelle Comunicazioni is supposed to monitor all stations' broadcast content and "guarantee" consumers' interests. RAI, meanwhile, is financed in roughly equal parts by a licence fee of about C$135 a year and by advertising.

But Italy's reality overshadows those structural protections. The terms of RAI's working mandate are set in a contract with the Italian Ministry of Communications that must be periodically renewed. In May 2001, Berlusconi won election (for the second time) as Italy's prime minister—strongly supported by his own three private TV networks. His and RAI's channels together command about 90 per cent of the Italian television audience.

GERMANY

If France and Italy represent subtle or overt examples of political influence on public broadcasting in democracies, Germany's model reflects intense reaction against any such possibility. Public broadcasting in the federal republic was conceived in the shadow of the Second World War, when the dark potential of the state to influence its citizens through propaganda had become brutally apparent, and was shaped by occupiers who had no wish to see a reconstructed Reich with similar powers. As a result German law (initially in West Germany, but extended after reunification to the country as a whole) devolves authority over broadcasting to state—*Lander*—governments.

Neither of the two big German public television networks can in consequence be called strictly "national." The oldest, ARD, is an alliance of regional channels based in the *Lander* and answerable to regulators in each. The other, ZDF, was created in the 1960s by a treaty among the *Lander* (eleven originally, sixteen since unification), each of which nominates members to its governing board. There is no federal broadcast regulator, and commercial channels that began to appear in the 1980s are regulated separately from the public networks. The *Lander* do delegate the collection of a television licence fee (one of Europe's highest, at C$265 a household) to a national agency. The fees provide the majority of funding for both public networks, with limited advertising (at one point it was restricted to twenty minutes a day and banned altogether on Sundays and national holidays).

The overall arrangement makes for what analyst Carole Tongue describes as "the most tiered, complex, devolved system in Europe." And while *Lander*-level politics sometimes influence the choice of delegates to the various boards and oversight bodies that govern the two networks, Peter Humphreys found that "no single political party ever enjoyed undue influence over the entire public-service broadcasting system."

SWEDEN

Swedes take yet another approach to insulating their public broadcaster from the politics of the state. Sveriges Television (SVT) was initially structured as a conventional joint-stock company, with press interests and other private businesses each owning 20 per cent of its shares and various associations and community groups owning the other 60 per cent. It is now owned by a foundation that appoints the six members of its board of governors. The Swedish government appoints the board's chairman. The board's autonomy is further constrained by multiple institutional masters and statutory obligations. It must obey a Radio Act that sets general obligations for Swedish broadcasters as well as its own charter, renewable every five years, which sets more specific goals for promotion of Sweden's culture and minorities.

As with most other European public-service broadcasters, a licence fee on television-owning households provides most of SVT's funds. Sweden's parliament sets the fee, recently about C$190 a year.

NETHERLANDS

To Canadian eyes, the Dutch history of allocating public broadcasting assets according to corporatist notions of social "pillars" based on religious and political association is arguably one of Europe's oddest. In the 1930s, government shared out the radio spectrum to groups identified with different faiths or ideologies—Catholics, Protestants, Socialists and Liberals (who, further to confuse things, were actually conservative).

After 1969, a newly created Dutch Broadcasting Corporation, Nederlandse Omroep Stichting (NOS), centralized technical functions for the three national television channels. It also began producing news, sport and current affairs programming to fill about 20 per cent of available airtime. Corporations representing eight "pillar" social groups received rights to the other 80 per cent on a pro rata basis according to their size (determined by the sale of memberships or subscriptions to their program guides). Although the groups were permitted to reflect their ideological biases, they also had to meet statutory quotas for "information (25 per cent), culture (20 per cent), amusement (25 per cent) and education (5 per cent)" programming.

By the 1990s, however, most programming offered by the various NOS groups was ideologically neutral. Says Peter Humphreys: "Viewers no longer felt tied to any particular broadcaster. Increasing numbers, particularly the young, now preferred instead to 'view around.'"

AUSTRALIA

In sharp contrast to the Dutch experience, Australia's model most closely approximates the Canadian—though still with some differences. An independent agency—the Australian Broadcasting Authority (ABA)—allocates broadcast spectrum, frequencies and licences to radio and television operations of all kinds (although it does not regulate telecommunications). Like Canada's CRTC, the ABA sets content standards and monitors statutory caps on concentration and foreign ownership of media.

Australia has two separate public broadcasting corporations: the general-service Australian Broadcasting Corporation (ABC), and the multilingual Special Broadcasting Service (SBS). Both are funded from parliamentary appropriations. SBS is also allowed to sell advertising. Neither however, is subject to the ABA's program standards. Instead, they must meet their own statutory expectations. In the case of ABC, those expectations are to "contribute to a sense of national identity, inform, educate and entertain." In addition, SBS is expected to reflect the country's multicultural society.

THE SEEMING EVAPORATION of "spectrum scarcity" in the age of digital free-to-air, cable and satellite technologies has stripped public broadcasters of a core historic raison d'être. Other rationales for their existence face attack on ideological grounds—or from those who simply covet their audience.

Lord David Lipsey, a former political journalist and commissioner of public inquiry into the BBC, writes: "It is no longer obvious that what people can consume should be determined by some outside authority. People can decide for themselves ... through the magic of the market. They can buy the programmes they want to buy, and not buy those they don't want to buy."

That view is popular at the Fraser Institute, a Canadian think-tank with close ties to the American Republican Party and an unwavering belief in consumer sovereignty. "Canadians must be free to choose among competing cultural products and services," its director of regulatory studies, Fazil Mihlar, has asserted. "Ottawa, therefore, should begin by eliminating the Canada Council [a cultural grants agency] ... then complete the task by privatizing the CBC."

Mihlar and the like-minded hold it as an article of faith that a non-commercial agency cannot claim to serve any valid public interest without the endorsement of a commercial exchange. *The Economist,* in an editorial in May 2002, harrumphed: "Whether or not viewers benefit from the BBC's existence is debatable ... Other broadcasters certainly suffer, because they have to compete in the same market against a handsomely subsidized state operation." Its conclusion for the venerable BBC: "Privatise it."

Yet it is striking that by the turn of the century, no European country had followed France's lead in privatizing its major public-service broadcaster—"a step," as Peter Humphreys notes, "which had clearly incurred damaging unintended consequences." The examples cited above are all lively functioning democracies. It seems reasonable to conclude that their "state"-sponsored broadcasters would not have endured if their publics failed to find value in what they deliver.

At the same time, the variety of public-service broadcasting models is remarkable. It ranges from the corporatist Dutch NOS, through the provincially oriented German structure and even more dispersed American one, to the markedly more statist French and Italian frameworks.

Similarly, funding takes a variety of forms. The licence-fee revenues that sustain British, German and Italian public broadcasters are entirely alien to the contemporary Canadian and Australian systems, let alone the American model. Advertising and sponsorship are similarly a much greater presence on some systems than others. In a comparison of European public broadcasters extending beyond the above examples, Humphreys notes that in 1985–86, advertising represented between 12.4 per cent of their revenue (for France's FR3) and 97.6 per cent (for Spain's RTVE).

Different structures are not neutral in their effects, however. It is especially interesting to note that the licence-fee approach, a frequent target of right-wing critics who bitterly characterize it as a tax obliging people to pay for programs that many do not watch, may nonetheless be one of the most economical ways to produce television. In a 2000 study of the licence-fee-sustained British program market, David Graham and Associates noted "the extent to which television has been underpriced historically in the U.K."

Also notable is that European countries that either privatized or commercialized public broadcasters in the 1980s did not reap the wider selection of better programs that commentators such as Fazil Mihlar blithely anticipate. Rather, the opposite occurred.

Among new private broadcasters pressed to recoup substantial startup costs, Peter Humphreys notes, "it was reasonable to expect that—for a period at least—spending on programming would feature rather low down the new operators' scale of priorities ... Actually to produce programmes was more costly than to buy them in packages or run repeats: therefore there was unlikely to be much innovation."

Public broadcasters forced to rely on commercial advertising for the majority of their funding meanwhile felt compelled to meet private competitors largely on the same program turf. As a result, the "evidence suggest[ed] that broadcasting systems which [were] most dependent on advertising also schedule[d] the narrowest range of programming."

The private McKinsey Group reached a broadly similar conclusion after surveying twenty public-service broadcasters (PSBs) around the world. "PSBs can fulfill their mission," McKinsey noted, "only by making distinctive programs popular ... PSBs with the highest income per capita (that is, for each member of the national audience) have the best chance of producing popular programs that stand out, since these programs are invariably expensive to make." Evidence showed that in general, the more money a public broadcaster had to work with, the greater its audience share. But significantly, McKinsey also found that "the source of a broadcaster's money is important ... [R]eliance on advertising income leads to relatively indistinctive programming."

In Portugal, for instance, two commercial channels introduced in 1992 relied heavily on inexpensive imported programs. The country's public channel, RTP, which is mainly supported by advertising, responded by scheduling similarly commercial fare—and soon found its market share in decline. "Lately," the consultants reported, "RTP has adjusted its program mix back toward more public service programs and halted its slide in market share."

"The great promise of specialty channels is diversity," says Canadian television critic John Haslett Cuff. "But what is equally apparent from the U.S. and Canadian examples is the deluge of 'repurposed' inventory, better known as reruns. In a television world controlled by such mega-corporations as Disney there is no room for explorations of social, cultural and historical identity. These are concepts antithetical to the homogenizing ethos of Conglomerate TV, which seeks only to propagate the culture of consumers."

In the previous chapter, Canadian documentary producer John Kastner recalled the pressure he faced from commercial investors to delete Canadian references from a script in order to secure its sale to American commercial broadcasters. That alternative may have returned a higher profit for the picture, Kastner says, but only at the price of "taking Canada out of a Canadian story." Working instead for the CBC, he observes, "I could explore a Canadian problem without compromise. The experience goes to the heart of the reason why we badly need to strengthen public broadcasting."

But even some admirers of public broadcasting fear that years of attacks like Fazil Mihlar's have made the CBC into the "victim of a self-fulfilling prophecy, a kind of Catch-22," as David Taras wrote in a 2001 book, *Power & Betrayal in the Canadian Media*. Perennially starved of the funds required to produce the sort of programs that might sustain its legitimacy with audiences, the CBC now finds itself "so battered, so beleaguered, that its very weakness has become the rationale for closing it down."

Public broadcasters are under varying obligations either to support independent producers like Kastner or reflect their audience's "dreams, fears and folklore," to use Richard Pells's evocative phrase from the last chapter. Canada's CRTC sets explicit "Canadian content" minimum quotas for public as well as private broadcasters (the former higher than the latter). Australia's ABA, on the other hand, sets quotas only for private broadcasters; ABC and SBS are exempt. In another irony of America's PBS, it is subject to no formal content requirements, yet bases a significant part of its appeal on airing foreign—especially British—television fare.

In Europe, all public broadcasters are expected to meet the minimum standards of the 1989 "Television Without Frontiers" directive for "European works" and independent production. France and Britain set additional minima for the share of program spending that their public and private broadcasters must direct to either original French or regional (outside London) British producers.

A study by the European Audiovisual Observatory in 2000 further contradicts the assertion that private commercial television systems are necessarily more fertile for programming. The observatory compared television production in Europe's five largest countries. It found that Germany—dominated by licence-fee-supported public broadcasters—produced more than twice as much programming (by investment) as did France, with its advertising-supported broadcasters (despite that country's rigorous domestic quota system) and five times the level in Italy. Production in Britain was more than twice that in France and four times the Italian tally.

"When a financial crisis hit [Italian PSB] RAI in the early 1990s," reported Carole Tongue, "its support for film production was slashed. RAI was able to do this because no legal obligations underpinned its investment in films." By 1995, she calculated, "Italian TV provided five times less to Italian cinema than France provided for its native film industry." Italy's (pre-Berlusconi) government responded with new regulations that by 1999 obliged RAI to begin investing a minimum of 20 per cent of its licence-fee revenues in Italian or European films. (The subjects of content quotas and mandatory expenditure requirements will be revisited in later chapters.)

The widespread—if unproven—suspicion of Italian prime minister Berlusconi's behind-the-scenes influence over RAI underscores the potential vulnerability of public broadcasters to interference by those holding state office, even in democracies. The danger is more vividly demonstrated in authoritarian states. Among the first targets of every aspiring coup d'état is the transmitter of the state broadcaster. That the highly regarded programs of the BBC World Service (funded by the British Foreign Office), Radio Canada International or the U.S. State Department's Arabic-language Radio Sawa (broadcast to the

Persian Gulf) less deserve the descriptor "propaganda" may only be a matter of perception.

Certainly, public funding of itself provides no guarantee of either pluralism or respect for diversity. Egypt's state-owned television station provoked outrage in the West in 2002 when it broadcast a mini-series called *Horseman Without a Horse*, which presented the forged "Protocols of the Elders of Zion"—which purport to document a Jewish plot aimed at world domination—as historic fact. The Qatar-based Al-Jazeera Arabic satellite TV news channel has won some credit for flouting both censorship and the eye-glazingly dull conventions of much Mideast state broadcasting. But American observers in particular fault the channel, launched in 1996 with US$150 million from Qatar's Emir Sheik Hamad bin Khalifa Al Thani, for what they deem inflammatory coverage of al-Qaeda and the Palestinian resistance to Israeli occupation. Jon Alterman, director of the Middle East program at the Washington, D.C., Center for International and Strategic Studies, estimates that Persian Gulf governments invest almost $5 billion a year in regional broadcasters. Their programming, far from encouraging pluralism, often "seems directed toward promoting a sense of anger and alienation to the outside world."

Even in the United States, public radio may have been spared from Republican "zeroing out" only to fall prey to an ideological threat—from Christians with deep pockets. In Louisiana, Indiana and Oregon, conservative evangelical groups have used a long-ignored provision of the FCC's rules to force NPR to relinquish its local frequencies to them. "The result?" says Bill Roberts, president of Canada's multi-faith Vision TV: "A broadcasting service that stands for pluralism, tolerance and the free-ranging exploration of ideas is giving way to others that promote a socially restrictive agenda."

ROBERT McCHESNEY sees a threat of a different kind corroding public broadcasters everywhere. As public-service broadcasters face both increased commercial competition and the necessity of raising a greater share of their budgets from corporate sponsorships or their own advertising, he argues, they risk losing the very distinctions for which they are valued. "It is hard to see an endgame for this strategy," he worries, "that does not include the utter abandonment of public broadcasting."

McChesney's despair may be premature, but there is no question that public broadcasters face an ongoing dilemma. In an increasingly competitive environment, Peter Humphreys wrote as early as 1996, "How long could politicians be expected to support a licence fee [or parliamentary appropriation] high enough to meet their requirements, when viewers were watching fewer and fewer of their programmes?" But if public-service broadcasters succumb to the lure of competing with private stations for audience, they suffer other damaging consequences. "Competition for programmes and media stars in a free market can be expected to drive up certain strategic costs [and] the public broadcasters' ability to concentrate resources on in-house quality productions would suffer." At the same time, attempting to appeal to audiences on the same terms as private broadcasters would erode their very raison d'être.

Still, the persistence of public broadcasting suggests that for the citizens of most countries, neither the commercialized media menu nor the ideology of the right have—yet—been entirely persuasive. In a speech to the World Trade Organization (WTO) in Geneva in 2001, the chairman of Germany's public ARD network, Fritz Pleitgen, gave this eloquent defence of broadcasting in pursuit of public service rather than private profit:

> Cultural diversity is the very pre-requisite for the peaceful co-existence of nations. In the European Union, as much as we harmonize our internal market laws, our cultural policies are *not* harmonized. Such a policy would completely ignore the fact that cultural goods and services are *not* like all the other products that *are* fully subject to the rules of the EU internal market.
>
> Audio-visual services are among the most important cultural services in our modern societies given their omni-presence in each and every household. They influence our thinking, our tastes and our perceptions of the world from our earliest days onward. In Germany, in the Thirties and Forties we saw how a media monopoly in the wrong hands can turn into a powerful and evil propaganda machine. But in Europe, we are also convinced that such a psychologically influential instrument in the hands of just one or two media moguls or companies can pose a similar threat to our democracies.
>
> In Europe, we strongly believe that it *does* matter and that we *do* need to care whether we watch programmes that reflect our own

cultural identity, values and experiences, or whether we feed our minds on the images of the lives of people of foreign cultures, with different attitudes and value systems. This is why we have a European quota system [and] we promote European production. To be sure it is entirely up to the viewer to decide what he or she wants to watch. But if our citizens want programming reflecting their *own* lives, they will have *that* choice too.

No institution reflects all these policy goals more decisively than the institution of public-service broadcasting.

The WTO has not, by and large, been a sympathetic audience for such sentiments, as Chapter 16 will show. The EU, however, has formally recognized the primary role that public broadcasters play in its members' cultural priorities. In doing so, it explicitly emancipated the rationale for public broadcasting from its genesis in "spectrum scarcity" and rooted it instead in the core democratic value of pluralism.

Early in 2000, while the Dutch held the EU's revolving presidency, its representatives met in Amsterdam to affirm the central legitimacy of public broadcasting in Europe's political culture. "Public broadcasting," the Amsterdam Protocol read in part, "is directly related to the democratic, social and cultural needs of each society and to the need to preserve media pluralism." In respecting those needs, the protocol guarantees "the competence of Member States to provide for the funding of public service broadcasting" so long as that funding is in "fulfilment of the public service remit."

"All too often, international media debate has been about nothing but markets, producers and consumers," NOS chairman André van der Louw asserted during the debate that led to the Amsterdam Protocol. "For public broadcasting though, it is not just about markets, it is about societies and citizens."

Had they known about it, the cast of *This Hour Has 22 Minutes* would perhaps have had something to say about Europe's decision. Doubtless it would have been something rude, and it probably would not have travelled well beyond Canada. But those are precisely the qualities for which Canadians prize the irreverent CBC production— and the public service that broadcasts it.

9

SCHEDULING
QUOTAS

O F THE RANGE of policy prescriptions advanced as offering potential to secure cultural diversity in the face of market failure,
one measure attracts a disproportionate amount of hostility
from free-market advocates: the application of any sort of scheduling
quota to cultural service providers.

Advocates of liberalized international trade—whether of cultural
products or of anything else—argue that quotas violate the market's
"unseen hand." Quotas are condemned as arbitrary, inherently unfair
and antithetical to the all-trumping economic value of "efficiency."

In Canada, critics of national cultural policies routinely attack the
requirement that broadcasters air a minimum quota of domestic content as authoritarian. The requirements are excoriated for being a
command-and-control policy of "coercion" that attempts to decide
which cultural products Canadians can consume and "force people at
home to watch them." They are regarded as "shackles" that "infringe
the constitutional right of freedom of expression."

Aside from the moral dudgeon that arises from such criticism, there
is also the accusation that quotas don't work. As Alex Strachan, media
critic for *The Vancouver Sun*, wrote: "Quotas reward quantity at the expense of quality. They foster mediocrity. They send a message that

Canadian programs aren't good enough to stand on their own feet. They exist because the law says they must, not because they deserve to."

The heat and vitriol of all this hostility is especially remarkable given the globally widespread resort to one form or another of what might be described as quotas in pursuit of cultural sovereignty. Some applications, like the maximum of twenty Hollywood films that China's authoritarian government allows to be imported each year (a ceiling doubled from ten in 2002), are unquestionably restrictive and exclusionary. Outside the paranoid hysteria of ideologues, however, it is difficult to make the same charge stick against the pluralistic markets for ideas, entertainment and capital that flourish in Canada, Australia, Great Britain, Germany—or the United States. Yet all those nations also employ quotas at least to some degree as a policy tool to achieve cultural diversity.

A quota is also the only cultural security measure given explicit endorsement in the General Agreement on Tariffs and Trade (GATT). Since 1947, that agreement has permitted the employment of domestic-content quotas on cinema screens. At one time many countries, including Canada and Britain, had cinema screen quotas. At present, however, cinema quotas for national films are applied in only a few countries, including Spain, South Korea and Brazil. Italy will shortly join that list as well.

These days, the most common setting for scheduling quotas is in the area of broadcasting, whether on radio or in television.

As was noted in Chapter 8, many countries first addressed the need for diversity of expression in broadcasting by creating a state-owned public broadcaster. Typically, a written mandate, charter or "remit" requires such public-service broadcasters to air programs of interest to minorities or programs that might not be provided in a system funded solely by advertising. Such programming flows rationally from the public's ownership of such a broadcaster. Citizens are a public broadcaster's ultimate "shareholders." By airing programs that respond to an audience's needs *as citizens* over those that play only to their needs *as consumers,* a public broadcaster clearly serves the interests of its shareholders.

Private broadcasters operate under different imperatives. A private broadcaster's only "mandate" is to maximize the monetary return to that subset (frequently a very small subset) of a country's citizens who own its shares.

In most countries, both public and private broadcasters now populate the broadcast airwaves. With deregulation and the profusion of digital technologies, more and more private broadcast services are being licensed everywhere. Around the world, they are taking a growing share of audiences—and reducing proportionately the numbers of people watching or listening to public broadcasters.

What can governments do in such an environment to serve the interests of public citizenship and provide for program diversity?

Historically, virtually every country with a functioning public administration has addressed this question by regulating private broadcasting. Usually, this is done through an independent regulatory agency vested with the power to award licences and impose program quotas in the public interest as a condition of a broadcaster's licence to operate.

A popular chorus among critics of any cultural regulation has been that such regimes are rapidly becoming technologically obsolete and unenforceable. Channel proliferation, they argue, makes spectrum-scarcity untenable as a basis for regulation and at the same time renders regulation unnecessary. The magic hand of the marketplace will provide for all.

But the alleged end of spectrum scarcity fails a reality check. Private free-to-air broadcasters that reach the entire population under their transmission footprint still operate over a limited spectrum of frequencies. And the number of would-be broadcast services that desire access to satellite or cable distribution exceeds those few that benefit from public rights-of-way or geo-stationary parking spots. Someone has to decide in each of these cases who will be permitted to launch a broadcast service and how it will be carried. Leaving those decisions entirely to the private sector or to a principle of "first come, first served" ignores the real-world failures of perfect-market theory that were laid bare in Chapter 3. To the extent that governments award broadcast franchises, they are able to mitigate those failures by imposing public-interest obligations on the franchisees.

This is not to say that quotas are without blemish as a policy device. Far from it. Typically, quota requirements are framed within general regulations or in the form of specific licence conditions. But any condition or regulation is open to interpretation. And it is axiomatic that every new rule carries in it the seeds of future loopholes. In order to be understandable and enforceable, quota regulations need to be in clear and unambiguous language. Yet this can be very difficult to accomplish in the subjective field of program content.

Just as other profit-motivated enterprises enlist lawyers and accountants to find gaps in tax codes, private broadcasters seek to minimize the intended impact of regulations and licence conditions, interpreting the letter of the rule in whatever way is least likely to lower revenue or reduce profit.

Nonetheless, there remain both strong motive and effective means to secure the public's interest in the output of private broadcasting. The balance of this chapter will survey how quotas work, where they succeed and where they fail. It will also put the charges most commonly levelled at broadcast quotas under closer scrutiny.

ABOUT FORTY YEARS AGO one of the present writers, then in law school, decided to undertake a research paper on the domestic-content requirement in force at the time for private television in Canada. The "Canadian content" rule was then all of four years old. By the time the paper was published in 1968, the rule had been amended seventeen times.

Like the programs they seek to regulate, content quotas are almost infinitely variable. And like complex broadcasting systems, they are constantly evolving to take account of changing circumstances.

Perhaps the most common form of quota requires private broadcasters to air a minimum amount of local or indigenous programming. This kind of quota is found in many countries; the most obvious exception is the United States, where it is deemed unnecessary, given that almost all programming aired in that country by mainstream commercial television stations is already domestic in origin.

Many other types of quota are also in force around the world. As will become clear in the pages ahead, there are quotas for programming in a particular language, quotas for certain genres of programming, quotas for programs directed to a certain audience and for programs produced by companies that are not linked by corporate ownership or vertical integration with the broadcaster.

Still, content quotas that assert some version of a local, domestic, national, or indigenous criterion are (outside the United States) often part of the bedrock of broadcast regulation. Already noted in Chapter 7 are the difficulties this raises for defining what is "local" or "national." There are many ways to determine where a cultural product comes from—what trade lawyers refer to as rules of origin. Some of these focus on the citizenship of the key creative contributors. Others consider subject matter, themes and settings. Still others rely on the locus of financing.

This variety is compounded by other considerations. Every jurisdiction confronts unique cultural, demographic, economic and industrial contexts. In addition, some apply additional tests for certain purposes: for example, tests for a certain work to qualify for a subsidy rather than fulfill a content quota.

However a jurisdiction chooses to define what local content *is,* the next question regulators face is *how much* of it to require from local broadcasters. That in turn generates a third issue: what should the quota denominator embrace? That is, will the requirement be placed across the whole program schedule, or only on particular times of day or genres of programming?

Since the dawn of broadcasting, Canada has wrestled with the risk that imported audiovisual products might completely supplant indigenous cultural expression. Even so, it took decades to learn the significance of the last of these questions.

Domestic-content requirements for television made their appearance in Canada at the same time as privately owned television broadcasting did, in 1961. The first regulation coincided with the issue of licences to the national CTV chain of private English-language TV stations. It required 40 per cent of the private broadcasters' overall on-air schedule to be Canadian-produced programming.

For the next decade, the CTV broadcasters largely complied with the Canadian content regulation as it stood. But the programs they aired to meet the requirement consisted almost exclusively of news, sports and game shows.

There was no mystery in the reason why. Canadian drama was hugely expensive. U.S. drama was cheap. It also benefited from high-profile stars already well known to Canadian audiences and from the overflow into Canada of promotional efforts aimed at American audiences. The CTV stations in any case had another mission for their limited resources that was, to their owners, far more pressing. In order to extend their signals' reach beyond the major cities to the rest of Canada they needed to erect dozens, if not hundreds, of rebroadcasting transmitters. These transmitters were costly. The undertaking simply left no room in the private stations' budgets for pricey Canadian drama.

In 1968, the Canadian government overhauled its system of broadcast governance. A new Broadcasting Act called explicitly for a high proportion of Canadian content. "The programming provided by each broadcaster," it asserted, "should be of high standard, using predominantly Canadian creative and other resources." Significantly, it also mandated programming that demonstrated both "variety" and "comprehensiveness." The object was not just to have a certain *quantity* of indigenous programming; it was also to have indigenous programs in *a broad range of genres.*

Simultaneously, the government created a new agency—the Canadian Radio-television and Telecommunications Commission (CRTC)—to regulate the broadcast industry. It received expanded powers to attach the new law's objectives to future broadcast permits as conditions of licence.

Two years later, after a major review of national broadcast policy, the CRTC revised its content requirements. Private broadcasters would now be expected to fill 60 per cent of their schedule between 6 AM and midnight with Canadian content. Evening schedules, between 6 PM and midnight, would have to be 50 per cent Canadian.

The private broadcasters strongly opposed the stiffer and more explicit Canadian-content requirement. But the regulator stood firm. Indeed, essentially the same rules remain in force today. (And it is interesting that in 1999, the same private broadcasters that once fiercely opposed the rules formally endorsed them in a presentation to the CRTC.)

But clarifying the Canadian content quota did not end the debate about whether its goals were being accomplished.

In the wake of the new requirement released in 1970, the CRTC undertook its first significant review of the private CTV chain's operations. In 1973, the commission renewed CTV's licence for three years, but noted its disappointment that CTV had failed to meet the "expectation" of "more drama programming with Canadian themes, concerns and locales." The CRTC restated its anticipation that the network would introduce at least "one new project of this nature" by the start of the 1973–74 season.

Three years later, CTV announced a network schedule without a single weekly drama produced in Canada.

This time, the CRTC was a little blunter in calling attention to the program deficit. "The Commission expects the network, in future schedules, to correct the deficiency of no weekly Canadian drama in the 1976–77 network schedule," it lectured. But it still renewed CTV's licence for another three years—without attaching any specific conditions regarding Canadian drama.

In 1979, the CTV licence was up for renewal once again. And the commission was appalled to discover there was still no Canadian drama in the private network's proposed weekly schedule. Nothing had changed.

That spring, the CRTC held hearings to gauge the public's and industry's views of the network. Four months later, it issued its decision. It was stark in rhetoric and impact:

"It will be a condition of the renewal," the decision bluntly ordered, "that 26 hours of original new Canadian drama be presented during the 1980–81 broadcasting year and 39 hours of original new Canadian drama be presented during the 1981–82 season. The primary orientation should be on Canadian themes."

CTV promptly announced it would appeal the CRTC decision to the courts. The network's lawyers claimed the commission had no right to require that the Canadian private broadcaster air Canadian dramatic programming.

For three years the matter moved slowly up the judicial receiving line, finally reaching the Supreme Court of Canada. On April 5, 1982, the country's highest court issued its decision. It unanimously concluded that the CRTC decree was justified. The law clearly did permit the commission to require Canada's largest private television network to broadcast a specified number of hours of original new Canadian drama in the coming season.

The court also addressed directly one of the most frequently aired criticisms of quotas: that they offend freedom of expression. Noting that the CRTC's decision was silent on the *content* of Canadian dramatic programming, the court dismissed the criticism as unfounded. Quotas, it found, did not offend freedom of expression.

By then, of course, the 1979 broadcast season over which CTV had drawn its line in the sand had long since come and gone. But the principle that the public's representative could require broadcasters to air specified hours of new original Canadian drama was now bolted to legal bedrock. It would help change the face of television broadcasting in Canada.

It is hard to overestimate the importance of the 1979 CRTC decision and the Supreme Court of Canada ruling three years later to uphold it. Since 1982, the CRTC has routinely made the licences it has granted to private broadcasters conditional on their meeting specific quotas in identified program categories—especially Canadian drama—that might otherwise be underrepresented. Just as significantly, the same authority has allowed the regulator to attach these requirements to licences granted for either radio or television, whether free-to-air or as specialty programming services delivered by cable or satellite.

In 1987, the CRTC granted CTV a five-year licence renewal. But it upped the ante for Canadian drama substantially. The licence required that the country's biggest private broadcaster (and by then its most-watched network) begin immediately to air 2½ hours of Canadian drama a week—rising by the end of the licence term to 4½ hours. Most of that, moreover, was to be broadcast between 8 PM and midnight. In addition, CTV was required to air twenty-four hours per year of Canadian feature films, made-for-TV movies or mini-series.

The CRTC has similarly tailored its Canadian-content requirements to the specific circumstances of other private broadcasters. In 1986, for instance, it required the Global Television Network (technically not a "network" at the time) to air three hours a week of first-run Canadian drama between 8 PM and midnight. That requirement was raised with each subsequent licence renewal for a decade thereafter.

Canadian content quotas for specialty programming services carried on the basic tier of cable services match those for free-to-air TV: 60 per cent overall and 50 per cent for evening hours. But pay- and specialty-television services are subject to more customized requirements reflecting their focus on particular genres or topic niches. Pay-channels, which rely heavily on feature films, are subject to a Canadian-content scheduling requirement ranging from 20 per cent to 30 per cent—acknowledging the comparatively small supply of Canadian-made feature films compared with available foreign (mainly

Hollywood) fare. Requirements for specialty services that focus on content niches have been set as low as 15 per cent and as high as 90 per cent, depending on the format.

Coupled with expanded subsidy programs from the federal government (discussed in Chapter 13), these broadcast requirements have resulted in the creation of thousands of hours of Canadian drama. In 1984, for example, Canadian drama (including comedy) represented only 2 per cent of the supply of drama on English television in Canada. By 2001, this proportion had increased to 17 per cent. During the same period, viewing of local drama increased from 2 per cent to 9 per cent of overall drama viewing. In French Canada, the supply of Canadian drama on television stations rose from 10 per cent to 20 per cent, and viewing of local drama increased from 10 per cent to 26 per cent.

The combination of subsidies and quota requirements for Canadian drama gave rise to another development: the rise of the independent program production industry in Canada. From tiny beginnings in the early 1980s, the independent production sector in Canada grew steadily. By 2002, it was producing c$2.4 billion in Canadian programming, almost half of the overall Canadian production output of c$5.1 billion (the remainder was accounted for by c$1.7 billion in foreign-location shoots and c$1 billion of in-house broadcasting production). Many factors have contributed to this success. But first and foremost has been the impact of government policy.

The lesson is unmistakable. Left to their own devices, private broadcasters will respond to a vaguely worded local-content quota that fails to distinguish between program genres by providing the least-expensive local fare possible. This will likely mean genres in which imported programs are in any event least popular—news and sports. They will not voluntarily undertake expensive drama programming, particularly when they can acquire popular work from foreign sources at a fraction of the cost.

Why, after all, would they do otherwise?

THIS LESSON was not lost on broadcast regulators in Europe in the decade that followed the Supreme Court of Canada's decision. It was a period of sweeping change rooted in new technology, liberalized markets, the collapse of communism and the rise of new, continent-wide political and cultural ambitions.

Up to then, broadcast regulation had been a strictly national concern. But the advent of satellite technology—at first to deliver signals to cable distributors and later broadcasting directly to homes—threatened to erase the containment that national borders provided, stripping national policies of any effect. Coincidentally, new governments came to power in France, Germany and Italy committed to opening up the continent's three biggest markets to privately owned broadcasting.

The advent of many new channels and a frankly for-profit programming ethic created an explosion in demand for popular shows that, at least initially, far exceeded the capacity of local producers to produce. The result was entirely predictable.

"Officials were well aware," broadcast historian Peter Humphreys writes, "of Europe's substantial trade deficit in television programmes, notably films and series, with the United States ... One of the main attractions of imported U.S. programmes was the fact that they were relatively cheap; to buy in such programmes was cheaper than to produce them domestically." While American producers benefited from their big home market to amortize the cost of films and series, selling them abroad for a fraction of their production cost, "Europe, by contrast was disadvantaged by the fragmented character of its audiovisual markets ... divided by linguistic and cultural heterogeneity."

The border-crashing capabilities of satellites seemed to offer one possible solution to that historic fragmentation. If commercial broadcasting had created a market highly favourable to imported fare, Humphreys records, "transfrontier broadcasting appeared to hold out a welcome opportunity to rebalance these historically unfavourable terms of competition between European and U.S. producers."

At the same time, communism's collapse in eastern Europe and the ascendant ambitions of western leaders—especially in France and Germany—to create a new, more unified European political entity on the world stage provided further impetus for taking a continental view of broadcasting. It was, Humphreys says, "the optimistic expectation—shared by members of the European Parliament, officials of the Commission of the European Communities, and other forces in favour of closer European union—that transfrontier broadcasting might give a welcome filip to the process of European cultural and political integration."

In 1984, the European Commission produced a discussion document entitled "Television Without Frontiers." Its primary thrust was to encourage the development of a continental market for small-screen entertainment: in its own words, the "opening up of intra-Community frontiers for national television programmes."

But enthusiasm for a Europe-wide cultural free-fire zone was not universally shared. "Many of Europe's small states," Humphreys notes, "were keen to see established in a European convention some regulatory protection for their cultural sovereignty."

In short, Europe faced the same contradictory pressures that have long confronted Canada. It wished to enjoy the variety of cultural offerings a free and open market can supply—but not to let that market fall under the effective monopoly of one low-cost provider. It wanted to offer its own cultural creators the biggest possible market and audience—but not at the cost of sacrificing smaller cultures to the larger whole.

In 1989, after much discussion, the European parliament enacted the "Television Without Frontiers" directive. Among its provisions, article 4 provided that EU member states

> shall ensure where practicable and by appropriate means, that broadcasters reserve for European works ... a majority proportion of their transmission time excluding the time appointed to news, sports events, games, advertising and teletext services.

Significantly, the European-quota rule explicitly ignored news, sports and game shows, genres where Europe has nothing to fear from Hollywood. The rule focuses directly and exclusively on fiction—the most expensive kind of programming to create and the category in which popular foreign imports can most easily be licensed for a fraction of their cost.

The "Television Without Frontiers" quota has undergone one major review since its inception. In 1996, the European Commission proposed a revision in which it was proposed to remove the words "where practicable," to extend the directive's coverage to include video-on-demand and to add a new provision for investment quotas to take into account the advent of thematic channels. For its part, the Motion

Picture Association of America worked feverishly to have the European content requirement (which *Variety* hyperbolically referred to as "quotas on U.S. movies and TV shows") dropped entirely.

Predictably, European producers, actors and directors strongly applauded the proposed clampdown and extension of the requirement. Private European broadcasters, like their Canadian counterparts before them, resisted.

After a long and contentious campaign, all the European Commission's proposals to tighten the quota provisions were narrowly defeated in the European parliament in 1996. The directive's coverage would not be extended to new transaction-based services and the weak language "wherever practicable" would remain—but so would the majority Euro-content requirement for fiction programs.

A 2001 study by the European Institute for the Media found that despite the use of the words "where practicable" in the directive, most European nations had instituted measures to meet the directive's goals. Indeed, it noted, "in most of the countries there are further (additional or stricter) provisions."

Many of those additional requirements focused on language. France, Greece, the Netherlands, Belgium (more precisely, its French-speaking Walloon community), Norway, Portugal, Spain and the United Kingdom all had imposed on their private broadcasters some form of quotas for programming made originally in an identified national or regional minority language. The amounts required ranged from 25 to 50 per cent of airtime.

Other quotas specified certain program genres. The Netherlands had specific quotas on educational and arts-related programs. France had quotas requiring a minimum allocation of the broadcast schedule to feature films.

Meanwhile, the developments that had originally prompted Europe to set a community television policy gathered momentum. In the decade following the directive's introduction, Europe consolidated its political union and opened its internal borders. Participation in its television market ïexploded. From 47 TV channels in 1989, Europe's airwaves and cable networks blossomed to carry more than 1,500 local, national and regional channels by 2002. Significantly however, only 50 of those—including most of the original 47—still drew three quarters of all viewers.

Against that sweeping market transformation, how well have the directive quotas accomplished their goals?

A survey of European broadcasters in 1999 and 2000 found that they were not only meeting the directive's quota for broadcasting "European works" but, on average, they were exceeding it. "The average broadcast time for European works was 60.7 per cent in 1999 and 62.2 per cent in 2000 for the fifteen [EU] Member States," the report stated.

Europe's private broadcasters, spurred initially by the quota, had also discovered the fact that audiences often *preferred* to watch shows that reflect their own countries' experiences, issues and settings. By 2000, domestic (European) programs anchored the prime-time schedules at most of the fifty major broadcasters. Cheaper imports were relegated to the less-watched "shoulder" and "off-prime" parts of the day. Between 1996 and 1999, meanwhile, the hours of new local television drama produced in Europe's five largest economies (Germany, France, Britain, Italy and Spain) rose by 26 per cent, with production jumping 90 per cent in Spain and an even more dramatic 228 per cent in Italy.

"This trend reflects increasing public demand for national and European works," observed European Commission member Viviane Reding, "especially of fiction." Nearly three quarters of all Europe's burgeoning host of television channels met or exceeded the domestic content quota.

Which did not? Some specialty channels serving thematic niches were unable to obtain the majority of their programs from European providers. Other individual channels within larger broadcast groups failed to achieve the quota—but the groups of which they were a part did so as a whole. And some new services also failed to meet the quota as they struggled to achieve profitability by airing cheaper imported programs. (Significantly, though, another group of start-ups "mostly broadcast European works right from the start in order to gain a foothold in the market by meeting the demand for them.")

But another category of exception was revealing. "Subsidiaries whose parent companies are located outside the European Union," the report observed, "systematically use their own catalogues and broadcast few European works." Among the examples cited, most were brands belonging to U.S. companies: Disney Channel, Bravo, Discovery Channel, Fox Kids and Nickelodeon. Ironically, the advent of the U.S.-owned, subscription-based children's channels put competitive pressures on the existing U.K. free-to-air channels carrying local children's programming, with the result that the ITV service reduced its children's TV budget.

YET ANOTHER COUNTRY that has found it desirable as well as possible to reconcile broadcast content quotas with pluralism, democracy and free markets is Australia.

Like Canada, Australia has placed a general requirement for Australian content on its private free-to-air broadcasters since the 1960s. For most of that time, the level has been set at 55 per cent of the program schedule from 6 AM to midnight. But on January 1, 1990, following the Canadian and European lead and addressing the same problem, Australia introduced a "sub-quota" focused on Australian drama.

Its mechanism, however, was a departure from those employed in Europe and Canada—both of which rely on a percentage of airtime. The Australian drama quota employed an innovative cumulative-points system. It awarded a different number of points for each broadcast hour of several different formats—serials, series, movies of the week and mini-series. Broadcasters were required to air programs that accumulated a minimum of 225 points in a year and 775 points over any three successive years. But it left to the broadcasters the decision of what specific mix of programs to air in order to achieve their target. To meet the benchmark, a broadcaster needed to air more than 80 original hours a year of the most expensive formats—mini-series and made-for-TV movies—but as many as 258 original hours of the least-expensive format, serial soap operas.

In addition to the points system for drama, the 1990 standard also included a number of more conventional, time-based requirements for other priority genres. Specifically, commercial broadcasters were obliged to air a minimum of 20 hours a year of first-run Australian-made documentaries; 260 hours of children's programming, of which half had to be first-run Australian productions (including 30 hours of drama); and 130 hours of first-run Australian programs aimed at pre-schoolers.

In 1999, after nearly a decade of experience with both the general and genre-specific requirements, a new Broadcasting Services (Australian Content) Standard came into force. It strongly reaffirmed the importance of maintaining the quota approach in general, "to promote the role of commercial television . . . in developing and reflecting a sense of Australian identity, character and cultural diversity, by supporting the community's continued access to television programs produced under Australian creative control."

With the new act in place, the Australian Broadcasting Authority (ABA) launched a review of how well genre-specific standards were working. In announcing its review, the regulatory agency restated the rationale for focusing on the most expensive and hard-to-do forms of television. "Diversity and quality are chiefly promoted by . . . drama, documentary and children's programs—categories that are culturally sensitive and most vulnerable to import replacement." Television fiction was particularly singled out for its capacity to "tell our stories, the stories that Australians want to see, the stories that become part of our sense of who we are as Australians—and constantly rate as the most popular productions with Australian audiences."

In late 2001, the ABA review released its findings, revealing a familiar picture of well-received domestic television dramas beset by challenging market economics. "Popular Australian drama," it found, "delivers high audiences to commercial television broadcasters. Local dramas such as *Blue Heelers* on the Seven Network are consistent ratings performers with loyal audiences." National audiences for the premier broadcasts of leading Australian TV dramas had shown a consistent upward trend during the previous decade. Domestic productions continued to fill about one third of drama hours on broadcast schedules.

That said, total airtime devoted to drama had slipped substantially in the decade between 1990 and 2000, from an industry average of 26.2 per cent of hours to 15.2 per cent. Meanwhile, the networks' spending on foreign drama was rising far faster than spending on local productions (2.4 per cent per year compared with 1.5 per cent per year). "Foreign drama," the report found, "represents the largest single category of program expenditure for the commercial networks." In all, the number of hours of Australian drama broadcast by the country's three commercial networks had fallen by nearly a third over the decade.

Closer analysis revealed a further story behind the decline in overall hours of Australian-made drama. Increasingly, broadcasters were opting to earn their point quota by investing in higher-cost mini-series and movies of the week instead of lower-cost, soap-opera-style serials.

The 2001 report also underscored a reality that was becoming familiar to producers in Canada, Britain and even to a degree the United States. In the competition for audiences, production budgets were relentlessly rising. Domestic-broadcast licence fees, however, were not keeping pace. For some types of production, available licence fees paid for as little as 25 per cent of a production budget (compared with as much as 100 per cent in the United States and, after subsidies, as much as 75 per cent even in Canada). Producers routinely sought to make up the difference from overseas sales. But those were becoming harder to find as broadcasters in foreign markets turned increasingly to their own local productions. (Thus the very success of the European directive has added to the woes of producers in Australia and Canada.)

In December 2002, the ABA released its regulatory conclusions. Based on the previous year's review, the Australian content standard not only remained in place—but the bar was going to rise. Beginning with 2002 (already almost over), Australian broadcasters were expected to achieve 830 total drama points over any three-year period and meet an annual target of at least 250 points. The three-year running benchmark would rise again in 2005, to 860 points. But in reflection of the rising costs of high-quality drama, the ABA would also adjust the "format factor" to increase the bonus for investment in the most expensive dramatic genres.

Although the 1999 review led to a general affirmation of the existing Australian content quota system, the events that triggered it bear a brief examination here for the light they shed on how trade agreements can affect such policies. In 1988, Australia and New Zealand had signed a Trade in Services Protocol to the existing Australia–New Zealand Closer Economic Relations Agreement (essentially a free-trade agreement), under which each country granted "national treatment" to an array of the other's service providers. Although the new Australian Broadcasting Act in 1992 purported to extend such treatment to New Zealand programs, a consortium of producers from the smaller country felt the ABA's content standard did not in fact live up to commitments made in the protocol. In 1994, they took their contention to court. After a chain of pro- and con-rulings by lower courts, the New Zealanders eventually won their case before Australia's highest court in April 1998. The following year, the ABA amended its standard to make clear that New Zealand programs would be treated as "Australian" for the purposes of determining whether broadcasters were meeting local-content obligations.

It is instructive at the same time to consider the picture on New Zealand's own small screen. With a population of only about four million people, that country confronts an especially acute challenge in funding television that reflects its own experience and competes in quality with the flood of imports available at marginal cost from other English-speaking markets. In the face of that challenge, successive New Zealand governments have until now opted to follow the model urged on them (and the rest of the world) by Hollywood's lobbyists in the Motion Picture Association and the U.S. Trade Representative's office. It has avoided content quotas in favour of subsidies for New Zealand productions.

In 2000, NZ On Air, the New Zealand crown agency established to administer those subsidies and encourage the country's commercial television broadcasters to "reflect and develop New Zealand culture and identity," conducted an exhaustive survey of what that policy was bringing to the country's television screens. Its results were devastating. "New Zealand citizens see less of themselves on air than do Australians, Canadians, Irish, British or American citizens," NZ On Air was obliged to report. Of total broadcast time, "less than a quarter" was filled with local productions. The percentage rose to 31 per cent if only the hours between 6 AM and midnight were considered.

NZ On Air's next move was illuminating. The agency began a new study, this time into whether or not to institute domestic-content quotas of the type found in most of the rest of the developed world. Strikingly, when New Zealanders themselves were polled on the matter in 2002, "more than 70 per cent of people surveyed favoured compulsory minimum screening levels for New Zealand made programs on free-to-air channels," NZ On Air chief executive Jo Tyndall reported. When those being surveyed were reminded that made-in-New Zealand programs cost more than imported ones, the number who supported quotas *increased* to nearly three quarters of the total.

Whether the will of New Zealanders ever passes into law may depend, however, on decisions taken far from their own shores. As Chapter 16 will demonstrate, restrictive rules pressed on other countries largely by the United States in the name of liberalized trade in services may preclude New Zealand from following where other democracies have led in adopting policies to secure its culture.

QUOTAS NEED NOT FOCUS only on domestic content. Singapore, for instance, requires its broadcasters to air a minimum number of hours of public-service programs—those that serve the public interest but may not be commercially viable. The requirement may be met with news and current affairs, educational and children's shows or minority-language programs as well as drama produced locally in either Chinese or English. But there is no specific requirement for domestic production.

More revealing still is another example.

No country embraces the "pure" market model more fiercely than the United States. Its broadcasting system is of a piece with the rest of the American reliance on commerce to answer all its citizens' cultural needs. Television in the United States emerged on a foundation of local stations that quickly coalesced into a complex system of national networks and market-by-market program syndication. To this, the last quarter-century has seen the addition of myriad specialty networks and premium pay-channels. While public broadcasting has long been undernourished, the U.S. system as a whole is large, rich, productive and extremely competitive.

U.S. broadcasters have historically been remarkably free from regulation. Content quotas would seem to be anathema to the less-is-more philosophy of regulation.

But that conclusion would be wrong.

Since the inception of the Federal Communications Commission (FCC) in the 1930s, U.S. broadcasters have also been seen as having public-interest responsibilities. In 1960, for example, the FCC set out detailed instructions to broadcast licensees about their public-interest obligations. The FCC insisted, among other matters, that licensees be "responsive to local needs," and it identified a laundry list of program categories that it deemed to be part of a balanced portfolio of programming. This included "the development and use of local talent," "programs for children" and "educational programs."

As high-minded as this pronouncement may have been, it is fair to say that it was never meaningfully enforced. In general, the FCC declined to regulate entertainment programming on the theory that the market can take care of it. However, the genre of educational programming for children could not be so easily dismissed. By the 1980s, despite occasional regulatory nudging, commercial TV broadcasters in the United States had largely abandoned educational programming for young viewers.

Finally, in 1990, the U.S. Congress passed the Children's Television Act, limiting the number of commercial minutes that could be broadcast in children's programming and directing the FCC to promulgate specific rules requiring TV licensees to present educational programming designed for children. The FCC responded by asking stations to increase their commitment to such programming voluntarily, without putting specific numbers on the table. Unsurprisingly, this produced no change in the broadcasters' schedules.

By the mid-1990s, the situation had grown intolerable. A study showed that many stations aired little or no educational programming for children. Some stations claimed that they aired such programs, but in fact they had merely relabelled titles such as *America's Funniest Home Videos, Mighty Morphin Power Rangers* and *Woody Woodpecker* as children's educational programming. Pressure mounted from lobby groups and the White House, responding to reports that American children spent nearly twice as much time in front of the television as they did in front of a teacher.

Finally, on August 8, 1996, the FCC issued a report and order setting a new requirement. Henceforth, TV broadcasters wishing to ensure renewal of their licences would need to air at least three hours a week of regularly scheduled programming between 7 AM and 10 PM "that has as a significant purpose serving the educational and informational needs of children." The order was consistent with a proposal submitted by President Bill Clinton and agreed to by the National Association of Broadcasters the month before.

The new rule set what amounted to a three-hour quota for children's educational programming. The rationale was that broadcasting had public-interest obligations, that the commercially driven marketplace did not provide a sufficient amount of educational programming targeted to children and that the new quota would be the best measure to address the unmet need.

The immediate effect was to create a new market for educational programming for children. Major players like Disney and Viacom, as well as a number of smaller producers, immediately geared up to meet the new demand. Some critics argued that making kids' programs more "educational" ("eat your spinach TV," some called it) would drive young audiences away from the free-to-air channels to cable networks not subject to the quota. In fact, nothing of the sort happened. Indeed, the ABC television network, which was perhaps better positioned than its competitors to respond to the new requirement by tapping the archives of its corporate parent, Walt Disney Co., saw its Saturday morning ratings soar by 35 per cent.

In early 2001, the FCC reported that in the previous three years, the average airtime dedicated to educational programming for children on commercial stations had risen to four hours a week and that stations had complied with requirements that those hours be adequately promoted and identified. Although there have been mixed reviews on the educational value of the programming, there is also a sense that the FCC rule has led to far more "quality" shows than before, at least for pre-schoolers.

Observers have mixed opinions about the apparent compliance of American broadcasters to the FCC's children's quota. Some commentators view the absence of protest as motivated by a reluctance to alienate regulators that were about to forgo a public auction in awarding a second broadcast channel to existing stations as part of their conversion from analog to digital. Whether or not that is the case, the precedent is illuminating. It demonstrates that even in the United States, the idea that the broadcast market may be deficient in certain program genres—and that commercial broadcast licensees may be compelled by a regulator to air programs that would otherwise be underrepresented—is well recognized.

THE CHILDREN'S educational requirement has not been the only American flirtation with content regulation of one sort or another. Between 1970 and 1995, U.S. commercial networks were prevented from dominating the production of prime-time entertainment. "Fin-syn" (financing or syndication) rules effectively required the networks to obtain most comedy and drama series from independent third parties. A further rule, the "Prime-Time Access Rule," reserved the hour between 7 and 8 PM on both coasts and 6 and 7 PM in the Midwest for programs acquired by local stations and not provided by the networks.

Both rules were intended to encourage more diversity in programming by lessening the domination of the networks. However, they were both swept away in the mid-1990s, in a wave of deregulation that hastened the amalgamation of American broadcasting into the half-dozen giants that currently dominate the landscape.

U.S. cable systems are also subject to a number of content requirements that closely resemble quotas in their design and impact. Under existing FCC rules, U.S. cable systems must reserve (typically) three of the twenty-five channels available on most basic systems for "public access" community use, as well as carry designated public-broadcasting (PBS) channels and any terrestrial free-to-air signals that are available in the system's coverage area. These rules seek to implement the FCC's long-standing policy supporting "localism"—the support of local expression, a principle that has been described as "the most sacred cow of communications regulatory policy" in the United States.

Given these measures, it is intriguing to imagine the regulatory response if U.S. commercial television were to find itself in the same situation as television in other countries, airing little or no local drama because stations could acquire equally popular and much cheaper foreign drama. Can there be any doubt that the U.S. government, either through Congress or the FCC, would shortly use precisely the same arguments raised in defence of local and children's educational programming to impose a quota for national U.S. drama?

THE USE of broadcast scheduling quotas in countries around the world, even in the United States, demonstrates a broad consensus that a free marketplace does not automatically provide certain kinds of desired programs. It similarly reflects wide acceptance of a legitimate mitigating role for government in ensuring audience choice and space on the schedule for such underrepresented programs.

Despite their wide adoption, no other measure in the tool kit of cultural diversity attracts the degree of moral opprobrium directed at program quotas. Opponents condemn them as antithetical to freedom of expression and as the functional equivalents of censorship. At the extreme, television quotas are portrayed as a form of "command and control" social engineering, with the implication that jackbooted agents of government are brutally forcing unwanted images on unwilling and victimized viewers.

"Canadian content regulations violate the spirit, if not the letter, of the constitutional guarantee of freedom of expression," an economist recently wrote in a critique of the Canadian regime for the Fraser Institute. "Freedom of expression has two sides. The first side is the right of the speaker ... to say what they want to say, subject to very, very few constraints ... The second side is the right of people on the other side of the exchange: listeners, readers, viewers, and 'consumers' of what is expressed—that is the freedom to be informed ... If the Canadian government is allowed to constrain the nationality of programs on TV and musical recordings on radio, we can ask if it will stop there."

The premise is quite true. Freedom of expression is meaningful only when paired in practice with a corresponding freedom to hear or view what is expressed. But the writer's conclusion ignores two key distinctions, to say nothing of a globally evident empirical reality.

The first critical distinction is that between *categories* of programming and the *content* of that programming. A second is between positive quotas, designed to *enhance* audience choice, and negative quotas, designed to *restrict* choice. Both underlie the evident difference between the lively diversity of views in open democracies that employ reasonable measures to preserve pluralism of expression and the monologues of truly repressive regimes.

Courts and constitutional litigants have been readier to perceive the distinctions. It is telling, in fact, that the compatibility of broadcast quotas with democratic guarantees of freedom of expressions has rarely been challenged. No constitutional objection has been raised in the United States against the children's educational programming quota, for instance. Nor have the broadcast quotas imposed pursuant to the 1989 "Television Without Frontiers" directive been challenged in Europe. Where cases have gone to court, judgements have failed to find substance in the spectral threat that quotas are alleged to pose to freedoms of expression.

The 1982 Supreme Court of Canada case referred to earlier, for instance, upheld the legality of quotas for Canadian drama against a statutory protection for freedom of expression. There has never been a submission to the court that those quotas fail the test of the Canadian Charter of Rights and Freedoms, which came into force as a part of Canada's constitution later the same year.

In the United States, a series of cases invoked the constitutionally guaranteed freedom of expression to challenge the FCC's requirement that cable systems "must carry" local TV signals. In 1997, the U.S. Supreme Court upheld the rules. A majority of the court found that although they were premised on support for a particular *category* of content (local broadcasts), the rules were "content neutral" because they did not discriminate on the basis of program message or speaker identity. Hence, "must carry" did not offend free speech.

The lesson from both the Canadian and American jurisprudence is clear. It is nonsense to suggest that the identification of a category, such as drama, is prescriptive of the point of view, opinion, theme, style or aesthetics of any particular content within that category. That determination, the choice of what specific expressions to put to air, is left entirely to the broadcaster. If the broadcaster chooses a program no one wants to watch, that is its responsibility. Self-interest suggests that, to the contrary, a rational broadcaster will choose the programs that are most likely to attract the largest or highest-value audience possible.

The implication for regulators is similarly plain. Broadcast quotas that focus on program categories and not on particular program content are benign with respect to freedom of expression. Quotas should simply establish the equivalent of a minimal amount of "shelf space" for at-risk program categories—drama, children's, documentary, feature film. They should be silent as to whether any particular program should or should not be aired. In this respect, defensible quotas are more like requirements for nature preserves than edicts that everyone should keep a mountain goat in their backyard.

This lesson is also relevant to the problem discussed in Chapter 7, of defining what is "local" and what is "foreign." To the extent that regulations use the *subject* of a program as the test for national origin rather than the *citizenship* of the creators or the locus of artistic control, they risk violating freedom of expression. (This does not, however, exclude the use of more subjective factors in awarding subsidies, which are generally subject to lesser constitutional tests.)

The second important distinction the quota critics choose to ignore is between *positive* quotas that seek to give audiences a choice of certain underrepresented but valued content, without unduly limiting access to other programs, and *negative* quotas that effectively prohibit access to a diversity of cultural expression.

Quotas like the U.S. children's programming requirement or the European "Television Without Frontiers" directive are examples of positive quotas. These measures are *inclusive,* not *exclusive.* No content is prohibited. Rather, room on the menu is assured for additional choices that would not normally be provided by the pursuit of maximum corporate profit and the peculiar market behaviour of cultural products.

A quota like the Chinese rule limiting the import of Hollywood films to no more than twenty a year, on the other hand, is an example of a negative quota. It *excludes* foreign cultural products far more than necessary to make room for local cultural expression.

The profound difference between the two is apparent in the real world outside the critics' alarmed imaginations. Scan the television dial in Canada, the United States, Australia, Britain or France—all of which, as we have noted, employ some form of positive quotas—and it is immediately evident why these states set the international standard for freedom of expression, not oppression.

Consider once more the requirement that commercial broadcasters in the United States air three hours per week of educational children's programming between 7 AM and 10 PM. Nothing constrains the subjects they can address in that three hours (except that they must serve "the educational and informational needs of children"). And each broadcaster has more than one hundred hours per week in the same time period that are *not* subject to the quota. It cannot be seriously argued that this materially affects their freedom of expression—indeed, as noted above, the argument has not been attempted in a constitutional setting. Neither can one argue that these programs are forced on "unwilling viewers" when the quota exists solely in response to an evident demand for a highly valued program genre that would otherwise not be presented. From a viewer's perspective, the requirement enhances choice where otherwise there would be little or none.

That said, the regulator's task of identifying underrepresented program categories and determining an appropriate requirement is not simple. Quotas need to be both responsive to demand and achievable. The correct balance—just as with wildlife—will be different in each country and change over time. It is likely to require independent research as well as extensive consultation with industry and the public.

Quotas will enjoy their strongest case when local creators are able to demonstrate two conditions: first, that their work serves a public interest; and second, that market forces prevent them from reaching their audience. Where those conditions are met, quotas can serve rather than impede freedom of expression.

WHAT IS PLAIN from the foregoing is that the most frequently raised objections to the use of quotas are deficient.

The evidence of every developed democracy refutes the assertion that the quotas are inherently anti-democratic, coercive or destructive of free speech.

The experiences of Europe and Australia—especially in contrast to that of New Zealand—contradict the charge that quotas are ineffective or generate only mediocre programming.

The record in Canada demonstrates that quotas can be adapted to evolving circumstances and technologies. On the other hand, the Canadian experience also argues that while quotas may be necessary to a diverse choice of high-value cultural expression on television, they are not *sufficient* for its viability.

In sum, intelligently structured quotas, customized as necessary, can have a significant positive effect in mitigating the perverse outcomes for domestic cultures of the unique economics of creative goods. But they are neither panacea nor silver bullet in defence of cultural security.

Quota regulations, in fact, are only one tool in the policy box. To achieve a lively degree of cultural diversity, they may need to be combined with other tools. We will examine several more in the chapters ahead.

10

SPENDING
RULES

THE PREVIOUS CHAPTER revealed how content quotas for broad-casters can pry open schedules to ensure that diverse cultural ex-pression reaches the screen. But while time may be money, quantity is emphatically *not* quality. Programmers locked into the pur-suit of profit will still find it in their interest to fill quota-mandated time slots in their schedules at the lowest possible cost. The result may be a nominal diversity at the expense of anything worth watching.

One of the earliest and most infamous examples of this truism oc-curred in the United Kingdom as it struggled to emerge from the wreckage of the First World War. That conflict broke out barely thirty-six months after the exhibition (in Paris) of the world's first motion-picture feature. By the time the war ended, four years later, much of western Europe was in ruins. Britain's nascent movie business, like the rest of its economy, was in tatters. And Hollywood's pioneering film-makers had stolen a march on their European rivals from which the latter would never recover.

American studios captured British audiences with technically so-phisticated films. Backed by the U.S. Congress, they also strong-armed British cinema-owners into accepting block-booking agreements that further served to shut out local producers. By 1925, only 5 per cent of the films shown in Britain were British.

Within three years, the U.K. government took action to secure the cinema front. In 1928, it imposed a statutory obligation on film distributors and exhibitors to screen a minimum number of British films. The minimum quota started at 5 per cent of the total of British and foreign films acquired and screened, increasing progressively to 20 per cent by 1936. That line would waver back and forth, but essentially it would hold until 1982.

And at first, the legislation seemed to be effective. A number of talented British producers emerged in the early 1930s, making ambitious films that reached international markets.

But this success was soon clouded by a strategy universally adopted by the U.S.-owned film distributors who were active in Britain. As a group, they opted to fill their domestic British quotas with what were called "second features" in the United Kingdom and what were known in North America as B movies. In decades when the major U.S. studios were spending between £40,000 and £65,000 (at then-current exchange rates) to make a typical film in Hollywood, their British subsidiaries received an average of just £5,400—about one tenth as much to make each movie. Necessarily produced on the cheap with limited sets and production schedules, the films they made were generally greeted with derision. Contemptuous critics took to dismissing them as "quota quickies."

In 1938, the British government sought to end the "quickie" problem by revising its legislation. A new rule set a minimum budget for quota films. To qualify under the new quota, a British film had to incur labour costs of at least £7,500. And there was a bonus arrangement for movies made on even higher budgets. If a film cost at least £22,500, it would count for twice its actual running time in calculating compliance with the quota. A film with over £37,500 in labour costs could be counted *three* times.

The studios resisted the change, and to some effect. American pressure led to a reduction in the overall exhibition quota from 20 per cent of screen time to only 12.5 per cent. Coupled with the quota multiple for higher-budget productions, the concession made it much easier for Hollywood's U.K. subsidiaries to comply with the system by producing far fewer films. Those few, however, were also usually much better funded than the "quickies" that had gone before.

During the following decade, less (in time-quota terms) would turn out to be more for the British film industry. Two major studios emerged, and through the 1940s the Rank and Ealing organizations produced a wide range of successful films. Developments at the end of the decade bolstered their resources.

In 1949, Labour prime minister Clement Atlee created a National Film Finance Corporation (NFFC). A year later, he introduced a tax on cinema tickets that was designed to divert some money from Hollywood's revenue stream into the pockets of British filmmakers. Charged on all admissions, the "Eady Plan" (named after Atlee's finance minister) rewarded U.K. producers with payments based on the box-office gross achieved by their previous film.

The next twenty-five years are seen by many as the golden era of British moviemaking. In the 1950s, 1960s and into the 1970s, hundreds of popular British films were nursed into production with the support of the quota, ticket tax and NFFC.

In the 1980s, Margaret Thatcher's government did away with all three incentives. Britain abandoned the screen quota in 1982. A Films Act passed three years later abolished the NFFC and Eady Levy. Moviemaking in Britain has subsequently plunged back into a state of serial crises.

It is interesting to note that for all the scorn heaped on the quota quickies of the 1930s, a kinder view has emerged more recently. Reviewers of their own era typically condemned them as "unwatched and unwatchable." But after looking at them again, at least one contemporary critic has suggested that they "represent a corpus of British films which are constantly surprising in their ability to entertain, intrigue, engage and fascinate any historian with a little imagination and a passion for the popular culture of the 1930s."

But whatever the enduring value of Britain's inter-war B movies, the lesson for policy-makers is plain. Any cultural policy that requires only *quantity* may fail, if it can be satisfied by work produced on the cheap without regard for *quality*.

The lesson applies equally to broadcasting. To avoid cost, broadcasters subject to an overall transmission quota will inevitably turn to news, sports and game shows instead of investing in expensive local drama. One response, discussed in Chapter 9, is to implement a quota specifically for drama or other underrepresented program categories.

Britain's history suggests a different strategy.

A growing number of countries have taken a leaf from the U.K. experience and are turning to *minimum expenditure* quotas. Instead of setting a quota on the number of hours of defined programming a broadcaster airs, these set a quota on the number of dollars a broadcaster spends on the target genre.

Implicit in such rules is the notion that it takes real money to create good programs. That is not to say money can't be wasted on programs that end up being unwatchable—or that great actors can't occasionally bring a brilliant script to life on a skinny budget. Nor is it the case that all fiction programs require the same minimum budget. Soap operas, with sets amortized over many seasons, few rehearsals and assembly-line production, cost far less per hour to produce than do other episodic drama series. Movies of the week, by contrast, cost much more.

But few observers would quibble with the general rule that, other things being equal, higher production budgets that reach the screen make a difference that is clearly apparent to viewers. For evidence, just compare the cinematic results of *West Wing's* us$4 million per episode to the inevitably less extravagant programs made in Canada, Britain or Australia on budgets typically a sixth to, at best, a third of that amount.

By establishing a minimum expenditure for high-priority genres such as fiction, a regulator can at least begin to level the playing field by deterring the sacrifice of quality for quantity.

There are many ways to calculate the minimum expenditure. It may be set as a portion of "turnover"—either advertising or subscription revenue, or both. It may be a percentage of the programming budget. It may even be a specified minimum number of dollars that must be spent per year, subject to adjustment if the broadcaster's earnings are sharply higher or lower than expected.

The requirement may vary with the size of the undertaking. It may be fixed or increase steadily over time. Sometimes expenditure rules are used *instead* of scheduling quotas. Sometimes, they are used *in addition to* scheduling quotas.

All of the foregoing are legitimate choices. Deciding which of them—or which combination—to deploy will depend on the circumstances of the country as well as of the licensees to whom they will be directed. All—and more—have been tested in a number of countries around the world.

A GOOD EXAMPLE of the application of content and expenditure quotas can be found in article 5 of the European Union's "Television Without Frontiers" directive. That provision compels EU members (and non-EU signatories to the directive) to require broadcasters to reserve at least 10 per cent of their transmission time for European works created by independent producers. But the article also gives regulators an alternative. Instead of setting a 10 per cent of *time* quota, countries can require broadcasters to reserve at least 10 per cent of their programming *budget* for such works. While most countries have elected to impose the 10 per cent of airtime requirement for independent productions (in the case of the United Kingdom, the minimum is set at 25 per cent), some countries have adopted the alternative.

France has gone furthest. To meet the requirement of the directive, French free-to-air broadcasters must invest at least 10 per cent of their previous year's net turnover in independent European productions. In addition, all terrestrial channels must invest at least 17 per cent of the same base in acquired shows produced specifically in French, as well as at least 3 per cent in feature-length European works (of which 2.5 per cent must have been produced in French). All broadcasters are also required to set aside 5.5 per cent of their income, whether from advertising, subscription or licence fees, to be paid into an investment fund for French feature films run by the Centre National de la Cinématographie (CNC).

Some services are subject to specific requirements. Encrypted pay-channel Canal+, which relies especially heavily on feature-length programming, must spend 25 per cent of its cash flow on broadcast licences for European films, of which 75 per cent should be produced in French. Public-service broadcasters France 2 and France 3 also have individual quotas of 11.5 per cent of cash flow that must be spent on independent productions. Cable and satellite channels have the option to dedicate 10 per cent of either their airtime or their acquisition budget to independent productions.

Other EU members place more limited requirements on their broadcasters.

All Italian commercial channels must spend 40 per cent of their advertising revenue on European or Italian feature films. Public broadcaster RAI must do the same with 20 per cent of the licence fees it receives. As well, Italian broadcasters are obligated to invest at least

10 per cent of their previous year's advertising profit in either in-house or acquired European children's programming.

In addition to their obligations under the "Television Without Frontiers" directive, Spanish broadcasters are mandated to earmark 5 per cent of their previous year's revenue for financing European feature films and movies-of-the-week.

In Sweden, Finland, Denmark and Iceland, individual broadcasters may make their own choice under the directive: 10 per cent of time or 10 per cent of their acquisition budget for "independent" European works. In Iceland, private broadcasters are also required to devote 10 per cent of their ad revenue to a fund for the production of cultural and educational programming.

Australia has also moved to enact a mandatory expenditure requirement on its pay-TV broadcasters in recent years. After an earlier voluntary expectation was ineffective, the Australian broadcasting authority moved in 2000 to require all "predominantly drama" pay-services to devote 10 per cent of their program acquisition budget to new Australian productions. Channels that fail to reach the target in any given year must meet the unmet portion of their obligation in the following year.

It is intriguing to note that the idea of expenditure requirements has even surfaced in the United States, although it has not taken hold there. In 1998, a commission led by then vice-president Al Gore produced a report, *Charting the Digital Broadcasting Future,* that proposed a measure it dubbed "pay or play." It would have placed an obligation on private broadcasters either to produce and air a certain minimum amount of public-interest programming or to pay other broadcasters in their market to provide equivalent programming.

CANADA HAS the world's most complex expenditure requirements for broadcasters. The country introduced its first such requirement more than twenty years ago. The system has evolved since then to tailor specific requirements to the circumstances of each Canadian broadcaster.

The first expenditure quota was introduced in 1982, with the licensing in Canada of pay-TV premium movie services. The quota was set as a fixed percentage of subscription revenue that was to be spent on acquiring Canadian programming. But when the number of subscribers who signed up for those early services failed to match rosy predictions, the licensees sought relief from the quota burden. In 1987, the services persuaded the CRTC to reduce, but not eliminate, the expenditure obligation.

The mandate, however, remains in place. The current rules for pay television services in Canada, updated most recently in 2001, require licensees to spend a specified percentage of their subscription revenues on Canadian programming. The percentage starts at 22 per cent and increases to 32 per cent as the number of subscribers to the service increases.

Over the twenty years from 1982 to 2002, the CRTC licensed dozens of new specialty-television services for carriage on analog cable systems. On almost every one, it imposed both Canadian scheduling requirements and program expenditure requirements.

Obligations derived under this formula have typically ranged between 35 per cent and 45 per cent of gross income. The lowest current commitment is 32 per cent, for TreeHouse; the highest is 71 per cent, for Life Network. Tables 10.1, 10.2 and 10.3 set out both the expenditure and scheduling requirements for a number of Canadian pay and specialty services.

TABLE 10.1: *Local Content Requirements Applicable to Canadian English-Language Analog Specialty Programming Services*

Name of Service	Genre of Service	Local Program Scheduling Quota for Broadcast Day (6 AM–midnight) (%)	Local Program Scheduling Quota for Evening Hours (6 PM–midnight) (%)	Local Program Expenditures Quota (% of Previous Year's Revenue)	Total Revenue from Advertising and Subscriptions (2002) (C$)
Bravo!	Arts/culture	60%	50%	33%	$28.7 million
Canadian Learning Television	Adult education	60%	50%	36%	$9.2 million
CBC Newsworld	News and information	90%	90%	—	$68.1 million
The Comedy Network	Comedy	58%	72%	41%	$29.6 million

Country Music Television	Country music videos	60%	50%	22%	$14.2 million
CTV Newsnet	Headline news	100%	100%	—	$12.7 million
The Discovery Channel	Nature and science	60%	50%	45%	$56.6 million
Food Network Canada	Food and nutrition	50%	50%	40%	$13.3 million
HGTV Canada	Home and garden	50%	50%	50%	$21.7 million
History Television	History	50%	33%	34%	$22.5 million
Life Network	Lifestyle information	82.5%	82.5%	71%	$30.7 million
MuchMusic	Teenage music video	60%	50%	—	$44.9 million
MuchMoreMusic	Adult contemp. video	60%	50%	—	$11.2 million
Outdoor Life	Outdoor recreation	30%	30%	37%	$11.4 million
PrimeTV	Seniors (50+)	50%	50%	40%	$24.7 million
Pulse 24	Local news	90%	90%	—	$6.2 million
Report on Business TV	Business/finance news	75%	75%	50%	$14.9 million
The Score	Headline sports	80%	60%	45%	$17.4 million
Showcase	Can./overseas fiction	60%	60%	42%	$34.6 million
Space: The Imagination Station	Science fiction	50%	40%	40%	$32.9 million
The Sports Network (TSN)	National sports	55%	60%	44%	$173.6 million
Sportsnet	Regional sports	60%	50%	54%	$95.6 million
Star TV	Entertainment news	35%	30%	39%	$12.0 million
TalkTV	Talk programs	68%	71%	36%	$3.0 million

TELETOON	Animation	60%	60%	40%	$55.4 million
TreeHouse	Pre-school children	70%	60%	32%	$9.0 million
Vision TV	Religious	60%	60%	45%	$15.5 million
W	Women's	70%	60%	41%	$38.4 million
The Weather Network	Weather	100%	100%	37%	$36.8 million
YTV	Children's/youth	60%	60%	35%	$80.2 million

TABLE 10.2: *Local Content Requirements Applicable to Canadian French-Language Analog Specialty Programming Services*

Name of Service	Genre of Service	Local Program Scheduling Quota for Broadcast Day (6 AM–midnight) (%)	Local Program Scheduling Quota for Evening Hours (6 PM–midnight) (%)	Local Program Expenditures Quota (% of Previous Year's Revenue)	Total Revenue from Advertising and Subscriptions (2002) (C$)
ARTV	Arts/culture	50%	50%	46%	$8.8 million
Canal D	Documentaries, films and performing arts	45%	45%	40%	$23.2 million
Canal Evasion	Tourism and adventure	60%	60%	50%	$3.5 million
Le Canal Nouvelles	Headline news	100%	100%	—	$14.3 million
Canal Vie	Lifestyle, health and outdoor	50%	60%	45%	$25.9 million
Canal Z	Science, nature and exploration	50%	40%	48%	$7.3 million
Historia	History	40%	40%	35%	$5.9 million
Météomédia	Weather	100%	100%	37%	$36.8 million
Musimax	Adult contemporary video	60%	60%	—	$6.9 million

MusiquePlus	Teenage music video	60%	—	—	$14.5 million
RDI	News/information	90%	90%	—	$40.8 million
RDS	Sports	65%	60%	50%	$63.9 million
Séries+	Canadian/ overseas fiction	25%	25%	22%	$9.8 million
TELETOON	Animation	60%	60%	40%	$55.4 million
TV-5	Francophonie	15%	15%	40%	$14.0 million
VRAK-TV	Children's/youth	60%	—	35%	$16.8 million

TABLE 10.3: *Local Content Requirements Applicable to Canadian Movie-Based Pay Television Services*

Name of Service	Language	Nature of Service	Region	Local Program Scheduling Quota (%)	Local Program Expenditures Quota (% of Previous Year's Revenue)	Total Revenue from Subscriptions in 2002 (C$)
Family Channel	English	Disney/family	National	25%	30%	$41.5 million
Movie Central	English	Recent movies	West	30% (6p–11p); 25% otherwise	31%	$61.4 million
MovieMax!	English	Older movies	West	20%	25%	$10.7 million
MoviePix	English	Older movies	East	20%	25%	$16.3 million
Super Ecran	French	Recent movies	National	30% (6p–11p); 25% otherwise	24%	$39.2 million
The Movie Network (TMN)	English	Recent movies	East	30% (6p–11p); 25% otherwise	32%	$77.0 million

These requirements have been widely accepted by Canadian broadcasters. And as we will see, they have contributed enormously to a sustained increase in Canadian audiovisual production across most genres of programming. Still, the CRTC's experience with expenditure requirements begs a number of comments.

A critical point is that the requirements were generally imposed following a competitive bidding process. In that process, more than one applicant seeks a licence to operate a specialty service in a particular format, but the CRTC selects only one winner. The effect is to create an auction scenario in which a higher commitment to Canadian content weighs positively in a bidder's prospect of success. An applicant that purposely lowballs its proposed spending on Canadian programs to avoid being saddled with the expenses if it wins the licence may lose out to an applicant who promises more Canadian content. The result is that the expenditure requirement that eventually comes into force is set at the highest level that is considered realistic by applicants.

Further, the process does not produce a one-time ruling. The CRTC has the authority to amend any broadcaster's expenditure requirement every five years to take account of changing circumstances.

BUT JUST as profit-maximizing broadcasters will find it in their interest to minimize the impact on their bottom line from scheduling quotas, they will also be strongly motivated to interpret expenditure requirements in whatever way they believe will least reduce their income. If requirements are to be meaningful, therefore, regulators must anticipate and counter the most likely gambits for avoidance.

These are limited otherwise only by a broadcaster's ingenuity.

A requirement that only vaguely specifies what rights it applies to may invite a broadcaster to buy rights to a program for more than its own territory. This allows the company to attribute the full gross cost of those rights against its quota obligation while offsetting the expense against sales outside the territory. This lowers the effective net cost to the broadcaster and reduces its real spending obligation.

Arbitrary cost allocations can also make expenditure rules difficult to apply. For example, a broadcaster might buy a package of local and foreign programs from a particular distributor for a flat sum. If the broadcaster then attributes most of the expense to the local programs included in the package, it gets credit for money actually spent on foreign productions. Similarly, a broadcaster operating two services (both a free-to-air and a satellite specialty channel, for instance), only one of them subject to a spending requirement, might buy rights to air a show on both services. But if it allocates most of the cost to the one with the spending obligation, it inflates its credit while artificially boosting the profit of the other service.

This hardly exhausts the possibilities. Creative broadcasters can take equity in the production of a local film they plan to air, claim that investment as an expense, then later recoup the money from foreign sales. Alternatively money may be loaned to a local producer; the loan is repaid later with interest, but meanwhile it is also claimed towards an expenditure requirement.

In Canada, after a number of examples of double-counting had come to its attention, the CRTC moved in 1993 to rein in a variety of avoidance techniques. The agency issued a public notice clarifying what would qualify as an "expenditure." The policy required broadcasters to claim only costs that a "reasonable allocation" could attribute to programs actually aired to Canadian audiences, "net of recoveries from sales," "after recognition of recoupments" and with any payments to related companies accounted for "at no more than cost." These rules were not perfect—the concept of "reasonable" allocation allows for considerable subjective scope, even when auditors are involved—but they did effectively eliminate most "double counting."

Creative accounting to minimize expenditure requirements is not unique to Canada. In the United Kingdom, for example, the government for a period imposed a higher tax rate on profits from broadcasting than on other businesses. The privately owned ITV companies quickly realized that it would make sense to claim as a "broadcasting" expense all the production costs of their domestic drama programs, even though a significant portion of those costs was recovered from export sales. An economist analyzing the situation could defensibly conclude that the cost to be attributed to the export market was the minimal expense of setting up a sales office and duplicating the tape, not the sunk cost of producing the original program. On this basis, the business of "domestic broadcasting" bore all the production expenses and produced little profit on which to pay the higher tax. In contrast, the business of international TV program sales bore none of the costs, made a huge profit and was taxed at the ordinary rate. The loser was the U.K. exchequer.

That loopholes in expenditure requirements can be closed, however, does not mean they have escaped controversy. Broadcasters, not to put too fine a point on it, are hardly thrilled to be told how much money they must spend—especially when a condition of the expense is that it not be recouped.

Requiring that Canadian pay- and specialty-TV services commit a certain level of expenditures to Canadian programs has been generally well accepted. The idea of applying comparable spending mandates to free-to-air TV stations has been more hotly contested. In 1986 and 1987, the CRTC did apply an expenditures requirement to the major free-to-air private television owners, Global and CTV. Then in 1989, it applied the concept to *all* major local television stations as part of their licence-renewal decisions.

In 1999, however, the CRTC once again reviewed all of these rules and issued a new omnibus television policy. To the disappointment of independent producers, it dropped the annual expenditure requirements for the free-to-air TV stations. In place of the general expenditure requirement, it implemented a scheduling sub-quota requiring eight hours per week of "priority" programming to be broadcast from 7 to 11 PM. By 2003, however, that policy was increasingly subject to criticism. English-language private free-to-air TV broadcasters had lowered their expenditures on Canadian drama, increased the use of documentaries and drama repeats to fill their scheduling quota, and spent more than ever before on new U.S. drama series. In the face of disappointing ratings for Canadian English-language drama series, the CRTC, having commissioned a number of studies on the matter, sought comments on possible new approaches to address the problems of Canadian drama in the fall of 2003.

The situation was different for the pay and specialty programming services. The 1999 television policy continued to require expenditure obligations of those services along with scheduling rules. Their contribution to Canadian programming has steadily risen along with their success. In renewal hearings for the services in 2002 and 2003, the commission generally sought increases in the percentages to be expended on Canadian content and was pressed by interveners to eliminate reporting loopholes.

GIVEN THEIR COMPLEXITY and apparent susceptibility to creative accounting, are expenditure rules worth the trouble? Can well-drafted spending mandates actually result in a net increase in the production of diverse, domestic and local television programs of high quality? Do they, in brief, *work?*

A comparison of experience in the two countries where the mechanism is most fully developed—France and Canada—is instructive.

France has by far the most sweeping obligations. Its broadcasters, in consequence, pour a large and steady stream of investment into French film and television. According to an examination of French and Italian film funding conducted by Eurocinema, a regional film-development agency, "Of approximately FF1.2 billion [c$300 million] invested per annum in France, 48 per cent comes from obligations levied on the different free-to-air channels." Separately, Canal+ spends £100 million a year on European production, contributing a quarter of all annual investment in French film.

Carole Tongue, in a survey of public service broadcasting in OECD countries, noted: "In France, investment obligations on television channels are much more important financially than any other form of support for film production. The advantage is that the film industry is guaranteed high and stable resources." It is probably not coincidental that, as Tongue also noted, "In 2001, France was the only EU country to achieve over 50 per cent cinema box office admissions for its own national films."

The Canadian experience with pay-television has also been positive. Since the first movie-based pay-television channels were licensed in 1982, the five Canadian pay-services have expended more than $250 million on Canadian feature film and other Canadian programs. Over the years, they have exhibited virtually every feature film produced in Canada. In 2002, the pay-services spent a collective amount of $43.2 million—the largest single private source of feature-film investment in Canada. This support is projected to rise significantly in the decade ahead, in step with growing subscriptions and escalating conditions of licence.

Experience with specialty programming services in Canada has been even more striking. Overall, these services spent more than $584 million on Canadian programming in 2002, out of total revenue of $1.37 billion. Their acquisitions have anchored the creation of an enormous volume of diverse programming for particular audiences.

Four services that broadcast to children as a major part of their mandate—YTV, TELETOON, TreeHouse and Family Channel—

together spent $57.4 million in 2002 on shows produced in Canada. YTV, for one, airs series that range from the high-tech cyber-fantasy of *Reboot* and teen-life-oriented *Girl Stuff/Boy Stuff*, to the quintessentially Canadian *Yvon of the Yukon* (the Popeye-meets-Beavis adventures of a 300-year-old frozen fur-trader who is freed from the northern permafrost when a husky pees on him).

History Television spent $6.4 million in 2002 airing accounts of Canadian current and historical events. Domestic content on its schedule has ranged from retellings of the epic adventures of real-life coureurs de bois (the original Yvons), through retrospectives on the Klondike gold rush to contemporary subjects such as the experience of Canadians at war in Afghanistan.

The Discovery Channel's $21.8 million Canadian programming expenditure focuses on science and nature. Among other projects, veteran Canadian science reporter Jay Ingram has explored how *Castor canadensis*—the Canadian beaver whose pelts those same coureurs-de-bois so avidly sought—has radically transformed the Canadian landscape. On a combined basis, Life Network (*Weird Homes*), HGTV Canada (*Mark Cullen Gardening*) and Food Canada (*Inn Chef*, shot on location in Prince Edward Island) spent $29.5 million in 2002 on Canadian programs about food, home, gardens and hobbies.

The French-language specialty services have also contributed to diversity in Canada. Services like ARTV, Canal Vie, Canal Z, Historia, Series+ and VRAK-TV spent $39 million in 2002 on French-language programs made in Canada about the arts, lifestyle, science, nature, history and children's issues, all pursuant to the spending obligations spelled out in their conditions of licence.

Some of these programs are exported around the world. Others are not, but nonetheless enrich the experience of Canadian viewers with stories that have a strong but purely local resonance.

Greater controversy has surrounded the relaxation in 1999 of expenditure requirements specifically directed at Canadian free-to-air television broadcasters. As noted earlier, private TV broadcasters in English Canada have been criticized for reducing their expenditures on original high-cost Canadian dramas and focusing more on lower-cost drama and documentary productions.

The problems faced by Canadian drama are more complex than this, however. Two related trends in North American broadcasting have conspired to erode the status of mid-budget drama series. Lavishly financed series like *West Wing, c.s.i.* and *The Agency* have sharply raised the standard of production values by which audiences judge television drama. Broadcasters everywhere have reacted by scheduling fewer, albeit more expensive such shows, and filling the air with cheap but popular "reality TV" fare. As investment thus gravitates to the extremes of program quality, it has become even more difficult for comparatively low-budget local series to compete.

Nonetheless, expenditure rules in Canada and France, carefully crafted to be realistic, meaningful and enforceable, have proven to be a powerful instrument in the tool kit of measures that can maintain or enhance cultural diversity. Equally: when that tool has been put away, domestic voices have paid a price.

11

NATIONAL
OWNERSHIP

O NE OF THE best-known brands in Canada appears on the
nation's oldest private television chain. Red, blue and green
banners ripple in an invisible wind. A booming baritone an-
nounces: "C.T.V.—*Canadian* television." The emphasis on the middle
word is pronounced. But so is the disconnect.

The CTV network does present some well-known Canadian television programs. On Wednesday nights at 8:30 PM, for example,
Degrassi: The Next Generation lights up the screen. And CTV's national
newscast, presented every night at 11 PM, is the highest-rated news
program in the country. But most of the prime-time hours on CTV,
like those on the other private English-language TV stations across
Canada, are devoted to programs from another country. CTV's colourful flowing banners are frequently mixed with the images of U.S. stars
from series like *The West Wing* or *Law & Order*. And most of CTV's
audience is for those imported programs.

So, *Canadian* television? The claim begs a little explanation. What
CTV *is,* of course, is a Canadian-*owned* television network.

But ownership, national identity and significance to the diversity of
culture do not always line up neatly in place. It is possible, as was discussed in Chapter 7, to draw conflicting conclusions from the citizenship of a particular work's creators, the ownership of its production

company, the source of financing behind it, the story line or imagery, even the locus of filming or recording.

The citizenship of the corporations that serve as delivery channels, intermediaries, "green lights" or bottlenecks between creators and consumers of cultural goods is often no easier to determine with certainty. Even less their loyalty.

Yet of all the public-policy devices intended to secure national culture against foreign domination, none is more nearly universal than controls, limits or the outright prohibition of "foreign" ownership of important national media, especially broadcasting.

Most countries in the world insist that their free-to-air radio and TV stations be owned and controlled by their own citizens. This is true for many nations in Europe, Africa, Asia and the Americas. In South America, the list includes countries like Argentina, Brazil and Venezuela. Australia and South Africa both do it. So do Mexico and Canada, the North American Free Trade Agreement signed between them notwithstanding.

Even that champion of bare-knuckle free enterprise, the United States, restricts conventional broadcasting to its own nationals. "Originally," one observer has noted, "the U.S. government feared that foreign ownership of radio broadcast stations would lead to the dissemination of subversive propaganda, the conveyance of sensitive military information to foreign enemies and the possible interference with the government's military transmissions."

"Today," argues another observer, the U.S. national ownership policy "represents an anachronistic attempt to limit free speech in America based on xenophobic fears of foreign ideas and influence."

The United States does not restrict the ownership of satellite-delivered pay- or specialty-subscription television programming services. In the American view, those are not "broadcasting" services. But many other countries—Canada among them—disagree, and they require such services to obtain a broadcasting licence and abide by foreign-investment limits.

Many nations limit foreign investment in other cultural sectors. Some limit the foreign ownership of retail bookstores. In Quebec, local ownership of bookstores is encouraged by a rule (Bill 51) that compels public libraries to buy their books at full price from Quebec-owned bookstores. Other countries require the local ownership of cinemas.

But apart from broadcasting, the most common restriction is on the ownership of newspapers. Australia limits the foreign ownership of "mass circulation" newspapers to 30 per cent—with no single foreign shareholder permitted to own more than 25 per cent. A number of European countries do not restrict media ownership narrowly to their own citizens, but do limit it to individual or corporate citizens of members of the European Union. Such rules are in force in Austria, France, Greece, Italy and Sweden. Canada does not restrict the foreign ownership of newspapers per se, but it achieves much the same result through tax legislation that disallows deductions for expenses incurred by Canadian companies targeting Canadian readers with ads in newspapers that are not Canadian-owned and -controlled.

National-ownership limits are hardly exotic. Historically, most nations have restricted foreign ownership in a variety of industrial sectors deemed important to national security, such as telephone companies, banks, airlines and oil or mining companies. It is hardly surprising that information and cultural enterprises—particularly broadcasting and newspapers—are also high on this list.

Over the years, however, many governments have loosened investment restrictions in some other sectors. A particular example is the telecommunications sector. Common carriers (telephone and data network systems) have historically been monopoly state enterprises in many countries. In the last decade, the sector has increasingly been opened up to foreign investment and competition, impelled in large measure by the 1995 WTO Basic Telecommunications Agreement.

Some countries have also relaxed or at least re-examined their limits on non-national ownership of media. New Zealand opened up its broadcast market to foreign owners in the early 1990s. Australia has flirted with the same idea, but by early 2003 it had not yet taken any action. Britain introduced legislation in 2002 to ease foreign-ownership restrictions in television. That same year, India, which had no restrictions on foreign ownership in television or Internet services, overturned a half-century-old policy limiting foreign investment in newspapers. It would henceforth allow foreigners to hold up to 26 per cent of a national newspaper company's stock and up to 74 per cent of a regional, scientific or technical publication. Even China, which restricts most other investments in its media and allows only twenty foreign films into its market each year, committed itself, as a condition of entry into the World Trade Organization, to allow foreigners to make joint-venture minority investments (up to 49 per cent) in movie theatres.

Russian legislators, meanwhile, voted in 2001 to reject a bill that would have curtailed foreign ownership in television networks, currently unrestricted to 49 per cent. The initiative had been sparked by reports that CNN's founder and Time Warner shareholder Ted Turner was considering buying the leading private Russian television channel, NTV.

Other nations do not limit non-national media ownership. In Europe, for instance, Belgium, Denmark, Finland, Germany, Ireland, Luxembourg, the Netherlands, Portugal and Spain permit unrestricted foreign media ownership. So does Japan by law, although in practice all five of its commercial TV networks are owned by or affiliated with one of its big five daily newspapers, whose entrenched corporate owners have staunchly resisted outside investors.

Yet broadcasting continues to be a sensitive sector for many nations. And as concern has heightened for the future of diverse cultural expression in the context of globalization, support for restricting broadcasting—and other cultural industries—to national ownership continues to be widely voiced.

The subject often arises in tandem with two related subjects: *concentration* of media ownership (few hands controlling much of a market's media) and *cross-media* ownership (that is, common control of many different media in the same market). Both raise alarm. The consequences of excessive horizontal as well as vertical corporate integration are examined in the following chapter.

The pages just ahead will consider whether the specifically *foreign* ownership of cultural industries threatens diversity of expression. They will review the arguments most commonly raised to make the case that it does pose a threat—as well as some evidence that points in the other direction.

THE DEBATE over foreign ownership and control is not, of course, unique to the cultural sector. There is a broad literature on foreign ownership generated as countries everywhere have grappled with foreign takeovers of domestic companies. Even the United States has not been immune—witness its decision, on national-security grounds, to quash the takeover of an American railroad by a Canadian one (or, more humorously, the opposition that arose to kill a foreign takeover of the much-loved Hershey candy brand).

With the rise of multinationals in every economic sector, concerns have centred on the retrenchment of research and development by subsidiaries, the loss of investment decision-making to remote head offices and the proverbial "giant sucking sound" of shop-floor jobs lost to lower-wage countries. As such transfers take place and formerly independent companies become mere units of multinational conglomerates, governments find their ability to recruit domestic industries in pursuit of domestic interests sharply constrained. Capital carries no passport. That raises troubling questions for national sovereignty.

Those questions are especially sharp for the cultural sector. As has been made clear throughout this account, stories are not neutral. Unlike capital, the most important stories often *do* carry a passport. The stories that speak intimately and resonantly to audiences in Nigeria will be different from those that evoke the deepest response in Finland. Some stories do speak powerfully to audiences in many countries and cultures, but they are of necessity keyed to the most general of human emotions. They cannot probe deeply into the "dreams, fears and folklore" of any particular culture or community, let alone explore its burning social or political issues of the day. Consequently, the question of who decides what story gets told, heard or seen is not a neutral one.

Why trust only a locally owned company with that decision? There are two main arguments.

The first asserts that a local firm is more likely than a foreign one to develop and nurture local creative expression. It is premised on the belief that a local company, closer to the ground and more sensitive to local tastes, interests and talent, will better reflect those realities. A foreign-controlled firm will tend to make its important decisions about the broadcast, sale or publication of cultural products in a distant headquarters, unfamiliar with those local facts and priorities, and motivated mainly by the pursuit of a global audience. In the result, local culture will suffer.

This was the view held in 2002 by a British parliamentary committee that opposed that country's easing of foreign-ownership limits on television broadcasting. The committee was chaired by respected British producer Lord David Puttnam, whose movie credits include *The Killing Fields, Chariots of Fire* and *Midnight Express.* "What is likely" at the hands of foreign owners, the committee forecast, "is a determined and sophisticated attempt—backed by enormous marketing expense—to shift away from domestic content produced primarily with a British audience in mind, towards a more internationally focused product mix. The inescapable reality is that a U.S. media company investing in the United Kingdom would be concerned every bit as much with enhancing the wide market value of its domestic [U.S.] content as with increasing its return on investment in the British marketplace."

Michael MacMillan, the chairman of Canada's Alliance Atlantis Communications, made similar points before a Canadian parliamentary committee examining the possibility of loosening Canada's foreign-ownership rules later the same year. "This is about attracting new shareholders who want active, strategic, operating control," MacMillan stated.

> If I were in their shoes, I would immediately want to program my Canadian channel as similarly as possible [to] my U.S. or my British or my German channel. I'd want to use as much as possible similar resources, same programming. Ideally, I'd want to amortize the cost across a wide audience. In our business, he who pays the piper calls the tune. Most of those programs would very naturally, predictably and properly be aimed at the largest audience where most of the cost is being paid.

The second argument in favour of restricting foreign ownership holds that a domestic firm is more likely to reinvest its profits in new works by local creators. This is particularly important in the casino of popular culture. As Chapter 4 noted, most books, sound recordings, TV shows and films are not commercial successes. Those few that are profitable must not only recoup the money lost on previous bad bets but finance future gambles. At the high stakes table of movie and TV fiction, script and concept ("development") financing—the showbiz equivalent of R&D—is particularly hard to raise and typically generated by prior successes. When the copyright and cash flow from one domestic winner wind up in foreign hands, so does the green light for future projects. Those foreign investors may simply take the money and run—or invest it in a project in some other country. Local firms with libraries of local hits, so the argument goes, are more likely to reinvest their profits in local creative expression.

These sound like compelling arguments. And on their strength, legislators and regulators in dozens of countries have imposed rules to keep cultural enterprises in local hands. But neither the rules nor the arguments have proven to be entirely watertight.

TYPICALLY, rules on foreign ownership limit the percentage of shares in certain kinds of companies to defined maxima. Australia, for instance, limits individual foreign holdings in pay-television services to 20 per cent, with a maximum combined foreign ownership of 35 per cent. But often there are other stipulations. The directors and officers of the local company, for instance, may have to be local citizens. Australia, again, allows up to a 20 per cent combined foreign shareholding in conventional TV licensees, but it also requires that 80 per cent of the affected broadcaster's board of directors be Australians. India allows foreign companies or individuals to own up to 26 per cent of a newspaper company—but only if an Indian citizen or corporation also owns a voting block of more than 26 per cent.

Such strict caps on local *ownership* would seem to ensure local *control*. But do they? Experience suggests that in this, as in the evasion of content and spending requirements, much ingenuity can be expended to make the reality depart from the appearance.

Imagine a local company in the book-retail business. A foreign company acquires 20 per cent of its shares. The remaining 80 per cent are owned by local citizens. This would appear to be an enterprise clearly locally owned and controlled. But what if the foreign investor is also in the book-distribution business and wants to expand into the local country? Does that change things?

Let's add a few more facts. The local company is eager to expand. To finance its ambitions, it borrows several million dollars from its 20 per cent foreign owner. But the financing comes with some conditions attached. Namely: the local company must acquire all of its books through a warehouse that is in the foreign country and is owned by the foreign company, and it must use the foreign company's computer system.

Who controls the operations of the local company now?

There are myriad other ways that a foreign company owning just 20 per cent of a local one, and complying strictly with all the legal rules, may nonetheless exert effective control over its nominally "independent" junior. The more critical question revolves not around who owns the shares, but around corporate governance. Who actually makes the decisions? Who has veto rights? Who determines the operating budget?

To answer those questions and ensure that limited foreign ownership also means effectively limited foreign control, governments need to include what lawyers refer to as a de facto control test. This requires a review of whether a foreign owner may be exerting control over a domestic company not just by owning a majority of the voting shares but by any other means. To make such a review effective in circumstances that may change, it is also necessary to set up a regime in which an independent arbiter can adjudicate instances on a case-by-case basis.

Even then, cases may not be clear. The determination of foreign corporate "control" has been at the heart of some of the past decade's most epic regulatory battles. One of those saw a succession of giant beverage and media companies gird for battle over a Canadian sports-TV channel.

The Sports Network (TSN) started out in 1984 as a fledgling TV sports service licensed by the CRTC. It was owned and controlled by the Labatt Brewing Co., a major Canadian brewer that at the time also had an interest in a number of professional sports teams and advertised heavily during televised sports events. Over the next ten years, TSN emerged as one of Canada's most popular and profitable channels, with over six million subscribers. TSN's fortunes particularly soared in 1987, when the CRTC allowed its English-language service to be distributed on basic cable and granted it a second licence to operate Réseau des Sports (RDS), a sister service in French.

After a decade in business, TSN in 1994 applied successfully for a licence to operate The Discovery Channel in Canada. TSN would own 80 per cent of the new operation. The other 20 per cent would belong to Discovery Communications Inc. (DCI), operator of The Discovery Channel and The Learning Channel in the United States.

There was only one glitch. DCI wanted a right of veto over the appointment or removal of the new channel's president. The CRTC approved the licence. But not before demanding to see a shareholders' agreement stipulating that DCI did *not* in fact possess any such executive veto.

That skirmish proved only to be the overture to what followed.

The following year a Belgian brewer, Interbrew, acquired Labatt in a takeover. Canadian law allowed a Belgian company to own a *brewery,* but not a *broadcasting company* in Canada. So what to do with TSN, RDS and The Discovery Channel?

TSN's Canadian management developed a solution: a takeover of TSN's name and broadcast assets in which they would own only a small percentage of the shares. Almost 80 per cent of the voting shares were divided among three Canadian investment groups. ESPN, the U.S. sports service whose programs the Canadian channel regularly distributed, would own another 20 per cent of the voting shares.

The Canadian government had forbidden the CRTC to issue broadcast licences to "non-Canadian" applicants. A licensee would be deemed "non-Canadian" if, after an inquiry, the agency determined it was "controlled by a non-Canadian, whether on the basis of personal, financial, contractual or business relations or any other consideration relevant to determining control." The wording was a classic example of a de facto control test.

The commission held a hearing to consider whether the proposed new ownership arrangement was acceptable. A few interveners expressed concern, but the CRTC approved the arrangement in 1996, subject to relatively minor change in the shareholders' agreement.

By 2001, however, TSN's Canadian investors wanted to take out their profits and leave the broadcasting field. The only investor that wanted to stay in was American-held ESPN. It had a strategic interest in owning part of Canada's most popular sports channel.

The Canadian owners shopped their interest around and found a willing buyer in CanWest Global, a Canadian company controlled by the Asper family. But ESPN was not happy with the choice, reportedly because of concern over Asper litigiousness. Under the shareholders' agreement that the CRTC had approved, ESPN had three months to find another qualified Canadian buyer willing to match the price CanWest had offered.

Enter CTV Inc., a Toronto company known until months earlier as Baton, which had recently acquired control of the CTV Network (it of the flowing red, blue and green logo). Baton–CTV had long coveted TSN. It happily agreed to take up all the Canadian shares that CanWest had spoken for. ESPN had found its Canadian dance partner.

But that was not to be the end of it. CTV already owned a 40 per cent interest in a competing sports channel, SportsNet. (In a delicious irony, 20 per cent of *that* channel was owned by Molson, another Canadian brewer, while Fox, an ESPN rival in the United States, also owned 20 per cent.) To satisfy competition concerns, CTV agreed to divest the less-lucrative SportsNet. (Eventually its interest and that of Molsons were acquired by Rogers Media).

The CRTC held yet another hearing to consider the licence transfer to CTV. This, however, also illuminated the terms the Canadian channel had conceded to its U.S. investor. CTV had agreed to change TSN's name to "ESPN Canada" or pay a penalty. Another clause allowed ESPN to shop the company around if CTV later wanted to sell its interest. The second point in particular troubled the CRTC. Was it altogether seemly that an American company could end up deciding who might own and control a Canadian sports service?

In the event, the Canadian regulator struck that clause out of the shareholders' agreement. It also moderated the terms of ESPN's leverage over the trademark licence before approving CTV's acquisition on March 24, 2000.

AN EVEN MORE contentious ownership proceeding took place in Australia and also involved CanWest Global. At stake were broadcast licences in five Australian cities: Sydney, Melbourne, Brisbane, Adelaide and Perth.

The Canadian company had first invested in Australian commercial television in late 1992, taking a minority position in the Ten Network. Australia, like Canada, prohibits a foreign "person" (natural or corporate) from being in a position to exercise control of a TV licence. And like Canada, Australia used a variant of the de facto test. In Australia, "control" was defined expansively: it included any case in which a person "is in a position to exercise, whether directly or indirectly, direction or restraint over any substantial issue affecting the management or affairs of the licensee or the company."

Following complaints from a former Ten Network employee, the Australian Broadcasting Authority (ABA) began an exhaustive investigation into whether CanWest was in a position of "control" over the Ten Network. The facts, on their face, suggested it was. While CanWest owned less than 15 per cent of the voting shares of holding company

The Ten Group Ltd. (TGL), it owned additional voting shares indirectly (a CanWest entity named Fulcrum Capital Corp. held shares in another Australian broadcast company, Telecasters North Queensland Ltd., which owned a piece of TGL). CanWest also owned thousands of non-voting shares as well as subordinate and convertible debentures that, combined, gave it what the ABA described as a "57 per cent economic interest" in TGL. Further, TGL had signed a consulting agreement with CanWest that gave the latter an advisory voice in the Australian network's management; and former CanWest president Stephen Gross had become a director and deputy chairman of the TGL board.

Notwithstanding those facts, the ABA, in a report issued in November 1995, found that CanWest "was not in a position to exercise direction or restraint over any substantial issue affecting the management of affairs" of Network Ten. Of the eleven directors on Ten's board, the report pointed out that nine were Australians, including the chairman. While the consultancy agreement (which had been terminated by 1995 in any case) gave CanWest a voice in Ten, that voice was advisory only; it did not convey a veto over any management decisions. The ABA added: "Neither Mr. Gross nor CanWest controlled the selection or the provision of programs broadcast by Ten."

Two years later, however, CanWest was back under the ABA's microscope. And in April 1997, the regulator reversed its earlier conclusion. Its report detailed a complex series of transactions late the previous year that had the result of delivering "52.49 per cent of the votes cast on a poll at a shareholders' meeting of the Ten Group Ltd." to an assortment of specially created shell companies all ultimately controlled by CanWest.

The ABA's investigators found that the previous autumn CanWest had incorporated one wholly owned subsidiary, Drie Sterren Kapitaal (Nederland) B.V., in the Netherlands and a series of others in Australia. The main entity in the latter group was named Selli Pty. Ltd. Between November 1996 and January 1997, CanWest had used the Dutch company, Drie Sterren, to finance a series of purchases of Ten Network stock from three TGL shareholders by Selli and its other Australian shells.

"The ABA found that the idea for setting up the structure which became Selli originated in CanWest," the regulator stated in a public release. "Selli is a special purpose company. Its function is to acquire and hold shares and other securities in the Ten Group Ltd. . . . CanWest is in a position to exercise control of the votes cast in the Ten Group Ltd. by Selli [and its subsidiaries] ... Adding these voting interests together gives CanWest a total voting interest of 52.49 per cent in The Ten Group Ltd."

The extent of that holding clearly exceeded what Australian law allowed. The ABA directed CanWest to remedy the breach of legislation.

CanWest initially appealed the ABA's conclusions. But when its appeals failed, the company executed a series of transactions to comply. Despite one hiccup, by August 1998, CanWest had finally brought itself into compliance with Australian law.

LABATT'S EXPERIENCE WITH TSN illustrates the unintended complications that can arise from ownership restrictions. The CanWest–Ten saga shows the corporate complexity that needs to be examined in order to make such restrictions effective. Yet a third story demonstrates the tortured projections of "nationality" to which they can lead.

This one involves the chameleon-like figure of Rupert Murdoch. Through his company, News Corp., the Melbourne-born mogul controls Fox Television and 20th Century–Fox movie studios in the United States, Britain's BSkyB and prestigious London *Times,* HarperCollins publishing, India's ZEE TV, Hong Kong's Star TV and dozens of lesser media holdings around the world.

Murdoch's ambiguous corporate citizenship has its roots in his appetite, beginning in the early 1980s, for a thick slice of the world's richest media pie, the United States. When Murdoch first acquired control of 20th Century–Fox in 1985, no ownership regulation stood in his way. No law requires Hollywood studios to be owned by U.S. citizens; indeed, foreign companies own a number of studios.

But soon Murdoch's American dreams expanded. With an eye to creating a fourth U.S. television network to distribute his new studio's products, he targeted a chain of local stations owned by Metromedia Corp. Later, he would convert them into the fledgling Fox Network.

As Murdoch contemplated the deal, however, his plans hit a legal wall. The U.S. Communications Act of 1934 limits foreign ownership of television stations in the United States. Against that prohibition, how could Murdoch—an Australian—acquire the Metromedia stations?

For a peripatetic traveller and deep-pocketed investor like Rupert Murdoch, the solution was simple: become a U.S. citizen. And so on

September 3, 1985, Murdoch took the oath of loyalty to the republic. (His wife and children were naturalized a few years later.) Forsaking his Australian citizenship did carry a cost—albeit a small one. As an American, he could not expect to own television stations in Australia, as he had in the 1970s. But that was not much of a sacrifice, given the alternative of owning a network in the United States. And in any case, Australia's cross-ownership restrictions already kept him from having a controlling interest both in newspapers, which he also owned, and in Aussie television.

But that did not quite settle matters. News Corp., Murdoch's principal holding company, was a publicly traded Australian-based company. It was essential to Murdoch's tax planning that this continue to be the case. Given his new U.S. citizenship, how would this be finessed?

The answer illuminates the many ways in which one can interpret foreign-ownership rules. Citizenship, at least of the corporate kind, can lie entirely in the ear of the listener. As Neil Chenowith noted in his recent biography of Murdoch, "who Rupert Murdoch was, would depend on to whom he was talking." Chenowith describes how this worked:

> [S]ince 1986, [Murdoch] has described himself as an American or as "at heart" an Australian, as the occasion demanded. To help Americanize News Corp. in 1985, Murdoch bought more stock to lift his stake in the company to 50.1 percent. Within weeks of receiving FCC approval for the deal, Murdoch sold the extra stock again, so as to be able to tell the Internal Revenue Service that for tax purposes News Corp. was Australian-owned.
>
> Murdoch's lawyers would pioneer a form of virtual law that allowed him to assure the FCC in 1985 and every year since then that the Metromedia television stations were American-owned because he and Barry Diller owned 75 percent of the voting stock of 20th Holdings Corporation, the holding company for the stations, and thus he and Diller controlled the stations. At the same time the News lawyers would tell the U.S. Securities and Exchange Commission that News Corp., a foreign company, controlled 20th Holdings. It held 99.9 percent of the company as nonvoting stock and could force Diller and Murdoch to sell the voting stock back to it at any time.

WHAT ALL THREE of these cases demonstrate is that it is plainly not enough simply to count shares to determine whether or not a "foreign" investor dictates decisions to a local producer or distributor of cultural goods. Purely "legal" rules are not enough. A de facto test is absolutely essential.

Even a strong de facto test may not always easily determine whether a cultural undertaking is controlled by nationals. In the end, the answer may take subjective judgement by an independent court or agency.

In that light, if foreign-ownership restrictions are to be meaningful, legislation must require that any share transactions above certain thresholds be reviewed by an agency capable of examining *all* the relevant factors *before* control changes hands.

A major country that enacts relatively clear foreign-ownership restrictions and that empanels an independent agency to interpret and enforce them poses a challenge to a multinational company based in another country. Unable to enter the market directly, the multinational is forced to deal with a local partner.

This at the very least bolsters local control over cultural decisions. A domestic company with local management gets to decide what programs to broadcast, whether local or foreign, what books to put on display, what records to sell. Since these gatekeepers are local, it may be presumed that they will consider local creators favourably (although, as Chapter 6 made clear, profit may well trump patriotism in the result).

The multinational company will be less pleased. Armed with a library of creative works produced (and usually largely amortized) in its home market, it will naturally seek to exploit the low marginal cost of repeat sales in other markets. The most attractive course is simply to own direct channels of distribution to consumers in those markets: local bookstores, film distributors and cinemas, local broadcasters. That degree of vertical integration not only ensures that the widest possible range of the multinational's inventory is passed through to the local consumer, but also that the greatest possible share of the potential profit is retained on its corporate bottom line.

Foreign-ownership rules foreclose that course. But a middle way is possible.

The solution is for a multinational to seek a *joint venture* relationship with the local company. In a typical arrangement, a media multinational will take a minority equity position in a local television broadcaster and get the right to appoint one or two directors. The multinational will also usually enter into a long-term agreement to supply programs to the local broadcaster. The latter may also pay a fee to use the multinational's trademark and branding. Examples are the many "international" versions of such U.S.-originated brands as Bravo!, MTV, Discovery and Nickelodeon.

These arrangements are increasingly popular, particularly in pay-TV and specialty programming services. Table 11.1 presents a number of current examples in Canada.

TABLE 11.1: *Examples of Joint-Venture Arrangements between Canadian Broadcasters and Foreign Companies*

Name of Canadian Service	Program Genre	Canadian Controlling Shareholder	Non-Canadian Company	Nature of Relationship with Non-Canadian Company*
BBC Canada	British drama/comedy	Alliance Atlantis	BBC	B, P, O
The Biography Channel	Biography	Rogers, Shaw	A&E	B, P, O
Country Music Television	Country music videos	Corus Entertainment	Country Music Television	B, O
The Discovery Channel	Nature and science	CTV Inc.	Discovery Communications Inc.	B, P, O
Discovery Health	Health	Alliance Atlantis	Discovery Communications Inc.	B, P, O
Family Channel	Disney/family	Astral Media	Walt Disney	B, P
Food Network Canada	Food	Alliance Atlantis	Scripps Howard	B, P, O
HGTV Canada	Home and garden	Alliance Atlantis	Scripps Howard	B, P, O
MTV Canada	Teenage lifestyle	Craig Media	Viacom	B, P, O
Outdoor Life Network	Outdoor recreation	CTV, Rogers	Outdoor Life Network	B, P, O

SportsNet	Regional sports	Rogers Media	Fox Sports Net	P, O
The Sports Network (TSN)	National sports	CTV Inc.	ESPN	P, O
The Weather Network	Weather	Pelmorex Management	The Weather Channel Inc.	B, O

* B = branding and trademark arrangement; P = program licensing deal; O = minority ownership

Joint ventures deliver advantages to both sides. In addition to having a supply of (presumably popular) "international" programming, the local broadcaster benefits from an infusion of the multinational's capital and, it hopes, the increased visibility, audience and revenue that its brand may attract.

From the perspective of the domestic public interest, local managers determine the entire program schedule. They make their decisions on the basis of local demand while abiding by any local-content regulations. They commission local programs to reflect their perception of local interests—and subject to any domestic rules mandating acquisitions from independent producers. And although there may be an output deal with the multinational, local executives will decide which of that company's library of programs will be aired. In short, local control provides the opportunity to maintain the diversity of local cultural expression.

At the same time, the multinational company has a broadcast platform that allows it to make money from its rights library, as well as a return on its brand identification.

Preserving the separate corporate identities of a domestic broadcaster and its foreign joint-venture partner can lead to disputes, however—particularly on the touchy issue of territorial program rights. A Canadian case from 1996 offers an illustration.

Two competing groups each applied to the national broadcast regulator for a licence to operate a specialty-television channel focused on the "history" genre. One application was presented by TSN (yes, the same TSN), which had entered into a joint-venture arrangement with A&E, the owner of The History Channel in the United States. The other applicant was Alliance Communications Inc., which had no U.S. partner but had given a 12 per cent interest in its proposed service to CTV in exchange for access to the network's news tape and video archives.

Since the CRTC's policy was to give "niche" protection to licensees in the form of market exclusivity, only one bidder would get a licence. Which one?

Both applicants proposed significant Canadian programming. But only one had gone to New York and negotiated exclusive access to A&E's extensive library of historical programming in exchange for a minority American interest in the proposed new channel. The other applicant was wholly owned by Canadians.

When both applications were heard at an open hearing, the A&E-linked group used its promised access to U.S. programming to sharpen the distinction between the two bids. If the competing Alliance application were licensed, TSN intimated, A&E would deny the new channel access to its highly regarded library, including the North American rights it held to programs from the BBC.

Alliance countered that TSN had overpaid for A&E's library and would inevitably provide a U.S.-centric schedule. Alliance insisted that it could readily provide a Canadian history service without access to the New York library and could deal directly with the BBC to secure Canadian broadcast rights to its shows.

After reflecting on the competing claims, the CRTC eventually gave the nod to Alliance. Its service, History Television, was launched in 1997. In the event, TSN's implied threat turned out to be empty. The BBC was perfectly happy to supply programs directly to History Television. A&E tried to keep Alliance (later Alliance Atlantis) from using the generic word "history" in its name, but the gambit failed; still, bad blood endured between Alliance and A&E for a number of years. Canadian-owned and -controlled History Television is now one of the most popular specialty channels in the country.

THE SKIRMISH over who owned the rights to "history" (the word, not the events) highlights another source of potential contention for joint ventures: the value of corporate brands to multinational owners.

The best-known music video service in the world is undoubtedly MTV. The music video pioneer, now owned by Viacom, began operation in the United States in 1981. Over the next two decades MTV expanded around the world, providing its service on almost every continent. But it was not permitted to operate in Canada.

In 1984, the CRTC had licensed instead a Canadian music video service, owned by CHUM Ltd., called MuchMusic. The regulator's policy—then as now—does not allow cable or satellite distributors to carry foreign pay or specialty services that are totally or partially competitive with licensed Canadian services. MTV found itself locked out. MuchMusic rapidly became the music video channel of choice for Canadian teenagers. It aired all the video hits from international record labels but, compelled by a 30 per cent Canadian content quota, also played music videos from Canadian artists.

In early 2000, the CRTC invited applications for a new round of digital specialty services. Later that year, after public hearings, it awarded a licence to Craig Broadcast Systems, a company from western Canada, for a teenage lifestyle service to be called Connect. The service was to target viewers in the 12–24 age group with overall Canadian-content levels starting at 50 per cent and rising to 60 per cent by the end of the licence. MuchMusic raised no opposition to the new service. At the same time, Craig also applied for and won a separate digital licence for a "nostalgia" channel, to have a format similar to Viacom's U.S. specialty service, TV Land.

Shortly after receiving a licence for Connect, Craig representatives visited Viacom in New York to seek to negotiate a joint venture for the launch of its nostalgia service, based on a branding and programming deal with Viacom's TV Land. But the discussion soon turned to another idea. Viacom also owned MTV. Over the years, MTV had steadily reduced the number of music videos on its service and had itself become more of a teenage lifestyle channel, although a sister service, VH1, continued to be driven mainly by music videos. Could Craig work together with MTV to convert Connect into a Canadian-controlled joint venture? The terms of the Connect licence confirmed this was possible. So Craig entered into an agreement with Viacom to obtain the MTV name and some of its programming in exchange for Viacom acquiring an option to purchase a minority of the shares of the Craig subsidiary and other consideration. In October 2001, Craig launched its new teenage lifestyle service across Canada under the name MTV Canada.

Now MuchMusic did object.

The CRTC reviewed the matter the following year. Its decision was issued in February 2003. On the ownership side, it required some tinkering to the shareholder agreements but otherwise approved Via-com's participation. Craig, not Viacom, clearly controlled the Canadian MTV service. On the programming side, the CRTC required assurances that the service would run fewer music videos and not lose sight of its teenage lifestyle mandate. But the bottom line was positive for both joint-venture partners. For the first time since it had been launched in 1981, MTV's brand was available in Canada, albeit under Canadian control.

IN SUM, assuring domestic "national" control of cultural corporations is not a simple task. But neither is it an impossible one. The question is, is it also worth doing?

Recall the two main arguments in favour of making the effort.

➤ Local companies are more likely to identify, develop and pro-mote a diversity of expression by local cultural creators.

➤ Local companies are more likely to reinvest returns from those rare successes in the cultural casino in future bets on local talent.

These propositions may seem intuitive. But are they true? There are counterarguments.

The first is that capital is indifferent to citizenship. It seeks simply to maximize profit. There is no *necessary* relationship between the local ownership of shares in a company and support for local cultural expres-sion. Rational managers will pursue whatever course carries most rev-enue directly to the bottom line. Hence, as noted in Chapter 6, the appeal to television broadcasters of cheap imported drama series over expensive local ones. The very fact that governments find it necessary to impose local content regulations on such broadcasters demonstrates that local ownership alone is not enough to ensure local content.

Similarly, local ownership of a cultural business is no guarantee that its profits will be reinvested in local creative projects. In fact, two dynamics militate against it. First, as companies become larger, profes-sional corporate managers motivated narrowly by the interests of shareholders tend to supplant entrepreneurial founders willing to let personal passion overrule financial prudence in assessing risk. Second, as companies expand, they also undertake more expensive projects in competition with better-heeled rivals. These gambles demand ever-larger pools of capital, which investment restrictions may deny to purely local firms.

That said, there is evidence that local companies are more likely to seek out local talent. The recent experience with Canadian magazines provides a useful illustration. For many years, all the magazines with any significant Canadian content have been produced by Canadian-owned companies. Up to 1999, it might have been argued that was simply an artifact of the 1976 law barring foreign companies from selling tax-deductible advertising to Canadian advertisers. But the law was changed in 1999 and now allows foreign publishers access to such tax deductibility, provided they produce magazines with original Canadian content. In the ensuing four years, however, not a single foreign publisher has emerged to take advantage of these provisions. This is clear evidence that foreign owners do not have the same incentive to support local creative talent in the magazine sector as do domestic owners.

It is also relevant to consider the Canadian experience in music, books and broadcasting, and the lesson of Hollywood in movies.

FEW PEOPLE have a better sense of the view from both sides on this issue than Allan Gregg. As an executive for the Canadian subsidiary of Viacom in the 1990s, he witnessed the corporate process of identifying candidates for investment. As a backer and CEO of the failed independent Canadian music label Song Corp. and inveterate self-described "hobby" promoter of young Canadian bands, Gregg has a visceral knowledge of the purely domestic play. He sees an interesting contrast between Canada's fertile production of musical talent and the exceedingly short list of resoundingly successful and distinctly Canadian films or television programs.

"In the music industry, we have a very, very healthy *creative* community and *no* industry—I mean there is *no* Canadian [music] business, there truly is not. There is barely a cottage industry," Gregg argues. "In film, we have a relatively healthy industrial structure but we are getting nothing out of the creator community, nothing."

Various public policies—from rules on radio content to funding for annual music-industry awards—may have created a fertile environment for emerging musicians. But as Gregg notes, "You look at the young creators, no one wants a Canada-only deal. The artists all want North American distribution and that is something the domestic [labels] can't offer." And while not one major music label is Canadian-owned, he adds, "they are here, in that they play a very, very active role in the artists' development program. They sign lots and lots of acts. To their credit for the first time in their history, they are breaking acts that are signed or discovered here."

Gregg is correct that the major record labels do sign new Canadian acts. On the other hand, they are equally quick to drop them if their first album does not succeed. Some 180 small and independent Canadian labels, most of them owner-operated if not very nearly mom-and-pop enterprises, have a far stronger track record of sustaining Canadian talent. Examples include True North (Bruce Cockburn), Nettwerk (Sarah McLachlan) and Stony Plain (Ian Tyson). While the five music majors and another ten big international labels racked up 86 per cent of all CD sales in Canada in 1995–96, more than 80 per cent of Canadian recording artists relied on small Canadian labels to release their music. "The usual cycle," observes Richard Green, acting director of the National Library and Archives of Canada's music division, "is the independents bring out the new music, the majors catch on and buy out either the artist or the label."

Like their musical counterparts, Canadian authors enjoy an enviable international following. For every Celine Dion there is a Margaret Atwood, for every Avril Lavigne a Yann Martel. The book business in Canada, however, presents a picture only a little different from the "cottage industry" of local music labels operating in the shadow of multinational giants.

About 140 small Canadian-owned publishing houses in English Canada produce general-interest titles mainly by Canadian authors. About twenty "branch plant" publishing houses owned by large multinational companies also produce books by Canadians. But the *kind* of author each sector publishes, and the ways in which their books are marketed, are quite different.

The Canadian-owned sector releases by far the greater *number* of distinctly Canadian trade titles. In 1999, those publishers released more than 1,800 new Canadian-authored titles into retail bookstores. Their titles grossed about $570 million in retail sales.

Canada also has local arms of most of the major international publishing houses: Random/Knopf, Penguin, HarperCollins and others. Their main business is distributing all the same books as their New York or London affiliates, the heavily promoted blockbusters—by John Grisham, Danielle Steele, Stephen King and many others—seen in airport bookstores around the world. In 1999, the branch-plant publishers released more than ten thousand new titles into Canada. Random House alone brings in more imported titles—about two thousand a year—than are published by all the Canadian houses combined.

But these majors are also significant publishers of Canadian authors, to the extent that former *National Post* book columnist Patricia Pearson lauded the senior editors of Random House and Knopf Canada—Anne Collins and Louise Dennys—as "arguably [the] two most powerful women in Canadian publishing." The Random House–Knopf list includes Martel, Carol Shields, and now Michael Ondaatje. HarperCollins publishes novelists Richard Wright and Barbara Gowdy. Penguin lists John Ralston Saul, consort to Canada's governor general as well as a trenchant social philosopher. Collectively, the foreign houses release about two hundred Canadian-authored titles a year.

That does not place the foreign and domestic publishers on an even footing, however—nor does it lead them to take comparable risks on new talent or topics of uniquely Canadian interest. With few exceptions, it is the small, locally owned publishers that identify promising new writers and give them the first opportunity to develop their talent. Once those same authors have built a name and reputation, the foreign-owned houses, with their deep reserves of capital, easily outbid local publishers for the rising star's next book. So Michael Ondaatje went from Coach House to McClelland & Stewart to Knopf and Carol Shields from Borealis to Stoddart to Random House.

In effect, local publishers operate as farm teams to the majors. They find the talent. But as soon as writers prove their talent, they move on to the "big leagues" of a multinational imprint. The much greater profits that flow from their mature works and established reputation then accrue to the multinational, not the local house that first took the risk on their budding promise. That may not be a bad deal for authors: they can look forward to bigger advances from those deep multinational pockets. But it does suggest that without a thriving community of locally owned publishers as well, there would be fewer careers. And Canadians would be reading fewer books about their own experience.

Meanwhile, Canadian-owned publishers face a familiar woe of the farm leagues: a chronic shortage of working capital. This limits their ability both to bid against the multinationals for the best manuscripts and to exploit those promising books that do fall into their hands. The more ambitious publishers offset that disadvantage by pursuing exports much more aggressively than do their branch-plant rivals, who typically leave world markets to head office. Locally owned publishers account for more than 90 per cent of Canadian book exports.

But Canada's publishers are not in the same advantageous position that specialty broadcasters are to be courted by foreign joint-venture partners bearing marquee brands or properties. Because Canadian law obliges broadcasters to be licensed—and denies licences to any company not majority-controlled by Canadians—a foreign television vendor cannot enter the Canadian market except in partnership with a local player. In book publishing, however, although Canada has prohibited foreign-owned publishers from entering its market since 1985, all the existing foreign-owned houses were permitted to continue their operations. Thus, almost all of the major global publishers are able to sell their titles directly in Canada.

In short, there is little to motivate a big foreign publisher to woo a small local house. The model instead has been to buy them outright— or more often simply to lure away their rising stars.

BROADCASTING IN CANADA presents another face of the issue again. Canadian law dictates that Canadian operations must be Canadian-owned and -controlled. Unlike the book industry, Canada's broadcasters are well capitalized and quite profitable. At the same time, the CRTC has tailored schedule and expenditure rules to ensure that each licensee supports local programming. Given that detailed regulation, how likely is it that broadcasters would behave differently if they were foreign-owned?

Here it is possible to speculate. If foreign-ownership rules were relaxed, it is a certainty that many non-Canadian multinationals that now hold minority shares in Canadian broadcasters would extend those stakes to controlling interests, if not outright ownership. Companies like Walt Disney, Viacom, Fox (News Corp.), Discovery International (Liberty Media), Scripps Howard and ESPN Inc. would find it in their interest to take over specialty channels that already use their brands or marquee programming in Canada.

The foreign owners would presumably continue to comply with all applicable Canadian regulations and licence conditions. But it is also clear that certain things would change. First, the *selection* of foreign programming would be constrained. A foreign owner would have every incentive to utilize its own library to the exclusion of other non-Canadian content, as well as to manipulate the price charged to its Canadian subsidiary, in order to maximize its own return. It is worth recalling from Chapter 9 that when the European Audiovisual Observatory surveyed the continent's broadcasters for compliance with local-content quotas, it noted that the most systematic failure to meet those targets was among "subsidiaries whose parents are located outside the European Union."

Second, the selection of *Canadian* programming would also be likely to change. Even if executives based in Canada were allowed to set their own schedules, they would encounter strong pressure to acquire or produce programs that were less specific to Canadian audiences and more general in their references. Why? Because those programs could most profitably be added to the multinational parent's library and reused in third countries at minimal marginal cost.

None of this is necessarily terrible. Producing programs that air successfully to many audiences is obviously more profitable than producing them just for a local audience. Some policy-makers would even see this as a good thing. They argue that more export sales will help to finance more local creative projects that would otherwise not be produced.

However, this is not widely supported by experience. More often, multinational conglomerates make less innovative, more profit-driven and risk-averse choices than those that emerge from small, local and often owner-operated companies. They tend to focus on local creators whose success is already assured, not on the new, unknown talents who need nourishing or development.

And there is a further risk, one we have encountered before. If *all* domestic programs on a local service are export-oriented, something important is lost. Those programs that reflect and address uniquely local "dreams, fears and folklore" will be sacrificed.

Neurologist and botanist Oliver Sacks has remarked: "How crucial it is to see other cultures, to see how special, how local they are, how un-universal one's own is." A local owner is far more likely to appreciate that special *un*-universality of her native culture than is a multinational conglomerate in dogged pursuit of its next global hit.

The United Kingdom, while selectively opening its broadcast services up to foreign ownership, did not entirely lose sight of this hazard.

Even before the aforementioned change in regulation, America's Viacom and Austro-American News Corp. were reported to be interested in various British assets. British producers voiced alarm that foreign owners, intent on maximizing the value of their library, might "dump" U.S. programs on British television screens.

The U.K. broadcast regulator (then the ITC, but slated to be replaced by a new agency called Ofcom) issued a cautionary note:

> Industry-wide consultation in the U.K. and analysis of key overseas markets provided evidence that opening up the U.K. media markets to worldwide investments would produce benefits as well as risks. It was argued that foreign owners would not seek to impose programming that would not be valued by British audiences, and considerable economic evidence that broadcasters are most successful when they commission and schedule a preponderance of local programmes. Nevertheless, the ITC considers it prudent to give Ofcom a toolkit of reserve powers, to be used on a case by case basis, *to enforce and expand the levels of original, U.K. productions, and protect levels of investment, including: targets for investment in original production as well as hours transmitted* ... [Emphasis added]

At the same time, if the dynamics of foreign ownership present a perceptible threat to lively expressions of local culture, it cannot be said that in broadcasting, any more than in bookselling, local ownership necessarily translates into a corresponding bankable benefit for domestic creators. Although there may be good reason to expect foreign broadcasters to favour programming of generic appeal over vivid and distinct local shows, the reverse proposition—that domestic ones will reliably support local expression—cannot be relied on.

In fact, the more that privately owned cultural companies expand and diversify into a number of countries, the less "nationality" they often display in their decisions.

Consider one group of companies intentionally omitted from the discussion so far. A perceptive reader might well have asked, "Are there no large book publishers owned by Canadians that can compete head-to-head with the multinationals?" In fact, there are two: Thomson Corp. and Torstar Corp.

Controlled by Toronto resident Ken Thomson, the son of Lord Thomson of Fleet, the former is a major multinational player in the educational and professional publishing field. But Thomson Corp. has shrewdly avoided the riskiest area of the book business, general trade publishing, where profits are made only on large press runs and the price of admission includes large advances that may never pay out. So it has never been a factor in trade publishing—or in bringing Canadian authors of general interest to readers in Canada or anywhere else.

For its part, Torstar Corp. owns the world's largest publisher of romantic paperback fiction, Harlequin. Its titles sustain millions of (mostly) women in escapist fantasies of varying degrees of titillation. But like Thomson, Torstar has never strayed from the profitable niche it acquired in 1981 nor dipped its toe into the risky area of general trade publishing.

Other Canadian publishers have aspired to become larger players in the trade publishing field. But most of them have found their growth stymied by chronic undercapitalization and the inherent risk associated with the unpredictability of demand for general-interest titles in a small market.

The notion that size and international presence trumps nationality is nowhere better illustrated than by the "U.S." motion picture industry. It provides a fascinating study of the impact—or more accurately, lack of impact—of "foreign" ownership once companies reach a certain size.

Only twenty-five years ago, the Hollywood majors were all owned by U.S.-based companies. Their product, then as now, dominated world cinema markets. But over the past two decades, many of the Hollywood majors were sold to non-Americans. Did this change in corporate parentage in any way change the ways in which studios chose their film projects? When Sony bought Columbia Pictures, did its production slate begin to include projects developed in Japan? When Seagrams, a Canadian company, bought MCA–Universal Studios, did Edgar Bronfman Jr. begin to look at projects developed in Canada? Or when Rupert Murdoch acquired 20th Century–Fox, did the Fox studios suddenly begin to green-light Australian scripts?

The answer, of course, is no. The centre of project development and production approval stayed, as it always had, in Hollywood. A foreign-owned major studio still had to locate its key creative decision-makers there because that is where A-list talent is and where top projects are pitched. And in a perfect feedback loop, A-list talent from around the world still flocks there because that continues to be the only place where a major film project can find a green light.

SO IS FOREIGN OWNERSHIP good, bad or neutral for diversity of expression? And is domestic ownership worth protecting as a matter of public policy?

We have seen that *smaller* companies in the cultural field—particularly those with owner-managers in place—have an admirable track record of supporting local cultural expression. These are by nature also most likely to be domestically owned. A policy that secures their vigour in the overall cultural "ecology" will contribute significantly to a lively variety of creative diversity. Restriction on foreign ownership in domestic markets also serves to increase the total number of green lights available to creators globally.

But there is a caveat. The larger and more successful a locally owned private company is, and the more it expands into other markets, the more indistinguishable its choices become from those of a giant multinational. Size can trump citizenship.

Not only that, but large corporate scale in an ownership-protected climate may even introduce new hazards. To the extent that a local gatekeeper in the cultural industries becomes dominant in a particular sector or program genre, the number of potential green lights in that sector is sharply reduced. Worse, should the solitary "favoured son" fail, its collapse may threaten the viability of an entire sector. Canadian authors and small publishers have shivered through precisely this experience on more than one occasion in the past decade. For both reasons, legislation to counter market dominance may be more necessary in order to preserve diversity. We address that policy issue in the next chapter.

In sum, statutory limits on foreign ownership *may* be of value to the extent that they preserve a greater number of local gatekeepers able to bring new cultural expression before their domestic publics. But in contrast to other available measures, such as content rules, mandatory expenditure requirements and, as Chapter 13 will demonstrate, targeted subsidies, they are surely not the sharpest or surest tools in the kit.

12

COMPETITION
POLICY

O NE DAY IN 1924, a Chicago ophthalmologist named Dr. Jules
Stein abandoned eye charts for a more quixotic pursuit: booking one-night shows for touring dance bands from a tiny two-
room office. Unencumbered by modesty, Stein gave his infant company
the grandiose name Music Corporation of America (MCA).

As a small-time booking agent, Stein quickly realized that his success hinged on gaining exclusive rights to book as many A-list bands
as possible. One of the first was Guy Lombardo and the Royal Canadians, a still relatively unknown group that Stein discovered in Cleve-
land. When Lombardo broke out as the most popular band-leader in
America, hotels found they could book the Royal Canadians only if
they did business with Stein.

Then the perceptive former ophthalmologist turned his strategy
around. Armed with exclusive contracts that made him the sole bargaining agent for top A-list bands—and dispensing cash incentives—
Stein negotiated a new round of contracts that gave him exclusive
booking rights to major hotels, dance halls and pavilions, all of which
depended on live bands to draw customers. As one recent chronicler of
Stein's double-edged strategy noted:

> The more exclusives Stein was able to obtain, the more important
> clients flocked to him; the more important clients were his, the more

he obtained exclusives. It did not happen overnight, but it was a machine that kept feeding itself, growing larger and larger, and with it came a great deal of leverage. This was the dawn of "tie-ins," a practice that later would become almost synonymous with MCA.

The exclusive deals benefited MCA on both ends. A hotel that wanted a hot band like Guy Lombardo's for one weekend could be forced to take an unknown group the next. Those unknowns, however, would also be from MCA's stable. Other up-and-comers faced a daunting problem: instead of working in a market of many hotels and venues to whom they could offer their services, they increasingly faced a single gatekeeper—MCA.

Soon Stein extended his power further by offering hotels a season's entertainment for a single lump sum. MCA then paid the bands itself, pocketing far more in profit than just an agent's commission. Stein may not have originated this concept of "packaging" talent, but he did develop it to its ultimate potential—at a high cost to new performers. Acts that MCA did not represent had little chance of being part of the package.

With its exclusive lock on both talent and venues, MCA quickly outgrew its two-room offices to become the largest talent agency in America. In 1939, it took on Hollywood. Spearheading the new venture was a brilliant and mercurial young talent agent named Lew Wasserman, who became the agency's president at age thirty-three. Wasserman extended MCA's strategy of owning both sides of the deal to its new turf, securing a controversial waiver from the Screen Actors Guild that allowed the company to produce television programs as well as act as agent for the performers that appeared in them. Soon, MCA dominated movie packaging and television production in the United States in addition to the booking of live bands.

By 1960, Wasserman was contemplating fresh conquests. That year MCA acquired Universal Studios, putting it in position not only to package talent and creative properties but also to finance and distribute them. At last the U.S. Justice Department—the same agency that had ended the dominance of the studio system over a decade earlier—stepped in. Reluctantly, MCA withdrew from the agency business. But the concept of "packaging" remained.

Indeed, as the MCA story illustrates, using exclusive deals and various forms of block booking (a form of "tied selling") to reduce risk and increase profit is pervasive in virtually every sector of the cultural industries. Previous chapters have noted how the peculiar economics of popular culture favour the big, how a corporate focus on the infinitely exploitable, cross-promoted and merchandised blockbuster can draw investment away from a broader range of creative works, to the detriment of pluralism. Once they have acquired clout in the cultural marketplace, conglomerates will find it in their interest to indulge in a variety of practices that maintain and even increase their dominance. Tactics that can hurt or exclude smaller players include vertical integration, block booking, exclusive dealing, tied selling and mergers with competitors.

If such abuse is, at the very least, a lively risk, it seems reasonable to suggest that one way to support more diversity would be to apply competition law or, as it is often referred to in the United States, anti-trust law. After all, the very purpose of such law is to attack monopolies and reduce the clout of dominant players. Even ideologues of the right are prepared to accept an occasional intervention from regulators to ensure that competition does not decay into monopoly. Australian Terry Flew, in an analysis of the breakdown of what he calls the "social contract" view of media policy, notes that "neo-liberal policy discourses" critical of the notion of "public interest" also "point to an increasingly important role for competition policy as a 'generic' form of industry regulation."

Can competition policy be a tool to achieve greater cultural choice? Might creative application of anti-trust law advance diversity of expression?

At first blush, this looks like a fruitful idea. After all, we have seen that an increase in the number of firms able to green-light a cultural project may enhance the range of cultural works on offer. If competition policy abhors monopoly and promotes a rivalry among many companies in a field, why not harness it to ensure the maximum number of green lights for a wider choice in films, books, music and broadcast programs?

This is an attractive notion. But as with so much else within the unique economic field of creative products, a number of complications severely blunt the edge of competition policy in dealing with culture. In some paradoxical circumstances, a simple-minded adherence to maximum competition may *undermine* cultural diversity. There may be cases where cultural diversity is better served by allowing a dominant supplier to exist, provided that supplier takes, or is compelled to take, steps to support diversity.

The pages ahead examine how the market anomalies of creative products keep competition policy from constituting an all-purpose Swiss army knife in the tool kit of cultural policy.

THOSE ANOMALIES run deep. Let's begin with a very basic notion. What do we mean by "competition"?

That seems easy enough. In pure-market theology, "sovereign" consumers are free to exercise individual preference among many available offers of any given good or service. Competition means having a wide choice of providers making such offers.

If only it were that simple. In the real economy, in contrast to the rhetorical one, even the basic dynamics of trade in creative works are not so clear. Markets that appear to display vigorous competition may in fact be subject to monopoly decisions by offstage gatekeepers, or bottlenecks in distribution that in fact inhibit true consumer choice.

Consider the shelf of your local convenience store, where dozens of magazine titles "compete" for attention. In a typical city, a single wholesaler supplies those magazines to all the newsstands and variety outlets in town. That company has a geographic monopoly. Its decision alone determines the menu of titles from which consumers may choose. Similar "rack jobbers" supply mass-market paperbacks to variety stores, pharmacies and other outlets in a city or region; they have a monopoly in deciding which titles fill the limited number of paperback slots in any store.

In a city with a dozen radio stations, there may be only one station that programs country music. That station is the local gatekeeper for new releases in the country music genre. What its programmer chooses to turn down, local country music fans have no opportunity to embrace. And if no local radio stations choose to program country music at all, as recently happened in New York City, what choice is there for country music fans?

Perhaps the clearest example of such a local gatekeeper is the cable or satellite television company. It controls subscriber access to the many potentially available pay- and specialty-channels. What becomes of market competition and consumer sovereignty when the cable company declines to carry a particular service or gives a preferential position on its menu to a service from its own corporate parent?

Pay-TV and specialty-television services may, like your local country music radio station, themselves have dominant or even monopoly positions within a particular program niche. The presence of such a channel may indeed add choice to what is offered by the local free-to-air broadcaster. But that diversity may be at the price of creating a series of mini-monopolies in genres such as live sports, premium movies, children's programs, "lifestyle" shows, history or biography. In many countries, particular services within such program genres enjoy just such a dominant status by reason of exclusive distribution arrangements, regulatory fiat or "first-comer" effects that disadvantage later entrants.

These examples point to a critical difficulty for competition policy in coming to terms with cultural products. The central thesis of such policies is that consumer interest is best served by a choice of providers within a given market. But as we have just seen, in some cases what may appear to be a wide-open choice is, at best, a constrained subset of all possible choices determined for the consumer by a gatekeeper whose presence is largely concealed from view.

But once a concern arises over anti-competitive concentration of ownership, a further problem emerges in the attempt to respond to it. The most common approach is to impose restrictions or conditions on mergers or acquisitions above a certain size within identified markets. Typically, a regulator reviews each proposed merger, analyzes the relative size of the companies involved and their competitors, studies their share of the market before and after the merger and tries to forecast the likely impact their proposed combination will have on consumers or suppliers.

But this turns out to be trickier than it first appears. What, exactly, *is* the relevant "market"? The infinite variety of cultural products and services often makes this difficult to define.

In a sense, every copyright confers a perfectly legal monopoly on every creative work. If a consumer insists on, say, a copy of Michael

Crichton's latest thriller, the soundtrack of Eminem's latest movie or the DVD of the film, there will be only one ultimate legal source: the publisher or distributor who holds the rights to those properties in the consumer's country. From that perspective, the unique content of each particular cultural product could be seen as conferring a small monopoly in itself.

Stepping back, one might argue that all cultural products that share a particular subject matter or style constitute a "market." In that sense, distinct markets plainly exist for "world" music, cookbooks, nature documentaries, popular histories, romance fiction, detective thrillers, or annotated synopses of the classics. Taken further, there might be identifiable markets within these categories for histories about the Second World War or creole cookbooks.

If more than one publisher provides titles in each such area, they are competing for the consumer. But as publishers or distributors rationally pursue market share in their preferred genres, they gain more and more dominance.

Yet, in practice, competition regulators are deeply averse to "content" as a test for describing markets in any cultural product. It is far too subjective and open to interpretive challenge. It is far easier to refer to objective criteria. The easiest is physical format. A CD is different from a DVD. A hardcover book is different from a paperback. Both are different from a magazine—but all magazines tend to be alike to a competition regulator, whether they are *Playboy* or *Christian Parenting Today*.

Complicating the delineation of markets is the incongruent coverage of *exclusive* and *non-exclusive* rights. The pattern in most cultural industries is for distributors of cultural services (such as film exhibition and TV programs) to enjoy exclusive rights to geographic territories. (These rights provide one basis for the orderly marketplace of sequential windows described in Chapter 3.) Distributors of cultural goods (such as the physical copies of books, magazines or records), at least at the retail level, are non-exclusive. So a broadcast program is available only to one broadcaster in a particular territory; a movie is available only through one theatre chain in an area. But copies of the same magazine and book titles, CD or DVD may all be available from a number of bookshops, music stores and video outlets in the same city.

Advertiser-supported products such as newspapers, magazines, radio and television programs throw out yet another complication. These involve two quite different markets: the consumer and the advertiser. There may be lively competition in one market and a pure monopoly in the other. For example, for a consumer who wants to hear country music, there may be only one radio station in town. But an advertiser buys access to audiences of a certain demographic. It is immaterial whether they are Shania Twain or Avril Lavigne listeners. Any station that reaches the desired demographic will suffice. So if you ask the consumer, "Is there competition?" the answer will be no. But if you ask the advertiser, the answer will be yes. And this ignores the upstream market, where you may have competition between content creators (authors or syndicators of articles, music distributors, or program producers) to provide their content to the media that carry their titles.

Even objective criteria do not remove all uncertainty. Should radio be segregated from television? Should FM radio be considered a market distinct from AM radio? Is the big-box bookstore market different from the mall bookstore market? Is cable television different from direct-to-home satellite, or should both markets be treated as one?

Given such imprecision, it is perhaps understandable that competition regulators do not have a distinguished track record in addressing the implications of mergers and acquisitions in the cultural industries.

UNCERTAINTY ABOUT where one market ends and another begins bedevils one of the longest-standing policy questions affecting diversity of expression: whether to permit cross-ownership of different media. Should a local newspaper owner be permitted to own the local broadcaster? Should radio and television stations in a market be owned by different people?

Given the importance to democratic society of ensuring the fullest airing of different points of view, it is hardly surprising that governments around the world have frequently restricted cross-media ownership. Curiously, though, the matter is rarely taken up by competition regulators. The reason lies in their narrow vision of what constitutes a market. Since competition regulators normally view the "newspaper market" as distinct from the "television market," they see no problem when the owner of properties in one acquires assets in the other. In effect they are blind to issues of diversity played out across media sectors. Thus it generally falls to governments or media regulators, where those exist, to impose restrictions on cross-media ownership.

One of the most restrictive regimes has been in the United Kingdom. Until recently, it precluded newspapers with more than 20 per cent of the national market from owning any radio or television services. That posed a particular problem for Rupert Murdoch. Since acquiring the tabloid *Sun* and *News of the World* in 1969, and *The Times* and *Sunday Times* seven years later, Murdoch has also stalked a television presence in the British market. In 1982 his News Corp. bought struggling pioneer Satellite TV UK and later relaunched it as a pan-European service, Sky Channel. In 1989, Sky service returned to Britain on a new satellite as a joint venture with the European Broadcasting Union (EBU).

The following year, regulators licensed a second domestic U.K. satellite service, British Satellite Broadcasting (BSB). After several months of punishing competition and mutual bloodletting, the two merged to form BSkyB. News Corp. held a 37.5 per cent interest. But the cross-ownership ban still prohibited the Australian-American tycoon from extending his reach to free-to-air television.

In May 2002, the British government introduced a bill that relaxed but did not eliminate a variety of broadcast ownership restrictions. For the first time, the Communications Bill would allow a single company to own Britain's leading private television network, ITV. Until then, the law had required it to remain in the hands of a consortium. What many observers found more chilling was that the bill also dropped the prohibition on large newspaper groups owning the nation's fifth-placed network, Channel 5 (which at the time trailed two free-to-air BBC services and Channel 4 as well as ITV).

The Guardian's broadcasting columnist, Steven Barnett, was one of many commentators who read the development as an invitation to Murdoch. "Rupert will have his slice of terrestrial television after all," Barnett wrote. He anticipated that News Corp. would acquire Channel 5 and deploy BSkyB's coveted rights to air British soccer matches to pull up the network's ratings. "Within five years," Barnett forecast, "one organization and one individual could be controlling over a third of our national press and our most popular free-to-air television channel, as well as dictating terms for access to the dominant digital TV platform."

Other countries continue to restrict cross-media ownership. Italy prevents publishers of newspapers with more than 8 per cent of national circulation from owning more than one television station; publishers with more than 16 per cent may not own any. (Italian prime minister Silvio Berlusconi does, however, own the country's biggest general publishing house in addition to his television networks.) In France, publishers with broadcasting interests are limited to a daily newspaper circulation of 20 per cent of the national market. In the Netherlands, any broadcaster that reaches over 60 per cent of the national audience cannot own a newspaper with more than 25 per cent reach. Similar restrictions on cross-ownership between newspapers and broadcasters exist in Norway and South Korea.

In the United States, a long-standing FCC rule prohibited the common ownership of a broadcast station and a daily newspaper in the same local market. In February 2002, however, the D.C. Circuit of the U.S. Court of Appeals struck down two related restrictions on media ownership involving the integration of broadcasters and cable companies and the maximum market share allowed to a single television network. In that ruling's wake, the FCC ruled in a split decision in mid-2003 that its regulatory limits should be liberalized. Within days, however, the U.S. Congress moved to introduce legislation to restore the rules on media ownership.

The ultimate fate of the media ownership rules in the United States was uncertain at the time of writing. But if the United States opts to abandon its prohibition on the common ownership of print and electronic media, it will not be alone. Among other nations that have found it unnecessary are Germany, Belgium, Mexico, Spain and New Zealand.

THE CANADIAN PICTURE shows what can happen when a regulator has jurisdiction over one medium but not another. In a curiously lopsided jurisdiction, the CRTC has the authority to approve or disallow a newspaper's takeover of a broadcaster—but not a broadcaster's takeover of a newspaper.

In 1982, the Liberal government of the day directed the CRTC neither to grant nor to renew a broadcast licence to the proprietor of any newspaper serving the same market. The regulator promptly went after the Irving family of New Brunswick, a powerful clan that owned both newspapers and broadcasting stations as well as much else in that province. The CRTC ruled that as long as the Irvings owned newspapers in three New Brunswick cities, they could not retain broadcast licences in the same communities. The family appealed to the courts, at first without success. But in 1984, a Conservative government came to power. Before the Supreme Court of Canada could hear the matter, the new government revoked the earlier directive. The CRTC's licence denial became inoperative, and the commission was not prepared to make a new policy on its own.

So matters stood until the end of the century. By then, the relatively few broadcast stations that had been owned by newspaper proprietors—including the Irvings—had passed into other hands. The issue of cross-ownership seemingly became academic.

That changed dramatically in 2000. In July of that year, CanWest Global obtained regulatory approval to acquire a number of additional television stations. The acquisition for the first time gave CanWest a national reach, with television outlets in most major markets in Canada. Barely had the ink gone dry on the approval order, however, than CanWest announced a new and even more sweeping deal. This time the company proposed to acquire *The National Post* and more than a dozen other local newspapers across Canada from press baron Conrad Black.

Unlike the earlier acquisition, this one was *not* subject to CRTC approval. Nor did Canada's competition regulator see any significant reason to withhold its approval. In its view, the newspaper market was entirely different from the television market. Thus, neither authority was in a position to stop CanWest from owning both the country's leading newspaper chain and one of its two private English-language broadcast television networks.

A similar scenario played out after BCE Inc. announced that it proposed to acquire CTV Inc., Canada's largest private television network, in February 2000. The purchase required CRTC approval. With the regulator's decision still pending and just weeks after the CanWest–Black deal was announced, BCE suddenly revealed that it was merging with the owners of *The Globe and Mail*, the country's other national newspaper. Again the CRTC had no jurisdiction to intervene in the transaction. And once more, Canada's competition regulator saw no issue for it to deal with. The two markets were, after all, distinct.

The following year, after the dust had settled, both CanWest and the new Bell Globemedia came before the CRTC in hearings to seek renewals of their respective television licences. The commission devoted much of its time to reviewing the implications of each group's cross-media ownership. But in the end, its only action was to endorse a set of rules on newsroom separation that the parties themselves had come up with. Lacking any direction from the government or direct jurisdiction over the newspapers, the CRTC had little option but to endorse the *fait accompli.*

The CanWest–Bell duopoly did agree to two rules for separating their print and television newsrooms. First, the companies would "maintain separate and independent news management and presentation structures for television operations that are distinct from those of any affiliated newspapers. Decisions on journalistic content and presentation for [television] will be made solely by television news management." Second, the companies' "television news managers will not sit on the editorial board of any affiliated newspaper; nor will any member of the editorial board of any affiliated newspaper participate in the news management of television operations."

The prescribed separation applied only to news management and content. Left untouched were possible "synergies" in cross-promoting television programs and newspaper reports. Testifying late in 2002 to a standing committee of Parliament on Canadian heritage, a reporter from CanWest's Montreal *Gazette* gave evidence to suggest that practice goes on apace. "Around the CanWest organization," Jan Ravensbergen testified, " we understand there are about 20 television cameras installed inside [newspaper] newsrooms. They are operated remotely from Global TV technical facilities and they can focus and pan remotely. In *The Gazette* we call the camera Darth Vader. There are different [news] 'hits' being done, reporters sometimes give a little heads up on the local news and it's seen primarily as a way to cross- promote."

The line beyond which cross-promotion becomes a common editorial initiative is a blurry one, however. "There is a very strong directive to produce showcase pieces where they can cross-promote," Ravensbergen told the committee. "For instance recently there was a series of features in *The Gazette* tied to a series of TV clips on Global Television about the debate over drugs and marijuana. There's been four or five or six of these projects."

In the flippant world of news reporting—whether print or electronic—the trend has even acquired its own bawdy metaphor: the poodle and the St. Bernard. The poodle is television news, with its typically tiny staffs; the St. Bernard is the newspaper with its historically much larger complement. "So it's the poodle trying to get together with the St. Bernard," Ravensbergen explained, "and the wags in the office are saying that the poodle wants to be on top."

Formal separation agreements between the two media is a solution also being considered in Australia. For a number of years, Australia has prevented newspapers from owning radio or television stations. New legislation introduced in 2002 proposed to lift the ban, under some conditions. The Australian Broadcasting Authority (ABA) would be empowered to grant "exemption certificates" to cross-media owners. Before receiving an exemption, applicants would have to demonstrate the existence of "separate and publicly available editorial policies, appropriate and publicly available organizational charts, and separate editorial news management, news compilation processes and news gathering and interpretation capabilities."

As the Montreal *Gazette* experience indicates, such prophylactic measures may be of limited utility in protecting the editorial virtue of either the poodle or the St. Bernard. But even if they are effective at preserving the diversity in news coverage and political viewpoint that are fundamental democratic freedoms, they do not even attempt to address the consolidation of decision-making over other forms of cultural expression. It is significant to note that a study of entertainment coverage by another CanWest paper, *The Vancouver Sun*, found that it reviewed programs on its corporate sister network, Global, far more frequently than programs on rival CTV or public broadcaster CBC.

In brief, there seems good reason to conclude that restrictions on cross-media ownership do indeed deter the creep of corporate monoculture and further the goal of creative pluralism.

EVEN WITH such restrictions in place, dominant players frequently emerge in cultural markets. Their prominence may be an artifact of historic business models—the gatekeeping "rack-jobber," for instance—or reflect the incapacity of regulators to prevent or break up media monopolies and the cross-ownership of cultural distributors, or to restrain practices like tied selling, block-booking and packaging arrangements that have anti-competitive effects. Alternatively, it may be a public-policy choice to favour a locally dominant but also locally owned player. In each case, however, there is potential for abuse.

Can policy restrain that potential? Perhaps. Here we examine two areas where different approaches have been tried: the promotion of independent production in oligopolistic television markets, and the control of channel carriage in the cable and satellite industries. Each illustrates the benefits of and limitations in the use of competition policy to achieve a diversity of expression.

PROMOTING INDEPENDENT PRODUCTION IN TELEVISION

The television and film universe falls into two very broad parts: *making* shows and *showing* shows. The most direct way competition policy can secure a diversity of expression is to keep the two apart. Policies that limit the extent to which exhibitors of cultural products may own the production houses that supply films or television programs also prevent those exhibitors from favouring their own products and discriminating against others.

The classic example of such a policy was directed at the U.S. film industry. Within two decades of the appearance of the first feature film, half a dozen major studios dominated the industry. The Hollywood studios benefited from nearly complete vertical integration, controlling production, distribution and exhibition of their work. In 1938, the U.S. Department of Justice filed suit, charging studio-owned film distributors with conspiring illegally to restrain trade by, among other things, requiring exhibitors who wanted any of their pictures to take all of them (that is, "block booking" them). The Majors settled this first round out of court, signing a consent decree in 1940. The decree committed them to rein in their distribution practices but allowed them to keep their theatres. And not much changed. Five of the Majors retained effective control of about 70 per cent of the first-run theatres in the United States.

In the face of further complaints from independent movie houses, the Justice Department reactivated its suit. In 1948, the courts ruled against the studios. A new decree drew a distinction between the production and distribution of films and their exhibition. In the result, the studios kept the first (believing, rightly as it turned out, that the real money was in production and especially distribution), but agreed to sell off their interests in movie theatres across the United States.

Twenty years later, the situation arose again—but this time in a new setting.

By the 1960s, the small screen had become a cultural force in America's living rooms and an economic one in New York and Hollywood. Three commercial networks, ABC, CBS and NBC, dominated free-to-air television. The Big Three, like the Majors before them, found it very much in their interest to produce their own programming rather than buy it from independent producers.

This time it was not the Justice Department that responded, but the FCC. In the early 1970s, it prohibited the networks from financing the production of prime-time drama and comedy and from syndicating such programming across their own station chains. A companion regulation addressed the exhibition side of the equation. This, known as the Prime Time Access Rule, prohibited network affiliates in the top fifty markets from running series syndicated by the networks in the hour before 8 PM.

When the networks bridled at the new rules, the Department of Justice did enter the fray. It brought anti-trust suits against the Big Three television chains. In 1980, ABC, CBS and NBC, following the path of the studios two decades earlier, entered into consent decrees that contained provisions similar to those the FCC had required of them.

The "fin-syn" rules effectively required the networks to obtain all their prime-time dramas and sitcoms from independent producers. The Prime Time Access Rule opened up a mandatory sixty minutes of "shelf space" each evening that network affiliate stations were obliged to fill with independently produced first-run syndication programs.

The prime beneficiaries were the Hollywood studios. They created television production divisions and became the networks' leading suppliers of programming. But a number of smaller independent television creators, such as Mary Tyler Moore Productions and Norman Lear, also emerged and flourished.

In the decade that followed the 1980 consent decree, advancing cable, home video and satellite technology expanded the channel choices available to many American homes. By late in the decade, the networks began pressing vigorously to have the rules rescinded. They argued that in light of the new viewing alternatives, their position was no longer oligopolistic.

Despite bitter opposition from independent television producers, the FCC rescinded the fin-syn rules in 1993 and the Prime Time Access

Rule in 1996. The anti-trust consent decrees lapsed in 1995. Since 1996, there has once again been no regulatory bar to self-dealing by the U.S. television networks.

The result, entirely predictable, has been the networks' rampant rush back into vertical integration. In-house production has soared. And an informal but inescapable new rule has come into effect for those few independent producers still pitching to the now-five big networks: either trade off some equity in the production to the network, or give up any hope of a sale.

For independent producers, the experience has been a return to an unhappy past. "Consolidation and vertical integration of the large corporate media giants has created a barren landscape in program production that mirrors the 'vast wasteland' predicted in the 1960s," declared a brief to the FCC filed in early 2003 by the Writers Guild of America, the Producers Guild and six independent production companies. "In 1992, only 15 per cent of new prime time series were produced by the major networks. By 2002 that number has increased over five times to 77 per cent." The brief continued:

> While the Commission suggests that there are 230 cable program services available to viewers, it fails to note that only 91 of these services reach at least 16 million cable homes. And of those 91 services, almost 80 per cent (73 such networks) are owned or co-owned by only six companies. More significantly, five of these six companies are the very same companies that control the broadcasting network marketplace. Thus five companies are now the gatekeepers and decision makers for the programming choices of the vast majority of American people . . . By any standard, *source diversity has almost completely disappeared* from the American television scene. [Emphasis added]

While the U.S. experience ran its course, much the same set of issues presented itself in other countries. In most of those (the United States is the exception), television began as a state-run monopoly, opening up to competition only as new services were permitted in the last few decades. Free-to-air television stations remained relatively few, however, while continuing to capture the lion's share of audiences. Those outlets tended to monopolize the production of local programming.

The same alarm over potential oligopolies that was raised in the United States in the 1970s echoed in Europe in the 1980s. In 1989, the "Television Without Frontiers" directive took direct aim at the threat. Article 5 of the directive mandates member states to "ensure, where practicable and by appropriate means, that broadcasters reserve at least 10 per cent of their transmission time, excluding the time appointed to news, sports events, games, advertising, teletext services and teleshopping, or alternately at the discretion of the Member State, at least 10 per cent of their programming budget, *for European works created by producers who are independent of broadcasters*" (emphasis added). It is left to each country to determine how broadcasters under their jurisdiction will meet the requirement.

As in many other areas of cultural regulation, France has taken the most muscular approach. As noted in the discussion of mandatory expenditure rules in Chapter 10, French free-to-air broadcasters must invest 10 per cent of their prior year's "net turnover" in independently produced European works. To meet the standard for "independence," such acquisitions must pass three tests: the provider must be an independent production company; the network may not contribute financing, technical or creative inputs to the production, nor guarantee its output; and the network may not acquire broadcast rights to any program for more than four years, including the year it is delivered. French public-service broadcasters and its dominant pay-service, Canal+, must meet higher benchmarks for commissions or acquisitions from independent producers.

Italy, in contrast, chose to base its requirement of broadcasters on airtime. Thus, free-to-air Italian television broadcasters must devote at least 10 per cent of their transmission time to European works by indie producers. The requirement is doubled to 20 per cent of transmission time for public-service broadcasters.

In keeping with its highly decentralized regulatory arrangement, German national law places no explicit requirement on its broadcasters regarding independent productions. In fact, although broadcasters are expected to meet the directive's mandate, German law does not define "independent producer." On the other hand, German private broadcasters are required by the sixteen *Lander* (states) that regulate them to provide broadcast time to independent third parties designated by the relevant regulator.

Sweden exercises its obligations under the directive by signing individual undertakings between each broadcaster and the government, which place a variety of specific requirements on each outlet.

Private television came late to Spain, arriving only in 1992. There, the law does precisely define independent production and requires that broadcasters achieve the directive's 10 per cent minimum of independent content within four years of going on-air. It places one additional onus on them as well, aimed at discouraging excessive recourse to stale reruns: more than half the programs counted towards the quota must have been produced in the past five years.

Britain has gone beyond the directive's minimum. It requires its free-to-air broadcasters to fill at least 25 per cent of their program schedules with independent productions.

Given the wide skepticism from market purists over any form of quota, has the directive's indie rule been effective? The European Commission conducted research in 2002 to find out. The answer, contained in a report released that November, was a resounding yes, although with one qualification of striking relevance to the present discussion. "The percentage of broadcast time or programming budget allocated to the works of independent producers," it noted, "was way above the minimum of 10 per cent in all the Member States, with the national average ranging from 21 per cent (Greece) to 59 per cent (France) of broadcasting time. In 2000, as in 1999, 85 per cent of the European broadcasters met the target of Article 5."

The exceptions were specific. Prominent among the minority of broadcasters failing to meet the independent production minimum were "subsidiaries whose parent companies are located outside the European Union. These broadcasters systematically use their own catalogues." With few exceptions, "outside the European Union" meant that these were American-based. In Britain, for example, they included Biography Channel, Bravo!, Disney Channel, Playhouse Disney, Toon Disney, History Channel, National Geographic, Nickelodeon, Reality TV and Sci-Fi Channel.

In Australia, there are no requirements for independent production, but the Screen Producers Association of Australia has recently proposed that a model like the U.K. requirement be introduced.

In Canada, independent television production essentially did not exist before the early 1980s. The public sector—the CBC—created all its programming in-house. And as Chapter 9 showed, the private CTV network and other independent private stations did little or no drama or scripted comedy at all. There were no cable-only or specialty channels.

Two initiatives, both exercises of public policy, brought independent television production into being. One was the CRTC's imposition of drama requirements on private broadcasters. The other was the introduction of federal subsidies for Canadian television drama available only to independent production companies (more on that subject follows in Chapter 13). With this combination of stick and carrot, Canada's independent production sector grew like Topsy, giving birth to and nurturing such companies as Alliance Communications, Atlantis Communications (later to merge) and Nelvana in Toronto, and Montreal's Cinepix and Cinar.

But the market also began to change dramatically. New satellite-to-cable services appeared, starting with pay-TV in 1982. For the first time, Canada's broadcast regulator turned its mind to the conditions facing independent production.

In licensing Canada's first movie-based pay-services in 1982, the CRTC prohibited them from producing anything except short bursts of interstitial programming aired between films. That general ban remains in place to this day (although one of the pay-services was recently granted permission to produce up to 25 per cent of its Canadian programming).

As additional specialty-services emerged later, the CRTC placed custom requirements on each new licensee to acquire independent productions, taking each one's circumstances into account case by case.

Some requirements are highly specific. In the case of the popular TELETOON animation service, for instance, 25 per cent of Canadian programs broadcast in the first year of its operations (1997) had to be financed by parties other than the licensee, its shareholders, their shareholders or any of their affiliates. The ratio rises annually, reaching 50 per cent in the sixth and subsequent years of the licence.

In renewing Alliance Atlantis's licence for the Life Network in 2001, the CRTC required that "a minimum of 75 per cent of all Canadian programs broadcast by the licensee shall be produced by independent production companies. For the purpose of this condition an 'independent production company' is defined as a production company of which Alliance Atlantis Communications Inc. owns or controls, directly or indirectly, less than 30 per cent of the equity."

In 2001, the CRTC finally addressed the acquisition practices of private free-to-air TV services. Although the two national networks, CTV and CanWest Global, had rarely produced drama on their own in the past, both by the late 1990s were acquiring production companies. Independent Canadian producers expressed concerns that anticipated those noted above from their American counterparts. In the end, the CRTC renewed both networks' licences for seven years—subject to an "expectation" that at least 75 per cent of their programming, other than news, public affairs and sports, would be bought from unaffiliated producers.

CONTROL OF CHANNEL CARRIAGE

Cable and satellite companies may enjoy local or even national monopolies or duopolies that convey substantial gatekeeping power.

Until the mid-1970s, cable companies generally offered no more than improved reception of available free-to-air television signals. In order to supplement local signals, they would bring in distant free-to-air channels by microwave or cable circuits. This they did without permission from either the broadcaster or whoever owned the rights to the programs being distributed through their cables. In 1976, the United States amended its copyright law to require cable companies to pay a compulsory licence fee to copyright owners in compensation for those imported signals. (Canada followed suit in 1989.) A number of companies experimented in a limited way with movies made available by subscription. But the system was crude: couriers "bicycled" tapes to local cable head-ends, where they were played at set times, obliging subscribers to watch them then or not at all.

This began to change in 1976, when Home Box Office (HBO) put its subscription service up on a satellite, making it available simultaneously to cable systems across the United States. Rivals initially tried to force the satellite pioneer into the regulatory ambit of the FCC and require it to obtain a broadcast licence to operate. The FCC, however, took the view that HBO was not a broadcaster at all, and hence was subject to no special restrictions in U.S. law. The courts agreed, and the floodgates opened. Within a short time, dozens of new specialty program services came into being.

These presented cable systems with a vast menu of new programming options they might offer to subscribers. Some were premium services like HBO or Showtime. Others were news or music video services like CNN or MTV. Still others were adult services like Playboy that took full advantage of the new unregulated environment. At the same time, inexpensive "negative trap" technology allowed cable operators to block sets of channels that any particular subscriber chose not to pay for, thereby making it economically possible to offer the new channels either as add-ons to basic service or in extended "tiers."

The choice as to which services to offer rested entirely in the hands of the cable companies. So too did the pricing, packaging and marketing of the services. At the start, cable systems took every "first-comer" service in each program niche. But soon they began exercising more discrimination among newly launched services, playing one off against another for the most concessionary terms. As the gatekeeper, the cable company held most of the cards. Moreover, unlike the situation with free-to-air TV stations, where the FCC forbade cross-ownership of cable and broadcast stations and prohibited foreign ownership of the latter, no restrictions of any kind applied to the combination of satellite and cable services.

The result was entirely predictable. Soon, cable companies in the United States began demanding equity ownership in new program services as a condition of carriage. Then more. They insisted on the *exclusive* right to distribute the channels they accepted to their markets (later outlawed, when direct-to-home satellite services emerged). They extracted the right to sell local advertising on the satellite channels. They obtained free service for a multi-year introductory period—and in some cases even squeezed payment from the program service for the privilege of being carried.

And once they became part-owner of one program service, many cable systems refused to carry competing services in the same genre, or they carried those in less attractive packages. Anticipating this, some prospective new services even sought out investment from cable enterprises, hoping to ensure they were then carried on favourable terms.

What an American subscriber may view by cable now depends as much on her provider's corporate affiliations as on the exercise of any supposed consumer sovereignty. In a survey published in 2001, an economist found that "integrated operators tend to exclude rival program services, suggesting that certain program services cannot gain access to the distribution networks of vertically integrated cable system operators ... Operators who own premium services offer on average one fewer premium service and one to two fewer basic services than do other operators. In particular, operators who own premium movie services are less likely to carry the rival basic movie service."

Viewed from the other end of the cable, that means subscribers do not have access to services their provider has excluded. Reflecting an economist's sense of priorities, however, the same analyst suggested that while this "does result in some degree of market foreclosure," it "does not harm, and may actually benefit, consumers because of the associated efficiency gains." That is, captive consumers have less choice in what the integrated companies allow them to see—but they don't pay as much for it, either.

Valid or not as that assessment may be, such practices are surely understandable. They reflect precisely the same alignment of interests that motivated the integration of movie studios and theatres in the 1930s (until stopped in 1948) or of American television networks with program producers in the 1960s (until arrested from 1971 to 1995).

But as the familiar forces of integration played out across the cable landscape, no regulator emerged to put on the brakes. If anything, integration accelerated with the consolidation of cable ownership among a few large companies, restrained only by an FCC cap of 30 per cent on the portion of cabled homes in America that any single owner may serve. By the turn of the millennium, just six corporate entities—Time Warner, Viacom, Liberty Media, NBC, Disney and News Corp.—controlled the program choices available to 80 per cent of all cabled households. (Some eighty-five much smaller players scrambled after the remaining 20 per cent of homes.)

Today, U.S. cable systems face only one meaningful carriage obligation. They are required to carry all local TV signals (the "must-carry rule") unless the station involved chooses to negotiate carriage instead. From time to time, turf wars break out between the large owners. One such spat in early 2000 led Time Warner briefly to delete rival giant Disney's ABC network from its New York cable lineup in a dispute over whether Time Warner would carry the Disney Channel on its basic cable service.

Meanwhile, American media conglomerates have lost none of their appetite for further integration. It was just such a goal that prompted Time Warner to challenge a long-standing FCC prohibition on one company owning both a free-to-air television station and a cable system in the same market. The issue arose when Time Warner wanted to expand its free-to-air network into New York and other cities where it already owns cable companies. The case, heard in Washington, was one of two decided in February 2002 against the FCC, triggering a review of all that commission's media ownership rules.

AS CABLE AND SATELLITE have proliferated in other countries, those nations too have witnessed the same factors motivating anti-competitive practices. A number of them, however, have shown a greater desire than the United States to restrain them.

In the United Kingdom, the issues of abuse of dominant position first arose in the 1990s with the emergence of BSkyB as the dominant supplier of premium broadcast services to the English-language market. Created from the merger of Rupert Murdoch's Sky Television with British Satellite Broadcasting in 1989, BSkyB rapidly turned two money-losing enterprises into an immensely profitable undertaking. Its dominance arose from two sources. First, it controlled the company that provided the "conditional access system" (the set-top software that de-encrypted signals for paying subscribers and the "smart cards" that controlled the process). Second, it had secured exclusive rights to top sports events, including Premier League football matches, and to block-buster Hollywood films, which it exhibited on its vertically integrated programming services, Sky Sports 1, Sky MovieMax and Sky Premier.

It did not take long for complaints to flood in. Competing program services that wanted access to BSkyB's set-top decryption complained about its discriminatory rates and practices. Competing cable distributors complained that BSkyB favoured its direct-to-home satellite over their distribution networks and priced its premium channels so as to squeeze out their margins.

In 1995, the European Commission issued a Europe-wide directive for the regulation of conditional access services. In response, Britain gave its telecommunications regulator, Oftel, authority to ensure that charges to third parties for access to set-top decryption were set on a "fair, reasonable and non-discriminatory basis." Oftel eventually set guidelines for such charges in 1998.

The regulation of conditional access terms and conditions was not the end of the matter, however. Sky's competitors also complained about its channel pricing and packaging practices. In 1996, under pressure from the U.K. Office of Fair Trading, BSkyB entered into a number of undertakings. It agreed not to bundle certain channels and to publish a rate card showing its wholesale prices for cable companies, with a discount structure that the director general of fair trading had approved in advance. Its conduct as sole proprietary rights-holder to the U.K.-standard encryption technology for analog satellite TV would be regulated. And it agreed to submit separate accounts for its wholesale and retail businesses, showing a notional charge for the wholesale supply of its in-house channels to its retail business, that would help the director general determine whether the latter made a reasonable profit on the terms of the published rate card.

On March 1, 2000, the new U.K. Competition Act came into force, mirroring European Commission competition law on the subject. It prohibited anti-competitive agreements and the abuse of dominant market positions. Before the year was out, the U.K. Office of Fair Trading (OFT) opened a new investigation into BSkyB's practices. On December 17, 2002, it issued its finding, concluding that BSkyB was indeed "dominant" in the wholesale supply of certain premium sports and movie channels. However, it ruled that BSkyB had not abused that position by exerting any anti-competitive margin squeeze on rival distributors of pay television, by anti-competitive "mixed bundling" of its own channels, or by giving anti-competitive discounts to distributors. However, the watchdog described its ruling on margin squeeze as a "borderline result," underlining the problems of allocating costs in an area where fixed costs far exceed marginal costs.

IN CANADA, the tension between viability and competition in the expensive business of delivering television from space has been apparent since the very dawn of satellite services. Public policy has also evolved under one assumption that is critically different from what has existed in the United States.

From the outset, the CRTC considered satellite-to-cable programming services to be a form of broadcasting. That brought the emerging business under its purview and meant that new ventures had to seek a licence before they proceeded. In 1982, the CRTC issued the country's first pay-television licences to a pair of competing independent investor groups in preference to a third applicant that would have been controlled by a consortium of cable companies.

But independence did not guarantee success. In the wake of disappointing penetration numbers, First Choice and Superchannel, the initial two premium movie services, soon applied to reorganize themselves into regional non-competitive monopolies, and this application was approved in 1984. In the same year, two competing French-language premium movie services were permitted to merge into one.

In the wake of that experience, the CRTC settled on a new policy of "niche protection." Aspiring specialty-channels could apply for a licence to distribute programs in any format they wished, so long as they could demonstrate that consumer demand existed for it. The CRTC, however, would grant only one new licence for each format. That limit was based on the cold calculation that the Canadian audience (at least at that time) was too small to sustain two or more competing domestic providers in any given genre.

Moreover, the number of new licences issued would be limited to the carrying capacity of the cable industry at that moment. In turn, cable companies would be expected to carry every newly licensed service. As a supplement in program niches not already occupied by Canadian channels, the CRTC also approved a few U.S. services as eligible for cable carriage in non-competing genres. Finally, the commission indicated that it would strongly favour applicants that were *not* owned by cable companies.

Under these rules, the CRTC began to license new Canadian specialty-channels in a series of "rounds." Over half a dozen of these between 1984 and 2000, the ground rules changed to some degree. Companies were allowed to add specialty services licensed in the earlier rounds to "basic cable" for a regulated additional fee. Later, analog services were added in discretionary tiers secured with negative traps that prevented non-subscribers from watching them. Services licensed in the most recent round in 2000 were required to be delivered in digital form, which could be secured with addressable set-top boxes.

Apart from the open question of whether a regulator or a privately owned company makes a better gatekeeper, it is difficult to fault the outcome. Dozens of new and distinctive Canadian services were launched in genres from gardening to gay lifestyles. Virtually all the early analog services proved extremely successful, exceeding both their penetration and revenue expectations. While it is too soon to judge the digital services, the early evidence is that many, though not all, of those will thrive as well.

Still, the CRTC revisited its ban on cross-ownership of cable companies and program services. In 2001, responding to pressure from a newly consolidated cable industry, the commission decided to allow cable companies to acquire ownership and control of programming services. It acknowledged the potential for disputes between distributors and unaffiliated programming services. But regulations prohibit either entity from giving undue preference to corporate siblings and provide an arbitration mechanism when disagreements do occur.

BEFORE LEAVING the intersection of competition law and diversity of expression, it is worth noting that not all the traffic here runs one way. In the frequently counterintuitive economic world of creative products, there may be policies that purport to *increase competition* but that in practice *hinder diversity*. Equally, there are circumstances in which allowing greater concentration of ownership may actually enhance rather than diminish the effective choice of cultural expression.

One of these paradoxical measures is what is known as "resale price maintenance," the practice of forbidding a retailer from charging less for a book than the publisher's suggested retail price. That practice is prohibited by competition policy in many countries, including the United States and Canada. And for obvious reasons: resale price maintenance prevents retailers from offering promotions based on price discounts for new book titles.

The problem for diversity of choice is this. Higher margins of retail price over wholesale cost keep more bookstores in business and encourage them to hold a larger inventory. Where resale price maintenance is banned, competition among stores drives down the price of best sellers and reduces inventories of books that sell more slowly. The result is consolidation among bookstores, fewer competitors, a higher ratio of best-seller sales to sales of other books (since bestsellers are most likely to be discounted) and eventually a poorer selection of alternative titles which are more and more expensive.

This issue pits consumers in search of bargains against those in search of choice. It is a contest increasingly won by the bargain-seekers. A long-standing voluntary resale price maintenance policy in the United Kingdom, referred to as the Net Book Agreement, recently fell apart. British publishers argued in its defence that readers required to pay full price for the latest best-seller might forgo it and instead be led to a more exotic title. But in the end the policy proved unsustainable, battered down in large part by the ease of access to discounted books on the Internet.

A second policy that seems to promote competition but in fact may erode diversity is that of permitting retailers to import for resale books or records bought legally in other countries, rather than from the exclusive rights-holder in their own, a practice often referred to as "parallel importation." This dilemma arises from the collision of two long-standing commercial principles. The first is the so-called "first sale" doctrine: it holds that once a physical item—such as a copy of a book or CD—is sold, it can legally be resold to anyone else without the permission of the copyright owner. The other is the principle of territorial exclusivity under which copyright owners grant a distributor the exclusive right to resell a creative product or item of intellectual property in a certain territory and withhold the product from other distributors in the same territory in order to prevent consumers from "buying around" and undercutting those rights.

The injury to cultural diversity is more easily demonstrated here. As Chapter 6 demonstrated, demand for a particular creative product may differ significantly from country to country, depending on the cultural discount between them. Demand is usually highest in the country of origin, with the result that most cultural enterprises base their business model on the premise that the local market is their most important. To take an example, consider two volumes by the popular Canadian historian Pierre Berton. *The National Dream* and *The Last Spike* tell the story of Canada's first transcontinental railway, the Canadian Pacific. The books were instant best sellers in Canada when they were first published in 1972–73.

An abridged version of the two volumes was published in the United States by Knopf under the title *The Impossible Railway*. Had it been about the first continental American railroad, it might have been a bestseller. But being a Canadian story, Berton's book stayed in U.S. bookstores only briefly before moving to the remainder tables, where it sold below cost and earned the author no royalties.

At that point an enterprising remainder agent might easily have purchased thousands of copies of the book and shipped them to Canada, where the original volumes were still in demand and selling at full price. Consumers might snap up the bargains. But the flood of cut-price competition would devastate sales of the original product—to say nothing of its Canadian author and publisher.

Any creative industry looks first to its home market to recover its sunk costs, such as editing a book and paying an advance to its author. Allowing an importer to arbitrage the differential decay time of a creative good's value in a distant market by offloading surplus copies in its home market jeopardizes the fair return due both its creator and the indigenous producer, who risked an investment in its production. The consumer's bargain becomes the creator's bath.

With that in mind, a number of countries give the territorial rights of the copyright owner or distributor precedence over the "first sale" right of resale, prohibiting parallel importation in certain cases. This includes the United States, although the jurisprudence is extraordinarily confused on the point. In Canada, regulations under the Copyright Act prohibit the import of books for resale unless the Canadian distributor fails to make the title available on reasonable terms and conditions. (In both countries, exemptions allow travellers to import single copies for personal use.)

In Australia, a general prohibition regarding parallel imports was relaxed in 1991 but continued to protect books published first in Australia or published there within thirty days of being published overseas. The protection did not apply to books for which local orders went unfilled for more than ninety days, however. This arrangement was referred to as the "30/90 day rule."

Australia entirely removed a similar prohibition against the parallel importation of sound recordings in 1998, after studies indicated that multinational record companies were charging excessive prices in the country. In 2002, legislation was proposed to abolish the "30/90 day rule" for books, opening the door fully to parallel imports. Australian publishers have protested that the rule helped "give writers real choice among publishers and consumers real choice about the books they want to read at competitive prices." But the government appears to have found the prospect of cheaper prices, "especially for small businesses, parents and the education sector" more persuasive. Competition may have won out. But local writers and publishers plainly lost.

The foregoing examples show how policies meant to stimulate competition may, in practice, stifle diversity. A study for the U.S. National Association of Broadcasters (NAB) illustrated the opposite proposition: that reduced competition can sometimes lead to a wider choice for audiences. When U.S. regulators in 1996 increased the number of radio stations that a single owner was allowed to operate in a single market, critics warned that diversity would suffer. Lobbyists for the change argued the reverse: that multiple owners competed for the same audience by programming similar formats, whereas owners of multiple stations in one city "would not want to steal audiences from their commonly-owned stations and ... would [offer] other formats not being adequately provided."

The NAB surveyed radio formats available before and after the change in communities where previously independent stations became consolidated under fewer owners. Against intuition, the variety of formats aired in most communities surveyed had increased, by a national average of 11 per cent. That being said, there has been a strong backlash in the United States against the emergence of consolidated players in the radio industry. In particular, Clear Channel Communications Inc., which owns more than 1,200 stations across the country, has been criticized in Congress for engaging in anti-competitive practices.

WITH THESE EXAMPLES in mind, it is obvious that while competition policy can be a useful tool to address some cultural policy concerns, it is by no means a panacea, and in some cases can be counterproductive. A recent review by a U.K. observer of the application of the European Union's competition policy to the media reached the same conclusion:

> The application of competition rules to the media industry cannot always safeguard other values and objectives, such as plurality of sources and diversity of content, that are threatened by undue market concentration. While effective competition and merger law is a necessary component of a healthy media industry, its purpose is to

remedy the effects of anti-competitive behaviour rather than to ensure a pluralistic and diverse media sector. Precisely because competition and merger control rules cannot provide the certainty that a significant number of different media voices are heard, and that there exists real choice of media products and services, other policy instruments need to be enacted and enforced.

The competition regulator in Canada has taken the same view. "Diversity of voices is not an issue of economic competition and, consequently, does not fall within the purview of the [Competition] Bureau's mandate," the commissioner of competition flatly stated to a parliamentary committee in 2002. Confessing his inability to deal with issues affecting Canadian culture and pluralism, the commissioner indicated that those matters would be deferred to the CRTC.

So where does that leave us? The complex industries that create, distribute, sell and exhibit popular culture are replete with hidden and overt gatekeepers, monopolies both trivial and significant, and ample opportunity for the abuse of market dominance. But there is also an increasing consensus that competition tribunals are not the perfect venue to deal with the kind of abuse of market dominance found in the cultural industries. In many cases, the best remedy may not be to require divestment or other structural measures, but rather to impose behavioural remedies. Such performance requirements can harness the clout of the larger players or distributors to benefit the cause of diversity of expression. This more sophisticated form of oversight may be better suited to regulatory agencies with a broader public interest mandate than to competition tribunals with a more limited ambit of interest.

Corporate consolidation shows every sign of increasing in the years ahead, little evidence of slipping into reverse. We have seen here that competition policy does offer the tool kit of diversity some measures that can deter abuse of dominance. But like the other tools earlier, competition policy cannot do the job alone—and may even slip and injure the very pluralism it is meant to advance.

13

SUBSIDIES

B Y THE FIRST WEEKEND of 2003, it was already clear that a pair of diminutive, hairy-footed fugitives had run away with the holiday season box-office. Over twenty-one days, audiences in North America alone paid US$265,467,000 to escape for three bewitching hours into the adventures of Frodo the Ring-bearer and his loyal hobbit sidekick Sam Gamgee. The rapturous reception that greeted *The Two Towers* built on the success a year earlier of the first movie installment based on J.R.R. Tolkien's classic fantasy *The Lord of the Rings*. It was a safe bet that by Christmas 2003, audiences would be lining up for the last episode of the epic trilogy as well.

The five-year production of all three *Rings* episodes—the most expensive film project ever attempted—was an epic of another kind. That it reached the screen filled with images of mountains that in real life tower over the remote South Island of New Zealand was a feat of financial as well as technical wizardry. In addition to featuring live action, computer graphics and a heroic story line, it involved incantations from tax law and a creativity Gandalf himself might admire.

The relevant spells were found in the New Zealand tax code. In effect, they allowed New Line Cinema, a unit of Time Warner, to use money belonging to a New Zealand bank and a German investment fund to finance the high-stakes venture while laying off more than a third of the risk on taxpayers in both countries.

Happily for all, the bet paid off handsomely—but not before the details of the tax sorcery behind the movies' creation came to light, causing an uproar among New Zealand voters, who imagined themselves having to make good a $90 million hole in their government's tax expectations.

Still, the behind-the-lens fellowship of directors, producers, accountants and taxmen illustrates a growing intersection of public and private interests in producing big-screen dramatic feature films, the riskiest and most costly of all cultural products.

State subsidy of culture has a long history. Rome's emperors routinely added statuary, arches and public coliseums to their civic landscapes, either to cultivate their own popularity or to amuse and placate their citizens. Much of the legacy of "high" culture, from the magnificent mosques constructed under India's Mughal or Turkey's Ottoman empires to Shakespeare's *Twelfth Night* and Handel's *Water Music,* was created as a result of the patronage of the governing powers of their day.

In the twentieth century, the motivation for state support shifted. Where once omnipotent rulers ordered up monuments to their own power or personal entertainment that only incidentally enriched the public, modern states found ideological and economic reasons to subsidize popular culture aimed at the broadest measure of their citizens. Some of this was blatantly propagandistic. The stilted "social realism" of the Soviet Union and the People's Republic of China or Wagneresque pretensions of Nazi Germany were true attempts at "command and control" culture.

But since the middle of the last century, all the major democracies have also at one time or another subsidized both high and low culture. They have generally attached few or no overtly political or ideological strings to their aid, although sometimes other conditions have applied. As governments everywhere outside the United States have grappled with the implications for their national identity and cultural creators of the economic realities laid out in the opening chapters of this book, the subsidy tool has become increasingly popular.

In this, New Zealand is far from alone. Australia, Canada, the European Union and most of its member states, most member nations of the Organization for Economic Co-operation and Development (oecd), many Latin American countries and thirty-seven of the U.S.

states in addition to the U.S. federal government (through its support for public television), offer some form of public subsidy for the production of filmed entertainment.

Subsidies even have the approval of many sharp critics of other public-policy tools in support of cultural diversity. "If there is a need to make space for Canadian content on television," notes Canadian economist Christopher Maule, who opposes the use of quotas, "there are dispute-free ways of doing it that can make use of subsidies." As Maule notes elsewhere, "neither the GATT nor the WTO prohibit governments from using subsidies as instruments of policy. Only export subsidies and subsidies paid contingent upon using domestic goods are prohibited."

William Stanbury, another fierce critic of measures like content requirements on broadcasters, acknowledges: "There seems to be a reasonable case to be made for subsidizing the production of certain types of TV programs made by Canadians and which have recognizable Canadian themes."

"Subsidies," notes a report to the Australian Broadcasting Authority on the challenge of securing local content in new media, "have the advantage of transparency over quotas. As budgeted transfers, they are more likely than quotas to be the subject of continuing evaluation."

Perhaps it is merely the lure of cheap money, but even Hollywood's arch crusader against every other form of cultural security measure, Motion Picture Association of America president and CEO Jack Valenti, is in favour of subsidies for making movies. "I support the right of sovereign nations to offer enticements to producers," he has said on more than one occasion.

For all that, subsidies for popular culture are no more panaceas, silver bullets or free from unintended consequences than any other measure in the policy tool kit. They pose the difficulty of structuring a process of application and award that will be neutral and transparent. Another problem arises in allocating public support among competing projects, some of which might proceed without help while others perhaps should not proceed at all. Together, those hazards court a third: developing a "culture" shaped more by the pursuit of grants than the pursuit of either artistic or popular merit.

Briton Martin Dale describes something approaching a worst-case outcome in the experience of European film in the decades between

1960 and the mid-1990s. As one European country after another cre-ated national funding bureaucracies dominated by intellectual cliques, film auteurs turned increasingly to introspective, self-consciously "cul-tural" stories and audiences plummeted. "Today," Dale wrote in 1997's *The Movie Game,* "the films that are made are increasingly provincial. There has been an almost total destruction of the cultural fabric of the film industry and this has coincided with massive intervention by the state under the guise of defending the cinema."

Dale's criticism turned out to be somewhat shortsighted. In the next five years, with the support of subsidies, there was a strong resur-gence in the popularity of local European films. By 2001, the box-office share of Hollywood films in Europe had dropped from over 80 per cent to 66 per cent. And in France, where subsidies for local films are sup-plemented by other support measures, the box-office share of U.S. films dropped to only 47 per cent in 2001, while films by French film-makers were able to garner a box-office share of 42 per cent.

The recent European experience has demonstrated that the combi-nation of subsidies with other support measures can generate films and television programs that get a very positive response from local audiences, although the overall numbers vary year to year. For many countries, however, subsidies represent an unavailable policy choice for the most basic of reasons: they take money. Where citizens must struggle to acquire even basic services, administrations often have higher priorities for scarce resources.

THE FINANCIAL WIZARDRY that allowed the world's biggest media empire to undertake history's most expensive movie project with (mostly) other people's money illustrates how complex the subsidies for the most expensive cultural forms can become.

At the heart of the deal was a provision in the pre-1999 New Zealand tax code that allowed firms not usually involved in show busi-ness to buy shares in film-production companies. Those companies were in turn expected to use the money they received for their shares to make a movie in New Zealand. If the movie made a profit, great. If it didn't, the initial company got to write off the cost of its shares—that is, the cost of making the film—against other profits, saving itself the 33 per cent corporate tax it would otherwise have paid on that income.

In this way the mechanism was designed to mitigate the downside of the cultural-goods lottery by delegating some of the risk to the tax-payer. (The mechanism in fact worked very much like "flow-through" shares that some countries, including Canada, have been used to en-courage investment in oil and gas exploration, another inherently risky field.) But it was another feature of the law that made it possible for U.S.-based Time Warner to access the tax magic.

Production companies created under the New Zealand law were also allowed to sell their movie, *in advance of actually making it*, to a foreign distributor. Critically, the transaction could close on pre-set terms at a later date, and the money for the sale could change hands later still and over a number of years. Together, the provisions meant that instead of a New Zealand company making a movie "on spec" and then seeking a distributor for it, a foreign studio could engage a New Zealand partner to create a company for the sole purpose of making a movie to order.

Which is exactly what Time Warner's New Line and New Zealand director Peter Jackson did to bring *The Lord of the Rings* to the screen. Most of the money to make the movies came from a New Zealand bank (the rest came from a German investment fund created under that country's own tax-shelter laws). New Line did not have to take possession of the film until it was made (giving it a chance to reject the film if it had been poorly executed) and did not have to make most of its payments until even later, after box-office revenue began to flow. Al-though the New Zealand bank now stands to recoup, through its stock in the production company, a small share of the three films' eventual profits, if the movies had flopped the bank would have been allowed to write off its entire investment against other income.

Subsidies for popular culture needn't necessarily be that complex. The European Union, for instance, was in 2003 considering a proposal that its otherwise universal value-added (sales) tax (VAT) be reduced or dropped for all cultural products and services. Movie tickets are al-ready exempt from VAT in some European countries. Similarly, some Canadian provinces do not charge this country's equivalent, the goods and services tax (GST), on the sale of books.

Targeted sales and hotel tax exemptions are popular among U.S. states seeking to encourage filmmaking within their borders. Accord-ing to a survey by the California State Library in 2001, half of all U.S.

states exempt some or all purchases made for film-production pur-poses from state sales tax. Twenty-two offer reduced hotel-room taxes to visiting productions. New York, Texas and Mississippi classify film productions as "manufacturing"—a designation that eliminates sales tax on some costs, such as materials used in set construction.

Ireland offers a variant on this device: it declares any movie for which three quarters or more of the production work occurred on Irish soil a "manufactured product." The benefit of the designation: income earned on the film is taxed at the "manufacturing" rate of 10 per cent, instead of the going corporate tax rate of 24 per cent.

Not all subsidies need be financial. Both the massive U.S. military and the more modest forces of other nations have been known to offer a range of support and assistance to movie productions. Troops of the New Zealand Defence Forces moved earth, planted and tended gar-dens and helped build sets to create Jackson's screen Hobbiton; three hundred of them appeared in costume in the trilogy's various battle scenes. None received more than their customary soldier's pay for the tour of film duty.

Many state and provincial administrations—and even individual cities such as South Africa's Cape Town—staff full-time bureaus to help visiting film productions find local service providers and camera-friendly filming locations. In France, several regional authorities wel-come film productions with free accommodation or local facilities made available gratis. Such support-in-kind is particularly attractive to comparatively cash-strapped jurisdictions.

But aid can be even less direct. Canada's government, for instance, subsidizes a variety of events designed not to increase the *production* of cultural goods but the *visibility* of the country's creators. Those events range from such national cultural awards as the Junos (for recorded music), Genies (movies) and Geminis (television) to subsi-dized book authors' tours. Lying somewhere between a subsidy for cre-ation and one for promotion is a modest but meaningful amount of aid for Canadian recording artists to make music videos, critical to any contemporary musician's or group's chances of popular success.

In a similar vein, Eurimages, an agency of the Council of Europe, supports thirty-seven cinemas for the exhibition of European movies in nine European countries. Media +, a similar agency created by the

European Union, with a budget of €400 million for 2001–05, supports the development, distribution and exhibition of European audiovisual works and, along with the "Television Without Frontiers" directive, is the main instrument of the European Union's positive audiovisual policy.

Governments in many places, among them Canada, have also contributed to the capital cost of erecting studios and sound stages for filming and invested public funds in the training of audiovisual technical specialists.

MORE OFTEN, however, subsidies are designed to dangle a purely financial carrot in front of a well-defined target.

One straightforward approach entails a sort of top-up bonus designed simply to enrich the market's own reward system. Such arrangements are especially popular in Europe. Spain, France, Belgium and Germany all have one form or another of this kind of subsidy for filmmakers. Under the Spanish scheme, filmmakers get a payment from a state agency worth 15 per cent of their film's first-year box-office receipts in Spain, to a maximum of 50 per cent of the film's production budget. Belgian films made in French qualify for a similar program of "automatic" support proportional to ticket sales. Germany's national Filmforderungsanstalt (FFA) administers what it calls a "success grant" to German producers whose films sell more than 100,000 tickets in German movie houses; amounts range in proportion to the film's popularity from US$98,000 to $1.2 million.

France, the country with the world's richest support framework for filmmaking, predictably has the most highly evolved—or just complicated—"automatic" box-office supplement program. That country's Centre National de la Cinématographie (CNC) maintains a register of every French filmmaker's oeuvre. It also collects a tax of approximately 11 per cent on every cinema ticket sold in France. In a triumph of Gallic bookkeeping, the CNC tracks admissions to each French film and credits an account in each French filmmaker's name for an amount based on a multiple of his or her films' theatre admissions. The multiple varies according to a formula based on the proportion of the films' "French" content (that is, how much of the work was done by French individuals or in France). Producers may take money out of their accounts to finance up to 50 per cent of the production budget of further films, or use the cash expected to flow into the account as a soft form of collateral to borrow production advances from other investors. "The *compte de soutien* is a massively generous scheme," commented British film-trade magazine *Screen Digest*, "which effectively means that once a producer has released his or her second film in France, they are set up financially."

Canada operates a subsidy for book publishers loosely based on the same principle. The Book Publishing Industry Development Program (BPIDP—known among its beneficiaries as "Bippydip") is open only to publishers that are predominantly Canadian owned. Other criteria limit it to established companies publishing more than a minimum number of titles annually (the number varies, depending on the genre of book) but below a maximum sales volume and profit margin—effectively targeting smaller houses that focus on distinctive Canadian titles and new authors. The program distributes about C$32 million a year according to a formula that allocates the lion's share of the money to publishers that can demonstrate the highest sales.

MORE COMMON than such "automatic" subsidies are discretionary programs that contribute public funds in some form of loan, equity investment or straight-up cash grant to film or television productions that must qualify for the support on an individual basis.

The European Union's Media + program provides what amount to semi-forgivable loans of up to €763,000 in the form of cash advances repayable from the "first dollar" of a production's box-office receipts.

Similarly, French producers can get funds from that country's CNC at either the development or production stage of filmmaking. The system of "advances on receipts" was started in 1959 and takes the form of an interest-free loan repayable with the film's receipts or using the automatic support fund discussed earlier. About eighty French films a year are supported in this way.

Britain's government-backed Film Council gives an assortment of cash subsidies. One funds script development.The grant must be repaid—plus a bonus of 50 per cent—only if the script is made into a movie, in which case the fund also expects a percentage of any eventual profits. Two other funds amount to sources of equity investments. They contribute money directly to productions in return for a share of a film's profits, if any.

Portugal's government directs aid to that country's filmmakers through the country's free-to-air broadcasters, reimbursing them for the production costs of domestic made-for-TV movies. Next door in Spain, the Instituto de la Cinematografia y de las Artes Audiovisuales gives comparatively small but non-repayable grants to up to two dozen "new directors or . . . experimental work of remarkable artistic and cultural content" a year.

According to some estimates, a diligent applicant who taps into a combination of Europe-wide and national subsidies can raise as much as 80 per cent of a medium-sized movie budget entirely from public funds.

New Zealand's Film Fund and Film Commission inject lesser amounts of equity into "feature films with *significant New Zealand content.*" The agencies also sometimes make loans against a film's sales or distribution guarantee. They limit aid to "New Zealand filmmakers who have already made one feature film," however, and to one production per filmmaker. NZ On Air, the country's vehicle to support the creation of domestic television fiction, takes the same approach. NZ On Air invests public money on an equity basis in series and television movies that it selects.

Canada subsidizes both film and television through the Canadian Television Fund (CTF), an agency financed with both public money and mandatory contributions from cable and satellite distribution undertakings. The CTF has a hand in a third of all English-language and half of all French-language Canadian TV shows (including a striking 93 per cent of all television drama shot in French). Money is injected into television programs in two ways. One part of the organization invests equity that is recouped only out of a production's profit. Another "tops up" broadcast licence fees for qualifying programs to as much as 35 per cent of production budgets, and is not recouped. The same agency also invests in feature films—typically taking a percentage of revenue from the "first dollar" of a movie's receipts. Over the years, several Canadian provinces have also created funds to make equity investments in films shot within their borders.

THE CREATORS of *The Lord of the Rings* tapped into the third major vector of public subsidy: preferential tax provisions. Governments like these mechanisms because they do not involve actual spending, but instead leverage the incentive power of forgone tax revenue. They are often more complex for creators to access than are direct subsidies. And, like subsidies for production infrastructure or cultural awards, their effectiveness can be unclear. But because they rely on deep pools of private capital instead of the limited funds at the disposal of most public granting agencies, they can also generate the large-scale investment required to finance an international blockbuster.

Three models of tax-based incentive are especially popular among investors, producers and governments—although each group gets somewhat different returns from each of those models. One offers a tax write-off tied to a direct investment in a production project. Another offers tax credits linked to some aspect of production, typically labour costs—which may also be refundable and therefore can be treated as anticipated revenue against which to borrow other financing. The last and most common model gives third-party investors a tax incentive for putting their money into investment pools that in turn act as sources of risk capital for filmmakers. The New Zealand scheme that financed *The Lord of the Rings* was an example of the latter.

Canada had a version of the first of these for more than two decades. Introduced in 1974, the "capital cost allowance" allowed investors to write off up to 100 per cent of their investment in a qualifying film production against other income in as little as one year. In effect, the scheme generated a tax benefit equal to slightly more than a quarter of the value of a film budget. The benefit was usually split three ways, among the producer, an outside investor and the middleman who put the two of them together. The allowance died when policymakers decided other mechanisms would drive more benefits to the actual production.

Similar tax breaks remained available elsewhere. Britain's Inland Revenue let investors in feature films made in that country with production budgets up to US$23 million write off 100 per cent of that cost. Ireland offered a comparable scheme for the deduction of 80 per cent of an investment, capped at 80 per cent of the budget, in a movie for which at least three quarters of the production work took place in Ireland. Australia offered a 100 per cent write-off for investment in a feature, made-for-TV movie or documentary "made substantially in

Australia which has significant Australian content." Films made under the terms of a co-production treaty between Australia and another country also qualified for the accelerated write-off.

Canada replaced its capital cost allowance scheme in 1995 with a refundable tax credit calculated on the amount a qualifying film production spent on labour in Canada. Several provinces offer similar tax credits that can be tapped in addition to the federal one, allowing Canadian productions to recoup a varying proportion of their overall budgets, depending on the province.

At least three U.S. states grant subsidies in a comparable form. Minnesota, as of 2001, returned 10 per cent of in-state expenses, to a cap of US$100,000, to visiting feature film, movie-of-the-week or TV series productions. The state billed its "Snowbate" as a "direct counteroffensive" to the Canadian tax credit. Missouri's Production Tax Credit is even richer. It returns 25 per cent of money spent in the state, up to US$250,000, on location budgets above $300,000. Oklahoma also rebates a portion of production spending within its borders. At 15 per cent, the portion rebated is lower than in Missouri, but there is no upper limit to the amount that can be claimed (although the state has earmarked a maximum of $2 million a year for the program).

In 2001, Australia introduced a similar regime. Any film production spending A$15 million or more in the country qualifies for a rebate from the government of 12.5 per cent of defined Australian expenses. As occurs in Canada, Australian states offer additional subsidies. New South Wales, for instance, established a fund that covers up to half the cost of shoots of at least a week's duration in the state, to a ceiling of A$100,000 for shooting in Sydney and A$500,000 for shoots outside the city.

Both the foregoing mechanisms reduce the private investor's risk of putting money into individual productions. The third widely adopted tax-incentive model encourages the creation of venture capital funds dedicated specifically to investing in multiple film productions.

Germany's version of this system allows taxpayers to deduct 100 per cent of their investment from other income in the year the investment is made. The 1999 provision opened a spigot from German wallets into three dozen film-investment funds around the country. The funds are not limited to investing only in German productions—which is how a Hanover-based pool came to share the financing of *The Lord of the Rings* with a New Zealand bank. Canadian studio Lions Gate Films also dipped into the German cash pools for a series of smaller productions.

A French version of this kind of tax-sheltered film-investment pool is known as the Sofica (Sociétés pour le financement du cinéma et de l'audiovisuel) system. France's seven Sofica funds collect money from individual and corporate investors and reinvest it—through interest-bearing loans—in film projects the CNC approves. The incentive for individual investors is a 100 per cent tax write-off of investments that can be as much as a quarter of their total income. For both individuals and companies, income from the amount invested is taxed at half the normal rate. Further reducing investors' risk, large French film companies like Canal+ and Gaumont guarantee the investments for as long as eight years.

Creative British financiers have adapted that country's rapid tax write-down of investments in film-production companies to achieve a similar effect. There, what is known as a "sale and lease-back" system allows British investors to reduce their income taxes by risking funds on film productions backed by foreign studios in much the same way that the New Zealand bank did. An additional twist lets them leverage their cash by borrowing more than 80 per cent of the amount they write off against other income.

To access the British system, financial middlemen assemble a pool of investors who each put up, say, £19,000 in cash, and borrow an additional £81,000 each to invest a total of £100,000 in the financing pool. For their £19,000 investment, each investor then gets to shelter £100,000 of other income from taxes. Meanwhile, producers looking for money *sell* their film (or, often, entire slates of films) to the group before shooting begins. At the same time, they secure an agreement to *lease back* the rights to "exploit" the film (collect box-office receipts, distribution revenue or broadcast licence fees) for a period, typically fifteen years. The producers get to keep—and sink into the production—about 14 per cent of the cash they receive. The rest goes into a bank as security for the lease payments to the pool. As those lease payments come into the pool, they go to service the original investors' bank loans. (For their efforts, the financiers who put these deals together also wind up with about 5 per cent of the cash that flows through them.)

Funds from several such schemes may be combined to finance any one production. According to the British Treasury, upwards of £100 million a year flow through such tax shelters into U.K. productions, and observers estimate that as much as 75 per cent of the budget of many British films is tax-subsidized. But only feature films are covered by the scheme; the rules had to be tightened after it was discovered that TV channels were using the system to make soap operas.

AS MUCH AS trade theorists endorse subsidies for their supposed "transparency," all these mechanisms are as vulnerable to unintended consequences as others designed to remedy market failure in the production of popular culture.

Subsidies may miss the desired target, motivating instead activities that either need no encouragement or court reprisals from trade partners. Subsidies given according to "automatic" formulae risk rewarding the undeserving. Subjective systems court the corruption of the gatekeepers. Then there is the question, never trivial, of where the money will come from.

The last point is especially relevant to less developed nations. "Some argue that subsidy is the more efficient way to promote cultural diversity," remarked Hyungjin Kim of South Korea's International Institute of Cultural Content at a 2001 seminar in Geneva. "However, subsidies also have limited utility. Governments must have money in order to provide subsidies." In practice, many of the countries most vulnerable to foreign domination of their audio-visual markets in particular—South American and Caribbean nations and those in Africa and central Asia—are also the ones with the most limited resources and most pressing humanitarian needs.

But the challenge can confront even wealthy countries. When Canada experienced a burgeoning of new television channels in the 1990s, many of the aspiring ventures promised to air schedules loaded with made-in-Canada programs. Most made those commitments expecting to receive subsidies from the Canadian Television Fund for the anticipated shows. In the event, the fund was heavily oversubscribed for much of the second half of the decade, and the commitments proved harder to fulfill than was anticipated.

Tax breaks possess offsetting advantages and disadvantages on the question of money supply. Politically sensitive finance ministries escape the opprobrium of taking money from one sector of the economy in order to give it away to another. On the other hand, forgone tax revenue is money that is not available to spend for other purposes. Moreover, because the mechanism depends on the decisions of many individual taxpayers, neither the amount forgone nor the amount that will reach the intended beneficiary can easily be forecast with precision. Finally, as appears to be the case in the example of Britain's sale-and-lease-back investment pools, the sums that actually reach the intended target—in this case, film production—may only be a fraction of the amounts that creative accountants manage to shuffle through the tax shelter.

Nonetheless, governments have shown remarkable ingenuity in raising money for targeted cultural subsidies.

Ireland funds its subsidies for film and television production in part from a tax on broadcast ad revenues. France, Germany and Argentina all charge a tax on movie tickets. Germany also levies a tax on the sale and rental of pre-recorded videos. Mexico's president Vicente Fox received a sharp protest note from the Motion Picture Association of America shortly after Mexico began imposing a one-peso levy on every cinema ticket sold in January 2003; the money was to be channeled by the state-backed Mexican Film Instititute into local production.

For nearly thirty years, Britain also taxed cinema admissions. The "Eady Plan," named after the cabinet minister who introduced it, directed a portion of cinema box-office receipts to the production in Britain of movies that included many of the early James Bond adventures and Stanley Kubrick's *2001: A Space Odyssey.* The plan was eventually repealed under Margaret Thatcher. Now in the United Kingdom, a portion of receipts from the national lottery is directed into film subsidies, passed on by the nation's Film Council.

Canada raises money for its array of cultural subsidies from a number of sources. Owners of "broadcast distribution undertakings" (better known as cable and satellite distribution systems) are required to pay a portion of their revenues into the Canadian Television Fund. One rationale for this levy is that these businesses profit handsomely from importing inexpensive foreign programs and exhibiting them to Canadian audiences in place of domestic programs that would be more expensive to produce. (Despite these cash flows, the fund early in 2003 blamed limited resources for its inability to finance more than half the proposals before it.) Large media enterprises are expected to commit additional funds as public benefits in order to secure regulatory approval of mergers or acquisitions that would otherwise benefit only shareholders.

FINDING THE MONEY is one thing. Giving it away again—fairly, efficiently and effectively—raises another distinct set of issues. Prominent among them is a tension that has surfaced repeatedly in these pages, particularly in Chapter 7: the desirability and difficulty of drawing a clear line between two broad categories of cultural product.

Into the first fall works most likely to be failed by the commercial market: distinctively local films or television series that strongly evoke the images and issues, "hopes, fears and dreams" of their place of origin. This is the category of the "visibly" Canadian (or Swedish, Australian or Taiwanese) movie, the one that has only a remote prospect of appealing to audiences unfamiliar with its world.

Into the other group fall those productions generic enough to appeal to wide audiences in many cultures. Science fiction, slapstick animation and special-effects action movies all go in this category.

As Chapter 7 demonstrated, most countries will treat either type of program as national product, provided the creators are nationals of their country and the artistic direction is exercised by local creators. However, when it comes to allocating subsidies, many countries will try to distinguish between the two categories, providing more financial support for culturally distinctive productions likely to have only a domestic audience than they do for generic productions likely to be exported to many foreign audiences.

In making this distinction, these nations recognize that while the culturally distinctive local drama might not get made without public assistance, the internationally generic entertainment probably will. In that case, why should the public contribute its good money to add to the profits of a project that would happen anyway?

The trouble, of course, is that the dividing line between the two categories is seldom bright and clear. *The Lord of the Rings* may convey more about the fictional culture of Middle Earth than it does about New Zealand. But defenders of the decision to let a New Zealand bank plunge tax-exempt dollars into its creation point to the showcase it affords the country's spectacular scenery—and an anticipated surge in tourism as a result. Some film version of the Tolkien epic, which has sold more than 100 million copies in print, might seem to have been inevitable. But "without the tax-incentive support," director Peter Jackson has told fellow Kiwis, "*Lord of the Rings* would not have been made here."

Similarly, television producers like *Degrassi*'s Linda Schuyler speak of the Catch-22 in which they sometimes feel trapped. The desire to reflect and speak to their home audience is in tension with the need to blur strictly domestic references for other markets. Yet, without those foreign sales, it would be financially impossible to put anything on the screen at home at all. They ask whether there is not a legitimate role for public subsidies to make possible a middle way: compensating them for some loss of foreign sales, in order to preserve some greater degree of local reflection.

Trade officials, of course, like to make a clear distinction between domestic and export subsidies in which the latter are potentially actionable under the WTO Agreement on Subsidies and Countervailing Measures if they apply to goods. However, as Chapter 16 will make clear, these provisions are difficult to apply to cultural products. In almost all cases, subsidies for cultural productions apply to the cost of creating the intellectual property in the original master work, efforts that in trade-law terms are considered a service, not a good. Few if any subsidies apply to making copies of the master, the "good" that is actually exported.

PLAIN IN ALL OF THIS is the difficulty of constructing a subsidy regime that accomplishes all the desired goals in terms of either ends or process. A wide range of formats nonetheless make the attempt.

"We have always had to strike a balance between our cultural mandate and the need to invest in winners," then-executive director of Telefilm Canada, Francois Macerola, said in 1998. "That is a matter of constant discussion." Telefilm's response has been to offer different measures of subsidy for projects that demonstrate different degrees of "Canadian-ness" according to the point-system described in Chapter 7: more money for projects with more "Canadian" points, less for those with fewer.

All of Telefilm Canada's television and film investments are expected to seek at least a measure of commercial success, however.

Canada maintains a separate agency, the National Film Board, with a mandate to support clearly experimental films and foster young talent.

A more common approach is for a single agency to provide film subsidies separately to two sets of candidates. The Council of Europe's Eurimages program does this. "Eurimages now awards assistance under two schemes," its Web site explains. "One for films with real circulation potential; one for films reflecting the cultural diversity of European cinema." The former are eligible for more money (a maximum of €763,000) than the latter (€460,000). The European Union (EU) guidelines for national film subsidy programs generally limit state aid for feature productions to 50 per cent of their budget. But that cap may be lifted for what the EU describes as "difficult and low-budget films" (what constitutes a difficult and low-budget movie is for each member state to determine) and for "films produced in a limited linguistic or cultural area."

Similarly, Britain's Film Council has a New Cinema Fund that invests smaller amounts in more experimental films and projects by new filmmakers, and a Premiere Fund with higher ceilings for commercial films that aim at international audiences. Spain, as noted earlier, grants an "automatic" subsidy that rewards films with box-office appeal and gives discretionary aid to "new directors or to experimental works of remarkable artistic and cultural content."

What such distinctions cannot do is duck the difficult and necessarily subjective task of selecting among competing applicants the relative few that will get the green light for funding. Most agencies establish guidelines that typically make reference to the prior experience of senior creative participants in a project, the presence or absence of broadcast or cinema-distribution commitments and the existence of independent private financing. But such factors do not take account of innumerable other relevant but unquantifiable variables. Is there good chemistry among the key creative partners? Have audiences recently been hot or cold towards movies of the proposed genre? Does the plot involve a high risk of unpredictable production costs? (Kids, water shots and animals are three danger signs.) Is the script any good?

In the end, it is always a judgement call. And usually it is made by a panel of "peer" experts, often drawn from the same pool of local film-industry types that contributes most of the candidates for the agency's support. These "experts," inevitably, are only human—and hence fallible. Chapter 4 emphasized that even commercially driven producers have a lamentable track record in predicting audience demand: *nobody knows.* The track record for juries made up of industry peers is no more stellar. Moreover, the potential for cronyism, mutual back-scratching and influence wielded by cliques assembled around particular aesthetic or political views is high. (This again is a phenomenon hardly foreign to Hollywood.)

"When you say you've never heard a word of criticism from producers about Eurimages," remarked French director Jacques Fansten in the early 1990s, "I immediately thought of the story of a Chinese emperor who insisted that he be criticized and then immediately executed anyone who did so."

In Britain in that era, director Mike Figgis charged, the film-funding system was "so inundated with class and snobbery and nepotism that all the talent that is there waiting to be used, waiting to be involved, waiting to be creative . . . is not welcome."

Of Canada's Cable Production Fund (a predecessor to the CTF in the same decade, financed by a levy on cable systems), Toronto media consultant David Ellis fulminated: "It services the old-boy network, the players who already have access to capital markets."

That many funding agencies—like the British Film Council, French CNC or Canadian Telefilm—exist at arm's-length from government, does not insulate them from political influence. Chief executives and members of their governing boards often hold their positions at the grace and favour of the government of the day. "The pre-eminent role of political patronage," says Martin Dale in his critique of mid-1990s European film financing, "means that commissioning editors, particularly for cinema, are often appointed because of political connections rather than from any prior expertise . . . One film tsar, when attacked by the press for knowing nothing about cinema, used the defence that the previous head knew nothing about cinema either!"

Britain tried to resolve the problem in the second half of the past decade by injecting more than £95 million raised by the state lottery into three organizations with private-sector roots. Policy-makers hoped that the commercial instincts of these "favourite son" companies would prove more astute than the judgement of bureaucratic funding panels. They didn't. Only one of fourteen films the three companies made between 1997 and 2000 turned a profit.

Canada's Telefilm in the same period sought to reduce the discretionary uncertainty in awarding its broadcast licence-fee top-up subsidy for TV productions. Its solution was to grant the awards on a first-come, first-served basis, starting on a certain date each spring (usually the date was April 1—April Fool's Day—an unintended irony occasioned by the start of the federal government's fiscal year). The unhappy result was lineups that formed outside the agency's Toronto offices up to a week in advance of the awards, with better-off applicants hiring place-sitters to keep their spot in line. Worthy projects whose representatives failed to show up in time lost out to more dubious candidates whose eager producers had spent a week camped out in sleeping bags.

Governments and funding agencies continue to search for better ways. Since the mid-1990s, Canada's Telefilm has required applicants to its Television Fund to produce a letter from a Canadian broadcaster committed to airing what they produce. The letter is meant to act as a proxy test for the project's appeal to real audiences. And under new executive director Richard Stursberg, Telefilm restructured its internal operations in 2002, promising Canadian filmmakers a simpler and more straightforward application mechanism with a more standardized commitment of funds. Britain dumped the ill-fated Arts Council that had funded the three hapless favourite sons in the late 1990s in favour of a new Film Council led by experienced director Sir Alan Parker (*Bugsy Malone; Evita*), although smaller U.K. filmmakers are not entirely happy with the new focus on "safer" films.

STRUCTURAL SUBSIDIES such as tax-credit or tax-shelter systems might seem to avoid the hazards of cronyism that plague funding agencies. But they too can suffer from opaque selection procedures.

Germany's tax-sheltered funds raise enormous amounts of money: an estimated US$1.95 billion in each of 2001 and 2002. "But there is a huge lack of transparency about exactly what and where these funds are," *Screen Digest* commented in a late-2002 survey. "Although an international producer does not need a German co-producer to access the funds, most will find it necessary to consult a local German expert to even find a telephone number for each."

Britain's sale and lease-back system has generated substantial amounts for film production in that country, but it may not be doing much for their exhibition. Nearly 60 per cent of the films made in the

United Kingdom in 2000 were not released, the third year running in which the portion of unreleased films climbed. The reason, *Evening Standard* critic Alexander Walker suggested in 2002, might be that so many got made, not on their merits, but so that investors could claim tax breaks. "A producer can put together a syndicate whose individual members take a legitimate tax write-off on the whole that's in excess of their individual investment by 10 or more percent. The producer also pays himself a premium. The film needn't be shown: in fact, it's safer not to risk it. It might turn out to be a hit: the investors would then have to pay tax on their profits."

Canada's tax-credit system for productions that score high on its Canadian-content ratings turned out to be no more watertight in the case of one high-flying and well-regarded Montreal animation house. Cinar Corp. soared in the 1990s on the strength of such popular children's series as *Arthur* and *The Busy World of Richard Scarry.* In 1997, *Hollywood Reporter* listed co-founder Micheline Charest at number 19 in its list of the 50 most powerful women in show business, above Madonna. Then, in late 1999, the company's stock and reputation tumbled to earth together on the disclosure that, among other schemes, the company had paid Canadians to lend their names to scripts written by Americans. With these *prête-noms* standing in for foreign writers, the productions received tax credits available only to "Canadian" scripts.

THERE IS, FINALLY, a risk that adheres to every sort of subsidy. It is the same one that traps generations of the same family and sometimes entire communities in the initiative-destroying grip of welfare dependency. Anticipating exclusion from commercial contention, cinema auteurs turn instead to introverted themes that are of limited interest to anyone but their artistic peers on funding panels.

"The point of a film is to be seen, it's not to massage the ego of the director," asserts *Screen Digest* research director and former Eurimage administrator David Hancock. "French producers until quite recently had so much money going into public funding they haven't really been exposed to a need to make films for the audience."

Some observers find the same symptoms in Canada. "You see the applications that come into the Centre [for Film Studies]," says Wayne Clarkson, director of Canada's pre-eminent graduate school for moviemaking. "They're all [about] dysfunctional families, demoralizing, despairing, antisocial, angry. You want to pay twelve bucks to see that?"

Mexican B-movie director Guillermo del Toro feels much the same way about the "fossilized" state system that until recently dominated film financing in his country. "Under the old system," del Toro told *The Guardian,* "the state would put [a state-financed movie] on at maybe two or three cinemas and then forget about it. It was tax money so they probably didn't even want it back anyway. When you let in private investors, you're suddenly dealing with people who'll make an effort to recoup their capital."

These criticisms were all too common in the early 1990s. More recently, however, they have faded as more refined subsidy systems in a number of countries increasingly supported a new generation of filmmakers strongly responsive to audiences. Nowhere has the success been more evident than in France, which managed through its generous support systems to achieve a cinema market share for its national films of 42 per cent in 2001, a record unmatched since 1986.

Other European countries also saw their local films enjoy growing box-office success. The most remarkable hit may have been in Finland. A nation with a population of only 5 million, it nonetheless supports production of as many as ten national films a year, subsidizing 60–70 per cent of their costs. In 2002, those few films achieved a domestic box office share of 20 per cent, led by the performance of a feature called *Pahat pojat* (*Bad Boys*), the third-highest-grossing feature film in Finland's history.

Just as with privately financed films, the audience response to subsidized films is inherently unpredictable. The market share for national films competing with star-driven Hollywood films that cost five or ten times more to produce will inevitably rise and fall. But in the cinema field, the subsidy systems around the world have made a key contribution to diversity in popular culture.

IT IS CERTAINLY true that governments can never create great art. Individuals create great art. But governments have always supported individuals who created great art.

It is equally true that when it comes to popular culture, most people neither expect nor receive great art—from Hollywood any more than from their national arts agency. What they receive may be good. It may just as easily be terrible, uplifting, irritating, boring or fascinating.

But it is important that enough of what people get to read, hear and watch be created by, for and about *them*. And as we have seen with regard to feature films, subsidies—judiciously invested—can do much to accomplish that. The success of Canadian authors, and the pleasure of Canadian readers, is further evidence of the benefit of subsidies.

Canada's book market may be one of the most competitive—and overstocked with titles—anywhere. Big international publishers release in Canada virtually all of the titles they publish in the United States, as well as titles from the United Kingdom and Australia. With "an incredible number of books coming over the U.S. border, plus all the British books, I can't think of a market anywhere that has so much going on," John Neale, president of (German-owned) Doubleday Canada told U.S.-based *Publishers Weekly* in 1998. Yet against that flood of imported titles, including every hot international best seller, Canadian readers in 1995 bought twice as many fiction books written by other Canadians as they had in 1985. Their purchases of Canadian non-fiction grew by 73 per cent in the same period.

"What we believe," Gordon Platt, head of the writing and publishing arm of the Canada Council for the Arts told an interviewer in 2000, "is that for literature to flourish, you have to have a functioning ecosystem."

"By that," commented *The Globe and Mail*'s Sandra Martin, who interviewed him,

> he means that the country needs small-circulation literary magazines where beginning writers can test their skills and their imaginations, and literary festivals and readings where they can connect with other writers and perform their works for potential readers. Then you need small publishers, based in local communities, from St. John's to Victoria, that are willing to take risks on emerging writers. The next step is mid-sized publishers to up the ante for writers and to provide them with a larger market. Finally you need major publishers who are able to expose writers to an even higher level of editing and marketing expertise.

To sustain that ecosystem, the Canadian government in 2002 invested less than c$50 million a year—the price of a single low-budget

Hollywood movie. From it, the same government reaped taxes, paid by Canadian publishers, of about c$100 million.

Canadian readers and appreciative counterparts around the world harvested the rich works of Alice Munro, Carol Shields, Rohinton Mistry, Michael Ondaatje and hundreds of other talented minds.

Doubling the public's money is not bad. Expanding the human imagination beyond the measure of accountants might well be called truly priceless.

New Zealand's government has since thought twice about leaving its taxpayers open to unlimited liability from some future *Lord of the Rings*. While the cameras were still rolling on that production, New Zealand amended its tax law. The loophole that allowed a Kiwi bank to put up the cash for the world's most expensive movie project snapped shut like the gates of Tolkien's fabled mines of Moria. However, the gates did not stay entirely shut for long. In June 2003, the government announced a less expensive support measure. Producers who chose New Zealand as a location for their big-budget films would be handed back 12.5 per cent of their production expenditure.

14

THE
TOOL KIT
AT
WORK

WHO WE ARE TODAY is not who we were yesterday or will be tomorrow. We are not static as individuals. Neither is culture. To the chagrin of economists, culture is a moving target, a rich garden of interconnections and dynamic influences, evolving themes and motifs that restlessly feed on and nourish each other in glorious unpredictability.

To borrow a term from Chapter 13, culture at large is more "ecosystem" than object, more process than product. An observation from biologist and broadcaster David Suzuki is apt. "Nature is in constant flux," Suzuki notes, "and diversity is key to survival. If change is inevitable but unpredictable then the best tactic for survival is to act in ways that retain the most diversity. Then, when circumstances do change, there will be a chance that a set of genes, a species or a society will be able to continue under the new conditions. Diversity confers resilience, adaptability, and the capacity for regeneration."

The past seven chapters have outlined the "tool kit" of measures that governments can take to sustain the diversity of thought and expression essential to their societies' resilience, adaptation, regeneration and growth. These measures include supporting public broadcasting, making reasonable scheduling or expenditure requirements of private broadcasters and other gatekeepers, supporting the creation of popular works in underrepresented genres through subsidies or tax incentives, limiting foreign ownership in certain sectors and enforcing competition policy to increase the number of green lights available to creators.

These measures have weaknesses as well as strengths. All of them need to be done right. Rules must be drafted with care to be effective. They must be implemented reasonably to be fair. They must be monitored and when necessary revisited and revised. Just as every national market is unique, what is appropriate to one society may be quite different from what is relevant in another.

There are some things these tools do *not* do. Those things are in many ways just as important as what they *do* accomplish. First, these policies do not stop cultures from changing, either from within or from without. Societies that desire to keep their unique cultures frozen in time will gain no comfort from these measures. Nor should they. Our case does not support the notion that cultures must—or can—be saved harmless from change.

Nor do these tools stop foreign cultural products from being heard and seen in any country. *Positive* quotas can ensure space on the shelf for domestic expression that would go unheard if pure market forces prevailed. *Negative* quotas whose effect is to prohibit access to foreign products cannot be supported. Cultural diversity is vastly enriched by the free flow of ideas across borders, even when those ideas challenge local thinking. The tool kit of policies we have identified seeks to provide space and choice for both domestic *and* foreign popular culture, not to prohibit the latter.

And finally, the tool kit does not guarantee that a particular expression by local creators will contribute overtly or obviously to a country's prior sense of its own "cultural identity," however that identity may be defined. Certainly, many stories, themes, images and ideas will be rooted in the unique cultural ethos of their creator's national context. But others will not. Like Canada's Michael Ondaatje or Britain's V.S. Naipaul, some creators may elect to write about the cultures from which they have come. Others may set their stories in a distant past or future. Or, like Yann Martel and J.K. Rowling, they may set them in a completely imaginary present. Nor will their works always support social cohesion. They may tell uncomfortable truths. They may seek to change and reform societies in ways that others will resist. Or yet again, they may seek simply to entertain and amuse.

All this may be problematic even for those economists who concede that cultural products bring "external" values to a society that the marketplace does not capture. What quantum value can they assign to ideas that upset society? How can they justify giving the nation's money to a cultural product that seems to display no visible cultural markers? Or to works that entertain more than they edify?

These are legitimate questions, and many countries may choose to limit their support to products that seem more cultural than commercial. But we must disagree with the ideology that what cannot be quantified can simply be discounted. Racial equality was once an idea that upset society; in some societies, gender equality remains so. How does one pro-rate the rich variety of cultural infusions in an allegorical tale like Martel's *Life of Pi?* In the face of a Disneyfied *Mulan,* who can assert that entertainment does not also transmit cultural values?

The freedom to create popular culture is empty without the opportunity for that culture to be exposed to an audience. Culture needs both freedom and opportunity to breathe. Nations must be entitled to ensure that their citizens have the capacity both to create and to be heard, read or watched. If they wish their creators to be able to do their best work on their own soil, in the presence of their own roots and influences and fellow citizens, that too is surely justifiable.

Creators are citizens of the world. The tool kit of measures seeks solely to give them room to grow and flourish. Following Suzuki's analysis, we take it as a given that it is in the interest of all humanity for creators from every country to add their voices to the widest possible diversity of expression. Any government prepared to support its own creators without limiting their freedom of expression surely then deserves the gratitude of other nations, not their criticism.

THERE ARE SOME who argue that market forces, aided by globalization, are in fact delivering cultural diversity. Perhaps the most eloquent supporter of this thesis is U.S. economist Tyler Cowen, whose 1998 book *In Praise of Commercial Culture* argued that the market economy provides vital and underappreciated support for a variety of artistic visions. Contemporary culture, he argued, is flourishing as never before because of the marketplace.

In a more recent book, *Creative Destruction: How Globalization Is Changing the World's Cultures,* Cowen expands his case. Far from being

in conflict with cultural diversity, globalization might instead promote, revive and broaden traditional cultures, he argues. While acknowledging that market forces put pressure on national or
communal cultures, Cowen asserts that trade enhances the range of
individual choice, yielding forms of expression within cultures that
flower as never before. This certainly is an effect to embrace; as we
have noted above, the tool kit set out in these pages seeks pluralism
of choice and expression, not exclusion. Cowen is also right to assert
that "invoking an absolute 'right' to one's original culture involves too
strong a moral claim, given that cultures are both synthetic and ever
changing." Again, no argument here.

But Cowen's analysis is fraught with contradiction. His case for the
benefits of "cross-cultural trade" rests largely on the example of cinema—a sector in which "trade" is a lopsided flow in only one direction.
Acknowledging the world dominance of Hollywood movies, Cowen argues paradoxically that this actually supports a diversity of style
around the globe. To give his example, European movies, shut out of
world markets, are forced to focus on "nuances of language and culture" that distinguish them from the products of Hollywood.

But having celebrated the diversity represented by European films,
Cowen opposes the very policies that have allowed them to be produced, whether those policies take the form of subsidies or structural
measures. In regard to films, he concedes that most European productions would not be able to survive without government assistance, although he criticizes those support measures as leading to "weaker
product" and forcing European taxpayers to underwrite "poorly
scripted films they don't want to see." Cowen suggests that if support
measures were withdrawn, this would induce European moviemakers
to make "a more commercially appealing product" in the long run (although he concedes it would lead to greater Hollywood presence in
European theatres in the short run).

The French support system for its local films, concededly a complex and expensive system, gives rise to Cowen's greatest hostility. But
it is also one of the most successful in delivering culturally diverse cinema that local audiences want to see. In the year 2000, for example, the
total production cost of the 171 feature films made in France was
US$742 million. Perhaps 65 per cent of that amount came from subsi-
dies, box-office levies, TV expenditure rules and other public-policy

support measures. Those films competed for French audiences against all the best films from Hollywood, which cost US $10.4 billion to make in the same year.

The box-office results were revealing. Hollywood films, which typically garner over 80 per cent of the domestic box-office around the world (and often far higher), obtained only a 63 per cent share in France. Films made by French filmmakers garnered fully 28 per cent of the domestic box-office in France. In other words, competing with Hollywood films that cost fifteen times more to make, French filmmakers still managed to achieve significant box-office results. Of course the French subsidy system ended up supporting many domestic films that were "weak" and that failed miserably at the local box-office. But as we have seen, the same is true of most films greenlit by Hollywood: "nobody knows." In fact, 2000 was considered a rather poor year for French films. The following year, the domestic share of French films shot up to 42 per cent, and the box-office share of Hollywood films declined to 47 per cent. Based on these numbers, which translate into more than 77 million tickets sold for French films out of 186 million tickets sold in total, the overall result of French cultural policy must be judged as an impressive success at the domestic level.

The one area where the French films "failed" was in getting significant box-office outside France. French films only made about US$72 million in export revenue in 2000, although this number increased in 2001 with the unexpected international success of *Amélie*. Most European films, like European TV fiction, face the same problem. Even if they are popular locally, they have difficulty in achieving success outside their national borders. The reasons for this, described in earlier chapters, include the dominance of Hollywood distributors, the difficulty in getting screen time for films without perceived stars and expensive ad campaigns, and the cultural discount in other countries for films too specifically rooted in a particular culture.

When Cowen condemns domestic support systems for not developing a "more commercially appealing product," then, he is not talking about commercial success at home; rather, he is referring to the lack of export success. The problem with a regime of subsidies, he argues, is that it "encourages producers to serve domestic demand ... rather than produce movies for international export." But if the purpose of cultural policy is to promote diverse local cultural expression, it is hardly a ground for criticism when domestic support structures lead to the creation of a range of culturally diverse films and television programs that succeed in telling a country's stories to its own citizens, without denying access to the best films from the rest of the world. Although export success is always welcome, it can never be predicted or assured, and the first responsibility of cultural policy-makers must be to ensure that their local creators at least have the space to tell their stories at home. Arguably, this is what truly adds to cultural diversity.

Cowen celebrates the contribution of capitalism to cultural diversity but ignores the many examples in which the tool kit of government measures allowed creative variety to flourish, both in the United States and elsewhere. As one critic has suggested, "Cowen has provided a libertarian view of culture which will be useful to anyone wishing to find out what libertarians think." But Cowen's analysis misses the importance of structural and other support measures in developing, maintaining and enhancing cultural divesity.

POTENTIALLY MORE TELLING is the charge levelled by other economists that no research demonstrates conclusively that the tool kit for cultural diversity produces results.

This line of attack is particularly popular in Canada among those who oppose cultural policy on ideological grounds. "Far too much is claimed on behalf of Canadian content regulations," William Stanbury asserts, in the absence of "any studies showing a link between Canadian content requirements and any measure of national identity or cultural sovereignty."

Others point to the "astounding imprecision" of statistics on cultural production and trade. In one telling comparison, two data sources (one from UNESCO, the other from the Canadian government) provided estimates of Canada's cultural trade in 1997 as either US$32.5 billion or US$7 billion—a fourfold difference. As even Harold Vogel notes in his authoritative *Entertainment Industry Economics:* "Most serious examinations of the economics of entertainment are desultorily scattered among various pamphlets, trade publications and journals, stockbrokers' reports, and incidental chapters in books on other topics."

In short, the critics are right that authoritative research is lacking. But absence of certain proof is no proof of certain absence. It must be acknowledged that the tool kit does not *guarantee* that diversity will flourish in every instance. Governments may make poor choices of inappropriate tools. They may draft rules badly. Poorly implemented policies may have unintended negative consequences for freedom of expression. And there is a limit to the ability of small countries to give financial support to expensive forms of popular culture, though even then the results can be inspiring, as we saw with Finland's local blockbuster *Pahat pojat.*

On this score, Canada's track record in implementing the full range of policy tools deserves further discussion. It is a record of stunning success in some areas and disappointing results in others. Perhaps the most disappointing is the track record in regard to Canadian movies. Although Canadian talent can be seen front and centre in many Hollywood movies, films that qualify as "Canadian" in terms of national origin garner less than 3 per cent of the cinema box-office in Canada.

Canadian policy-makers continue to experiment with new approaches to improve this number. But at the same time, they can take some satisfaction in the fact that over the years, a number of Canadian films have scored real success. A number of significant Canadian filmmakers—Denys Arcand, David Cronenberg, Atom Egoyan, François Girard, Bruce McDonald, Don McKellar—have elected to stay home to make their films and now have an enviable body of work. Films produced in French for the Quebec market have outperformed English-language films in Canada and have been box-office winners. And culturally specific Canadian films like *Atanarjuat (The Fast Runner)* continue to garner worldwide critical acclaim.

The field of English-language Canadian TV drama has also been a problematic area. Since 1984, with the rise of the independent production sector in Canada, Canadian television producers have become highly successful in a number of genres, including children's and family drama, animation, sketch comedy, and long-form documentary. The track record in series drama in English Canada has been a more checkered one, however. The late 1980s and early to mid-1990s saw some real successes in this area, from *Due South* to *Street Legal* to *The Boys of St. Vincent.* In the last three years, however, ratings for indigenous drama series have declined in English Canada and the number of new drama series has diminished. In the face of this, as noted earlier, the CRTC sought comments on possible new approaches to address the problems of Canadian drama in the fall of 2003.

The story is quite different in French Canada. Made-in-Quebec French-language dramatic series like *Blanche, Les Filles de Caleb, Lance et compte, La Petite Vie* and *Scoop* have consistently beaten the best U.S. dramatic series in ratings. A study released by the CRTC in 2003 noted that "the French-language broadcasters take it as a given that original dramas are largely responsible for maintaining audience loyalty and drive the entire programming schedule." Nor has drama been the only success story in Quebec. In early 2003, *Star Académie*, a nine-part music series featuring fourteen unknown singers, was a runaway success on the TVA network, with ratings exceeding 50 per cent of the Quebec population. But broadcasters and producers continue to be concerned with the growing cost of drama and the stability of government assistance.

Given the success of local drama in French Canada and in many other countries, what accounts for the problems encountered by English-language drama in Canada? The answer is not a simple one, since the puzzle has many moving parts. But among the reasons are these:

➤ U.S. networks can afford to develop, test with focus groups, "pilot" and then reject far more series than Canadian networks can. Hence, more failures are weeded out before they reach the screen, and only the most promising go to air. Those few successes are also seen on Canadian schedules. By contrast, less-wealthy Canadian networks are much more likely to feel obliged to air every program they have committed scarce resources to.

➤ Private television networks in English Canada build their schedules around "simulcasts" of the most popular American shows at the same hours in Canada that they air on U.S. networks. By doing so, they maximize audience since their signals (including the Canadian ads) are then substituted for the U.S. signals when they are delivered into the homes of Canadian cable or satellite subscribers. In consequence, however, their prime-time schedules are effectively set in Los Angeles and Canadian shows are relegated to any left-over slots.

➤ Canadian networks tend to order fewer episodes of new series than do U.S. networks—and then repeat those episodes more often. This has two pernicious effects: Canadian series have fewer episodes on which to build an audience, and those audiences quickly lose interest in overexposed reruns.

Both Canadian television and Canadian film confront another problem that is, if not unique to Canada, more severely felt here than elsewhere: the powerful lure of Hollywood for Canadian actors, writers and directors. Many of these creators make personal contacts in the American industry while working on "industrial" productions shot in Canada for U.S. studios or networks. English-speaking Canadians share a common language and cultural context with their U.S. counterparts. Industry practice makes it relatively easy to relocate from Toronto or Vancouver to Los Angeles. As a result, the magnet of Hollywood draws away more of Canada's best creative talent than that of any other more distant centres of audiovisual production.

Filmed drama, whether for the big or the little screen, is also the most expensive by far and the hardest of all forms of popular culture to get right. It requires the availability of by far the greatest number of different skills, all performed to a high level of excellence, in order to achieve maximum effect.

Canada is not alone in struggling to find the formula for making popular cultural products profitably and sustainably, even on strong drafts of public policy. Britain deploys a considerable number of policies from the tool kit. It is the world's second-most-populous English-speaking nation, with sophisticated financiers, a centuries-long creative legacy and some of the world's best film technicians. Yet, after decades of fitful successes and box-office disappointments, the prospects for British film reached such a nadir in late 2002 that the House of Commons struck a committee to examine its perilous condition.

Other big, rich and culturally sophisticated nations have similar troubles with film. In 2000, not a single Italian feature was judged good enough to appear in the main competition at Cannes. And although 2001 was a bellwether year for French films in terms of domestic market share, led by the art-house hit *Amélie,* French industry observers were alarmed to note an 18 per cent drop in ticket sales to French movies in the first quarter of 2003. Nothing is predictable.

But the picture on the wide screen does not necessarily reflect the tool kit's failure. For one thing, it is in the extraordinarily high-stakes gamble of film production that the greatest advantages accrue to the cultural conglomerates' size, scale and global integration. For another, thanks largely to the tool kit's existence, movies continue to be made in Canada, Italy, Britain, France and many other nations—some of which succeed in finding their audiences. Diverse bets get made in the casino of popular culture. And *nobody knows* when one of those will pay off.

Meanwhile, other sectors provide strong empirical evidence that where the tool kit is at work, so are creators, producing works of popular music, print fiction and television that delight millions of listeners, readers and viewers around the world.

Earlier chapters of this book referred to the striking success of Canadian musical performers and writers. Those successes owe much to the existence of scheduling requirements for radio and music television (in the case of musicians) and subsidies (for Canadian authors and publishers). A parliamentary committee report issued in June 2003 had particularly strong praise for the 35 per cent Canadian-content quota for music on radio. "[T]he measure of success for the [quota] is that it continues, year after year, in all its styles, to foster the development of great musicians and great Canadian music. It is, arguably, the single most successful policy measure in the history of Canadian broadcasting." It is intriguing to read, from one critic of those policies, that "the vitality of the [Canadian] culture sector speaks for itself. Over 640,000 people are employed in the cultural industries (compared to 557,700 in construction and 255,500 in transportation equipment) and cultural exports have increased by 38 per cent (current dollars) since 1995 to $4.5 billion." Yet, succumbing to the same error as Cowen, that critic then advances the very success the Canadian cultural sector enjoys as a reason to abandon the tool kit that helped make its success possible.

Beyond Canada, the positive effects of the tool kit at work can easily be measured on television. Prime-time viewing on most free-to-air TV stations in Europe was dominated in the 1980s by U.S. series like *Dallas*. Europe began to apply scheduling quotas in the 1990s, and the amount of local drama on television in countries with quotas soon went up. In the four years from 1996 to 1999, the number of original hours of first-run local-drama programs being produced in Germany, Spain, France, the United Kingdom and Italy rose by 26 per cent. The increases in local drama production were particularly notable in Spain (up 90 per cent) and Italy (up 228 per cent). By 2000, television broadcasters in Europe were devoting an average of 62 per cent of their fiction hours to European works.

More striking, however, has been the rising popularity of local drama. In Germany, Italy and Spain, where U.S. television drama had formerly dominated prime time, attractive and well-crafted local drama produced in response to the quota has reversed this position. Prime-time television in Germany, France, Spain and Italy is now dominated by local domestic drama. U.S. series continue to be aired and watched. But they now are largely relegated to off-prime periods on the free-to-air TV channels.

The popularity of European drama in these countries is shown in the top-ten listings of drama programs. In the United Kingdom, *all* of the ten top-rated prime-time dramas and comedies were produced locally. The same is true for Germany.

In Australia, the Australian Broadcasting Authority (ABA) introduced a drama quota in that country for the first time in the late 1980s. Australian dramas now account for five of the top-ten-rated prime-time dramas in Australia. (U.S. series account for three and U.K. series account for two of the top-ten slots.)

Around the globe, the results are the same. A survey released in 2003 by Nielsen Media Research found that 71 per cent of the top-ten programs in sixty countries were locally produced.

Other tools have also been used with effect. In much of Europe, South Africa, Australia and Canada, as well as in the United States, public-service broadcasters retain wide popular support for programming that serves to "inform, educate and entertain" their audiences as citizens, as well as consumers. Quotas to ensure that local films in South Korea are screened (but that do not guarantee ticket sales) have helped them also attract more than 45 per cent of that country's box-office. Australia applied national-ownership legislation to keep effective control of its Ten television network in Australian, not Canadian hands. Comparable tools keep the green lights of American free-to-air radio and television broadcasters and Canadian broadcasters of all kinds in the hands of their respective citizens. Spain, Britain and the United States, as well as Canada, have deployed a variety of competition-policy measures to reconcile a diversity of program content with a concentration of program carriage via cable or satellite.

WE WOULD AGREE with those who say that the effectiveness of all of these tools deserves more study. Public resources of political as well as financial capital are too valuable to waste on ineffective strategies. The better the mechanism of each tool in the kit is understood, the more precisely and appropriately it can be deployed in the interest of diversity.

What will *not* change, we believe, is the need for the tool kit itself. This, for the reason noted in Part One of this book: the market behaviour of cultural products demands it. People change. Societies change. Creative expression is a critical tool for the management of those changes. Diversity of expression is a vital resource for promoting the sustainability of societies and their peaceful accommodation of internal and external differences. Television in particular is a window on the world and a medium that can encourage an understanding of other cultures.

Thanks to the tool kit of policies that exist in many nations, diversity of expression is flourishing. But like the biodiversity in whose defence David Suzuki has so often and eloquently raised his voice, the diversity of creative expression cannot be taken for granted. Some of the same global forces that appear to many to threaten the biosphere also pose a threat to the symbolic and spiritual environment of cultural expression.

International efforts are under way to forestall those threats. We examine those forces and threats, and the possibility of containing them, in the concluding part of this book.

PART THREE

THE
CHALLENGE

15

TECHNOLOGY

A^{S THESE WORDS} were being typed into a laptop computer in early 2003, speakers attached to the same machine wafted out a fluid jazz composition. The writer was working in Vancouver, Canada. The music originated from a radio station in Mission Viejo, Orange County, California. Open at the same time on another screen on the same computer was a news page that the British Broadcasting Corporation asserted was "updated every minute of every day" from somewhere in the United Kingdom. Earlier, the same writer had checked the latest events being reported by *La Nacion,* a newspaper published in the capital city of Costa Rica, where he anticipated travelling.

Such is the everyday and quite unexceptional experience of the "borderless" world of the Internet. In less than a decade, since the invention of the browser software that first opened the online "virtual" universe to non-technicians, the Internet and its offspring the World Wide Web have revolutionized communication in a manner unmatched since the advent of radio. In that time, e-mail has gone from novelty to a necessity of modern economic life. In developed countries, young people spend more time surfing the Web than the TV and keep in touch with their peers more often through instant messaging than by phone. The network reaches into every corner of Earth. The destitute African nation of Eritrea manages ten thousand Internet accounts, Kazakhstan more than a hundred thousand.

Along with that ubiquity has arrived the virtually unchallenged modern truism that the world of the Internet is, as the cliché has it, indeed borderless. To many media commentators, the notion is self-evident and beyond serious dispute.

If any of these commentators have stayed with us while the previous pages detailed how intelligent domestic regulation can nourish diverse creative expression, they are surely by now itching to voice an obvious protest. Are not all—or at least many—of the tools in the regulatory kit doomed to obsolescence in the face of digitally channeled globalization?

In fact, evangelists for a digital tomorrow might reasonably point to not one but two technologies that seem to toll the death knell for any attempt to regulate the markets for popular culture. Satellite broadcasting is also a border-leaping technology. Satellites sitting over the equator and pointing downward have "footprints" that blanket entire continents instead of mere countries. Signal overlap is inevitable.

To the extent that satellites or the Internet distribute audiovisual or any other cultural content directly from foreign creators to domestic consumers, the threat to national rules predicated on borders must surely be evident. That was, certainly, the conventional early wisdom on the potential of both technologies.

Alarmists on the Canadian cultural scene dubbed the new generation of direct-broadcast satellites launched in the mid-1990s "death stars" for their anticipated lethal effect on local broadcasters and Canadian television content.

Others applauded. "The technical revolution ... effectively renders 99 per cent of Ottawa's telecom and broadcast regime irrelevant," crowed columnist Terence Corcoran in late 1996. "The main regulatory framework of Canada's broadcast industry—the Soviet-style content rules and the system of broadcast licences that protect industry participants—is rapidly becoming unenforceable."

"Vietnam, China and others that are trying to control the Internet—even our own government—have no chance," James Kimsey, one of the founders of America Online Inc., declared in March 2000.

"For the content industry," Sheridan Scott and David Elder of telecom giant Bell Canada wrote in 2001, "an increasingly global marketplace for communications services challenges existing legal and regulatory schemes that rely on largely on geographic borders."

"Technology has breached the protectionist walls of domestic policy initiatives," economist Christopher Maule told a conference on trade and culture in early 2002.

"Canada's jerry-built extravaganza of tax-credits, production quotas and ownership restrictions is going to come tumbling down," yet another columnist, Drew Fagan, enthused three months later. "The inexorable force of new technologies makes that inevitable."

At the height of enthusiasm for the supposed inevitability of this "inexorable force" some went further still. French diplomat Jean-Marie Guehenno argued that the Internet would render obsolete not only national policy, but the entire system of nation states. "This new revolution in information and communications technologies," the author of *The End of the Nation State* asserted in 1997, "destroys the idea of territorial sovereignty."

But does it? Has it?

On more sober examination, "death star" satellites and the global reach of the World Wide Web appear to have changed things rather less than much. Reports of the death of national cultural policy, to say nothing of the end of the nation state, turn out to have been greatly exaggerated.

There are reasons for this. One may perhaps be the events of 9/11, which in a single morning brought the world's most powerful nation state to a tight focus on its sovereignty and security. But the other is money. Territories defined around national geography are a prime factor in determining how money is made from intellectual property. Financial interest, as it turns out, trumps technology.

LET'S BEGIN with satellite technology. Satellites began delivering programs to cable television systems in the United States in 1976. But it soon dawned on others that those signals were not beamed exclusively to cable systems. In fact they beamed down widely. Any individual prepared to put up a six-foot dish could trap the same signals the cable companies were picking up. Reception was made even easier by the fact that the signals were in analog form—the form receivable by regular TV sets—and broadcast in the clear. That realization spawned an avid counter-culture of direct-to-home (DTH) satellite dish owners, mostly in rural areas, who were capturing signals intended for cable head ends.

By 1986, the number of DTH dish owners capturing television from satellite feeds without paying for it had reached proportions that alarmed program suppliers. They insisted that U.S. satellite services begin encrypting their signals. That significantly slowed down the growth of the big dishes. But it was not long before enterprising pirates figured out how to defeat the analog encryption systems. And over the next few years, the illegal satellite dish community continued to grow as hackers successfully defeated each new advance in encryption.

Several ventures attempted to provide consumers with a more legitimate alternative. Legal DTH services allowed viewers to buy packages of services on an authorized subscription basis. But their expansion was constrained by the unwieldy size of the dish and the continuing ease of illegal access to the same programs.

In 1994, that picture finally changed. A new generation of high-powered direct-broadcast satellites (DBS) used digitally compressed and highly encrypted signals to deliver programs to much smaller reception dishes. Suddenly a broader range of consumers could get a cheap convenient package of satellite programming. In the United States, competition devolved into two players, DirecTV and Echostar. By the beginning of 2003, less than ten years after their launch in 1994, they had achieved a penetration in the United States of 20 million subscribers, compared with 65 million households served by cable.

In the United Kingdom, the same development occurred. BSkyB changed from an analog satellite platform to a high-powered satellite using digital technology in 1998. Using a marketing approach that almost gave away the satellite dishes, and with a monopoly on Premier League football rights, BSkyB reached a penetration of 6.3 million U.K. households by the beginning of 2003, compared with 3.4 million served by cable.

This take-up of encrypted digital subscription services did not change one long-standing fact about DBS technology. Transmission coverage by and large remained broad and essentially borderless. The footprint of the American DirecTV and Echostar satellites easily reached the populated areas of Canada. The footprint of British satellite BSkyB reached many European countries other than the United Kingdom.

But, contrary to many expectations, this did not prevent national jurisdictions from regulating the DTH and DBS systems. In fact, quite the opposite happened.

In the United States, although the program offerings on the two DTH systems, DirecTV and Echostar, are not directly regulated, both companies need government and legislative approvals to operate. Moreover, they must abide by special copyright provisions relating to the carriage of local free-to-air signals. And when Echostar attempted to merge with DirecTV in 2002, their union was subject to approval by both the Federal Communications Commission (FCC) and the U.S. Department of Justice. In the event, both withheld their blessing and the merger did not proceed.

Europe's largest DTH operator, BSkyB, is classified as a domestic satellite operator under U.K. law and is regulated by a number of entities, including the Independent Television Commission (ITC), the Office of Telecommunications (Oftel) and the U.K. Office of Fair Trading. In addition, all European satellite operators, including BSkyB, are subject to domestic legislation that must itself meet the standards set by the "Television Without Frontiers" directive.

Canada regards satellite transmission as a form of broadcasting. Hence, legislation requires all DTH satellite operators offering service to Canadian homes to obtain a CRTC licence, no matter where the satellite may be located.

A year before its launch in 1994, DirecTV sought the CRTC's approval to serve Canadian subscribers directly. But under Canadian policy, DirecTV was forced to take a minority investment in a Canadian licensee that would offer a combination of authorized U.S. services from DirecTV's satellite and Canadian services from a Canadian satellite. With that in view, DirecTV found a Canadian partner and put forward such an application. In 1995, the CRTC granted it a licence. But the new venture wanted Canadian program services to subsidize the company's Canadian satellite transponder costs. When the CRTC declined to issue such an order, DirecTV and its partner abandoned their plans.

Since then, five all-Canadian companies have applied for and obtained such licences, although only two currently operate: Bell ExpressVu and Star Choice. Both licensees are subject to detailed conditions of licence comparable to those placed on cable operators. Among other terms—some referred to in earlier chapters—those specify what services the satellites may carry and oblige the companies to contribute to a fund for the production of Canadian programming.

But where, a skeptic might well ask, is the traction? How can a country exert jurisdiction over foreign satellites whose signals originate outside it? It is all very well to regulate what satellite channels a *cable* television system can or cannot provide; after all, the cable system is locally licensed and has earthbound assets. But a foreign satellite's signal travels directly from space to the home. Most nations shy away from regulating their citizens' actual ownership of satellite dishes. And if they went after the DBS operator, how would they regulate an entity with no physical assets on national soil?

The Canadian experience provides some answers. Canada's definition of "broadcasting" includes any undertaking "carried on in whole *or in part* within Canada" (emphasis added). And courts in Canada and elsewhere have ruled many times that assets need not be physically located in a country for an enterprise to "carry on business" there.

As early as 1993, the CRTC issued the following statement:

A DBS service provider whose signal is receivable in Canada could be found to be carrying on a broadcasting undertaking in Canada in whole or in part where, for example, it has some or all of the following characteristics:

➤ it acquires program rights for Canada;
➤ it solicits subscribers in Canada;
➤ it solicits advertising in Canada;
➤ it activates and deactivates the decoders of Canadian subscribers.

The Commission will apply the appropriate enforcement tools to assert its jurisdiction over these undertakings should they enter the Canadian market without making contributions to the Canadian system as required of all broadcasting undertakings under the Act. In the case of U.S. DBS ... the Commission has determined that where a non-Canadian satellite programming service authorized for cable distribution in Canada is also distributed in Canada by a DBS operator not authorized by the Commission, the service may be removed from the lists of Eligible Satellite Services.

Yet, how could the CRTC enforce its orders on a DBS system based in the United States? It had, as it turns out, a number of levers at its disposal.

First, any person "aiding or abetting" a breach of the Broadcasting Act could be prosecuted. That included anyone importing or selling DirecTV equipment in Canada or taking subscription orders. The effect of such potential prosecution was to drive those activities underground, since any retail store selling or advertising the equipment in Canada could face charges.

The same approach proved effective in the United Kingdom. There, a number of pornographic channels based in countries with more permissive standards attempted to reach subscribers in Britain. The British government asserted jurisdiction under provisions of its 1990 Broadcasting Act, which gave it the power to declare particular channels "proscribed satellite services" and to penalize suppliers, advertisers and equipment retailers who abetted their delivery. Prosecutions and threatened prosecutions soon drove the pornographers out of business.

But penalties have a poor track record against activities driven by consumer demand—as witness the perennial, costly and generally ineffectual "war on drugs." A more effective strategy leveraged a truism older and more certain than the one about borderless technology: *money talks*. It enlisted the financial self-interest of companies that owned the programs being illegally broadcast to Canadian homes.

A number of U.S. program services enjoyed privileged access to 8 million cable households in Canada by reason of their inclusion on the CRTC's "Eligible" list. As quoted above, the CRTC indicated that "where a non-Canadian ... service authorized for cable distribution in Canada is also distributed ... by a DBS operator not authorized by the Commission, *the service may be removed* from the [Eligible] lists" (emphasis added).

In other words, any program service that permitted DirecTV or Echostar to retail their channels illegally to a handful of customers in Canada stood to lose a far larger number of legal Canadian cable viewers. The result was entirely predictable. Services such as CNN, A&E, TNN and TLC—all listed on the "Eligible" list and distributed legally by Canadian cable systems—immediately notified the U.S. satellite services that the program-distribution rights they had purchased extended only to residents of the United States, not to Canadians. Other U.S. programming services, although not carried directly on Canadian cable, had nonetheless licensed their content to Canadian services. Many faced a similar trade-off of interests and soon reached the same conclusion.

In short, copyright owners found it decidedly in their interest to support meaningful borders. The importance of territorial rights "windows" exceeded the small incidental value of a few cross-border subscriptions.

The result was that far from offering service to Canadian residents, U.S. DBS operators have actively sought to curtail such services, even though their signals continue to cover Canadian centres.

The experience since 1995 has been instructive.

The launch of all-Canadian DTH television was at first delayed by bad luck. When one of Telesat Canada's satellites suffered a major power failure in orbit in March 1996, Canadian DTH licensees were forced to postpone their planned launch by a year. By the time Bell ExpressVu and Star Choice did go to air in 1997, many Canadian households had already begun subscribing illegally to DirecTV. The Canadian services had trouble winning them back. But after moving to a new high-power DBS satellite in 1999, their take-up accelerated.

By 2003, Canadian DTH services subject to Canadian program rules were a success. Bell ExpressVu and Star Choice had a combined total of over 2.2 million subscribers, representing a penetration level higher in Canada than DirecTV and Echostar had achieved by that time in the United States. The Canadian cable industry, with 8 million subscribers, suf-fered some initial losses to DTH but soon stabilized with the introduction of digital cable packages.

Canadian residents willing to act illegally continue to receive U.S. DBS signals. To do so they must either arrange a fraudulent U.S. accommodation address or, more commonly, acquire a cloned "smart card" and hope to avoid any payment at all. The extent of such illegal subscriptions is hard to estimate, but as of late 2003, it was believed to be in the 400,000–700,000 range, including a number who illegally capture the signals of Canadian DTH services as well. While the figure is disconcerting, it represents less than 5 per cent of all Canadian television households. Furthermore, recent enforcement efforts supported by the Canadian courts, both Canadian and U.S. satellite services and program rights-holders are likely to drive that number down.

But the Canadian experience already demonstrates several key lessons. It is clearly crucial to "occupy the field" early with one or more domestic services that satisfy local demand at a reasonable price. Second, the financial interests of copyright holders afford a critical source of policy support. And as a matter of practice as well as law, the exercise of national legal jurisdiction over this purportedly "borderless" technology is not only feasible, but increasingly common and effective.

This should not be so surprising. The United States, for one, has a long history of extraterritorial application of its laws, from tax statutes to competition policy. Many countries quarrel with those measures as invading their own sovereignty. But in the area of satellites, even the United States has recognized that national jurisdiction can and does apply. As one critic noted recently, "The most publicized form [of globalization], satellite television, is in the vast majority of cases bounded by states in terms of its regulation and programming, if not in terms of its footprint."

Further, as technology introduced the supposedly borderless satellite footprint, technology may also redefine it within a more limited perimeter. In a study for the Council of Europe, Christopher Marsden reports that "new satellite technology permits 'spot beam' transmission, which would allow the signal to broadcast to only a portion" of a satellite's total potential coverage area. Marsden notes that this capacity could soon allow individual European regulators to exert "must-carry" requirements on satellite services that would be effective within specific national borders.

Another dimension of the belief that satellites are creating a new "borderless" media environment also deserves closer scrutiny.

When television satellites were first launched, many observers believed they were witnessing the birth of a new era of global media. These would be on a scale quite beyond that of the first broadcasting age of state-based systems, and of another character. After all, one critic noted, globalization implies "distinctive aspects of media operations that take place across a range of countries, with the same or similar content being used in each case, thus realising economies of scale to a greater extent even than is characteristic of all media."

But has this universal voice emerged?

Not on the evidence. "The majority of satellite broadcasting, and certainly that which has been most successful in terms of audience-size," records global media analyst Daya Kishan Thussu, "has had a distinctly national content."

Two widely seen logos serve as poster children for this notion of media globalization: those of CNN and MTV. Both purportedly reach over 100 million subscriber households outside the United States. But in each of the countries where the two are broadcast, their actual share of audience is tiny in comparison with that of national channels. In most places, services like CNN and MTV typically attract less than 1 per cent of viewers. When, as in Canada, a service like MTV must work with a partner in order to be received legally, its local content can be regulated. (Even when that is not the case, both CNN and MTV have discovered that adding local content to U.S. or generic international fare produces higher ratings.)

Nor have satellite services as a whole achieved as significant a presence as often depicted. In most countries, satellite services reach only a small proportion of the country's population. Penetration is limited in many markets—especially in Africa, Latin America and South and Central Asia—by the cost of service, a lack of channels in local languages, poor infrastructure or other factors. Of the fifty-three DTH satellite platforms in service around the world as of January 2001, only nine actually reached more than a million subscribers. Among the top thirty satellite platforms, the two biggest African services combined reached fewer than 0.2 per cent of that continent's 392 million sub-Saharan residents. China's CBTV reached barely 0.02 per cent of that nation's 1.2 billion people. In most nations, fewer than 5 per cent of people subscribe to satellite services.

Even more telling is the amount of time that viewers in most countries actually spend watching broadcasts originated elsewhere. Despite globalization, the overwhelming majority of television viewing in most of the world is to local services regulated by a domestic authority.

Some European audiences do spend significant time viewing out-of-country signals. Viewers in the Scandinavian countries and the Netherlands, for instance, watch foreign signals about 20 per cent of the time, reflecting their capacity to understand languages other than their own. Viewing of foreign channels also increases when a smaller country is next to a larger one with the same language. Channels from France account for 43 per cent of viewing in French-speaking Belgium, for instance. Austrians spend 44 per cent of couch time watching channels from Germany. And in Luxembourg and Switzerland, more than half of viewing time is dedicated to foreign channels. (In all these cases, "foreign" means originating in another European country; there is no viewing whatever of non-European channels.)

But these are the exceptions. The real story is told in the larger European nations. The TV audience share in 2001 of foreign-source channels in countries like Britain, France, Germany, Italy, Greece, Spain and Portugal was less than 5 per cent. In a number of cases, it was effectively nil.

Clearly, despite the introduction of direct-broadcast satellites, Europe has maintained control of its broadcast destiny. National regulation governs the system.

The same is even more true for countries throughout Asia, Africa, Latin America and Oceania. Despite the introduction in all those regions of DBS systems, local channels continue to garner over 95 per cent of the audience.

In sum, "the irresistible tide of supranational globalization" at the point of a satellite beam turns out to be much more resistible than was forecast. DBS systems are not in fact under the remote guidance of corporate Darth Vaders. They are owned by conventional earth-bound companies, accessible to reasonable policies in support of national objectives. Moreover, for them as well as for their customers, the value in the transaction lies in the program content transmitted and received. Historically, the owners of that content have extracted a financial return through its sequential exposure in territorial "windows." There is no incentive to abandon that system. To the contrary, it provides every incentive for every player involved to uphold the sanctity of borders and the national territories they define.

Audiences, meanwhile, show a clear preference for locally originated services that have a mix of national and imported programming. This lends merit to the licensing of such services in order to "occupy the field" and satisfy local demand.

It also underscores, yet again, a central tenet of our thesis. The desirable outcome is neither the "irresistible tide" of globalized homogeneity nor the inbred provincialism of isolation. It is a healthy and diverse mix of both.

FOR MANY early enthusiasts, no greater or more open diversity could be imagined than the grand virtual commons of cyberspace. At the same time, the emergence of the Internet as a universally accessible global network linked by computers around the world has seemed to pose an even more forceful challenge to national sovereignty than satellites do.

On July 23, 1997, Ira Magaziner, then U.S. president Bill Clinton's special adviser on electronic commerce, famously said that any attempt to regulate content on the Internet would be futile. "We believe the Internet, broadcast and telecommunications are going to converge within the next five years, maybe ten at the latest," he said. His assessment has since been echoed repeatedly as the "inexorable force of new technologies" has nowhere appeared to march forward more irresistibly than through the Internet.

The Internet's central idea—that computers could break data up into digital "packets" and send them by different routes to other computers that would reassemble them into replicas of the original—has in fact been around for a while. It was developed four decades ago to help the U.S. Air Force protect its command structure from Cold War attack. The first physical network of what would become the World Wide Web was strung in 1969, linking three university campuses in California and one in Utah. It operated more slowly than today's dial-up telephone modems.

The first e-mail program was developed in 1972. A year later, programmers developed a protocol that allowed different kinds of computers to connect to the same network. And in 1976, the early Internet leapt the Atlantic to connect with a number of computer labs in Europe.

It would take two more decades for the network to come to wider public attention. One critical step occurred when researchers at the University of Wisconsin created the Domain Name System that allowed users to identify Internet addresses with memorable words instead of strings of numbers. Another occurred in 1990, when a researcher in Geneva implemented an Internet version of hypertext, which allowed users to follow a link from one word or phrase to a document somewhere else, and invented the phrase "World Wide Web" to describe the interconnected weave of information that resulted. And in 1993, a programmer at the University of Illinois developed the first graphic interface—the predecessor of today's Netscape or Explorer browser software—that began to make it all accessible to ordinary people disinclined to learn alphanumeric programming code.

With this last innovation, what had been a convenience for researchers began an explosive breakout into a new role as the central piece of infrastructure for a post-industrial age. In 1990, a mere 313,000 host sites were connected to the Internet. By 1995, there were 6.6 million.

At last count, there were a guesstimated 2 *billion* pages of information accessible over the Internet, but no one really knows for certain. It is a bit like asking how many pencils there are in the world. Which is also something of an indicator of how integral the Internet has become to contemporary life.

The last half of the last decade of the twentieth century witnessed a speculative bubble in "new economy" business plans that was unmatched since the radio craze of the 1920s. Like that one, this bubble also burst, leaving behind it a cruel economic hangover. But like radio, the Internet is plainly here to stay.

Yet six years after Ira Magaziner's assessment, his forecast begs the same question posed by the "death star" satellites.

Have broadcasting, telecommunications and the Internet become one? Do households around the world routinely download their radio or television shows off the Internet? Has "Web-casting" eclipsed conventional off-air broadcasting, siphoned away local television's ad revenue or made national regulators irrelevant?

Are borders meaningless in cyberia?

Of course not.

Much to the surprise (and in some cases regret) of the doomsayers, the Internet has turned out to be something entirely different. Far from being a threat to conventional broadcasting, the Internet has exhibited unique weaknesses as well as strengths. It is a powerful new medium. But it shows no more likelihood of killing off television than television does of destroying radio, or than either of those older "new" media do of rendering books extinct. And, for the same reasons, it has not proven to be a threat to the *regulation* of broadcasting.

Of most interest to the present discussion, virtual space, far from being borderless, turns out to be just as susceptible to the erection of borders as physical space. The reason why is instructive. Once again, money, in the end, trumps technology.

As often before with revolutionary new forms of communication, Canada was the scene of an early test case.

This one began in December 1999. An enterprising company based in Toronto announced a new Internet Web site to be called iCraveTv.com. Visitors to the site would be able to watch a selection of Canadian and U.S. free-to-air TV channels on their home computers. iCraveTV proposed to capture the signals on antennas at its "head end" north of Toronto in much the same way that conventional cable companies do. Only it would then "stream" the signals onto the Internet, where interested viewers would be able to watch each channel in an inset box on their computer screen. The service would be free to viewers. But the screen box would include banner advertising that iCraveTV hoped to sell and insert.

In offering their service, the owners of iCraveTV benefited from a decision of the CRTC earlier that year to exempt the Internet from the Broadcasting Act. The ruling meant that iCraveTV did not need to secure a broadcasting licence from the agency before launching its new venture.

There was one problem. iCraveTV's owners had not troubled to obtain permission from the rights holders for the programs they proposed to stream over the Internet to the public. They had not entirely disregarded the issue. But they believed they had a solution. iCraveTV argued that its service was really no different from that of a cable company. Cable companies were already permitted to retransmit local and distant TV signals without any explicit authorization from rights holders. That was allowed thanks to a "compulsory licence" under the Canadian Copyright Act. In return for an automatic right to rebroadcast copyright material, cable companies paid a compulsory licence fee set by the Canadian Copyright Board. Why couldn't iCraveTV proceed on the same basis, relying on the same compulsory licence?

The answer came soon enough as, once again, money spoke. iCraveTV was hit with massive lawsuits from rights holders on both sides of the Canada–U.S. border. In the United States, a number of major movie studios and sports leagues obtained a temporary restraining order shutting down the company's Web site. In Canada, broadcasters and program rights holders obtained a shotgun settlement on the courthouse steps in which iCraveTV agreed not to proceed with its plan.

Even more directly than in the case of cross-border satellite signals, "iCraveTV vs. the copyright industry" raised the essential issues explored in Chapters 5 and 6. Rights holders rely on the territories created by geographic borders to maximize revenue from their programs. Any technology that threatens to erase borders also threatens to annul territories, and with them the ability of copyright owners to fully exploit their intellectual property.

Canadian rights holders had paid good money for the right to exploit copyrighted material in Canada. They simply didn't want to see the value of those rights eroded by any more "free" exhibition of that material than they could forestall.

A different aspect of the same erosion of territorial boundaries alarmed rights holders in the United States. iCraveTV's Web site was accessible to any Internet user. Its technology would stream first-run U.S. programs aired on Canadian and U.S. networks as easily into homes in Paris as in Peoria. Shows sold for exhibition only to American or Canadian audiences could be delivered gratis to markets where no one had paid for them. To add insult to injury, they would be accompanied by banner ads competing with the commercials already in the program, further undermining the economic basis of the television industry.

For rights holders, this raised a particularly ominous spectre. Distributors sell programs like *c.s.i.* at different prices around the world; a broadcaster in a small developing country can buy the right to broadcast *c.s.i.* for as little as a few thousand dollars. Suppose that a local Webcaster in that developing country were to pick up the program off-air and, like iCraveTV, retransmit it around the world, relying on some minimal compulsory licence fee paid under local copyright legislation. What would be left of *c.s.i.* for its owners to sell to broadcasters in other countries, at much higher prices, if the audiences in those countries had already seen the program on the Internet?

The same issue confronted the Canadian rights owners to programs like *Degrassi: The Next Generation.* What price would their series fetch from a broadcaster in the United Kingdom if British viewers had already watched it streamed into their home PC?

iCraveTV's owners in fact recognized that it would not be politic to stream their signals into the United States, where copyright law does not provide a compulsory licence for Internet retransmission. To screen out American viewers, they required users to enter their local telephone area code before gaining access to iCraveTV's service. Anyone with a U.S. area code would be excluded. But this attempt at border control by the honour system proved laughably ineffective. Hundreds of thousands of U.S. residents simply punched in a Canadian area code. Presented with evidence that this was so, the U.S. court hearing the application for a restraining order against the Canadian service was not amused. It issued the order.

But iCraveTv's signoff did not end the issue of Internet retransmission. A year later, a new Canadian company calling itself JumpTv proposed a similar service. Once again, it sought to invoke the compulsory licence available in Canada for cable and satellite retransmission. Taking the matter further than iCraveTv had, JumpTv applied to the Canadian Copyright Board for a special tariff to be declared for Internet retransmission. During the proceeding, JumpTv claimed that its plan was different from iCraveTv's. First, JumpTv would drop the idea of banner advertising. Instead, it would be a subscription service (as it happened, the months following iCraveTv's demise had also witnessed a general collapse of dot-com advertising). Second, and more important, JumpTv claimed it had found an effective way to secure its Web site against subscribers from other countries. It argued that it would use proprietary software that could determine a user's geographic location and deny access to those outside Canada.

By 2001, with the Copyright Board still considering its application, JumpTv decided to drop the notion of relying on a compulsory licence. It withdrew its application, and the board terminated its proceeding.

Broadcasters and rights holders remained unsatisfied and simply shifted their attack to lawmakers. In late 2002, Parliament amended the Canadian Copyright Act to make it clear that the CRTC's internet exemption did not permit compulsory licensing for online retransmission. Any future attempt at Internet retransmission of free-to-air television would require either a new exemption order or a CRTC distribution licence. In a report to the government on January 17, 2003, the CRTC indicated that it intended to offer neither.

The regulator's main rationale was that it frankly doubted JumpTv's claims. In the agency's view, Internet "border controls" remained ineffective. Without such control, and given the potential disruption to the program-rights marketplace, the CRTC saw no public benefit in extending legal signal retransmission to the Internet.

The fate of these two ventures sends a clear message. Ventures in the new economic space of the Internet that plan to use filmed entertainment must still get authorization the old-fashioned way—from rights holders. If copyright owners decline to make rights available because of inadequate border controls on the Internet, their decision can be made effective through the courts.

Eventually, effective border control technology for the Internet is likely to emerge. When that moment will come is a matter for the marketplace to resolve.

It may be sooner rather than later. Although the motives may not always be savory, technology is emerging from a variety of quarters to fence in the open range of cyberspace. The Internet as "a parallel universe of pure data, an exciting new frontier where a lawless freedom prevailed," turns out to have been no more than a glorious illusion for the first cyber-sodbusters.

Even *The Economist* has conceded the point. In a 2001 issue entitled "The Internet's New Borders," it described the new reality:

> [I]t turns out that governments do, in fact, have a great deal of sovereignty over cyberspace. The Internet is often perceived as being everywhere yet nowhere, as free-floating as a cloud—but in fact it is subject to geography after all, and therefore to law . . .
>
> Though it is inspiring to think of the Internet as a placeless datasphere, the Internet is part of the real world. Like all frontiers, it was wild for a while, but policemen always show up eventually.

The realities bringing the law to the wild frontier of the Web are the same ones that brought it to the plains: money and power.

Not all of it meets western standards of political morality. In dozens of countries, authoritarian regimes mistrust their citizens' access to the Web's cornucopia of opinion and data. "The explosion of news and information on the World Wide Web is tempting governments, developed and developing, politically free and not free, to consider restricting content on the Internet," the human-rights group Freedom House reported in 2000. More-repressive tactics range from restricting access to the Net and licensing modems, to filtering Internet content as it passes through server points under a government's control. Among nations that restrict or control access to the Web are China, Saudi Arabia, Libya, Turkmenistan, Belarus and Cuba. In some instances, the motivation is nakedly political. But some Asian states, such as

Singapore, filter content in the interest of "Asian cultural values." Middle Eastern states promote censorship as a means of protecting public morality.

The last rationale is not entirely unknown in nations with better civil-rights records than those of Saudi Arabia or Iran. The United States and Britain, to name two, prohibit child pornography online. In 2000, France famously exerted its jurisdiction in obliging Yahoo!, an American company, to prevent French Internet users from gaining access to auction sites where Nazi paraphernalia was for sale. And in 2002, an official with the popular Google search engine acknowledged that it blocked citations for more than a hundred sites—mainly U.S.-based sites featuring racist material—when presenting results to users from Germany and France.

The other factor pushing fences out onto the open prairie of cyberspace is money. As occurred in the case of iCraveTV, the interests of copyright owners align strongly with the emergence of borders on the Internet. As e-commerce expands and enterprises such as Amazon and e-Bay begin to turn profits, legislators are also beginning to give thought to the inevitable question of how to levy taxes on transactions conducted online. California's governor, struggling to close a yawning US$34.6 billion budget shortfall, indicated in January 2003 that his state might be the first to impose an Internet sales tax. Necessary to such a levy is a means to determine where in the "borderless" world of the Web a particular transaction has taken place.

Meanwhile, a growing roster of commercial disputes arising from online transactions is coming before courts in every country—and creating a growing jurisprudence of cyberlaw.

Even the example most often cited by those who insist that the digital environment portends an epochal shift in the market dynamics of creative products—illicit music downloads—may not be going quite the way they expect. It is true that an early victory for rights holders—driving the file-sharing pioneer Napster out of business—proved not to be the end of the war. A virtual posse of even more dispersed successors rapidly took Napster's place, and within months more music files were changing hands than before. The loss to legitimate rights owners was measurable and large. According to Neilsen SoundScan, the big music labels sold 13 per cent fewer CDs in 2002 than in the previous year.

But copyright owners have fought back on a number of fronts. Some have tested the proposition that hackers will inevitably defeat any new copy-protection scheme with a variety of new "codecs" (compression-decompression algorithms) that, if not beyond all possibility of breaking, make the job difficult and time-consuming. Others have sought to poison the file-swapping pool with "spoof" files that, once downloaded, turn out not to be the songs being sought. More directly, the Recording Industry Association of America (RIAA), the labels' primary lobby group, announced in early 2003 that it was launching a legal assault on "the 10 per cent of users who offer 90 per cent of the files" online. The RIAA planned to use software "bots" to troll the Internet for those high-volume offenders. Once it identified such individuals, the group planned first to send a cease-and-desist letter and then to sue.

Music vendors have moved more slowly to follow a strategy suggested by the Canadian playbook on satellite service. Although the labels have gone after the pirate market in downloads, they have been slower to occupy the field by making music available legally online. By 2003, however, a number of labels and big North American music retailers had either launched or planned to launch such ventures.

And despite dire predictions, the Napsterizing of digitized movies has failed to emerge as a widespread concern. Pirated versions of many new films have appeared in the darker reaches of the Internet, in some cases even before their official release. But the difficulty of acquiring them, the exceedingly long download times required (overnight or longer for those with dial-up connections) and the inadequate experience of watching a special-effects blockbuster on a fifteen-inch computer screen all help explain why the phenomenon has not taken off.

Technology may yet have the last laugh. It is possible that novel compression techniques, the wide adoption of high-speed Internet connections and new breakthroughs by hackers in cracking encryption codes will turn back the forces of law and legitimate commerce.

But the evidence so far leads to a different conclusion: that a bet on the money is seldom misplaced. If the world of the Internet *is* as strongly "bordered" as the physical one, the implications for diversity of expression are twofold.

First: the "new economy" changes nothing fundamental in the market for creative property. *Sunk cost, near-zero marginal cost* and *arbitrary pricing* all still apply as forcefully as ever. And they carry the same inevitable consequence: a huge advantage to the scale and vertical integration of the international cultural oligopoly.

But second: neither has the "new economy" neutered the nation state. Public-policy tools that nourish diversity in broadcasting, books or the recording industry offline retain their traction online.

THERE IS ANOTHER SIDE to the Internet's potential for increasing the diversity of cultural expression. Optimists have speculated that several of its features make possible a new creative Renaissance.

Web sites are cheap and relatively easy to create. Together with the plummeting cost of digital photography, audio recording and editing, could not this dramatically lower the cost barrier to entry for many future Polanskis and Fellinis?

Some believe so. "I really expect that technological innovations are going to help tremendously," suggests indie filmmaker Allison Anders. "And I don't just mean getting a digital camera. I think about the huge places we used to have to edit in. Now you're sitting at a computer in a little tiny corner of your room. Kids can be doing that in their dorms. But the big thing is how they're going to get audiences to see those movies. And I'm really hoping the Internet may help with that. If people can get access to ways to distribute their work, that's the key."

Variety editor-in-chief Peter Bart shares some of that hope. "Consider the fact that the basic process of shooting a movie was exactly the same between 1920 and 1998. Nothing changed. Now, all of a sudden, everything has changed. It could change a lot for the better. These changes in technology could loosen the chokehold of the major companies on the pop culture. That's what could happen."

But there are at least a couple of flaws in this line of thinking.

Supply, first, has seldom been the problem in creative goods. Chapter 4 discussed how the risk-reward ratio for cultural products has always ensured that more products vie to enter the market than are either realized or brought to consumers' attention. Cheaper digital production may carry more creative ideas forward to completion. That has been the experience in print. But as high-volume retailers come to dominate North American book sales, they pass on fewer titles to consumers, not more. It is far from clear, moreover, that comparable reductions can be achieved in the cost of producing video entertainment. Actors, makeup artists, costumes and props do not lend themselves to being digitized.

The Internet may provide essentially limitless shelf space, but it does not solve the *too much information* problem. Consumers are already overburdened with choices and partial information. They rely for a manageable menu on taste-makers and other gatekeepers acutely susceptible to conglomerate manipulation. More titles, therefore, do not in themselves mean more diversity in effective consumer choice.

Similarly, adding another page to the 2 billion already on the Internet is a very long way from ensuring that anyone ever discovers it. Creators who hope to bypass the gatekeepers and deal directly with audiences over the Web quickly discover that cyberspace is not so egalitarian after all. Just as in other arenas of popular culture, most consumers flock to only a few branded sources. Even the most individualistic sites on the Net—Weblogs, or "blogs"—turn out to follow the same iron rule. A small handful of "blogs" get most of the eyeballs.

Even if a Web site does list many thousands of book, video, audio or CD titles, most consumers will have heard of only a few of them. Advertising and promotion, in other words, still rule. That does not change because of the World Wide Web. If anything, the Internet in many respects has served mainly to amplify and reinforce the status of traditional media. Each of the big multinational culture conglomerates has its own Web site or portal devoted to its program listings, its artists, its catalogue, advertising and promotion. Of the twenty most-visited Web sites in the United States in March 2003, according to a survey by Neilsen/Net Ratings, nineteen were affiliated with large conventional media chains (the sole exception being the far-from-fringe Yahoo! News portal).

And there is another profound problem facing this new flowering of creators. True: they can build it. Perhaps audiences will come. But will they pay?

The Internet may be a superb tool for delivering information. But with limited exceptions, it has so far proven a fool's paradise for creators who hope to be paid in exchange for the downloading of their work. Expectations for online advertising burst along with the dot-com bubble. Subscription models for online magazines have also failed. E-books are still parked on the tarmac somewhere short of liftoff.

If anything, the Internet has proven better at facilitating copyright theft than at creating new markets for innovative creators. Napster and its file-sharing clones, for all their rhetoric about bypassing the control of the major record labels, have put no money in the pockets of musicians.

When creators go unpaid, the result is to undermine cultural diversity, not foster it. In this fight, all creators of popular culture, whether large or small, have common cause. (One of the plaintiffs seeking to close down the iCraveTV Web site was the producer of *Degrassi*.)

Cyberlaw—or technology—may yet disarm the Internet's copyright pirates. Enterprises looking for a way to stream or download books, sound recordings, films or TV programs on a "pay-as-you-go" basis may find a model that is both consumer- and copyright-friendly. Recent legal music services like iTunes and Napster 2.0 have presented some hopeful signs. But those services will not be at all like traditional broadcasting. Digital downloads invite consumers to "pull" the program of their choice. This is very different from the traditional broadcaster's "push" of a predetermined schedule of shows.

In this "pull" environment, policies to regulate program schedules are irrelevant. But nations have other ways of ensuring that their citizens have a choice of local cultural products and that their creators enjoy shelf space for their work. They can require that works included on a file server include a reasonable proportion of local titles, that the menu provided to the consumer promotes local expression or that the undertaking supports local creators in other ways.

In this, digital downloads on the Internet are akin to the "video on demand" services that have already begun to appear in developed markets, typically delivered over cable systems. Many countries treat these as a telecommunications service rather than as broadcasting. Canada has taken an opposite approach.

The CRTC has licensed a number of video-on-demand services under the Broadcasting Act. These are now beginning to be offered by cable companies using hybrid optical fibre–coaxial cable systems with sufficient security to satisfy the needs of rights holders. The CRTC, however, has required that 5 per cent of the available titles in English and 8 per cent of those in French be Canadian, and has added other conditions. In keeping with its exemption from the Broadcasting Act of all Internet services, however, the CRTC chose not to impose such rules on services that may deliver movies online in the future. In its view, the Internet is unlikely to compete directly with more traditional forms of broadcasting anytime soon and hence needs no regulation.

It is too early to tell whether the CRTC was entirely right in that assessment. What is evident so far at least is that other fears—notably, how to get paid and not have their copyright infringed—have deterred most movie and television producers from trying their hand at video-on-demand-online.

THE GOOD NEWS, however, is that to the extent that the tool kit of cultural diversity maintains pluralism in conventional media, the choices, range and varieties of expression are likely to carry through to the Internet.

Degrassi: The Next Generation also has an active Web site where teenagers can connect with the stars of the show. That site exists only because *Degrassi* exists, but it also enhances the program's presence around the world. Similarly, most of the world's public broadcasters operate admirable Web sites. Of course, those Web sites too would not exist if the public broadcasters did not exist.

In short, just as it amplifies the reach of the culture oligopoly, the Internet also serves as a force-multiplier for policies that secure and sustain a diversity of expression in other media.

As it turns out, the Internet did not render the tool kit of cultural policy obsolete, ineffective or irrelevant. But neither did it alter the need for those measures.

Chicken Little was wrong. The sky is not falling in on the nation state or on its capacity for effective policy. But if the heavens are not collapsing on creative diversity, that does not mean it is not in danger. In the name of trade liberalization, some nation states may choose to set aside the tools that technology has failed to blunt.

We turn to that subject next.

16

TRADE
WARS

O N CNN a fresh-faced pilot, newly returned from an air strike, talks to a reporter. He describes a "tremendous light show" that lit up Baghdad as bombs burst amid bright puffs of anti-aircraft fire beneath his wings. Then the U.S. news channel cuts away to a slowly spinning graphic of the aviator's plane, cataloguing its arsenal of weapons. In a moment there will be an interview with the worried but stoic mother of a captured American soldier.

Down the dial CBC Newsworld, the continuous news service of Canada's public broadcaster, is also running an interview. This one features a woman in a hajib very like one the Iraqi-Canadian character "Fareeza" wore in the *Degrassi* episode filmed the previous summer. This woman is somewhere in the Middle East. She speaks with evident distress about the danger and suffering that Iraqi civilians face under bombardment.

On yet another channel, a London-based anchor for the BBC's World Service holds a sober conversation with its Washington correspondent. They are discussing the setbacks encountered by the American-led invasion. Over their shoulders are images of British troops landing at a beach somewhere in the war zone.

The battles raging in Iraq in early 2003 put into perspective the rhetoric so often wrapped around conflicts of merely economic interest. Whatever other casualties "trade wars" cause, bullets do not fly across negotiating tables and bystanders need not fear being shredded by shrapnel.

And yet the theatres of economic and military conflict are not entirely separate. One frequently bleeds into the other. And although this is not a book about war, the relevance of its themes to the diversity of views in a free democracy could hardly be more evident than in the very different perspectives provided on the action in Iraq by CNN, CBC Newsworld and BBC World Service.

The frontier between trade interests and military methods—to say nothing of martial metaphors—has long been indistinct. "War," Karl von Clausewitz famously observed, is nothing more than the advancement of national interest "by other means." The "Trade Wars" of our own title are a commonplace of headlines in the business pages. And when not engaged in fighting real wars, many governments have placed their security forces at the service of significant national enterprises.

Since the end of the Cold War, both China and Russia are known to have used their spy services to obtain commercial intelligence on trade partners. The United States has done the same. In 1993, French counter-espionage agents discovered that a team of five CIA operatives had tried to bribe French trade officials for insight into their bargaining positions in the 1986 Uruguay Round of trade negotiations. According to *The New York Times,* the CIA later "boasted to Congressional intelligence committees ... that it is able to obtain scoops on trade talks [and] diplomatic negotiations."

Another account of the same incident is given in British film producer David Puttnam's analysis of "Hollywood's extraordinary dominance in the field of filmed entertainment." Puttnam also finds it not the least surprising that later in 1993, MPAA chief executive Jack Valenti was a backroom member of a delegation led by U.S. Trade Representative Mickey Kantor trying to finalize a new trade pact in Geneva on terms favourable to the Hollywood studios. "For despite all the talk of globalization," Puttnam notes, "the political interests of those studios remain irreducibly identified with those of America as a whole."

Puttnam called his book *The Undeclared War: The Struggle for Control of the World's Film Industry.* That was the title in Britain. The book's editors renamed it *Movies and Money* for release in the United States (where it is no longer in print).

But if spies can affect a negotiation one way or another, outright war can completely remake the economic landscape. Already some analysts have begun to speculate that disagreements between continental Europe and Britain and the United States—or indeed between the United States and Canada—over their handling of Iraq will derail half a century of progress towards expanded international trade rules.

History's lesson, however, is that war can also lead to a new and better order. In fact, the very trade rules over which some analysts now fret are a legacy of the last great world war. In its ashes, the victorious western Allies put in place a new global economic system whose three pillars included the International Bank for Reconstruction and Development (now the World Bank), an International Monetary Fund to stabilize currencies and the General Agreement on Tariffs and Trade (GATT). The last of these institutions set the coordinates for sixty years of what we now call "trade liberalization."

Other elements, including the World Trade Organization, have been added since. Still, GATT endures, now with some 142 signatories. Its principles continue to govern international transactions in the conventional commodities that dominated mid-twentieth-century industry: steel, oil and machine goods.

As the previous chapters have made clear, however, popular culture does not behave like steel, oil or machinery in the marketplace. As a consequence, it has become increasingly apparent that the multiplying institutional descendants of the original GATT now pose a mounting threat to the world's diversity of cultural voices.

The war in Iraq concluded in just a few short weeks. Despite differences of opinion on how it was waged, there was a general hope that the world could now move on to an era of greater peace and understanding. But it was also clear that such an understanding would not advance if cultural pluralism was threatened. Accordingly, governments, citizens and creators have increasingly sought out cultural policies that enhance access to both domestic and foreign expression. High on the agenda in this decade will be the treatment of cultural products under both present and prospective trade agreements.

ALTHOUGH ITS AMBIT was confined to goods, not services, the original GATT, signed in 1947, contained a number of key principles that continue to govern trade relationships today. Three were central:

- *tariff reduction* (reducing customs duties on the importation of goods);
- *most-favoured nation treatment* (treating imported products from one country no differently than those from another); and
- *national treatment* (treating imported products no differently than domestic products).

The first principle simply enshrined in international agreement one of the harsher lessons of the Great Depression. Then, trading nations had unleashed a crippling cycle of tariff "protections" that all but shut down the world's commercial economy. Those nations undertook to eschew such measures in the future.

The second and third principles, however, significantly augmented the scope of the agreement. They dealt with what are referred to as "non-tariff" barriers to trade. It was increasingly realized that if products were to be traded freely across borders, it was not enough simply to reduce customs duties. It was necessary to strike down hidden barriers that discriminated against imported products. So Article II of GATT required that any concessions offered to one ("most favoured") country must be offered to all. And Article III required that internal taxation and regulation be applied to imported goods on equal terms with domestic ones ("national treatment"). Paragraph 3 of that article stipulated:

> The products of the territory of any contracting party imported into the territory of any other contracting party shall be accorded treatment no less favourable than that accorded to like products of national origin in respect of all laws, regulations and requirements affecting their internal sale, offering for sale, purchase, transportation, distribution or use.

Trade in 1947 was overwhelmingly an exchange of conventional goods. Trade in the products of popular culture was a tiny fraction of what it has become. It did not loom large in the thinking of those drafting GATT. With one exception: in one area, several nations at the table perceived a real threat to the survival of their cultural industries if the principles of GATT were to be strictly applied. That was cinema.

Europe's film industry had not yet recovered from two world wars and a devastating economic depression. Hollywood had come to dominate European screens between the wars. American armies were based throughout western Europe, and French observers in particular worried aloud about the "coca-colonization" of their culture. Their apprehension focused on a renewed influx of Hollywood feature films. France, along with many other countries, had begun to set quotas for the screening of local films in theatres.

French negotiators argued strongly for the adoption of a "cultural exclusion" in GATT—a clause setting cultural industries apart from its general provisions. American negotiators fought back, arguing that "entertainment products" should be treated no differently than others.

In the end, negotiators added a provision—Article IV—that permitted countries to reserve screen time "for films of national origin." A paragraph was then added to Article III of the agreement to make it clear that the rules for national treatment in that article did not apply to such screen quotas.

Only one other provision in GATT addressed cultural products: Article XX stipulated that nothing in the agreement prevented the enforcement of measures "necessary to protect public morals" or "imposed for the protection of national treasures of artistic, historic or archaeological value."

But there was no "cultural exception." GATT therefore applied—and continues to apply—to trade in cultural goods such as books, newspapers, magazines, sound recordings and film (subject only to the provision allowing screen quotas in theatres).

Rounding out its provisions was GATT's Article VI, which provided for countries to levy countervailing duties against trade partners that were guilty of dumping their products. The offence was defined as pricing an exported product at less than the price charged in the exporting country for a like product.

THE BELIEFS UNDERLYING GATT were based on the high-minded theory of "comparative advantage." First developed in the nineteenth century, that theory remains the fundamental faith of liberalization and is spelled out in every international trade text. The theory asserts that each country should specialize in producing and exporting goods in which its comparative advantage is greater, or its comparative disadvantage is smallest, and should import goods in which its comparative disadvantage is greatest. For most conventional goods, this specialization leads to higher real incomes for all—lending force to arguments for free trade.

The theory rests on classic economic assumptions, including the assumptions that the goods being compared are readily substitutable, whether they be bushels of wheat or computer chips, and that the relative efficiency of countries can be measured by looking at the marginal cost of the commodities they produce. These classic economic assumptions do not, however, hold for cultural products. With those, the symbolic content (the intellectual property) that provides the value in each copy is unique. The language and ideas of each product can have cultural specificity, increasing demand in certain societies and lowering it in others. Moreover, having "public good" attributes, these products typically have a marginal cost per unit close to zero and therefore are priced at discriminatory levels that have little or no relation to cost. As Chapter 3 demonstrated, cultural products behave quite differently than ordinary commodities not only in these respects but in many more.

However valid the theory of comparative advantage may be for ordinary commodities, it breaks down entirely in regard to cultural products. Unrestrained free trade in the cultural sector, far from yielding higher real income for all participants, would simply institutionalize the dominance of a few advantaged producers and prevent governments from taking effective measures to ensure space and choice for a diversity of cultural expression.

Within fifteen years of the forging of the GATT framework, new developments brought an increased sense of urgency to both perspectives. The evolution of television (viewed as a live "service" and therefore beyond GATT's scope) led to a growing and very valuable global commerce in pre-recorded programs. And in general, the service sector of developed economies grew much faster than their goods sector, drawing attention to the absence of international ground rules in that arena.

In the early 1960s, the United States submitted to its GATT partners that television broadcast quotas offended Article III and were not protected by the cinema provisions of Article IV. The matter was referred to a working party, which failed to reach a consensus. In any case, most countries felt that any decision concerning trade in television programs should await further technological developments. Accordingly, no action was taken and the matter rested.

By the mid-1980s, however, the growth of services had sparked efforts to achieve a much more ambitious project: the negotiation of a General Agreement on Trade in Services (GATS). This was a more logical forum for arguments about broadcast quotas. Broadcasting is a perfect example of a service. And although video tapes of television programs are, like release prints of films, "goods" in a physical sense, the intellectual property of television programs was increasingly being transmitted by satellite, which involved no goods being imported at all.

Multilateral trade negotiations began in Uruguay in 1986, and by 1994 the parties were nearing a series of agreements. One created the World Trade Organization to administer the entire bundle of accords. The GATT itself, as originally worded in 1947, was reaffirmed and now became enforceable by virtue of a new separate agreement providing for binding dispute resolution. Copyright owners also benefited from what was called the TRIPS (Trade-Related Aspects of Intellectual Property Rights) agreement. It permitted trade retaliation against countries that breach the national treatment granted to the authors of copyright works under a number of existing international agreements.

But as the target for agreement loomed, negotiators struggled to resolve one last item: the issue of broadcast quotas. The United States, led by its trade representative Mickey Kantor, a former Hollywood attorney, sought to apply the principle of national treatment to the audiovisual sector. That would outlaw broadcast quotas for local productions. The European Union and most other countries refused to give in.

"Creations of the spirit are not just commodities," French president Francois Mitterand asserted. "What is at stake is the cultural identity of all our nations ... it is the freedom to create and choose our own images."

In the end, the two sides effectively agreed to disagree on the narrow point. A new GATS came into force in 1994. Like GATT, it rested on the principles of *national treatment* and *most-favoured nation*. But while it did not contain a "cultural exception" either, GATS required national treatment only in service sectors for which countries made specific binding commitments. Most declined to make such commitments in the audiovisual sector. Most also invoked a special provision allowing them to make one-time exceptions to the most-favoured nation principle in order to protect their international co-production treaties.

The MPAA was furious. "In a global treaty supposed to reduce trade barriers," fumed Jack Valenti, "the European Community erected a wall to keep out the works of non-European creative men and women ... This negotiation had nothing to do with culture, unless European soap operas and game shows are the equivalent of Molière. This is all about the hard business of money."

But the MPAA's own tactics had severely undermined its position. Its arguments had been so doctrinaire—opposing discriminatory subsidies as well as quotas—that they left little room for compromise. Even some of its erstwhile friends in Europe were unable to support its hardline position. A last-minute offer to settle for national treatment only for video-on-demand and "new media" proved to be too little, too late.

In the end, most countries made no commitments whatever in the audiovisual sector. One of the few that did was New Zealand, to its later regret. But most nations that sought to ensure a diverse choice of expression on television without fear of retaliation were able to claim a victory.

The Uruguay Round negotiations brought the contradictions between cultural policy and free trade to public attention in a way that had never before happened. Groups representing creators suddenly began to look more closely at trade agreements. In doing so, they began to appreciate the implications for their own nations' cultural security of commitments such as "national treatment," and the difficulties inherent in applying trade-law tests to specific creative products.

By 1998, when trade interests under the aegis of the Organization for Economic Co-operation and Development began negotiating a new Multilateral Agreement on Investment (MAI), these groups were galvanized into action, finding common cause with activists in the environment and other areas. The Société des Auteurs et Compositeurs Dramatiques (SACD), a French-based authors collective, spearheaded a campaign from the arts community in Europe to oppose the agreement. The SACD argued that in the guise of giving national treatment to foreign investors seeking to exploit intellectual property rights, the MAI could well undermine governments' ability to assure space and choice for their own citizens' cultural expression. French prime minister Lionel Jospin also commissioned a high-profile study that showed that the MAI could undermine the sovereignty of nations in regard to social, labour and environmental issues as well as cultural issues.

THE CAMPAIGN against the MAI was ultimately successful and the promoters of the agreement conceded defeat. But as the debate gathered steam, cultural industries around the world were in a sense only catching up to their counterparts in Canada. For this country, the issues were familiar ones. Canada had weathered a series of confrontations with the United States over culture and trade dating back to the 1970s.

Canada's sense of its own culture as a prism of national identity had come of age in the 1960s. Over the next decade, it adopted a variety of measures to strengthen its own voice.

Following the passage of a new Broadcasting Act in 1968, the federal government announced that it would require all broadcasting undertakings to be owned and controlled by Canadians. A number of broadcasting stations and cable television systems had been owned by foreign investors. They were given time to find Canadian buyers, but by 1975 the entire sector was in Canadian hands. The U.S. government could hardly object to the Canadianization of broadcast ownership, since it had imposed similar restrictions on the ownership of free-to-air broadcasting (although not on cable ownership).

In the mid-1970s, Canada addressed another growing problem. This one arose from the existence of many U.S. television stations along the northern border that had large overflow audiences in Canada. A number of these stations had begun to sell air time to Canadian advertisers who wanted to reach Canadian viewers of those U.S.-based signals. In 1976, the Canadian government amended its legislation (in a measure still referred to as "Bill c-58") to disentitle Canadian advertisers from claiming a tax deduction for the cost of such ads.

At the same time, the broadcast authority adopted "simulcast" rules that required Canadian cable companies to substitute a local Canadian television signal for a U.S. signal when Canadian and U.S. broadcasters were carrying the same program. Most controversial of all was a practice known as "commercial deletion," which allowed cable companies to randomly delete ads from the signals of U.S. border stations and replace them with public-service announcements.

U.S. border broadcasters were outraged. They appealed the policies in the Canadian courts on a variety of grounds. The case reached the Supreme Court of Canada, which upheld the federal authority to regulate cable television. The American broadcasters also lobbied the U.S.

government to take retaliatory steps and petitioned the Federal Communications Commission (FCC) to forbid Canadian television stations to buy U.S. programs on a "pre-release" basis (which allowed a Canadian station to broadcast a show before its U.S. counterpart). But this effort similarly went nowhere. Indeed, in turning down the petition, one FCC commissioner famously quipped that if this was gunboat diplomacy the gunboats were in Los Angeles harbour with their guns trained on Hollywood, since the stations' demand would simply rob Hollywood studios of the ability to sell their programs as they saw fit.

In the end, the CRTC abandoned its commercial deletion policy. But the other measures remain in force to this day. (Although in response to a complaint brought by the U.S. border broadcasters under section 301 of the U.S. Trade Act of 1974, the United States enacted "mirror legislation" in 1984 that disentitled U.S. advertisers from tax deductions for ads placed on Canadian border stations.)

By the mid-1980s, new frictions had arisen over Canada's cultural policies. But they were merely background to a much more ambitious effort: the negotiation of a comprehensive free-trade agreement between Canada and the United States. Sensitized to the vulnerabilities of cultural industries, the Canadian government of the day sought to keep culture off the negotiating table. Analysts continue to debate the extent of its success.

When it was eventually signed in 1988, the Canada–United States Free Trade Agreement (FTA) did contain a "cultural exception" of sorts—a clause that specifically excepts measures respecting cultural industries from obligations otherwise imposed by the agreement. But in fact the clause did not entirely exclude cultural measures. Canada agreed to zero-rate its customs tariffs on imported cultural goods (copies of books, records, magazines, films and tapes). It also agreed to require cable and other television distributors to pay royalties for the retransmission of distant signals, as well as agreeing to certain investment disciplines in regard to its book publishing policy.

But there was a more contentious tradeoff. Canada also agreed that if it took any measure that would, in the absence of the "exception," breach other terms of the FTA, the United States would be entitled to retaliate with measures "of equivalent commercial effect."

Some commentators have suggested that this provision totally vitiated the exception's effectiveness. What new cultural measures will

Canada ever introduce, they demand to know, if the result would be to invite retaliation?

Some of this criticism is misplaced. Carefully analyzed, the clause permits U.S. retaliation only for measures that otherwise would be inconsistent with the 1988 agreement. Since Canada made no national treatment commitments in the audiovisual services sector in the 1988 FTA, it is therefore free to introduce new measures affecting such services, including broadcasting, without triggering a right of retaliation. And, in fact, it has done so more than once.

On the other side of the coin, American entertainment interests have heavily criticized their government for agreeing to the exemption. Washington has since insisted that the Canadian precedent was misconceived and that it will never again accede to such an exception in any future free-trade agreements.

Still, when the FTA was superseded by the North American Free Trade Agreement (NAFTA) in 1994, adding Mexico to the mix, Canada's cultural exemption was "grandfathered" into the new pact. It now governs Canada's relationship with both the United States and Mexico. Separate negotiations took place between Mexico and the United States, at the end of which Mexico preserved certain of its cinema and terrestrial broadcasting policies but agreed to free trade in direct satellite broadcasting.

DESPITE THOSE continental agreements, Canada and the United States have continued to find themselves in dispute over cultural policy. The cases provide telling insight into the way in which trade law treats cultural products.

The first case to erupt was a dispute over periodicals. The second centred on the rights of a U.S. specialty television service operating in Canada.

The magazine case arose from a Canadian policy designed to mitigate the particularly perverse effect of cultural economics on periodicals. Those effects are closely parallel to the situation examined at length in Chapter 6 regarding audiovisual products. They work like this. A huge domestic market allows American publishers to amortize the original-copy costs of making any magazine—its editorial content and the "mechanical cost" of preparing to print it—across a very large potential circulation. The marginal cost of printing additional copies of any single issue for sale across the northern border is minimal—pennies per copy.

A low cultural discount on American subject matter among Canadian consumers means that most U.S. magazines can easily attract additional readers in Canada. Those readers make it possible to attract additional Canadian advertisers as well. At the same time, the magazine's publisher can set a price for that advertising space based on the marked-down marginal cost of the extra copies, typically a fraction of what must be charged to cover the full production cost of a magazine originating in Canada and intended for Canadian readers. In short, both in pursuit of readers and in pursuit of advertisers, such "split-run" editions (so called because a press run is "split" to insert different ads in the Canadian edition) are able to sharply underprice any local competitor.

The unsurprising result is that exported split-run editions can reap profit margins for American publishers of up to 80 per cent on Canadian ad sales. By contrast, a Canadian magazine, amortizing its original editorial cost only over the smaller Canadian market, is typically hard-pressed to scrape out a 10 percent margin. Nor do Canadian magazines have much room to make up the difference through higher prices.

For decades, those dynamics have meant that U.S. titles outnumber domestic ones on Canadian newstands. As early as 1925, American magazines outsold Canadian titles by a factor of eight to one.

For almost as long, Canadian governments have sought ways to balance the playing field somewhat for Canadian publications without excluding American ones.

The effort first found traction in the 1960s. At the start of that decade, 80 per cent of the magazines Canadians read were American. Only eight domestic titles had significant national sales. In 1965, Canada outlawed the import of split-run editions of foreign magazines that contained ads directed specifically at Canadian readers while continuing to allow editions that did not contain such ads freely into the country. It also disallowed the deduction of the cost of ads bought in foreign split-run magazines for Canadian business-tax purposes. With two exceptions, split runs disappeared from the Canadian market. Special "grandfather" rules that remained in place for ten years and some accommodations by the two titles permitted long-established *Time* and *Reader's Digest* to continue their Canadian editions.

Fast-forward to 1993: 80 per cent of the titles on store shelves in Canada continued to be American. The ratio revealed corporate clout as well as Canadian tastes. Clearly, Canadians desired a wide choice of imported reading: they were spending c$700 million a year on U.S. magazines. But the newsstand dominance of U.S. titles also reflected the ability of deep-pocketed American publishers to pay placement fees to magazine distributors—effectively buying shelf space.

However, the ratio of magazines Canadians actually *read* was strikingly different. Of those, almost half were Canadian. In fact, the twenty biggest Canadian titles had a combined circulation five times that of the twenty top-selling U.S. magazines in Canada. The difference was made up of titles to which readers subscribed or that employed controlled circulation. Thus, in a marketplace where the unbalancing effect of discriminatory pricing was contained, Canadians showed a strong appetite for material that spoke to their own experience.

But technology had also moved forward. By the early 1990s, digital pre-press techniques had freed publishers from the physical layout of paper pages that until then had been a necessary step in the printing process. In 1993, Time Warner decided to use new technology to do a digital end run. Instead of importing split-run copies of its *Sports Illustrated* from a printing plant in the United States, the company simply beamed digital versions of the magazine's pages by satellite to a Canadian printing plant. There it digitally inserted ads purchased by Canadian companies before printing a Canadian edition of the popular title. The customs prohibition against split-run magazines did not apply because no physical copies of the split-run magazine had been imported at all.

A weightless stream of digital bits had vaporized the effect of a policy that had worked well for a quarter-century. Cassandras predicted the same fate for Canadian magazines. Advertisers and publishers anticipated that as many as a hundred U.S. titles would follow the lead of *Sports Illustrated*, draining off as much as 40 per cent of the revenue supporting Canadian titles.

After consulting the industry, the Canadian government fired back. It amended Canada's tax codes to impose an 80 per cent excise tax on Canadian advertising revenue from split-run editions—in essence sweeping up all of the anticipated margin that made the editions so attractive to begin with.

In March 1996, U.S. trade representative Mickey Kantor invoked the year-old World Trade Organization (WTO) process to challenge both the new tax and two other Canadian measures of longer standing. In Kantor's view the excise tax, the old import prohibition on split-run editions and a postal subsidy for Canadian periodicals "had nothing to do with culture." The magazine policy was instead "purely a matter of commercial interest" that violated Canada's commitments under GATT.

In particular, the United States challenged the tax as being contrary to Canada's national treatment obligations under Article III, paragraph 2, of GATT. The matter was heard by a WTO dispute-resolution panel whose decision was later reconsidered by a WTO appellate body. Canada's position was that the excise tax was a tax on services (the advertising in the magazines), not on goods (the magazines themselves). It also argued that in any event, magazines with Canadian editorial matter are not "like products" to U.S. split-run magazines.

In the end, the WTO appellate body sided with the United States. It concluded that the excise tax had a sufficient connection with the goods to be caught within Article III of GATT. (This was not entirely unexpected, since Canada had structured the tax so that it was levied against the publisher and tied to the magazine itself.)

More controversially, however, the appellate body also ruled in favour of the United States on the issue of whether Canadian magazines were direct substitutes for U.S. split-run magazines. The original panel had fumbled the issue of "like products," examining a hypothetical comparison that upon review turned out to be unrealistic. The appellate body declined to uphold this ruling. Instead, it focused on a second test in Article III, namely whether Canadian magazines were "directly competitive or substitutable products" for foreign split-run magazines. This was a looser test than the test for "like products," and on it the appellate body decided in favour of the United States.

During the hearing, Canada had conceded that magazines of different kinds compete with each other for advertising revenue, since advertisers generally focus on the penetration of a certain demographic, not the subject matter of the publication. But at the same time, Canada argued that for consumers, subject matter was crucial and Canadian magazines were not "like" U.S. periodicals. To support that argument, Canada compared *Time* (in both its foreign and split-run editions) with the Canadian newsmagazine *Maclean's*. In any typical week, the magazines have very different editorial matter. *Maclean's* covers Canadian current news, while *Time* focuses on U.S. and international news. Even when they occasionally cover the same story, their perspectives on events are usually widely divergent.

A writer for *The Toronto Star*, Greg Quill, demonstrated the point by comparing single issues of the two magazines published in the same week. Both *Maclean's* and *Time* had featured the same topic on their cover: the proposed mergers of big banks in both countries. "But," Quill noted, "the two stories were nothing alike. While *Maclean's* focused on the mergers of Canadian banks and placed them in the context of both domestic and global business affairs, *Time* focused only on what the move toward megabanks in the U.S. would mean to American business and American bank customers. *Time Canada* didn't even mention the Canadian mergers."

However, to the WTO appellate body, this was irrelevant. "Our conclusion that imported split-run periodicals and domestic non-split-run periodicals are 'directly competitive or substitutable' does not mean that all periodicals belong to the same relevant market, whatever their editorial content," it conceded. "A periodical containing mainly current news is not directly competitive or substitutable with a periodical devoted to gardening, chess, sports, music or cuisine. But"—and here was the clincher—"newsmagazines, like *Time, Time Canada* and *Maclean's,* are directly competitive or substitutable in spite of the 'Canadian' content of *Maclean's.*"

Recall from Chapter 12 that one of the difficulties in applying competition law to cultural products is determining which marketplace they should be considered in the context of. In the case of magazines, there are several possible choices: the marketplace of readers, of advertisers and even of freelance suppliers of content. The WTO opted to flatly ignore the first and last, and to consider only whether the two magazines might look the same or different from the standpoint of advertisers.

This conclusion—whatever its validity in trade law—illustrates a key reality: a WTO panel cannot be relied upon to appreciate distinctions of cultural specificity. No Canadian consumer familiar with the two publications would see *Maclean's* as a direct substitute for *Time,* either in its U.S. or Canadian edition. But the panel members were trade law practitioners with no background in cultural matters and came from countries where language barriers effectively protect local periodicals against foreign split-run editions. Their ruling betrayed their lack of understanding.

In response to the panel's finding, Canada dutifully rescinded the 80 per cent excise tax. However, it introduced a new measure, Bill C-55, to prohibit the sale of advertising services directed solely at the Canadian market except by Canadian publishers. This was no longer a tax and was no longer tied to the sale of magazines per se. As such, its fate would be determined under a different paragraph of Article III of GATT, where only the more limited "like products" test applied. In doing this, Canada felt it would have a better chance of success before the WTO.

The United States declined to take the new measure before the WTO. Instead, it simply threatened unilateral trade retaliation in order to drive Canada to the bargaining table. In particular, the United States threatened to impose retaliatory duties on up to $4 billion worth of Canadian exports to the United States of textiles, plastics, wood products and steel.

The last target was aimed directly at the Canadian legislator responsible for cultural policy who had co-sponsored Bill C-55: Sheila Copps, the minister of Canadian heritage. Copps represented a riding in Hamilton, Ontario—the centre of Canada's steel industry. The threatened U.S. retaliation would strike her voters especially hard and force her to explain to them why she was risking their paycheques to protect jobs in the magazine trade mainly located elsewhere (in fact in Toronto, Hamilton's historic rival across Lake Ontario).

In the end both sides pulled back from the brink. In May 1999, more than six years after the "magazine war" began, it ended in a negotiated truce. Canada passed its legislation, but with significant amendments. The United States withdrew its threat of retaliation.

Foreign magazine publishers won a partial victory. They would be allowed to sell advertising to Canadian businesses up to a capped limit of 12 per cent of their total advertising revenue (which increased after three years to 18 per cent). Before they could sell more ads than the cap allowed, foreign magazines would have to demonstrate that at least half of the editorial content in their Canadian edition was "original." At that point, Canadian businesses that bought ads in the Canadianized issues could also deduct 50 per cent of their cost from their taxable income. Deductions could reach 100 per cent if a magazine carried 80 per cent "original" content. In a final Canadian concession, the limit on foreign ownership of Canadian magazine publishers was raised to 49 per cent.

Canadian nationalists fumed. "This is total capitulation," railed one arch-critic of Canada's trade commitments. Some magazine publishers expressed fear that even the limited ad sales permitted by the new pact would drain away more advertising than they could afford to lose, although the government also created a subsidy program for Canadian magazine publishers to alleviate any harm.

But four years after the pact was signed, those dire impacts have not materialized. Relatively few American magazines have found the limited revenue allowed under the Canadian law worth pursuing. There has been no devastating epidemic of Canadian magazine failures. Indeed, new titles have appeared and found Canadian readers and advertisers in sustainable numbers. *Maclean's* continues to thrive and provide a unique focus on Canadian news and issues.

In early 2003, Michael Elliot, the new editor of *Time*'s Canadian edition, spoke about that magazine's role. "*Time Canada*'s mission as I see it," he said, "is to be the great international newsmagazine of Canada. I doubt if Canadians look to us to tell them, on a weekly basis, detailed coverage of a wide range of Canadian issues. *Time Canada* is there because, in terms of magazines, *Time* has an absolutely unparalleled range of correspondents from around the world, and we can bring that international perspective, and American perspective, into the Canadian market."

By its own admission, in other words, *Time Canada* is not a substitute for *Maclean's*, despite the wto decision to the contrary.

THE OTHER TRADE DISPUTE between Canada and the United States in the 1990s related to Canada's broadcast policies.

In 1984, the crtc had permitted Canadian cable companies to distribute a limited list of U.S. specialty-programming services to Canadian subscribers. The services were in genres not considered to compete with either present or then-proposed Canadian cable channels. But inclusion on the "Eligible List" was explicitly not made permanent. If a Canadian service were licensed in the future in a format competitive with an authorized non-Canadian service, the CRTC made clear that the latter could be dropped from the list, terminating the authority for it to be carried on cable. One of the first services listed was Country Music Television (CMT), a music-video channel operated by a partnership of Gaylord Entertainment and Westinghouse.

Ten years later, however, the moment the CRTC had foreseen finally came. Five Canadian companies applied to the CRTC for a licence to operate a Canadian country music–video service. At a public hearing in February 1994, the CRTC reviewed and compared the applications. Each proposed a different level of Canadian content and different expectations as to its revenue. But all five applicants made plain that they expected CMT to cease distribution in Canada by virtue of the CRTC policy.

On June 6, 1994, the CRTC awarded a licence to The Country Network. The partnership of Rawlco and Maclean Hunter had proposed the highest Canadian content level and the lowest wholesale charge to cable carriers of any of the five applicants. Following its policy, the CRTC also deleted CMT from the Eligible List, effective on the launch date of the new service.

But CMT was not about to hang up its Stetson that easily. Gaylord Entertainment saddled up a posse of lawyers and lobbyists to press its case before Congress and the U.S. administration. CMT argued that the United States had the right to retaliate under the cultural exemption clause of NAFTA. Its argument, for the reasons noted above, was flawed; but U.S. trade law tends to ignore such niceties. This time, the U.S. government did not bother pursuing a remedy through the WTO. It simply threatened retaliation for what it alleged was an unjustified confiscation.

Under pressure, the owners of the newly licensed Canadian country music channel negotiated a compromise. CMT received a 20 per cent interest in the Canadian channel, which was branded Country Music Television Canada. Washington backed off. Canadian nationalists criticized the outcome as another instance of Canada caving in to American pressure. But rather than undermining Canadian cultural policy, the negotiated "compromise" strongly supported it.

The new channel prospered, rising from fewer than 2 million

subscribers in 1994 to 7.9 million in 2002, helped by the fact that since it was a Canadian service all Canadian cable and satellite distributors were required to carry it. CMT Canada's ownership went through a number of changes, ending with 90 per cent of the voting shares being held by Calgary-based Corus Entertainment. Country Music Television Inc., the U.S. company, ended up with a 10 per cent voting interest—but of a much more profitable service than it had before. True, the service carried the U.S. brand. But it was originated and controlled entirely in Canada. Licence conditions required at least 40 per cent of the music videos it broadcast to be Canadian and at least 22 per cent of its gross revenue to be invested in Canadian video and program production. The content and spending requirements offer crucial support to Canada's musical talent in this genre.

During the height of the dispute, one of the writers debated the U.S. trade lawyer acting for CMT in a panel discussion. The U.S. advocate—who later acted for the American lumber industry to oppose softwood lumber imports from Canada—scoffed at the notion that the CRTC policy could be said to support "Canadian" music. "Country music is American and comes from Nashville," he argued. How could Canada suggest it had its own country music?

He revealed a deep ignorance of musical history. Country music has roots in Canada at least as deep as those in the Appalachians. Irish, Gaelic and Breton folk tunes—all among the antecedents of modern country music—go back more than two centuries in Canada. George Wade and His Cornhuskers first broadcast over the predecessor of the CBC in 1933. Don Messer first appeared on radio the following year. Wilf Carter first recorded in 1932, Hank Snow in 1936. Over the next six decades, many hundreds of country artists have emerged and become successful in Canada. They include the Rhythm Pals, Tommy Hunter, Gary Buck, the Mercey Brothers, Family Brown, Carroll Baker, Patricia Conroy, Stompin' Tom Connors, Michelle Wright, George Fox and many others.

The U.S. trade lawyer knew none of this. But why would he? There is not much opportunity to experience Canadian country music in Washington.

Of course, some Canadian country artists become popular in the United States and worldwide: Hank Snow, Anne Murray and most recently the diva of "New Country," Shania Twain. But many more are known only to Canadians. Their most potent form of advertising is to be heard on Canadian country music radio stations, where there is a 35 per cent Canadian-music quota, and to have their music videos watched on Country Music Television, where 40 per cent of the music videos presented must be Canadian. From there on, it is up to their own talent to reach and resonate with Canadian audiences.

Canada's broadcast policy ensures that the keeper at the gate to those showcases is a Canadian broadcaster, interested in a Canadian audience—not a foreign interest serving a predominantly foreign audience.

THAT POLICY and others like it around the world are now in the crosshairs of trade practitioners who, like the U.S. lawyer and the WTO appellate body, are simply blind to such ends.

In 1994, most nations declined to make any commitments in the audiovisual or broadcasting sectors under GATS. But built into the agreement on trade in services was a ticking clock. By setting up a variety of deadlines, expiry dates for exemptions and the presumption of future negotiating rounds, GATS is designed to maintain pressure on its members to progressively reduce all domestic policies that regulate trade to a theoretical null point.

In late 2000, parties to GATS began exchanging negotiating proposals. Packages of "requests" and "offers" followed in 2002 and early 2003. A round-robin process of demands and concessions is expected to lead to an initial set of locked-in commitments by mid-decade. This is just the beginning. Once the first set of commitments is locked in, the GATS framework contemplates the immediate resumption of negotiations in a new round of offers and requests. Any services not committed to liberalization under the current round will be vulnerable under the next.

Nonetheless, no sector is automatically committed to the terms of GATS. Market access and national treatment are among the specific commitments that parties may make or withhold during negotiations. It is possible for nations simply to withhold commitments on sectors that implicate culture, such as broadcasting and "audiovisual services." Many have indicated they will do just that.

Yet, the American determination to bring culture within the ambit of national treatment and most-favoured nation remains undiminished. A 2002 document compiled by the office of the U.S. trade representative lists "foreign trade barriers" that remain in its cross-hairs. It cites the EU "Television Without Frontiers" directive, French broadcast quotas, a Spanish reservation of minimal cinema space for European films, and broadcast quotas in Canada and Australia, among dozens of pages of other targets.

The United States has also sought to eliminate the GATS exemption of film and television (technically: "audiovisual and related services"). In December 2000, the U.S. Trade Representative's Office released a proposal it said was directed at "ensuring an open and predictable environment that recognizes public concern for the preservation and promotion of cultural values and identity."

It advanced a number of arguments. New technologies like digital compression "have transformed the audiovisual sector," it asserted. Nonetheless, "creating audiovisual content is costly and commercial success is uncertain. Access to international markets is necessary to help recoup production costs. Predictable and clearly defined trade rules will foster international exhibition and distribution opportunities and provide commercial benefits that audiovisual service providers must have to continue their artistic endeavors."

The U.S. proposal insisted that "the WTO['s] four cornerstones—the GATT, the GATS, TRIPS and dispute settlement—apply to the audiovisual sector." It argued that "other sectors also have unique characteristics for the purpose of fulfilling important social policy objectives . . . that the GATS has shown the flexibility to accommodate." As examples it cited the "special and unique" GATT exception for cinema films, the general allowance for governments to regulate in the interest of public morals and GATS "annexes" on financial services and telecommunications. (It did not acknowledge, however, that the United States had earlier refused to agree to a similar annex for culture.)

In three concluding paragraphs, the American document itemized its specific proposals. One called for the creation of a "clear, accurate and comprehensive" classification of what, exactly, GATS parties mean by "audiovisual services." The second, insisting again that "GATS disciplines are relevant to the audiovisual sector as they are to virtually any services," restated the American goal of "negotiated commitments . . . that establish clear, dependable, and predictable trade rules with due account taken of the sector's specific sensitivities." Finally, it seemed to offer an olive branch of sorts on "subsidies that will respect each nation's need to foster its cultural identity by creating an environment to nurture local culture." The paper noted that "there is precedent in the WTO" to recognize such subsidies, as long as they are "carefully circumscribed ... for specifically defined purposes, all the while ensuring that the potential for trade distortive effects is effectively contained or significantly neutralized."

Some analysts have endorsed the American contention. They insist it is indeed possible to frame policies that will secure cultural diversity and yet comply with the GATS. One suggestion is to subsidize the *promotion* rather than the *production* of films and television programs that express culturally distinct points of view. This might at least be inexpensive, since there is likely to be little enough produced under those circumstances. Others argue that foreign sales can sustain authentic local expressions without the need for any support—ignoring the practical experience that export markets never provide more than a small fraction of the financing to make such programs, and do so at the expense of much authentically local detail.

It is telling, however, that this line of thinking has been unable to fully articulate a pragmatic proposal to square the theoretical circle. More often it has reached the non-specific—not to say non-helpful—conclusion that, in one analyst's words: "Policy choices that are not offensive to commitments under international trade agreements must be increasingly sought out."

THE UNITED STATES does not stand entirely alone among nations in seeking to extend GATS with minimal limitations to cultural products. Japan has also urged that "all registered MFN exemptions should be eliminated by the end of 2004 or the conclusion of the current negotiations, whichever comes earlier." It bears observing, however, that audiences and creators in Japan, with its near-homogeneous ethnicity, unique language and script, are protected from foreign competition by one of the steepest "cultural discounts" in the world.

Other nations have greeted the U.S. proposal to reopen the GATS audiovisual exemption with little enthusiasm.

The European Broadcasting Union (EBU), in a detailed commentary on the proposal, found it deeply wanting. In particular it questioned the American assertion that the GATS, as it stands, is capable of accommodating concerns for the "democratic, cultural and social aspects" of trade. "With regard to measures whose aim is to preserve and promote cultural diversity, to guarantee access to impartial news and information and to a diverse, pluralistic and comprehensive choice of content, or to provide public broadcasting services, [GATS] Articles . . . are of hardly any relevance," the commentary acerbically noted. It took exception as well to the necessity of listing audiovisual services, fearing that such a list might preclude the introduction of new cultural policies to deal with as-yet-unforeseen technologies. And it insisted that "cultural and audiovisual policy measures must not be limited to subsidies alone. They should include the establishment of public services, programming obligations, access to frequencies, must-carry rules and taxation measures."

Indeed, Europe's broadcasters said: "In giving the impression that WTO members which followed U.S. demands . . . would . . . keep the necessary power and flexibility for measures protecting and promoting cultural diversity, the U.S. paper has a tendency to create dangerous delusions."

"In return for irrevocable liberalization commitments," the EBU concluded, "the U.S. does not seem willing to provide any guarantees which could dispel concerns that legally binding trade liberalization in this sector . . . has no purpose other than to perpetuate the already dominant position of the U.S. industry in this area."

Since 2000, Canadian and European ministers, among others, have restated their resolve to maintain cultural policies and shield them from erosion by rules designed for the economics of merchandise rather than those of ideas, values and expressions of identity.

Faced with that resolve and increasingly dissatisfied with its lack of progress in liberalizing the audiovisual sector through the GATS, the United States has recently embarked on a mission to try to accomplish the same objective through bilateral negotiations and agreements.

In December 2002, this strategy scored its first success with the announcement of a Chile–U.S. free-trade agreement. Although the new treaty grandfathers a 40 per cent domestic-content quota for free-to-air television stations, it also grants unrestrained market access for other audiovisual services and foreswears any future local quotas for satellite or cable programming services.

Flush with victory, the MPAA hailed the agreement. "[It] represents a landmark achievement on market access for the filmed entertainment industry," Jack Valenti stated. He went on to add that "this ... demonstrates that a trade agreement can harmonize two important objectives—trade liberalization and the promotion of cultural diversity ... In stark contrast to some earlier trade agreements, this Agreement avoids the 'cultural exceptions' approach, while demonstrating that a trade agreement has sufficient flexibility to take into account countries' cultural promotion interests."

The contrast between the MPAA's professed support for cultural diversity and the effect of what it seeks to achieve in trade negotiations should by now be evident. Far from supporting expressive pluralism, the Chile–U.S. agreement will invite the United States to threaten trade retaliation if Chile ever wishes to implement a number of the widely accepted structural measures outlined in previous chapters. The agreement would, for instance, preclude Chile from copying a model used in Europe, Canada and Australia by requiring a Spanish-language, movie-based pay-TV service targeting Chile either to include Chilean films in its schedule or to invest in the production of Chilean films.

In January 2003, the U.S. Trade Representative announced the conclusion of a free-trade agreement with Singapore. In an early draft released to the public, it appears that Singapore managed to exempt its broadcasting sector from national-treatment obligations. However, under the heading "electronic commerce," Singapore committed itself to grant national-treatment to "digital products," defined to mean "computer programs, text, *video, images, sound recordings* and other products that are digitally encoded" (emphasis added). This wording will preclude Singapore from giving preferential treatment to CDs or films made by its own nationals. Again, the MPAA trumpeted the agreement as "striking an appropriate balance between trade liberalization and the promotion of cultural diversity."

At around the same time, the U.S. Trade Representative announced a short list of regions and countries with which the United States would seek bilateral free-trade agreements. They included Central America (El Savador, Nicaragua, Guatemala, Honduras and Costa Rica), Morocco, Australia and the South African Customs Union (Botswana, Lesotho, Namibia, South Africa and Swaziland).

In March 2003, a new U.S. organization, the Entertainment Industry Coalition for Free Trade (EIC), was formed in Washington, D.C. The EIC included all the Hollywood studios and multinational record companies as well as the five big U.S. entertainment industry craft guilds. Supported by U.S. Trade Representative Robert Zoellick and a number of U.S. senators, the new organization had a simple mission: to lobby members of Congress on "the importance of free trade" and "drive awareness of the benefits of free trade for the entertainment community and the entire nation." Included in this objective were aims that many creators around the world would broadly support, including "providing strong protection of intellectual property in the digital age" and "strengthening copyright enforcement."

Other objectives were more likely to raise hackles in creative communities beyond American borders. They included "increasing market access . . . for all U.S. entertainment products" and "demonstrating that trade agreements can be constructed to incorporate commitments on opening up service markets while addressing specific cultural related concerns at the same time."

One member of the new U.S. lobby group found the U.S.–Chile free-trade agreement especially praiseworthy. "These agreements hold the key to future investment and growth in the pay television industry in Latin America," Sean Spencer, president of the Television Association of Programmers–Latin America, was quoted as saying. "And it's especially reassuring to have USTR supporting this Coalition." The Television Association of Programmers represents most U.S. satellite TV services—the same companies eyeing Latin American for expansion. The new trade agreement with Chile appears to protect them from any requirement that they support Chilean creators in return for profiting from the Chilean market.

THESE ATTEMPTS to achieve Hollywood's objectives through flanking manoeuvres executed against bilateral targets are understandable. In tactical terms, they allow the United States to concentrate its diplomatic force on smaller, weaker countries one by one. This is a much easier task than meeting a coalition of bargaining partners in the wider theatre of a multilateral negotiation. As Australian Terry Flew has observed: "Small and open countries [are] less vulnerable in an environment of multilaterally endorsed trading rules than 'in the dog-eat-dog world of bilateral trade wars.'"

Writes David Puttnam in his *Undeclared War:* "Stories and images are among the principal means by which human society has always transmitted its values and beliefs. If the largest and most influential element of our entertainment business has inexorably shifted abroad, what will become of our, or for that matter any other nation's, cultural identity?"

So is it a "rock or a hard place" for policies that seek to sustain cultural diversity—either endure a bilateral shakedown or be stripped naked in the arena of global trade law?

Perhaps neither.

17

A NEW
DIRECTION

T HE CARIBBEAN NATION of Trinidad and Tobago offers another
illustration of what happens when culture-as-identity and cul-
ture-as-commodity collide in the cauldron of trade globalization.
In the 1980s, about 30 per cent of the programming aired on the nation's single public-television broadcaster was produced locally—by,
for and about the two islands' roughly 1.2 million citizens. In the following decade, new technology and market liberalization brought
viewers a second locally owned private television signal and upward of
sixty more foreign-originated cable channels. But local expression
plummeted to less than 10 per cent of airtime, even on local channels.

"If they can get a Tom Cruise film for $300, why should they pay any
more for a local film?" Trinidadian television producer and broadcast
consultant Bruce Paddington laments. "It's gotten so bad that if I or
one my colleagues wants to get a film shown on television, *we have to
pay them.*"

As the 1990s became the 2000s, a joint business–government
agency named TIDCO set about developing strategies to improve the
Trinidadian and Tobagonian economy. It hired Paddington to work up
a plan for the audiovisual sector. As he drafted recommendations, he
toyed with a proposal for local-content quotas in island movie
houses—a policy clearly permitted under the terms of GATT.

Then the draft reached the desk of TIDCO executives. The response was swift and sharp.

"I was told, 'No!'" Paddington recounts. "'It will affect our trade deals.' They feared it could go against us at the WTO and in the Free Trade Area of the Americas agreement."

"Small countries are frightened, intimidated and bullied by the American pressure that says, 'If you start to protect your cultural industries, we'll put up more barriers against your trade goods,'" Paddington asserts.

He is right about the pressure, but wrong in believing it is limited to David-and-Goliath encounters. Other trading partners as small as Croatia and as substantial as Canada and Australia have found themselves under similar real or implied threats. Indeed, the muscularity of U.S. pressure to enshrine in writing what its negotiators like to call "free and open" trade in "entertainment and leisure services" can be perplexing, given that in many cases American cultural works already dominate the markets in question.

The explanation lies once again in the money trail mapped by economics and the predatory potential of arbitrary pricing. As the example of Tom Cruise on Trinidadian TV illustrates, foreign producers of expensive motion pictures can, as Paddington says, "use the so-called 'level playing field' as a way of dumping their films at very low cost."

The rest of the explanation lies in the critical importance of cultural exports to the United States' balance of trade. "These sectors generate significant numbers of jobs and revenue," observes U.S. trade consultant and former deputy secretary of the treasury William S. Merkin. He continues:

> Measures or policies which are implemented in the name of protecting culture but which end up restricting the movement of cultural products from one country to another are viewed very critically by the United States. Harsh American reactions are based not just on commercial harm being inflicted on United States economic interests, but also because *actions by one country set precedents for others* around the world. [Emphasis added]

In other words, it is not the profits at stake in Croatia or Tobago—or even Canada—that harden the U.S. bargaining stance. Rather, it is fear of a kind of economic domino effect: if *even one* country establishes its right to protect its cultural diversity, others may do the same, possibly affecting more lucrative markets. In American eyes, tiny Trinidad is a tripwire for the defence of its $80 billion annual trade surplus in cultural products.

But the principles at stake cut two ways. In securing its own revenue stream, Washington is also in a position to establish standards for the rest of the world. As noted in Chapter 16, the most-favoured nation principle dictates that whatever concessions the United States extracts from one GATS partner in one-on-one bargaining must be extended to all that country's other trade partners (some exceptions apply to concessions granted to partners in regional free-trade agreements). The eventual and irrevocable outcome of that process, U.S. trade negotiators clearly hope, must be the creation of a "free, open and level" playing field that permanently locks in a crushing economic advantage for U.S. cultural exports.

That remains a highly possible, if not indeed a probable, outcome. But it is not inevitable.

SINCE 1998, an alternative process has been quietly gathering strength. Its organic roots can be traced to meetings in Stockholm and Ottawa. Its philosophical model hails from Rio de Janeiro. And by the start of 2003, it had enlisted support from more than fifty nations— including two of the United States' three biggest trade partners.

In contrast to the broadly constituted "anti-globalization" cause, this has not been a mass movement. It has gained its momentum for the most part below the radar of media notice and celebrity. That is perhaps because its goals are not, in fact, so radical. It is not out to stop or reverse progress towards a common and transparent set of world trading rules. To the contrary, it could help secure those gains by removing a good deal of the cause for animus among people who believe a global economy necessarily destroys local values.

"What is needed is no doubt an 'economic constitution for an open world,'" France's Elie Cohen wrote of the emerging trade regime in the *World Culture Report* for 2000. "But it must be a world which can combine the values of trade, democracy and identity."

The emerging international view shares Cohen's conviction. It recognizes that *both* culture-as-commerce and culture-as-identity are essential to expanding wealth and well-being. But it acknowledges that the two values do not flourish equally under the same conditions, with the result that competition between them for priority in policy-setting has often been viewed in a bipolar, zero-sum frame. The search is on for a new view that would reconcile these two imperatives.

In 2002, that goal began to acquire substance. Meeting in South Africa, a group of activist culture ministers from five continents reviewed the first draft of a new kind of international trade instrument. It would for the first time establish unequivocally the legitimacy of both economic and cultural interests. And it would lay out in clear, accountable and transparent terms how trading partners might secure the first without jeopardizing the second.

The meeting in Cape Town brought to fruition a conversation with deep roots in international dialogue. Calls for more focused attention to the interplay of culture, development, wealth and power are decades old. They first became insistent with the reassertion of national and ethnic identities that coincided with the retreat of classical European colonialism.

During the 1970s, the United Nations Educational Social and Cultural Organization (UNESCO) began to look beyond its early preoccupation with learning and living conditions to focus on the interaction between culture and development. In 1982, it hosted a world conference on the topic in Mexico City. The declaration that emerged from it was in some ways poetic and in others prophetic. Much of it remains relevant.

"Culture," UNESCO observed, "is dialogue, the exchange of ideas and experience and the appreciation of other values and traditions; it withers and dies in isolation."

But in a remark that prefigured contemporary concerns, it also warned: "Growth has frequently been conceived in quantitative terms, without taking into account its necessary qualitative dimension, namely the satisfaction of man's spiritual and cultural aspirations." And, it added, "the universal cannot be postulated in the abstract by any single culture: it emerges from the experience of all the world's peoples as each affirms its own identity. *Cultural identity and cultural diversity are inseparable* ... All of this points to the need for cultural policies that will protect, stimulate and enrich each people's identity and cultural heritage" (emphasis added).

Two years after the world's trading nations launched the Uruguay Round of talks aimed at accelerating liberalization and increasing international commerce, UNESCO launched another initiative, the "World Decade for Cultural Development." Its top goals were to acknowledge the cultural dimension in development, assert and enhance cultural identities and broaden participation in cultural life.

By the time the World Decade for Cultural Development drew to a close, the trading system had acquired ambitious new rules and extended its reach far into hitherto cordoned-off realms of culture and services. As for the protection of culture and diversity, nothing existed that had not been there a decade earlier.

In 1998, UNESCO hosted another international conference, this one in Stockholm. Its concluding declaration made explicit the rising tension between the expansion of liberalized trade and long-standing cultural values. "Globalization link[s] cultures ever more closely and enrich[es] the interaction between them," it reflected, "but [it] may also be detrimental to our creative diversity and to cultural pluralism."

Among the specific concerns UNESCO noted were "the risks and challenges arising from the promotion of cultural industries and trade in cultural products. Participation in cultural life being a fundamental right of individuals in all communities, governments have a duty to create conditions for the full exercise of this right." And, echoing Samuel Huntington, UNESCO issued a forecast for the years ahead: "The dialogue between cultures appears to be one of the fundamental cultural and political challenges for the world today; it is an essential condition of peaceful coexistence."

Coincidentally, at that moment, the dialogue between the United States and Canada over the latter's magazine industry had sunk into strained silence. *Sports Illustrated* had launched an edition in Canada, intending to sell advertising in it to Canadian businesses. Canada had responded with a prohibitory tax on any advertising targeted to Canada that the U.S. magazine sold. Washington had complained under GATT and secured a favourable first ruling from the WTO in Geneva. Canada had appealed.

By late June of 1998, both sides had dug in, awaiting a final verdict. But in Ottawa, Canadian political and bureaucratic minds were already bracing for a loss—and thinking ahead. Legal draftsmen were preparing a new measure for Canada's magazine culture. It shifted the point of legal leverage from the physical *goods* of periodicals to the *service* they rendered to advertisers.

Politicians, meanwhile, focused on a longer-term challenge. With negotiations pending under the three-year-old GATS agreement, it was likely that Canada would sooner or later face mounting pressure to expose services as well as goods to the discipline of "national treatment." The legislation being drafted for magazines, in other words, might succeed only as a temporary evasion.

In that climate, Canada's minister of heritage, Sheila Copps, convened a meeting in Ottawa to resume a conversation begun two months earlier at the UNESCO conference in Stockholm. With counterparts from other nations, Copps wanted to explore whether there might be a way to frame, under international auspices, a permanent solution to the recurring frictions between Canada and the United States over culture—of which the magazine war was only the most recent. Culture ministers from nineteen other countries were invited.

Among them were delegates from Mexico, Sweden, Great Britain and Greece—but not the United States. Copps and her officials gave two reasons for the omission. The formal explanation was that the United States, in keeping with its trade posture that "culture" is indistinguishable from "entertainment" or "leisure" goods and services, regards the subject as unworthy of a cabinet-level authority. Washington, therefore, simply had no one to send. A more significant but unofficial second reason was so that those who did attend could debate the issue unrestrained by the presence of a powerful emissary unsympathetic to their ends.

By the time they left Ottawa, the ministers had agreed to establish a loose but ongoing association to pursue a variety of common concerns involving cultural policy. Those initiatives ranged from prodding the World Bank to lend more money to poor nations for cultural programs to fostering co-operation among their respective television producers. A concluding statement did not explicitly address the tensions between trade and culture. But in agreeing to establish the International Network for Cultural Policy (INCP) and to meet again in a year's time, the ministers had created an arena where that topic could fruitfully be taken up.

The Canada–U.S. magazine war was still raging eight months later when another meeting in Ottawa—this one private—brought a precise new focus to Canadian treatment of the issue. Ever since negotiating a free-trade agreement with the United States more than a decade earlier—followed by the NAFTA, which added Mexico's signature—the Canadian government had routinely sought advice on trade matters from leading figures in various areas of the economy. These inelegantly named Sectoral Advisory Groups on International Trade had come to be better known by their acronym as SAGITs.

In February 1999, with the threat of American trade retaliation hanging over $4 billion worth of Canadian wood, textile, plastic and steel exports, Canada's international trade minister sat down to receive a brief from the SAGIT representing cultural industries. Its members included senior executives from the film, television, music and publishing businesses, as well as several others long associated with those fields. (One of the writers is a member of the cultural-industries SAGIT).

After a few paragraphs of preliminaries, the SAGIT brief got to the point. "There is growing concern worldwide about the impact of international trade agreements on trade and investment on culture," it noted. "The tools and approaches used in the past to keep cultural goods and services from being subject to the same treatment as other goods and services may no longer be enough." The cultural exemption has its limits.

"Just as nations have come together to protect and promote biodiversity, it is time to come together to promote cultural and linguistic diversity. The time has come for Canada to call on other countries to develop a new international cultural instrument that would acknowledge the importance of cultural diversity and address the cultural policies designed to promote and protect that diversity."

The instrument the industry leaders had in mind would set several key assurances into the larger fabric of the international trading system. Among other things, those assurances would

> "acknowledge that cultural goods and services are significantly different from other products";

> accept that "policies intended to ensure access to a variety of indigenous cultural products" are defensible corrective interventions in the market;

> "set out rules on the kind of . . . measures that countries can and cannot use to enhance cultural and linguistic diversity"; and

➤ "establish how trade disciplines would apply or not apply to cultural measures that meet the agreed upon rules."

Eight months later, the idea became official Canadian policy. On October 19, 1999, the federal government confirmed that it had approved the pursuit of a new international instrument on cultural diversity. At the same time, it expressed the hope that a formal acknowledgment that culture deserved special treatment in trade rules would be endorsed by WTO trade ministers, who were scheduled to meet that December in Seattle.

That hope proved forlorn. The Seattle trade summit adjourned in disarray after thousands of anti-globalization protestors forced pitched battles on police who were guarding the summit's fortified venue. But even as the stinging haze of pepper spray flowed down the city's steep streets, leaving negotiators' hopes of launching a new round of negotiations for an expanded WTO accord as badly trashed as the Seattle centre, a new appreciation began to settle in of the popular and democratic challenges facing globalization.

Over the next few years, it became increasingly evident that to accomplish their goal of a more seamless, predictable and orderly rule-based trading system, advocates for the world's economic interests would need to become sharply more sensitive to other values that their ambitions might affect.

As a new millennium began, the unresolved friction between the global-trade objectives of culture-as-commerce and the global reassertion of culture-as-identity surfaced at a growing number of other international gatherings. In April 2001, protestors again met tear gas outside a barricaded conference centre—this one in Quebec City. But as hemispheric leaders departed the Summit of the Americas, they left behind them a declaration stating that cultural diversity "must be a cohesive factor that strengthens the social fabric and the development of our nations."

The following month, the European Commission and UNESCO sponsored a Forum on Globalization and Cultural Diversity in Valencia, Spain. Delegates from the audiovisual sector in countries from every continent (except Antarctica) attended. "Information and culture," its closing statement recognized, "have become important dimensions of the process of globalization. Media and the arts are increasingly under pressure. Vast new global markets and the ongoing corporate merger process provide not only rich opportunities but also new challenges, especially for cultural heritage and values." Significantly, the forum focused on the particular risk and potential from one particular medium. "The audiovisual and media industry provide strong instruments for the expression of cultural identity," it declared, "but can also be destructive to those cultures that are economically and socially more fragile."

With those observations in its preamble, the Valencia gathering concluded: "Cultural diversity deserves to be protected ... International forums and processes, including those focusing on international trade, must respect the need for nations to protect, nurture and support that diversity." To that end, it added, "there is an urgent need for the negotiation of a new international instrument on cultural diversity to address issues related to cultural products." This was the first international recognition of the concept of a new cultural-trade instrument.

The instrument the European delegates envisioned would, at its core, contain several of the same insights that infused the SAGIT proposal. As the forum communiqué put it:

➤ Cultural products are goods and services with a distinct specificity different from merchandise.

➤ The media play an important role in determining the state and conditions of cultural diversity.

➤ States have the primary responsibility to guarantee, protect and provide an enabling environment for the exercise and enjoyment of the right to cultural diversity.

➤ States are entitled to ensure a proper framework for cultural diversity and to address the emergence of dominant cultural configurations.

Two months later, in July 2000, the concluding communiqué of the Kyushu–Okinawa Summit of G-8 leaders acknowledged "the importance of diversity in linguistic and creative expressions ... [as] a source of social and economic dynamism."

Finally that year, the International Network on Cultural Policy (INCP) met on the Greek island of Santorini. There, Copps's department would later report to Parliament, a working group led by Canadian officials "presented a discussion paper and an illustrative list of principles to be used as a starting point for the development of an international instrument on cultural diversity." The ministers agreed to have their officials put flesh on the skeleton proposal during the following year.

Nearby, a second group—with its own roots in Stockholm and Ottawa—also met under the Greek sun. This one brought together delegates sent by seventy private non-governmental organizations (NGOS) representing artists' and cultural groups in twenty-one countries. Some of those present had attended the UNESCO summit in Stockholm two years earlier. A larger number had been in Ottawa for a conference of NGOS timed to coincide with the 1998 ministerial meeting that Copps had hosted. In Santorini, this loose collection of like-minded delegates coalesced into a formally constituted civil-society analogue to the international policy network. The newly minted International Network on Cultural Diversity (whose acronym, INCD, unhelpfully differed by only a consonant from that of the ministerial INCP), would be "dedicated to countering the homogenizing effects of globalization on culture."

On Santorini, the NGOS also voted to add two significant clauses to a founding statement that had been drafted in advance of their meeting. The first declared "that the network should endorse the creation of a new international treaty on cultural diversity with some form of enforceability"; a second, "that it should ask governments not to make any new commitments on cultural goods and services in trade negotiations."

Throughout the following year, the idea of a new international instrument on culture gathered steam, securing endorsements from increasingly senior diplomatic forums. In June 2001, culture ministers of La Francophonie, an international organization of fifty French-speaking countries (including Canada and most former French colonies), meeting in Benin, added their backing to "the principle of a universal international regulatory instrument that supported the promotion of cultural diversity."

That year's meeting of the INCP group, held in Lucerne, Switzerland, in the shocked fortnight following the attacks on New York and Washington, drew ministers or their seconds from twenty-two countries. Among those represented were the United States' two NAFTA partners, Mexico and Canada, as well as Russia, France and Brazil. Britain sent an observer, as did UNESCO, the Council of Europe and the European Union. In a closing statement, the culture ministers argued that the acts of terrorism against the United States, and the kidnapping as they met of a former INCP member in Colombia, underscored the urgency of "a greater understanding and respect for the differences inherent in our cultural diversity."

Of more substance were other conclusions that emerged from Lucerne. One was a clear endorsement of the right of governments to act to secure cultural diversity. "It is the legitimate role of government to preserve and promote cultural diversity through the development and implementation of cultural policies at all levels," the ministers' closing declaration read. "The further development of an International Instrument on Cultural Diversity which includes a common vision, objectives, and norm-setting elements is essential."

The ministers assigned to their officials the job of drafting such an instrument. Its focus would be "on the promotion and preservation of cultural diversity in the face of globalization—including the impact of trade liberalization, prejudicial trade practices and rapid technological advancement on cultural products and policies ... including the notion of its enforceability."

Meeting over the same few September days in Lucerne, the NGOs of the INCD felt similarly overshadowed by the events in the United States. "We oppose fanaticism and cultural absolutism in all forms," their closing communiqué noted. They also renewed their call for a new international instrument on cultural diversity—which by now had acquired an acronym of its own, NIICD. In contrast to the ministerial statement, the NGO sought a document with broader scope affirming artists' rights, the "fundamental importance to preserve language" and "the cultures and traditional knowledge of indigenous people."

But the civil-society group also sought something "more than a declaratory statement of principles." The new instrument, the NGO added, "must be an effective buffer from the trade agreements and provide a solid legal foundation for measures that promote cultural diversity. Signatories must agree that there can be no trade retaliation against measures adopted in conformity with the treaty."

Within eight weeks, the notion of the new cultural instrument—an NIICD—would get its most powerful endorsement to date. Meeting in Paris, the General Conference of UNESCO, on November 2, 2001, adopted a "Universal Declaration on Cultural Diversity." Its twelve articles brought together and articulated a coherent sweep of principles, many of which had flowed through or been implied in earlier declarations either from UNESCO-sponsored consultations or more junior diplomatic bodies. It noted in particular that the claim to cultural diversity cannot be allowed to trump every other value: "No one may invoke cultural diversity to infringe upon human rights guaranteed by international law, nor to limit their scope." It also affirmed the necessity of both the freedom *to access* and the freedom *to express* culture: "While ensuring the free flow of ideas by word and image, care should be exercised that all cultures can express themselves and make themselves known."

The United Nations agency went on to lend its weight to several of the same contentions the Canadian SAGIT had made. In Article 8— "Cultural goods and services: commodities of a unique kind"—the Universal Declaration stated in part: "particular attention must be paid ... to the specificity of cultural goods and services which, as vectors of identity, values and meaning, must not be treated as mere commodities or consumer goods."

In the following two articles, it elaborated the implications of that point for public policy. "It is for each State, with due regard to its international obligations, to define its cultural policy and to implement it," Article 9 stated. And in Article 11, it emphasized UNESCO's belief that "market forces alone cannot guarantee the preservation and promotion of cultural diversity ... From this perspective, the pre-eminence of public policy ... must be reaffirmed."

UNESCO also adopted a twenty-point action plan to implement its new Universal Declaration. Point 1 of the plan committed member states to co-operate in "deepening the international debate on questions relating to cultural diversity ... taking forward notably consideration of the opportunity of an international legal instrument on cultural diversity."

Lastly, in 2001, the Council of Europe, in a declaration on cultural diversity adopted that December, endorsed much of the same ground in only slightly more elliptical terms. A preamble noted that "new information technologies, globalization and evolving multilateral trade policies have an impact on cultural diversity" and added that "media pluralism is essential for democracy and cultural diversity." Then the council declared that "the legitimate objectives of member states to develop international agreements for cultural cooperation, which promote cultural diversity, must be respected." It further endorsed the right of states to enact domestic measures to secure culture: "Cultural and audiovisual policies, which promote and respect cultural diversity, are a necessary complement to trade policies."

As a closing flourish, the Council of Europe issued what amounted to a "stand-still" advisory not very different from the plea the INCD had earlier voiced. "Member states are urged to pay particular attention to the need to sustain and promote cultural diversity . . . in other international fora where they might be called on to undertake commitments which might prejudice these instruments." Diplomatically, the council did not specifically name either the WTO or GATS.

THE RATIONALE, foundation and core objectives of any new international instrument on culture are now clear. The need for such a vehicle rests in the nexus of the economic and symbolic characteristics of cultural goods.

Economically, cultural products are significantly different from conventional merchandise in ways that make them highly vulnerable to a variety of market effects that, singly and together, act to attenuate diversity of choice. At the same time, cultural products contain symbolic significance that may be closely specific or acutely foreign to particular audiences. As a result, the unregulated market will not only be inefficient by conventional economic standards but may be destructive of identity and community values. These effects are most strongly apparent in the distribution of the most expensive and psychologically potent cultural forms, the audiovisual products of film and television.

"Cultural identification, self-recognition and self-esteem are important to people," David Throsby notes in *Economics and Culture*, "and these values are impacted upon by trade. Economic policy in this area may need to accept that the ultimate goals of different societies extend beyond immediate economic concerns."

Put another way, cultural products are one of those not-so-rare instances in which the invisible hand of Adam Smith fails to deal a perfect outcome. In this case, the raw physics of commerce prevent audiences from being fairly presented with a full spectrum of choices— a menu unbiased by the pursuit of profit, which clearly is often driven by factors remote from audience preference. Corporate media further over-provide information relevant to *consumption* while under-providing information relevant to *citizenship*. This last issue is not in-consequential in today's increasingly complex democratic societies.

The right and the responsibility of governments to moderate market failure are well established in many other areas, from public health to the sale of corporate securities. Public policy can, as we have seen, be effective in correcting market failure in the supply of cultural products as well.

Since GATT's establishment in 1947, a growing body of international agreement has extended a common global understanding of the acceptable ambit of state activity in the economic arena. But until now the evolution of international trade law has proceeded with only limited regard for the difference between cultural products and conventional merchandise, or the social injury that may result from failing to observe that distinction.

Therein lies a danger for the economic agenda as much as the cultural one. Professor Ivan Bernier, formerly of Laval University's faculty of law, draws this point out well:

> Cultural expression is a key factor in the ability of various cultures to adapt to globalization. To address the question of the relationship between culture and commerce exclusively from the standpoint of commerce is to subject culture to commercial imperatives and thereby prevent it from playing its own role.
>
> By engendering a new economic structure that is based largely on competition and tends to impose a single commercial mould on all the expectations that citizens have in various realms of activity, globalization fosters new forms of social organization that call into question traditional ways of doing things and existing loyalties. If these changes upset people, economic globalization itself could suffer the consequences.

Of course, the problem of accommodating societal or non-commercial goals in the international trading system is not unique to the cultural field. The WTO is wrestling with similar confrontations in regard to environmental and labour standards, and its challenge will be to show that it has the flexibility to accommodate these concerns.

But the cultural imperative can no longer be ignored. In sum, the world community of trading nations confronts a demonstrable failure of market outcome. It possesses a set of pertinent remedies and a foundation in long-standing national practice and international law to support their application. What is lacking is only a mechanism to reconcile cultural security with trade liberalization.

"The challenge," as Bernier concludes, "is to bring about a rapprochement between the commercial perspective and the cultural perspective."

ANY SUCH RAPPROCHEMENT must satisfy both communities of interest. It must provide traders with transparent rules, fairly applied, that will minimally distort the objective merits of competing proffers in the international marketplace. It must ensure that publics retain, through governments, a corresponding right to mitigate the market's own distortions, particularly its erosion of diversity in choice and access.

Deciding how to square that circle—and questioning whether it can be done at all—has consumed hundreds of hours of international debate. The discussion has ranged far afield in the various fora that have tackled the issue. Three issues have proved salient.

The first concerns the form—the scope and remit—of any new instrument on culture. The second is how it should relate to the preexisting structure of international agreements on trade and culture. The third question is perhaps touchiest of all: how such an instrument might affect the long-standing United States position that cultural policies must take a back seat to trade negotiations.

Debate over the form of a new cultural trade instrument has proceeded along two primary dimensions. The first describes the scope of its coverage: should it be broad or narrow? The other presents a scale of enforceability: should it be merely declaratory, or should it entail positive obligations and a mechanism for enforcement?

The spectrum on coverage is staked out at one end by Canada's SAGIT. At the other are members of the NGOs that have gathered annually since 2000 in the shadow of the network of culture ministers.

The former presses for a narrow focus on the nexus of national policy and international trade law. It sees the key utility of an NIICD to be in clarifying how existing trade rules will interact with national measures to secure access to and the distribution of domestic cultural products. In their view, national governments must play a primary role as signatories to the existing trade regime and as the main actors on behalf of their national publics.

Social activists have demanded a much broader remit. "There must be special recognition of the need to preserve threatened cultures, especially languages, including those of indigenous peoples [as well as] of the need to protect traditional knowledge," delegates to the 2002 INCD meeting concluded.

Views on scope also differ from the perspective of developed and less-developed regions. A report prepared for the South African Department of Arts and Culture, for instance, noted that many national governments in less-developed regions lack either policies or resources to secure culture diversity. Some indeed "view social and economic development as contradictory to cultural diversity," to the extent even of encouraging "xenophobia or cultural exclusivity." To counter those conditions, the South African report urged that an NIICD should include "a set of guidelines to governments who wish to promote and preserve cultural diversity." It should also "provide a framework for support (financial and technical expertise) between North and South" and "direct member states away from cultural insularity and towards cross-cultural exchange."

The activist camp similarly takes a maximal view of the legal force an NIICD should seek to exert. The NGO network has urged that any instrument contain a variety of positive obligations on national governments, requiring them to take specific action to sustain cultural diversity. The same group also calls for third parties (that is, NGOs or even individuals) to have the right to trigger the international enforcement of those obligations.

This contrasts with the UNESCO and Council of Europe declarations issued thus far. Those declarations have been purely exhortatory, urging respect for cultural diversity but not suggesting any sanction for a failure to do so.

A middle view—held by the Canadian SAGIT, among others—rejects the idea that an NIICD should commit signatories to positive obligations. But it does insist that the instrument should provide an effective mechanism to resolve disputes between trading partners over cultural measures that appear to conflict with trade commitments—such as the one that arose between Canada and the United States over magazines.

Underlying the views opposed across the two dimensions of scope and force are different ways of framing the issue of diversity. They also impinge on the second major question hanging over the proposed NIICD: how it should relate to the existing structure of international agreements.

One view frames diversity in a diffuse, highly post-modern understanding of culture. At its extreme, this perspective rejects even nation states as legitimate actors on behalf of publics—which it regards as fragmented collections of "privileged" and "non-privileged" groups centred as much on lifestyle (such as gay and straight) as language or ethnicity. It considers culture in the least normative terms possible. Its exponents are inclined to place an international instrument within the context of uncompromising opposition to globalization and even to capitalism in general.

The alternative view (which these writers share) is sharply more limited. Aware that markets are imperfect and that globalization is often disruptive, it nevertheless regards both as desirable. It recognizes that there is internal diversity (sometimes insufficiently acknowledged) within national publics. But it also accepts that national governments remain the most effective agents of those publics and the only agents capable of securing commitments from international partners. It declines, for the purposes of a new instrument, to give the term "culture" its widest possible interpretation. Instead it concerns itself narrowly with the specific vulnerability of those high-impact, high-value modes of commercial culture that are most susceptible to market failure. Agreeing with Ivan Bernier, this view seeks rapprochement with the forces of trade liberalization, not resistance against them.

This polarity of frames is significant at two levels. One is the predictable tension between reach and grasp. In this instance, the present writers argue, the perfect ought not to become the enemy of the good.

But the different viewpoints also influence judgements about how a new international instrument on cultural diversity and trade would best relate to the existing fabric of multilateral agreements. Should it stand alone? Should it be an annex or attachment to the structure of GATS, and administered by the WTO? Should it be a creation of UNESCO and administered by that agency? Where, to put it in diplomatic terms, should this NIICD be housed?

The answer will largely determine whether any document ultimately adopted is regarded as a predominantly cultural statement of values or as an effective instrument capable of reconciling competing cultural *and* commercial imperatives.

The distinction is key. A statement of principle in favour of cultural diversity is all very well, but for an NIICD to establish predictable rules for how trade disciplines will or will not apply to cultural-security measures—a core objective on which all perspectives agree—it must as a practical matter engage those disciplines on some common ground. There must be some way to answer the inevitable question: in the event of conflict between actions taken in respect of an NIICD and obligations under the WTO, which instrument will prevail? Similarly, an NIICD needs to be compatible with international copyright treaties and obligations.

One way to provide such traction is simply to negotiate the cultural instrument directly under the authority of the WTO. In a comment on the UNESCO conference held in Valencia in 2000, the Motion Picture Association of America made just that point. "As a factual matter," Hollywood's lobby group noted, "a 'new international instrument on cultural diversity' could not affect the existing international 'acquis' [accepted practice] unless it were negotiated within the competent international organization by its members." In a similar vein, Canadian trade-policy analysts William Dymond and Michael Hart have observed:

> Multilateral and regional trade agreements have a long history of tolerating, even encouraging, special trade restrictive regimes for politically difficult sectors such as textiles and agriculture. If such regimes can exist within the architecture of international trade rules, there is every reason to believe that trade in cultural goods and services can be fitted within the system in a manner compatible with expanding trade and vibrant cultural expression.

But to expect the WTO to appreciate the importance of cultural policies is rash. Can a WTO dispute panel that cannot tell *Time Canada* from *Maclean's* be trusted to distinguish between *Degrassi: The Next Generation,* a half-hour drama focusing on the problems of teenagers in a Canadian school, and *Friends,* a half-hour sitcom focusing on the problems of twentysomething New York roommates? Yet *Degrassi* provides ideas, situations and cultural references entirely different from those portrayed on *Friends*—or anything else on television. And it would never have been made without the tool kit of measures to support it.

Similarly, can a WTO panel unable to distinguish between *Time Canada* and *Maclean's* be expected to see that *Generations*, a drama about families from all walks of life and ethnic origins living together in South Africa, is different from *Dallas*, a drama featuring the travails of a Texas oil millionaire and his dysfunctional family? To the WTO, on the basis of its decision in the periodicals case, both programs would simply be characterized as "dramatic series," indistinguishable for trade purposes.

Another difficulty in working with the WTO trade vocabulary is presented by the question of "proportionality," sometimes referred to as the "necessity test." Article VI, paragraph 5 of the GATS provides a test for determining whether domestic regulations governing services for which commitments have been made are valid. To pass, they must "not [be] more burdensome than necessary to ensure the quality of the service." If cultural services were brought under GATS and allowance was made for "reasonable" policies to provide space and choice for national cultural content, how would this be interpreted? Would it, as in the case we encountered earlier, place a panel of trade academics in Geneva in judgement over whether a Canadian (or Australian or South African) regulator, acting after public hearings in Canada (or Australia or South Africa) had set domestic content quotas on Canadian (or . . .) television at a level "more burdensome than necessary"?

This is not to defend unreasonable cultural policies. Still, the problem presented by the "necessity test" underlines the difficulty of articulating subjective cultural values within the rationalistic and purportedly objective analytic framework of international-trade rules. The tape measure and weigh scales appropriate to ordinary commodities and merchandise make poor registers of the symbolic significance of cultural goods.

Because of these and other limitations of the WTO process and structure, an alternative consensus has gathered momentum in favour of housing any possible instrument within the agency that laid much of the philosophical groundwork for its necessity: UNESCO.

This view was endorsed in October 2002, by the diplomatic forum that has most advanced the idea of an NIICD—the international network of culture ministers. After meeting in Cape Town, South Africa, that group, now bolstered by the presence of China's culture minister, asserted in a communiqué that "UNESCO is the appropriate international institution to house and implement an International Instrument on Cultural Diversity." It further undertook to "actively engage with UNESCO ... for the advancement of the Instrument."

The following week, the nations of La Francophonie, meeting in Beirut, added their endorsement:

> We have decided to contribute actively to the adoption by UNESCO of an international convention on cultural diversity, enshrining the right of states and governments to maintain, establish and develop policies for the support of culture and cultural diversity ... This convention must also underscore openness to other cultures and to their expression. [translation]

The world body responded the following year. On October 14, 2003, UNESCO's members unanimously passed a resolution calling on its director-general to develop a new "standard-setting instrument" whose goal will be the "protection of the diversity of cultural contents and artistic expressions." A draft international convention is to be brought back for review by the next general conference in 2005.

Pursuit of an NIICD within UNESCO has some advantages. The organization's established presence provides a firm and credible foundation on which the new instrument can take its place in the expanding web of international governance. UNESCO also has an active secretariat capable of sustained support for any new instrument's implementation.

But there are also two significant deficits. For one, UNESCO is not noted for reaching swift and decisive agreement. There is some risk that what the MPAA calls the "acquis" of disciplines obliged under GATS will take hold before an NIICD realized under UNESCO leadership can provide security for public policy in defence of cultural diversity.

More troubling still is the complete absence of any interface in international agreement between the authority of UNESCO and that of the WTO. UNESCO is an organization established under the United Nations with its own mandate and membership. The WTO is an autonomous agency created by agreement of its own members. While there is much overlap between the two groups of member states, neither organization extends explicit recognition to the other. Put another way: a declaration under UNESCO's imprimatur, however strongly phrased, simply carries no weight in deliberations at the WTO.

That gap must somehow be bridged if an NIICD realized through UNESCO is to have any prospect of achieving its central objective. One possibility is for signatories to the WTO to recognize a UNESCO-authorized NIICD in a supplemental agreement. But whether through that means or some other, the ultimate rapprochement of culture-as-commerce and culture-as-idea cannot be accomplished unless the world's trade regime takes explicit account of the competing imperatives accommodated in an instrument on diversity.

WINNING APPROVAL of the WTO may depend upon a no less problematic endorsement: that of the United States. How likely is America to agree to a convention that enshrines the right of other countries to maintain policies that ensure space and choice for local as well as imported cultural products?

In the eyes of most observers, the answer is: "Not likely at all."

In many (though not all) cases, it has been an unacceptable imbalance in favour of specifically American exports that has prompted other nations to take measures to secure their own culture. Countries from Trinidad to Chile can testify to the force of American exertions to foreclose the possibility of exactly such policies setting an international precedent. There seems good reason, then, to expect the United States to mount no less muscular a resistance to any instrument designed to enshrine a *right* to employ such policy tools in international law. "It is delusional," William Dymond and Michael Hart write, "to base any position on the prospect that the United States . . . will accept any dilution of the international trade rules to the disadvantage of their industries."

Adds Canadian Chris Maule: "Critics note that the U.S. government is not supportive of these initiatives and that without its involvement there is little chance of an agreement that will embrace most of the trade activity that has been the subject of problems to date. Having achieved success in the periodical dispute [against Canada] in the WTO, it is unlikely the U.S. would give up this approach in order to become part of an agreement that would be unlikely to have the teeth that the WTO dispute resolution mechanism has revealed."

This undoubtedly overstates the case. In fact, the United States did compromise its position in its settlement of the periodicals dispute, permitting the Canadian government to continue with a cultural policy that discriminated in favour of magazines with local content. But the question strikes to a deeper current of uncertainty. Quite apart from whether to surrender the high cards in any potential future confrontation over culture, the United States is profoundly conflicted over the terms of its entire relationship with the rest of the world.

In its 2002 National Security Strategy, the United States government articulated two bald precepts for a new doctrine. First: American foreign policy will for the foreseeable future be based on the exercise of an overwhelming power advantage (and the preservation of that advantage against all rivals). Second: the United States reserves to itself the right to determine the moment and manner of applying its power.

An analysis by Robert Kagan in *Policy Review* offered a widely circulated rationale for the new doctrine. "Great powers," Kagan observed, "often fear rules that may constrain them more than they fear the anarchy in which their power brings security." When, in other words, you are what U.S. secretary of state Colin Powell calls "the bully on the block," you have little to fear from the law of the jungle. It is easy to draw the inference that no administration with such an admitted penchant for fiat will be likely to accede to a new instrument constraining the hegemony of one of its nation's most successful and profitable export industries.

But while the thread of American internationalism that gave birth to the United Nations and the world trading regime itself may have frayed, it has not entirely run out. Joseph Nye, dean of the Kennedy School of Government and an assistant secretary of defence in the Clinton administration, is only one voice that continues to advocate for what he calls "soft power" exercised through international and multilateral organizations. In Nye's view, the nature of such twenty-first-century challenges as global terrorism, climate change and transnational migration of refugees will compel the United States to seek the willing co-operation of other states more often than it attempts to coerce them.

It is worth remembering that tides always change—even in the politics of a superpower. Administrations are voted in—but also out. Even as many Americans rallied around their president in a time of war in early 2003, numerous surveys revealed that many Americans had grave concerns about their country's growing estrangement from the family of nations. There are many constituencies in the United States who would benefit as much as any group from the provisions of a cultural instrument. Among them are the coalitions that successfully won a quota for children's educational television and fought for "source diversity" in television after the nation's networks began eliminating independent program production.

There is another dimension to consider. The United States in recent years has withheld or rescinded its endorsement from several agreements that the rest of the world held to be desirable. It stood off from the Kyoto environmental accord, the nuclear test ban treaty, the land mines treaty, an international accord to limit trade in small arms, the biological warfare protocol and the proposed International Criminal Court.

These decisions have been roundly criticized as examples of U.S. unilateralism and disdain for world opinion. But they also illustrate a countervailing theme: each of these agreements proceeded anyway. The absence of U.S. endorsement does not doom an instrument on cultural diversity to failure—if it finds wide support elsewhere. "The U.S. view is not a majority view at the international level," notes Canadian trade consultant Anne McCaskill.

Agrees trade lawyer Larry Herman: "While the U.S. is clearly the most important player, it's not the only player." It is notable that before UNESCO agreed in 2003 to develop a new cultural instrument, the United States—rejoining the agency after a nineteen-year absence—at first tried to undermine the idea. Faced with overwhelming support for the proposal from other nations, however, the United States in the end relented.

A NEW international instrument on cultural diversity is both achievable and gaining a growing body of diplomatic support. What, then, might it look like? Drawing from the various proposals and drafts in circulation by early 2003, it is possible to anticipate several key elements.

As most international accords do, an NIICD will doubtless open on a *preamble* establishing its rationale, fundamental objectives and relationship to other international undertakings. In the case of an NIICD, this will most likely establish at least three key principles:

➤ Cultural diversity is a common asset of humanity and is funda-mental to individual freedom and democracy.

➤ The products of cultural expression are significantly different from other goods.

➤ Governments have a right to secure their publics' access to the means of cultural expression.

At a minimum, the *body* of an NIICD will attempt to distinguish between those public policies that signatories agree a government *may* implement to secure cultural diversity, and those they have deter-mined it *may not* use.

This may be accomplished through a set of guidelines or general principles, or a more specific listing. In one model that could be adopted, the WTO agreement on subsidies and its agreement on agri-culture both place policy measures in three broad categories: those that are clearly permissible, those clearly prohibited and those that are permissible in specified circumstances or when they meet certain ne-gotiated limitations. (As a step towards establishing the range of measures that might be addressed in this section, both the INCP and the Council of Europe have undertaken surveys of cultural-security measures used by various countries.)

A final key element must set out a *mechanism to resolve disputes* over the application of the instrument. Such a mechanism could be es-tablished entirely within the framework of the NIICD itself, or it could refer disputes to some outside tribunal such as the process provided for by the WTO. It is likely also to specify who can trigger recourse to such a mechanism.

Various drafts of a possible NIICD have taken different approaches to all of these questions. One model, prepared by the Canadian SAGIT, takes note of UNESCO's Declaration on Cultural Diversity in its pream-ble but also takes care in the same section to place its concerns squarely in the trade domain. It notes, among other things, that:

➤ "clarifying the rules of the international trading system play[s] an important part in the social and economic prosperity of all nations";

➤ "there are some valid concerns that the forces of globalization may adversely affect cultural diversity if local cultural expression is overwhelmed by cultural products from other cultures";

➤ "at the same time the evolution of the global information society offers great social and economic opportunities if prosperity is built by the enabling forces of the market"; and

> "clarity, transparency and openness, achieved through management of the modern trading system, can contribute to the goal of enhancing cultural diversity."

The body of the Canadian SAGIT's draft establishes a variety of principles and objectives, a framework for permitted and prohibited cultural measures and an arrangement for resolving disputes. A central objective is: "To maintain the flexibility for governments to support, promote and preserve cultural diversity so that they may ensure choice, space and visibility for both domestic and foreign cultural content."

A section detailing what is permissible in policy opens with a definition of the "cultural content" it is intended to address. That definition embraces the work of individual artists and the contents of museums and galleries. But it also explicitly includes popular commercial media—"the sounds, images and texts of films, video, sound recordings, books, magazines, broadcast programs [and] multimedia works"—and makes provision for any other technologies, "whether now existing or to be invented." A subsequent section draws a distinction, however, between the cultural *content* of such products, and their physical manufacture—making it clear that the NIICD would not, for example, apply to a CD-pressing plant.

The same part of the Canadian draft would establish that "Member States have the right to take measures with respect to the creation, production, distribution and exhibition of cultural content... guided... in particular by the objective of ensuring choice, space and visibility for domestic and foreign cultural content." Critically, it also emphasizes that each government "may decide on the basis of its own circumstances what measures to take" and "what constitutes cultural content of national origin."

But the model also explicitly prohibits some measures. Policies that "would abridge legal guarantees of freedom of expression" or "expropriate the investment of non-nationals... without fair compensation" or be "inconsistent with international treaties respecting... intellectual property" would all be forbidden.

This draft envisages an executive council created by signatories to the NIICD with authority to create a dispute resolution body that would, in turn, establish panels to address specific cases. Member states would commit themselves to submit any disagreements arising from reliance on the terms of the NIICD first to those panels, before having recourse to any other tribunal. The panels' findings would be advisory only (that is, non-binding). States would be able to appeal them to the WTO or to any other court of competent jurisdiction.

Finally, and most importantly, the Canadian SAGIT draft offers an illustrative and non-exclusive list of measures it takes to meet the objectives and constraints of the agreement. These measures include subsidies, screen quotas, mandated support by "cultural undertakings" for the creation of national content, broadcast quotas for national content, public broadcasting services, requirements for national ownership of "cultural undertakings of a particular class" and requirements that market-dominant cultural providers ensure "equitable access [to] content . . . created . . . by independent creators."

THE LARGE MULTINATIONAL conglomerates that wish to dominate the field of popular culture, and their newly formed lobby group in Washington, are likely to be hostile to many of these terms. Acting as it historically has on their behalf, the United States government would likely oppose, dilute or minimize the impact of any agreement that contained them. Several reasons were noted above to hope that a future administration might be disposed even so to find some basis on which to enroll in a new cultural agreement. But let us assume the frankly likelier outcome that the United States does not ratify an NIICD.

Any eventual agreement therefore does not bind the United States or any other country that does not sign it. The new instrument also cannot affect any obligations that countries that *do* sign it may have previously made under the WTO towards those, like the United States, that did *not*. Would countries that support the right of free citizens, acting through their governments to secure their own cultural voice, still find value in proceeding?

The answer is still clearly yes, for several reasons.

First, and of elemental value, the pursuit alone of such an agreement will raise societies' awareness of the importance of indigenous cultural expression. It will bring home to them the threat to their identity and voice if trade agreements rob their governments of the right to do what can be done to ensure that there is space in the market for a diverse choice of foreign and domestic culture.

Leading that process must be creators and cultural industries themselves. Many have only belatedly awakened to the issues at stake and the threat to their future. The need for a treaty on trade and culture may be firmly founded on the "curious economics" of popular culture. But it will be up to the cultural industries to take that case to their customers, governments and officials. It will take effort and patience to explain why cultural products behave differently than ordinary commodities, and why trade laws' treatment of them is flawed. This effort will foster and require linkages across borders between creators who share a common cause.

A second reason to pursue such an agreement even without the United States is that it will promote a common understanding of what policies effectively promote cultural diversity without limiting free expression. The pursuit of an agreement will create a forum and motivate consensus among countries, creators and cultural industries on the extent to which trade rules should, or should not, apply to cultural policy.

Those benefits will emerge from the sheer pursuit of an instrument. Others would be gained by its accomplishment.

First, the ratification of an NIICD will make it harder to impose new obligations under GATS on countries that have declined so far to make commitments in their cultural sectors. "Signatories of such an instrument," noted an INCP research paper, "would conduct their WTO negotiations mindful of the principles, objectives and obligations of the instrument on cultural diversity and so would need to retain the flexibility to carry out those obligations under new WTO rules. Indeed, the instrument could provide a forum for consultation on the culture–trade interface that could assist signatories in future WTO negotiations."

Second, principles set out in an NIICD would have an indirect impact on how existing obligations under the WTO are applied or interpreted. Many WTO provisions are ambiguous, overlapping and even contradictory when applied to cultural products. To take a conundrum examined earlier, how do trade partners determine the country of origin of a cultural product when, say, the master is made in one country and the copy in another? Is a subsidy to a film production (generally categorized as a service) the same as a subsidy for making a release print of the film (generally categorized as a good)? Is the digital download of a TV program or a musical CD equivalent to the import of a good, or should it be categorized as the import of a service? Is the discriminatory price charged for exhibition rights to a film the equivalent of dumping or an intangible transaction to which the anti-dumping rules should not apply?

WTO dispute panels presented with problems like these frequently seek guidance from agreements outside the ambit of trade. To the extent that a significant number of countries reach a consensus on such issues in a treaty on cultural diversity, their views may influence the interpretation of existing WTO commitments.

Ultimately, the relationship of a new instrument on culture to existing and future trade disciplines would best be dealt with through explicit links. But developing a common understanding outside the WTO will mark an important first step in that process. It may also serve as a vital backstop if the WTO declines to engage the larger issues presented by trade in cultural products.

POPULAR CULTURE is at the confluence of two great contemporary tides in a rapidly globalizing world. The first is a retreat to culture as a primary marker of identity and guide to conduct for individuals and nations alike. The other is the evolution of national economies toward an integrated global marketplace governed by trade rules with an international ambit.

A treaty on cultural diversity is the first step in bringing these two competing visions together, to ensure that each of us is enriched by the cultural creativity of neighbours and strangers alike, and not driven into silence by the bullhorn of the most powerful.

18

ROOM
TO
GROW

THE FICTIONAL TEENAGERS in the Canadian drama that brought us into this account reflect a distinct perspective. It is animated by the fact that year after year, Canada welcomes more immigrants in proportion to its population than does any other country. Perhaps as a consequence, *Degrassi: The Next Generation* is at every level an exploration of how to live together.

In the same episode in which a teenager named Fareeza encounters hostility because of her Iraqi heritage and producers worried about exposing a Scot's kilt-bared knees to ridicule, another character, Spinner, reflects on the nature of identity.

"Last night, I asked my mom what my culture was," Spinner remarks to a friend as they head for their lockers through the multi-hued throng filling their high school hallway. "She pointed to a globe. Said I'm from Earth."

Call us hopelessly naive, but that is not a bad starting point from which to imagine a future with fewer conflicts than the present.

Yet, as a practical matter, that hopeful scene and the rest of the consciously idealistic *Degrassi* series would never have been made, much less have found responsive audiences from Alabama and Aberdeen to Beijing and Melbourne, were it not for the tool kit of cultural policy explored in this book. At one time or another, every one of the six types of policy measures examined here has made *Degrassi* possible.

A *public-service broadcaster*—the Canadian Broadcasting Corporation—commissioned the very first *Degrassi* series in 1979.

Left to pursue only maximum profit, private broadcaster CTV would fill its prime time with the imported shows that produce the widest margins, not necessarily the greatest ratings or the greatest contribution to social discourse. *Content quotas* instead oblige it to air Canadian drama and other underrepresented programs for at least eight hours a week in prime time. Competition did the rest, motivating CTV to acquire a series compelling enough to attract viewers and sell out its commercial slots before the first show went to air.

But even at the strongest share, an English-Canadian TV audience of just 25 million potential viewers simply does not deliver a broadcast licence fee rich enough to build a weekly scripted drama series on. Other financing existed because of *expenditure requirements* that obligate Canadian cable and satellite distributors to place money into an independent production fund to support Canadian drama.

No channel controlled by a foreign parent would have reason to commission a local production like *Degrassi*. Its motivation would instead be to fill its schedule with inventory already amortized at home. *Domestic ownership rules* preserved a broadcaster for whom Canada was the home market. Its executives' own teenage children attend schools that look a lot more like *Degrassi* than like the spoiled hothouse of *Beverly Hills 90210*. They were in a position to grasp the show's appeal.

Degrassi's producers are able to make creative decisions at relative arm's length from CTV, the BBC and their American broadcaster, Noggin Network (a Viacom company). Their company, Epitome Pictures Inc., owns the series' copyright, an asset they can use to finance future creative risks. Neither would be the case if *competition* values reflected in licence conditions did not require CTV to buy at least 75 per cent of its drama programming from independent producers.

Even with all those considerations on its side, Epitome lacked the cash to put on screen the glossy production values that let *Degrassi* stand up against more lavishly funded imported shows. *Subsidies* from Telefilm Canada, a Canadian government agency, closed that gap.

In short, *Degrassi* got made because Canada used every tool in the policy kit to nourish its producers and secure their opportunity. It succeeds, however, not for any of those reasons but for the only one that matters to its viewers. It speaks to the heart with powerful stories rooted in the audience's reality.

THE ULTIMATE CONCEIT of pure-market zealots is the assertion that "entertainment" is value-neutral and no different in quality or character from wheat, hammers or construction equipment.

The truth is the exact opposite. "Entertainment" is merely the popular face of culture, a candy-coated isotope of something more fundamental. It holds appeal only because it possesses symbolic power. It provides the map of emotional, social, spiritual and political values in which each of us locates our own reality. Entertainment, in short, is all about values.

That is what brings out, in one critic's view, "the high rhetoric and overdoses of testosterone that tend to dominate discussion of cultural policy issues." Economists may prefer to filter out of their equations whatever they cannot capture in a number, but people in the rest of the world get heated about culture precisely because they know it captures those non-numeric values worth fighting for. "Movies are more than fun, and more than big business. They are power," David Puttnam reminds us.

"U.S. broadcasting, publishing, film and recording corporations, whose objective is to maximize profits, exercise this power," Ajit Jain, associate editor of *India Abroad,* says in a column on the threat of trade to indigenous cultures. He adds: "People like me who object to culture becoming part of globalization . . . know the history of colonizers. First the trade—and then the missionaries and the colonial masters."

The export of culture is, in that sense, also a projection of power— an opinion shared, both implicitly and explicitly, by its leading exporter. It is not by accident that Radio Sawa, a propaganda project of the U.S. Office of Global Communications, continuously beams "America's story," wrapped in pop hits by J-Lo and Whitney Houston, into the Persian Gulf. A group of Hollywood film unions went further in a brief to the U.S. International Trade Administration protesting Canadian film subsidies: "American films and television programs promote freedom and democratic values, as well as workers' rights, environmental protection, antidiscrimination, free speech and free press."

But no single and particular cultural product—no book, no song, no movie, no television show—illuminates any more than one small part of the great map of human experience. Each is necessarily only a partial, incomplete and tentative contribution to the whole of mankind's understanding. It is the entire *ecology* of culture—sprawling, dynamic, interconnected—that counts.

How could it be otherwise? The human condition is not static or stable. As the emotional, spiritual, social and political condition of humanity changes, so must its maps. *Madame Bovary* may explain some truths. But so does Eminem.

"Creators of culture and cultural intermediaries play a key role in adapting cultures to change," international trade academic Ivan Bernier reminds us. "They create a space where national values and foreign values can confront one another, as can the values and behaviors of the past and those of the future . . . The massive influx of foreign cultural products (films, records or CDs, books etc.) to some extent stifle domestic cultural production, thereby depriving the affected communities of the symbolic discourse essential for their own development."

This holds not only between "advanced" or "developed" nations and the rest, or between the United States and every other nation. It is true within any pluralistic body politic that aspires to freedom. "It is premised on the notion, fundamental to our American democracy, that to assure a functioning marketplace of ideas, multiple speakers are preferred, if not crucial," declared a group of independent U.S. TV writers and producers pleading for the FCC to resist further concentration of power in their industry.

This is what makes the diversity of cultural expression more than merely of academic or recreational interest. More is at stake than our choice of prime-time popcorn viewing. At issue is the "R&D of the soul" that will, perhaps, allow a complicated world to find a way forward that avoids annihilation.

BUT AS THE HOLLYWOOD producers and screenwriters who appealed to the FCC understood, the jungle forces of the market do not favour this kind of diversity. "By any standard, source diversity has almost completely disappeared from the American television scene," they noted. The same holds true for the world's big-screen cineplexes.

As we saw in Chapters 2 to 6, this is not the result of conspiracy. It is the perfectly natural and predictable consequence of commercial market forces at work on the unique economics of culture.

Cultural goods are supply-driven. Creators create. There are always more goods on offer than audiences to receive them, always players in the cultural casino ready to sink time and talent into creating another new song, the next great American novel, another Bollywood music-and-dance spectacular, another take on the undying TV detective procedural. But for every one hundred eager players at the table, at most only one or two will walk away with a pot.

That is the *nobody knows* nature of popular culture. But the simplest of cultural products, a book, still requires a significant investment of physical and financial capital. The most complex and potent, those big-screen, star-studded and special-effects-laden blockbuster movies, suck up truly staggering sums of time and money.

But if art and Mammon drive the betting in the casino of culture, it is the curious and very nearly magical economics of creative goods that pay off the winners. The key features are those we met in Chapter 3. *Sunk cost:* virtually all the investment is committed beyond retrieval in the first copy. *Near-zero marginal cost:* subsequent copies cost next to nothing. *Public-good qualities:* one audience's enjoyment does not exhaust the product's value for the next, and may even enhance it. *Discriminatory pricing:* when *sunk cost* is paid down and *marginal cost* is next to nothing, owners can sell creative works in additional markets at any price that undercuts the cost of producing a competitive product from scratch.

Those are the economic qualities that allow the owners of the few hits in the cultural casino to earn back their losses—and much, much more—across the geographic and temporal windows of reproduction and exhibition rights. But they are the same qualities that also give overwhelming advantages to size.

"The great profit in media today comes from taking a movie or TV show and milking it for maximum return through spin-offs in books, CDs, video games, and merchandise," Robert McChesney and John Nichols remind us. "Hence it is virtually impossible to compete as a 'stand-alone' movie studio, TV network, or music company, when one's competitors are part of vast empires."

Only the very, very rich can afford to keep playing at $100 million a throw until a bet comes in. Only the very biggest can sustain the management infrastructure needed to play the winners across every single window and make sure the tables pay out.

But with size and conglomerate scale come endemic faults of corporate judgement. Risk-avoidance trumps risk-taking. The tried-and-true—the bankable A-list stars, the proven formats, the sequel, prequel and franchise story—eclipse the novel and experimental in the green-light conferences. Bulked-up special effects that play to the lowest visceral denominator of action-hero audiences across every language beat out the local, particular and closely observed human story. And more money goes into opening the big bets, while "small" movies scrounge for art-house screens.

These effects vary over the spectrum of cultural goods. They are least apparent—though not absent—in the lowest-cost sectors: books and recorded music. They are most pronounced where the bets and the prizes are biggest: in what a trade economist would call "scripted audiovisual products" but the rest of us know as movies and TV shows.

Blockbuster authors do get the best front-of-the-store, high-traffic shelf space. Music companies do put their resources behind the handful of prime acts that promise to move a million units a year. But the raw cost of making a book or recording a CD is low. Those relatively low costs ensure that a significant number of new expressions reach the market every year—although only a tiny fraction of those walk away with most of the rewards.

But books and recorded music represent the low-impact as well as the low-cost end of the spectrum of creative expression. The forms that come with the highest price tag—feature films and fictional television series—are also the forms with the highest potential impact on cultural norms and corporate profits. Hence the pernicious effects of corporate dominance, profit-taking across horizontal and vertical affiliates and a risk-averse dulling-down of vision become most pronounced among the very products that possess the greatest influence.

The dislocation these effects cause is not evenly distributed around the globe. It is least in countries with big audiences and high cultural discounts. They possess markets capable of sustaining indigenous creative industries that do not depend on foreign sales. Usually these countries also possess local cultures so strongly attached to distinctive values and aesthetics that imported creative products either hold limited appeal or pose little risk to indigenous expressions. But these nations are few: the United States, India, China and Japan. (There is also a handful of unenviable exceptions that exclude the "foreign" as a matter of ideology, such as North Korea.)

Smaller nations with limited cultural discounts and open political and social cultures feel the effects more profoundly on both scores. Canada is perhaps an extreme example. Canadian creative producers "must serve a diverse market without the economies of scale enjoyed by large, well-capitalized foreign service providers who enjoy a large presence within the domestic Canadian market," observes Philip Stone, director general of trade and investment in the Department of Canadian Heritage. "These challenges are particularly pronounced given that Canadians live next to the largest exporter of cultural products in the world—the United States—with whom we share a common language."

But Canada is not the only example. The same dynamics are in play with respect to the United States in Europe, Britain and the anglophone South Pacific nations as well as much of Latin America. Parallel dynamics, with the imbalance favouring Indian film and television productions, are at work in South Asia and East Africa. They recur in East Asia, from Malaysia to Korea, with respect to films from Japan and Hong Kong, and in smaller Latin American nations with respect to television shows made in Mexico, Spain and Brazil.

MARKETS SOMETIMES FAIL. This truth is troublesome only to ideologues of a certain narrow right-wing bent. More empirically minded people simply accept that this is so and move on to design public-health systems, subsidize the local buses and regulate air pollution. It is possible for public policy to achieve outcomes that markets cannot achieve on their own.

This is hardly radical thinking. There is no reason why applying it to culture should seem more revolutionary than doing so to any other public interest, especially when effective policy instruments exist: when there is a tool kit.

Tools without leverage are of limited use. But in fact there are multiple linkages between the cultural sector where market failure is most marked and pernicious, and the industry on which policy can exert its greatest traction: broadcasting. Television is an important arena of creative expression; it drives enormous financial flows. And it is a key window for the exploitation of feature films. For all three reasons, intelligent broadcast regulation is central to securing choice in audiovisual expression.

Chapters 8 to 13 examined in detail the six families of tools that the creative state can use to nourish the diversity of expression.

Commercial media pursue profit. They naturally address their audience within the paradigm of commerce—as consumers first, last and throughout. But that is not the only identity people possess. Individually they are also mothers, fathers, children—*citizens*. Their needs and interests in those roles are no less valid for failing to align with the goal of corporate profit. The mandates of *public-service broadcasting* canvassed in Chapter 8 address the needs of citizens through programming "that informs, educates, entertains and advances social equity" while maintaining "independence from vested interests and government." As that chapter showed, sufficiently well-funded public-service broadcasters are able to invest in distinctive programs; they also retain their audience well against private competitors. This may be the most universally employed tool in the cultural policy kit.

Content *quotas* inspire a truly startling amount of vitriol among unfettered-market purists. This may be related to their signal effectiveness. Chapter 9 pointed out that quotas may be general in scope, setting overall minima for domestically produced content, as in the European "Television Without Frontiers" directive. Or they may be very specific. Some quotas obligate licensees to air defined genres within certain daily periods. In Canada, requirements are tailored to the individual circumstances of each commercial service. But this tool can also be highly flexible: Australia's ingenious structure provides extra incentive for broadcasters to produce riskier and more expensive dramatic formats.

But such quotas risk encouraging quantity over quality. Chapter 10 showed that *spending rules* can mitigate that hazard in a variety of ways. Whether they are structured to mandate broadcasters' direct spending or to oblige them to flow funds through arm's-length agencies (as in both Canada and France), expenditure requirements can ensure that enough money is injected in production for works of real value to be created. As also noted, however, this tool is susceptible to inventive deceptions in accounting; its use demands well-thought-out regulations.

As ubiquitous as public-service broadcasting are *foreign-ownership exclusions* in broadcasting and other cultural industries. But as Chapter 11 made clear, these too have weaknesses as well as strengths. Rupert Murdoch epitomizes the creative projection of different national identities, depending on which regulator needs appeasing. Domestic owners may not in every case secure greater real diversity than foreign ones. In broadcasting, however, regulation is more likely to succeed in spirit as well as in form with domestic than with alien proprietors.

Like foreign-ownership controls, *competition policy* has a mixed record in advancing diversity of creative expression. Chapter 12 outlined how the complex and peculiar channels of distribution for cultural products create numerous hidden gatekeepers. Competition regulators are poorly equipped to discern domination in markets defined by subjective judgements of genre. Advertiser-supported products like magazines or broadcasting create multiple concurrent markets that further frustrate anti-trust agencies. Yet, neglecting this tool may lead to an intensity of vertical integration that can, as in the American network television experience, effectively eliminate what Hollywood's struggling independent creators refer to as "diversity of creative source."

The final tool in the kit offers the most precise effect—but at a price. Chapter 13 illustrated how *subsidies* permit policy-makers to direct public resources to highly specific goals. Critics of European films made in the 1970s and 1980s, and of many Canadian films in the present, justly charge that subsidies are prone to capture by aesthetic cliques and opaque award processes. They may prevent creators from learning the discipline of serving an audience. Yet that is not an inescapable outcome, as the internationally popular—and hugely subsidized—*Lord of the Rings* trilogy attests. And in a creative environment that is more nakedly dependent on dollars than any other, this tool may be indispensable to a diversity of filmed entertainment.

Not every one of these tools is equally effective. Not every one is suitable to every application. They are highly differentiated in effectiveness, scope and the resources required. It is said that freedom of the press is more meaningful to those who own a press than to those who don't. It is certainly true that subsidies are a rich nation's tool. Quotas, mandatory expenditures, restricted ownership and competition policy, in contrast, are open to any nation with the bureaucratic sophistication and discipline to exercise them. But in most countries, content quotas are difficult if not impossible to make effective in the retail sale of books; subsidies to authors and small publishers may provide the only tool with traction in that case.

And, as with any tool, the effectiveness of each depends largely on its application at the point of greatest leverage. This point differs in each cultural sector and with the particular structure of each nation's industry. When South Africa tried to institute a performance-rights payment system for its many superbly talented musicians, it found that most of the money involved would have gone to performers in other, much richer, countries to the north.

The best of these tools is no panacea. Not even in combination do they guarantee diverse popular expression: that is the role of creators, not of governments. Chapter 14 discussed some of the possible reasons why Canada, where all six tools in the kit are deployed in one way or another, has yet to launch a Fellini or a *Crouching Tiger* or even a *Full Monty* into the world's cinema firmament. In the casino of popular culture, the only absolutely unbreakable rule is that *nobody knows* what will lift an audience out of their seats.

Nonetheless, the dullest and most awkward of these tools can serve a purpose. Although competition policy is difficult to bring to bear on cultural industries, a failure to try may surrender the marketplace to arid choices driven solely by the imperatives of profit: *Bachelorette* versus *Temptation Island.* Even foreign-ownership restrictions may allow other tools in the kit to obtain better results than they would on corporations domiciled and controlled beyond domestic reach.

And perhaps it is necessary to emphasize here once more the clear and critical distinction—much blurred by pure-market theists—between well-regulated *markets of choice* in cultural expression and state-directed *cultures of command.* The latter exist in too many nations where dissent is forbidden and only "official" culture is tolerated. In contrast, every free and democratic nation maintains a wide variety of rules designed to bring order, transparency and trust to free markets. They minimize the distorting effects of what economists call "externalities" without constraining choice.

Critics who carp that Canada's use of its tool kit of cultural policy has created a "model totalitarian state" have been answered by *Toronto Star* columnist Richard Gwyn:

On your next trip to a sizable U.S. city, drop into a specialty magazine store. You'll notice, of course, the absence of the small range of Canadian magazines such as *Maclean's, Chatelaine,* and *Elm Street.*

But if you look more closely, you'll notice another cross-border difference. The racks of Canadian stores will include *a far wider range,* small but not insignificant, of "foreign magazines"—British, French, German, Italian, Spanish—and a wider selection of "foreign" newspapers.

Switch on the TV in your hotel room and you'll soon become aware that there are far fewer of those programs—"television for grown-ups" I would describe them—mostly British, that are regular fare on Canadian channels. (Radio's range there is even narrower.) [Emphasis added]

In short, it is simply *not* axiomatic that unfettered commercial markets necessarily outperform well-regulated ones in producing variety and choice. The opposite may be true.

What *has* been demonstrated is that the policy tool kit can deliver results. Intelligently constructed, thoughtfully implemented, adequately monitored and judiciously tweaked (conditions that apply to every other application of public policy), the tool kit that nourished *Degrassi* has a list of other credits.

In Britain, a well-funded public-service broadcaster bestrides its market and claims the wide affection and not inconsiderable national pride of its audience.

In Europe, the "Television Without Frontiers" directive established a market window that talented producers filled with a creative flowering that has forced imported fare to the scheduling sidelines. Comedy and drama made by, for and about Europeans themselves own prime time on free-to-air television. The ten top-rated shows in each of Britain, France and Germany are all domestic productions.

In Australia, which has a population of only 25 million people but canny and flexible drama quotas for broadcasters, half of the top ten TV hits are home-made.

Canada's audiovisual policies struggle against the gravitational pull of Hollywood—which is much closer to its talent pool than to Australia's or Britain's. But Canada's book culture is the envy of literate citizens—to say nothing of authors—in most other nations. Canada's popular recording stars enjoy even greater acclaim and career success. If any further affirmation were needed for this, Superbowl XXXVII, in January 2003, may have provided it. One Canadian, Celine Dion, sang America's national anthem to open the annual rite of commercialism, football and jingoism. Another, Shania Twain, anchored the half-time show.

In every one of these examples, tools from the policy kit of cultural diversity set the stage, established the market conditions or provided early exposure to the creators, whose talent eventually connected with audiences to secure success.

WHAT IS WORKING does not need to be fixed. Yet on the basis of a faulty appreciation of the economic behaviour of cultural products, international trade negotiators are driving to "liberate" creative expression from the very tool kit that in most nations has enabled its vitality.

Chapter 16 examined the history and future work plan of the General Agreement on Trade in Services (GATS). As we saw, this offshoot of the World Trade Organization and the General Agreement on Tariffs and Trade would impose a paradigm derived from trade in commodities and merchandise on the exchange of symbolic products.

Such a transposition ignores three salient realities. First: when cultural products are treated as conventional ones, their *public-good* characteristics lead to *market failure*. Second: people are cultural citizens as well as consumers of entertainment; hence, any analysis that registers only capital flows fails to account for significant social, emotional, political and spiritual qualities intrinsic to cultural products. Third: those qualities are inseparable from the trade value of creative goods, but they are also deeply significant to the identity, social integrity and cultural development—the "fears, dreams and folklore"—of nations, communities and individuals.

Misapplied market reductionism can only have damaging consequences for the undisciplined, contradictory but endlessly fertile bazaar of the human imagination. States that commit their cultural sectors to the discipline of GATS would be obliged to extend *national treatment* to foreign providers of creative products—in stark denial of the local particularity of much cultural expression. The effect would be to deprive policy-makers of the most effective measures in the tool kit of diversity: local-content quotas and requirements for mandatory expenditures on domestic productions. They would also be forced to surrender to foreign ownership creative industries that are critical to cultural security.

International trade law enshrines a presumption against the use of export subsidies. Although reasonable enough on its face, it would in practice be almost impossible to disentangle from public support for mainly domestic productions, since many of these productions depend on at least some export sales for financing.

Countries that succumb to pressure to commit their film and television sectors to the terms of GATS would see their tool kit reduced to two measures: competition law and public-service broadcasting. The first, as we have seen, is an awkward tool when applied to cultural diversity. And while public broadcasters can be very effective in nourishing diverse expression, they also rely on public resources on a scale that many countries may be unable to commit. Moreover, to the extent that countries do direct public funding to support such broadcasters, they could face the threat of trade challenges if that funding was seen as trade-distortive.

Chapter 16 also noted the "ticking clock" feature of the GATS process, which sets signatories on a forced march towards deadline-driven commitments. A related feature encourages the tradeoff of cultural-security policies for reciprocal commitments in other sectors. Finally, *most-favoured nation* status ensures that each nation must grant equally to all of its trade partners whatever concessions the strongest negotiator wrings from it.

Collectively, these features of the trade-liberalization agenda heavily favour the country with the most to win from persuading other nations to put aside the tools of cultural diversity. As observed in Chapter 6, the Hollywood-based culture oligopoly's exports of filmed entertainment anchor the United States' $89 billion surplus on trade of intellectual property—the biggest positive contributor to national accounts that otherwise run a deficit approaching half a trillion dollars. In contrast to its exports, the United States (as Richard Gwyn noticed) imports an insignificant amount of other nations' cultural products. GATS would chisel this stark imbalance in trade-law stone.

This need not be. A number of countries, Canada and France among them, have so far resisted the advance of the GATS agenda by withholding commitments. But time is not on the side of that strategy:

the clock is ticking. A better alternative would embed into the framework of international law an explicit acknowledgement of the significance and singularity of trade in popular culture.

Such a new international instrument on cultural diversity (NIICD) would build on an existing international recognition of the necessity of culture. Wide acceptance of the insight that a healthy biological environment relies as much on a diverse ecology as on the health of single species provides a conceptual framework for a parallel assertion about cultural diversity. A cornerstone of that thought was laid at UNESCO's conference in Mexico City in 1982. Its final communiqué declared: "The universal cannot be postulated in the abstract by any single culture: it emerges from the experience of all the world's peoples as each affirms its own identity. Cultural identity and cultural diversity are inseparable."

In 2003, a growing international consensus coalesced around the utility of an instrument that would accomplish three key tasks. It would establish in international convention the critical distinction between cultural products and conventional goods and services. It would articulate in clear terms the right of governments to avail themselves of all or most of the tools in the kit of effective cultural policy. And it would establish a framework to mediate between those rights and the obligations and claims of state signatories to trade agreements.

POPULAR CULTURE will never be merely neutral—nor everywhere the same. Societies and circumstances change.

"The world as we knew it is over," CBS president Les Moonves declared without irony early in 2003. He had in mind the advent of reality TV. *Joe Millionaire* and *Bachelorette* reduce emotion to game-show fodder—cheaply. And if they are hits, they can deliver enormous profit.

But since Moonves made his prediction, several flops have shown that one thing hasn't changed: *nobody knows* which reality show will be a hit either. Nor are they likely to displace well-scripted comedies and drama, which have afterlives in lucrative syndication if they are successful in their initial run.

Meanwhile the consequences of perverse cultural economics mount.

Media continue to consolidate. Vivendi surrendered Universal Entertainment to NBC. British broadcasters Carlton and Grenada merged into one company with half that country's TV ad sales. And the five companies dominating world music could shrink to four, if competition regulators approve Sony and Bertelsmann's desire to merge their music divisions into Sony BMG Music.

Creative clones edge out diversity. Hollywood released a record twenty-five sequels in 2003—twice as many as in 2001. The drama *Law and Order* became a video game. Madonna wrote a children's book, then "opened it wide" in one hundred countries and thirty languages.

The Internet less than ever resembles a new paradigm favourable to new voices. Surveys confirmed that most Web traffic flows to heavily promoted extensions of existing brands.

But there is also a growing realization that cultural products are different from other products, that choice and diversity are important, and there are reasonable measures that can be taken to address these concerns. Recently, CNN founder Ted Turner joined members of Congress in rebellion against letting corporate oligarchs own more American media. Doing so, he warned, would "stifle debate, inhibit new ideas and shut out smaller businesses."

Fundamental things do apply. Creative expression remains the laboratory of the soul. Stories in all their many forms remain the most powerful means that societies and individuals have to communicate identity. Culture is still the essential expression of who we are.

Giving space for individuals from all societies to tell their stories cannot alone ensure peace nor guarantee liberty and prosperity for all. But enforced silence is certain to beget only resentment. Societies that believe their culture is threatened will be inclined to strike back. A strong culture, confident of its future, is capable of accepting other views without fear.

Dialogue may not save the world. But monologue and exclusion will go far to destroy it.

SOURCES
AND
FURTHER
READINGS

THIS BOOK is based on interviews, personal experience and an extensive review of the growing literature, both academic and popular, concerning the impact of globalization on culture and trade and various government responses to this issue. Most of the regulatory and trade documents referred to here can be found on the Web sites of the regulatory agencies or international agencies involved. The principal sources relied on are described below, along with suggestions for further readings.

PREFACE

For a discussion and criticism of cultural relativism, see Roger Sandall, *The Culture Cult: Designer Tribalism and Other Essays* (Oxford: Westview, 2002). The issue of the conflict between cultural practices and human rights was a matter of dispute in the Johannesburg Earth Summit in September 2002, where a phrase in the declaration calling for better health services "consistent with national laws and cultural and religious values" was made subject to the words "in conformity with all human rights and fundamental freedoms." The phrase "curious economics" as applied to popular culture appears in a collection of articles from *The Economist* published under the title *Globalisation* (London: Profile Books, 2001), at p. 88.

CHAPTER 1: DISTINCT VOICES

The information on *Degrassi* at pp. 13–16 and pp. 18–20 was based on interviews with Linda Schuyler, Stephen Stohn and others on the Epitome Pictures production team in Toronto in August–September 2002. Ratings information is based on the Neilsen data for September 2002–January 2003, when *Degrassi* was broadcast on

Sunday nights. It was moved to Wednesday nights the following season. The reference to Bethune at p. 14 is to Norman Bethune, a twentieth-century Chinese Revolutionary War surgeon who was born in Canada who has long been an official symbol of Sino–Canadian goodwill. Canadian-born actor Donald Sutherland starred in a Canadian movie version of Bethune's life. For the Alan Murray quotation at p. 19, see *The Wall Street Journal,* September 16, 2003. For the Huntington quotation at p. 21, see Samuel P. Huntington, *The Clash of Civilizations: Remaking the World Order* (New York: Simon and Schuster, 1996). For the Ayton-Shenker quotation at p. 21, see Diana Ayton-Shenker, "The Challenge of Human Rights and Cultural Diversity," United Nations Background Note, at www.un.org/rights.

CHAPTER 2: CREATIVE CLUSTERS

The Baffin Island stunt referred to at pp. 25–26 is also described under the entry "The Asgard Jump" in Steven Jay Rubin's *The Complete James Bond Movie Encyclopedia* (New York: McGraw-Hill, 1990). The Pangnirtung Print Shop referred to at pp. 26–27 originated in 1969 with Canadian government support and financial assistance as part of an effort to create cash-based employment in developing Inuit communities. It has gone through a number of reorganizations, including a fire in the old print shop in 1994. For a history of the centre, see www.uqqurmiut.com/Printshop.html.

On the cluster theory referred to at p. 30, see Michael Porter, *The Competitive Advantage of Nations* (New York: Macmillan, 1990). The quote from Alfred Marshall at p. 30 appears in Masahisa Fujita, Paul Krugman and Anthony J. Venables, *The Spatial Economy: Cities, Regions and International Trade* (Cambridge, MA: MIT Press, 1999), at pp. 4–5. Other sources include Joel Kotkin, *The New Geography: How the Digital Revolution is Reshaping the American Landscape* (New York: Random House, 2000). The application of the cluster theory to the audiovisual sector in fifteen media centres around the world is examined in Hans-Joachim Braczyk, Gerhard Fuchs and Hans-Georg Wolf, eds., *Multimedia and Regional Economic Restructuring* (London: Routledge, 2001). The Hollywood cluster is examined in chapter 3, "Patterns of Employment in Southern California's Multimedia and Digital Visual-Effects Industry," by Allen J. Scott, at pp. 3–48, while the Toronto cluster is described in chapter 6, "The Digital Regional Economy: Emergence and Evolution of Toronto's Multimedia Cluster," by Shauna G. Brail and Meric S. Gertler, at pp. 97–130. The quote at p. 39 is from p. 122 of the latter study. Reference should also be made to Martha Jones, "Motion Picture Production in California," document presented to Select Committee on the Future of California's Film Industry, Burbank, February 1, 2002; available under CRB Reports at www.library.ca.gov.

For a description of the A-list effect, noted at p. 31, see Bruno S. Frey, *Arts & Economics: Analysis & Cultural Policy* (Berlin: Springer, 2000), at pp. 53–55. As applied to the film industry, see Mark Litwak, *Reel Power: The Struggle for Influence and Success in the New Hollywood* (New York: William Morrow, 1986), and Martin Dale, *The Movie Game: The Film Business in Britain, Europe and America* (London: Cassell, 1997), at pp. 39–40. The Dale quotation on p. 34 is from the latter book, at p. 39.

There are numerous sources for the history of the film industry in Hollywood, briefly described at pp. 32–34. Among those consulted were Thomas Schatz, *The Genius of the System* (New York: Pantheon, 1988); Neal Gabler, *An Empire of Their Own* (New York: Crown, 1988); Barry R. Litman, *The Motion Picture Mega-Industry* (Boston: Allyn and Bacon, 1998), and chapter 2 in Harold L. Vogel, *Entertainment Industry Economics: A Guide for Financial Analysis*, 5th ed. (Cambridge: Cambridge University Press, 2001). An industry primer that describes the roles of the participants in the film, television and music industries is Rodger W. Claire, *Entertainment 101* (Los Angeles: Pomegranate Press, 1999).

Current statistics on the output of the Hollywood majors, referred to at p. 35, can be found on the Motion Picture Association of America Web site at www.mpa.org. For statistics on the Canadian film and television industry, see *Profile 2003: An Economic Report on the Canadian Film and Television Production Industry* (Ottawa: CFTPA, 2003). For comparative statistics on world cinema, see *Screen Digest*, "Top 20 Countries Ranked by Production Investment in Feature Films, 1999, 2000," available at www.afc.gov.au/GTP/acompinvestment.html.

For further details on the making of *Atanarjuat*, referred to at pp. 40–41, see Raul Galvez, "Epic Inuit: In Conversation with Zacharias Kunuk," *Montage*, Spring 2002, at pp. 10–14. The quote from *The New York Times* review of the movie can be found in A.O. Scott, "A Far-Off Inuit World, in a Dozen Shades of White," *The New York Times*, March 30, 2002.

CHAPTER 3: CURIOUS ECONOMICS

This chapter focuses on the economics of popular culture, including the production and distribution of books, magazines, sound recordings, films and TV programs. It does not address the performing arts. For a path-breaking study on the economics of the performing arts, see William J. Baumol and William G. Bowen, *Performing Arts: The Economic Dilemma* (New York: Twentieth Century Fund, 1966). For a more recent treatise, see James Heilbrun and Charles M. Gray, *The Economics of Art and Culture*, 2nd ed. (Cambridge: Cambridge University Press, 2001), and David Throsby, *Economics and Culture* (Cambridge: Cambridge University Press, 2001). The *Journal of Cultural Economics*, which tends to focus on the arts, has been published since the 1970s.

Sources on the economics of popular culture have tended to focus on the specific structure of each cultural industry. The best-known general survey is Harold L. Vogel, *Entertainment Industry Economics: A Guide for Financial Analysis* (Cambridge: Cambridge University Press, 2001), now in its 5th edition. For works focused on the audiovisual sector, see Bruce M. Owen and Steven S. Wildman, *Video Economics* (Cambridge, MA: Harvard University Press, 1992), and Colin Hoskins et al., *Global Television and Film: An Introduction to the Economics of the Business* (Oxford: Oxford University Press, 1997). For a further description of the orderly marketplace for feature films, see Martin Dale, *The Movie Game: The Film Business in Britain, Europe and America* (London: Cassell, 1997), at p. 34. The economic organization of the arts and culture is brilliantly analyzed in Richard E.

Caves, *Creative Industries: Contracts Between Art and Commerce* (Cambridge, MA: Harvard University Press, 2000). As noted earlier, the phrase "curious economics" as applied to popular culture appears in a collection of articles from *The Economist* published under the title *Globalisation* (London: Profile Books, 2001), at p. 88.

The "nobody knows" quote by William Goldman at p. 48 is from his *Adventures in the Screen Trade* (New York: Warner Books, 1983), at p. 39. For the 1994 study on the selection of U.S. drama series, referred to at p. 48, see William T. Bielby and Denise D. Bielby, "All Hits Are Flukes," (1994) 99 *American Journal of Sociology* 1287–1313. See also Bernard Weinraub, "Low Ratings Haunt Sitcoms with High-Profile Stars," *The New York Times*, October 15, 2001. For a further discussion of the term "public good" in the context of cultural products, as noted at pp. 56–57, see Jeff Dayton-Johnson, "What's Different About Cultural Products? An Economic Framework," Study No. SRA-501, November 23, 2000, for the Department of Canadian Heritage, at pp. 8–9. For the article referring to "culture and other non-economic concerns" noted at p. 59, see W. Ming Shao, "Is There No Business Like Show Business?" (1995) 20 *Yale Journal of International Law* 105 at 112–113.

CHAPTER 4: WHY HITS ARE FLUKES

The material on the development of *C.S.I.: Crime Scene Investigation* came from author interviews with Peter Sussman in October 2002. For the Hollywood development statistics, see Richard E. Caves, *Creative Industries: Contracts Between Art and Commerce* (Cambridge, MA: Harvard University Press, 2000) at p. 113. For further information on the MCA/Hennessy story noted at p. 64, see Jennifer Ordonez, "Behind the Music: MCA Spent Millions on Carly Hennessy—Haven't Heard of Her?" *The Wall Street Journal*, February 26, 2002. The quote from *The Movie Game* at p. 65 is from Martin Dale, *The Movie Game: The Film Business in Britain, Europe and America* (London: Cassell, 1997), at p. 39. For the study by De Vany noted at p. 66, see Arthur De Vany, "Contracting in the Movies When 'Nobody Knows Anything': The Careers, Pay and Contract of Motion Picture Directors," paper presented at Conference of the Association of Cultural Economics International, Rotterdam, May 21, 2002. For the Ravid study quoted at p. 66, see S. Abraham Ravid, "Are They All Crazy or Just Risk Averse? Some Movie Puzzles and Possible Solutions," paper presented at Conference of the Association of Cultural Economics International, Rotterdam, May 21, 2002. The Dale quote at p. 66 is from Dale, *The Movie Game*, p. 22. For the 2002 study cited at p. 66, see Frank W. Rusco and W. David Walls, "Film Finance and the Distribution of Earnings," paper presented at Conference of the Association of Cultural Economics International, Rotterdam, May 21, 2002. The Alice Thomas Ellis quote at p. 68 is from a book review by Ellis entitled "Publish and Be Remaindered" in *The Telegraph* (U.K.), August 31, 2002. For the report of the Publishers Group merger, noted at p. 69, see David D. Kirkpatrick, "A Merger of Book Middlemen Could Deeply Influence Sales," *The New York Times*, January 17, 2002. The Branford Marsalis quote noted at p. 69 is from an article by Mark Miller, *The Globe and Mail*, September 26, 2002. The Ryan quote on p. 70 is from Dale, *The Movie Game*, at p. 88. The quotes from Allison Anders, Peter Bart, Michael Cieply,

Michael Douglas, Lucy Fisher, Larry Gerbrandt, Peter Guber, Elvis Mitchell, Kevin Smith and Howard Stringer, cited in this and the next chapter, are from the tapes and transcripts of the PBS *Frontline* program, "The Monster That Ate Hollywood," which first aired on PBS stations in the United States on November 2, 2001. The complete transcripts of the interviews made for this program can be accessed from www.pbs.org/wgbh/pages/ frontline/shows/hollywood. The Dale quote at p. 71 is from *The Movie Game*, at p. 30. For the Gruner+Jahr story at p. 72, see Gruner+Jahr president Daniel Brewster quoted in Araminta Wordsworth, "Rosie Abandons the Soccer Moms: The Queen of Nice No More," *The National Post*, October 3, 2002. The quotes from Victor Loewy at p. 72 are from an author interview in October 2002. For the Weinraub quote at pp. 73–74, see Bernard Weinraub, "On TV, A Loss of Independents," *The New York Times*, May 7, 2000. The Gillespie quote on p. 74 is from Nick Gillespie, "All Culture, All the Time," *Reason Online*, April 1999. For the quote from Korda at p. 76, see Michael Korda, *Making the List: A Cultural History of the American Bestseller 1900–1999* (New York: Barnes & Noble Books, 2001), at p. 196. For more on the French regulation referred to at p. 77, see Nancy Tartaglione, "France Resists TV Advertising for Films," *Screendaily.com*, April 8, 2003. The Caves quote at p. 77 is from Caves, *Creative Industries*, at pp. 178–180. For the quote by Dale, at p. 78, see *The Movie Game*, at p. 32.

CHAPTER 5: WHY BIG IS BEST
The material on Song Corporation at pp. 80–82 is based on an author interview with Allan Gregg in August 2002. For additional information, see David Hayes, "Song Corpse," *Toronto Life*, February 2002. For material on the FilmFour experience noted at pp. 82–83, see David Gritten, "How the Life was Sucked Out of Film-Four," *The Telegraph*, July 10, 2002; Matt Wells and Angelique Chrisafis, "FilmFour Scales Back," *The Guardian*, June 5, 2002; and Adam Minns, "New-look FilmFour Boasts Tantalizing Slate," *Screendaily.com*, May 16, 2003. The quotes from Allison Anders, Peter Bart, Michael Cieply, Michael Douglas, Lucy Fisher, Larry Gerbrandt, Peter Guber, Elvis Mitchell, Kevin Smith and Howard Stringer, cited in this and the previous chapter, are from the tapes and transcripts of the PBS *Frontline* program, "The Monster That Ate Hollywood," which first aired on PBS stations in the United States on November 2, 2001. The complete transcripts of the interviews made for this program can be accessed from www.pbs.org/wgbh/pages/frontline/shows/ hollywood. For the Les Moonves quote at p. 84, see Josef Adalian, "TV Traumas Trouble the Town," *Variety International*, June 24–30, 2002. For the Dale quote on p. 84, see Martin Dale, *The Movie Game: The Film Business in Britain, Europe and America* (London: Cassell, 1997), at p. 25. The David Hancock quote on p. 84 is from an author interview in August 2002. For the Thussu quote on p. 87, see Daya Kishan Thussu, *International Communication: Continuity and Change* (London: Arnold, 2000), at p. 120. Further information on the size of the major media companies may be found in Thussu, *International Communication*, at pp. 119–166. For the Rusco and Walls quotation at p. 94, see Frank W. Rusco and W. David Walls, "Film Finance and the Distribution of Earnings," paper presented at Conference of the

Association of Cultural Economics International, Rotterdam, May 21, 2002. For the Dale quote at p. 95, see Dale, *The Movie Game*, at p. 34. The quote from Peter Chernin at p. 95 appears in Robert W. McChesney, *Rich Media, Poor Democracy: Communications Politics in Dubious Times* (New York: New Press, 1999, 2000), at p. 16. For the U.K. numbers cited at p. 96, see Keith Damsell, *The Globe and Mail*, October 25, 2002. The Loewy quote at p. 97 was based on an author interview. For the Dale quote at p. 98, see Dale, *The Movie Game*, at p. 24. For the U.S. case study noted at p. 99, see "A Music Industry Case Study," *New York Daily News*, February 19, 2003. For the Dale quote at p. 100, see Dale, *The Movie Game*, at p. 20. For the Vogel quote at p. 101, see Harold L. Vogel, "Flickering Images: The Business of Holly-wood," chapter 9 in Joni M. Cherbo and Margaret J. Wyszomirski, eds., *The Public Life of the Arts in America* (New Brunswick, NJ: Rutgers University Press, 2000), at p. 239. For the Leigh quote at pp. 101–102, see Danny Leigh, "Usual Suspects," *The Guardian*, August 30, 2002. For the Dale quote at p. 102, see Dale, *The Movie Game*, at p. 23. For the TV producer quote in 2002 and the Robert Iger quote, both at p. 103, see Josef Adalian, "TV Traumas Trouble the Town," *Variety International*, June 24–30, 2002. For the reference to "Caves and others" at p. 103, see Richard E. Caves, *Creative Industries: Contracts Between Art and Commerce* (Cambridge, MA: Harvard University Press, 2000), at p. 142; Martin Arnold, "It's Not What It Used to Be," *The New York Times*, July 19, 2001; and Thomas Whiteside, *The Blockbuster Complex: Conglomerates, Show Business and Book Publishing* (Middletown, CT: Wesleyan University Press, 1980, 1981). For the Jilly Cooper, Luigi Bonomi and Danita Kean quotes at pp. 103–104, see Danuta Kean, "The Book Brokers," *This Is London*, June 8, 2002. For the Philip Noyce quote at p. 105, see Simon Houpt, "Doubling Back," *The Globe and Mail*, November 26, 2002. For the Gillian Blake quote at p. 105, see Martin Arnold, "It's Not What It Used to Be," *The New York Times*, July 19, 2001. For the *New York Times* quote at p. 106, see Alex Berenson and Matt Richtel, "Heartbreakers, Dream Makers," *The New York Times*, June 25, 2000. For the *Wall Street Journal* quote at p. 106, see Jennifer Ordonez, "Bands on the Run," *The Wall Street Journal*, October 25, 2002. For the Lions Gate quote at p. 107, see Johanna Schneller, "A Fine Film Whose Days Were Numbered," *The Globe and Mail*, March 14, 2003. For the Schechter, Miller, Johnson and Turner quotes at pp. 107–108, see Mark Crispin Miller, "What's Wrong With This Picture?" *The Nation*, January 7, 2002. For the Blethen quote at p. 108, see Frank A. Blethen, "Concentration of Media Ownership Is Eroding Our Democracy," *I Want Media*, September 12, 2002.

CHAPTER 6: GLOBAL VISIONS

The speech by R.H. Thomson referred to at p. 110 was made at a conference organized by the International Network for Cultural Diversity, and held in Cape Town, South Africa, October 11–13, 2002. The authors, travelling separately to the same conference from Frankfurt to Cape Town on South African Airways, were shown the U.S. films *Divine Secrets of the YaYa Sisterhood* and *North by Northwest*, episodes of the U.S. sitcom *Frasier*, and episodes of a British-made animated series based on the character of *Mr. Bean*. The Bollywood themes referred to at p. 114 are from Daya Kishan Thussu, *International Communication: Continuity and Change* (London: Arnold, 2000), at p. 220. The Thussu book referred to at p. 114 is Daya Kishan Thussu, ed., *Electronic Empires: Global Media and Local Resistance* (London: Arnold, 1998), an anthology of analysis and criticism. The TV Globo references at p. 116 are from Thussu, *International Communication*, at p. 216. For the report to the California legislature referred to at pp. 116 and 119, see Martha Jones, "Motion Picture Production in California," document presented to Select Committee on the Future of California's Film Industry, Burbank, February 1, 2002; available under CRB Reports at www.library.ca.gov. A different accounting by the Department of Canadian Heritage, the government department with responsibility for cultural industries, claims the figure for 2001 was C$4.5 billion. For the 2000 U.K. study referred to at p. 117, see David Graham & Associates, "Out of the Box: The Programme Supply Market in the Digital Age," a report for the Department of Culture, Media and Sport, December 2000. For the Pells quote at p. 118, see Richard Pells, *Not Like Us: How Europeans Have Loved, Hated, and Transformed American Culture Since World War II* (New York: Basic Books, 1997), at p. 211. The 1995 U.K. film statistics noted at p. 118 are from Madelaine Drohan, "Britain's Loss is Hollywood's Gain," *The Globe and Mail*, May 17, 1996. For the Irish study referred to at pp. 118–119, see Industry Strategic Review Group, *The Strategic Development of the Irish Film and Television Industry 2000–2010* (1999), p. 35, cited in Jones, "Motion Picture Production in California," at p. 52. For the statistics on the nine most-watched international TV channels referred to at p. 119, see Thussu, *International Communication*, p. 133. For the Canadian numbers cited at p. 119, see Anthony DePalma, "Tough Rules Stand Guard Over Canadian Culture," *The New York Times*, July 14, 1999. For the Latin American numbers cited at p. 120, see Thussu, *International Communication*, at pp. 174 and 187. The Thussu quotes from pp. 120 and 122 are from Thussu, *International Communication*, at pp. 176 and 182. For the quotation on the cultural discount at pp. 123–124, see Stuart McFadyen, Colin Hoskins and Adam Finn, "Measuring the Cultural Discount in the Price of Exported U.S. Television Programs," paper prepared for presentation at Association of Cultural Economics International, Conference, Rotterdam, June 12–15, 2002. For the Caves quote on p. 124, see Richard E. Caves, *Creative Industries: Contracts Between Art and Commerce* (Cambridge, MA: Harvard University Press, 2000), at p. 282. For the Kim quote at p. 124, see Jeongmee Kim, "Billy Elliot: Promoting British Cinema in the USA," paper presented at the Conference on "Trading Culture," Sheffield, England, July 18–20, 2002. The prices in Table 6.1 come from *Variety International*, March 24–30, 2003. Similar international price comparisons are presented annually in *Television Business International*. For the Graham study noted at p. 132, see David Graham & Associates, "Out of the Box: The Programme Supply Market in the Digital Age," a report for the U.K. Department of Culture, Media and Sport, December 2000. For the Canadian estimate noted at p. 135, see Brian D. Johnson, "The Canadian Patient," *Maclean's*, March 24, 1997. For the IIPA study noted at p. 135, see Stephen E. Siwek Economists Inc., *Copyright Industries in the U.S. Economy: The 2000 Report* (2002).

CHAPTER 7: THE NATIONALITY OF CULTURE

For further details on the making of *The Bridge on the River Kwai,* see Kevin Brown-low, *David Lean: A Biography* (New York: St. Martin's Press, 1996), at pp. 345–392, and Natasha Fraser-Cavassoni, *Sam Spiegel* (New York: Simon and Schuster, 2003), at pp. 177–200. David Lean also contributed to the script for the movie. For the OECD study noted at 142, see Organization for Economic Cooperation and Development, *The Economist,* November 2–8, 2002. Almost a quarter of working Australians are immigrants. For the Myers quote at p. 142–143, see Kevin Myers, "Salute to a Brave and Modest Nation," *The Sunday Telegraph,* April 21, 2002. For the Potter quote at p. 143, see Andrew Potter, "Let's Appease Cultural Minorities," *National Post,* June 16, 2001. For the dictionary referred to at p. 143, see Kwame Anthony Appiah and Henry Louis Gates Jr., eds., *The dictionary of global culture* (New York: Knopf, 1996). For the Shapiro quote on p. 143, see James Shapiro, "From Achebe to Zydeco," *The New York Times Book Review,* January 15, 1997. For the Kakutani quote at p. 144, see Michiko Kakutani, "Britons Chafe at Giving Americans a Shot at the Booker Prize," *The New York Times,* June 10, 2002. For the Pells quote on p. 145, see Richard Pells, "American Culture Goes Global, or Does It?" *The Chronicle Review,* April 12, 2002. For the German newspaper quote noted at p. 145, see Peter Kramer, "German Nationality/Hollywood Patriotism," paper presented at the Conference on "Trading Culture," Sheffield, England, July 18–20, 2002. For the *Economist* quotes at pp. 145 and 147, see "The Culture Wars," *The Economist,* September 12, 1998. For the Lucy Fisher quote at p. 147, see the reference to the PBS program "The Monster That Ate Hollywood," in the sources for Chapters 4 and 5 above. For the Berggreen study referred to at p. 146, see Dr. Shu-Ling C. Berggreen and Katalin Lustyik, "Building a Cultural Bridge in the Magic Kingdom: The Importance of Maintaining Cultural Integrity in a World of Global Disneyfication," unpublished 2002 research paper. For the Kastner quote at p. 148, see John Kastner, "Producers Pressured to Shed the Soul of Canadian Films," *The Globe and Mail,* January 2, 1997. For the Burke quote at p. 148, see Doug Saunders, "Exporting Canadian Culture," *The Globe and Mail,* January 25, 1997. For the relevant section of the 1994 WTO Agreement on Rules of Origin noted at p. 150, see Article 9.1(b). For the applicable Academy Awards rule noted at p. 152, see Academy of Motion Picture Arts and Sciences, 75th Academy Awards Rules, Rule 14. For the Australian rules noted at p. 153, see the Australian Broadcasting Authority Web site at www.aba.gov.au. For the Canadian rules noted at pp. 153–156, see Public Notice CRTC 2000-42, March 17, 2000, available from the CRTC Web site at www.crtc.gc.ca. For the quotation at p. 156 from the Report of the Standing Committee on Canadian Heritage, see *Our Cultural Sovereignty: The Second Century of Canadian Broadcasting* (Ottawa: House of Commons, Canada, 2003), at p. 164. For the 1963 directive noted at p. 157, see Council Directive of October 15, 1963; 63/607/EEC. For the EAO review referred to at p. 158, see Michael Gyory, *Making and Distributing Films in Europe: The Problem of Nationality* (Strasbourg: European Audiovisual Observatory, 2002), available at the EAO Web site, www.obs.coe.int.

CHAPTER 8: PUBLIC BROADCASTING

For the Flew quote at p. 169, see Terry Flew, "Broadcasting and the Social Contract," in Marc Raboy, ed., *Global Media Policy in the New Millennium* (Luton: University of Luton Press, 2002), at pp. 113–129. For the Humphreys quote at p. 170, see Peter J. Humphreys, "European Public-Service Broadcasting Systems," chapter 4 in *Mass Media and Media Policy in Western Europe* (Manchester: Manchester University Press, 1996), at pp. 121–158. The PBS Web site referred to at p. 171 is hosted by Radio Canada International, an arm of the CBC. See http://www.publicbroadcastersinter-national.org/cgi-bin/default.asp?M=whats. For the Holznagel quote on p. 172, see Bernd Holznagel, "The Mission of Public Service Broadcasters," *International Journal of Communications Law and Policy*, Issue 5 (Summer 2000). For the 1999 McKinsey study noted at p. 174, see Adrian D. Blake et al., "Keeping Baywatch at Bay," *McKinsey Quarterly* 1999, number 4, at pp. 18–27. For the Jon Snow quote at pp. 174–175, see Stuart Jeffries, "Gentle Giant?" *The Guardian*, July 17, 2002. For the BBC licence fee reference on p. 175, see David Lipsey, "In Defence of Public Broadcasting," from Philip Collins, ed., *Culture or Anarchy? The Future of Public Service Broadcasting* (London: Social Market Foundation, 2002), at pp. 1–25. The Gavin quote on p. 175 is from Charles Goldsmith, "As BBC Flourishes, U.K. is Shaking Up the Rest of the Dial," *The Wall Street Journal*, October 25, 2002. The Dyke quote at p. 175 and the BBC ratings referred to at p. 176 are noted in Alan Riding, "What Price Success for a Newly Popular BBC?" *The New York Times*, February 3, 2002. The Jowell quote at p. 175 is cited in Stuart Jeffries, "Gentle Giant?" *The Guardian*, July 17, 2002. The FCC report noted at p. 176 is noted in Robert McChesney, *Rich Media, Poor Democracy: Communications Politics in Dubious Times* (New York: New Press, 1999, 2000), at p. 73. For the McChesney quotes at p. 179, see McChesney, *Rich Media*, at pp. 248 and 250. For the quote at the top of p. 180, see ibid., at p. 231. For the CBC opinion survey noted at p. 182, see COMPAS Inc., "National Identity, TV, and CBC, a COMPAS Poll for CanWest–Southam Newspapers, Global TV and the *National Post*," April 29, 2002. For the parliamentary committee report noted at p. 182, see the Report of the Standing Committee on Canadian Heritage, *Our Cultural Sovereignty: The Second Century of Canadian Broadcasting* (Ottawa: House of Commons, Canada, 2003), at pp. 177–224.

For the court rulings referred to at pp. 182–183, see Holznagel, "The Mission of Public Service Broadcasters," noted above. For the Humphreys book referred to at p. 183, see Humphreys, *Mass Media and Media Policy in Western Europe*. For the Tongue article referred to at p. 183, see Carole Tongue, "Public Service Broadcasting: A Study of 8 OECD Countries," in Philip Collins, ed., *Culture or Anarchy? The Future of Public Service Broadcasting* (London: Social Market Foundation, 2002), at pp. 107–142 (hereafter *Public Service*). For the "malicious editing" quote at p. 183, see R. Kuhn, *The Media in France* (London: Routledge, 1995), quoted by Humphreys, *Mass Media*, at p. 147. For the "common mandates" referred to at p. 183, see Tongue, *Public Service*, at p. 113. For the Humphreys quote at p. 184, see Humphreys, *Mass Media*, at p. 149. For the National Users Council quote at p. 184, see Tongue,

Public Service, at p. 118. At p. 185 of the text, ARD is the acronym for *Arbeitsgemein-schaft der Offentlich-rechtlichen Rundfunksanstalten der Bundesrepublik Deutsch-land,* and ZDF stands for *Zweites Deutsches Fernsehen*—literally "Second German Television." For the Tongue quote at p. 186, see Tongue, *Public Service,* at p. 120. For the Humphreys quote at p. 185, see Humphreys, *Mass Media,* at p. 153. For the Netherlands statutory quotas referred to at p. 186 and the Humphreys quote, see Humphreys, *Mass Media,* at p. 142. For the ABC mandate referred to at p. 187, see Tongue, *Public Service,* at p. 112. For the Lipsey quote at p. 187, see in Philip Collins, ed., *Culture or Anarchy? The Future of Public Service Broadcasting* (London: Social Market Foundation, 2002), at pp. 1–25. For the Mihlar quote at p. 188, see Fazil Mihlar, "Cultural Institutions Must Be Freed from the Shackles of Regulation," *The Financial Post,* September 3, 1998. For the *Economist* quote on the same page, see "British Broadcasting, Free TV," *The Economist,* May 11, 2002. For the Humphreys quote at p. 188, see Humphreys, *Mass Media,* at p. 243. For the comparative ad revenue numbers on p. 188, see Humphreys, *Mass Media,* at p. 127. For the Graham quote on p. 188, see David Graham & Associates, "Out of the Box: The Programme Supply Market in the Digital Age," a report for the U.K. Department of Culture, Media and Sport, December 2000, at p. 8. For the Humphreys quote at p. 189, see Humphreys, *Mass Media,* at p. 230. For "the evidence suggested" quote at p. 189, see Blumle et al., quoted in Humphreys, *Mass Media,* p. 240. For the McKinsey study referred to at p. 189, see Adrian D. Blake et al., "Keeping Baywatch at Bay," *The McKinsey Quarterly* 1999, number 4, at p. 24. The imprecision of the relationship between income and audience share, however, is revealed in the strikingly different audience shares captured, for roughly the same income, by Canada's CBC and Sweden's SVT. One possible explanation: SVT's high cultural premium is based on the Swedish language, versus the many private and foreign-source alternatives available in English to Canadian audiences. For the Cuff quote at p. 189, see John Haslett Cuff, "The Value of Public Broadcasting," *The Globe and Mail,* July 3, 1996. For the Kastner quote at p. 190, see John Kastner, "Producers Pressured to Shed the Soul of Canadian Films," *The Globe and Mail,* January 2, 1997. For the Taras quote at p. 190, see David Taras, *Power and Betrayal in the Canadian Media* (Toronto: Broadview Press, 2001), at p. 196. For the EAO study cited at p. 191, see European Audiovisual Observatory Press Release, "European TV Fiction Production Valued at 2.7 Billion Euros," December 18, 2000, available from the EAO Web site at www.obs.coe.int. For the Tongue quote at p. 191, see Tongue, *Public Service,* at p. 119. For the Alterman quote at p. 192, see John Alterman, "Slouching Toward Ramallah," *The Wall Street Journal,* November 21, 2002. For the Bill Roberts quote at p. 192, see *The Globe and Mail,* October 24, 2002. For the McChesney quote at p. 192, see McChesney, *Rich Media,* at p. 254. For the Humphreys quotes at p. 192, see Humphreys, *Mass Media,* at p. 231. For the Pleitgen quote at p. 193 (reprinted with permission), see Fritz Pleitgen, "Cultural Diversity and Pluralism—The European Audiovisual Model," speech to the WTO Audiovisual Industry Seminar, July 4, 2001, available from the WTO Web site: www.wto.org. For the van der Louw quotation at p. 194, see *Hilversummary,* March 1998, available at ww.omroep.nl/nos/rtv/voorlichting/hsumm/hs5_5.html.

CHAPTER 9: SCHEDULING QUOTAS

For illustrative critiques of quotas, see William Stanbury, *Canadian Content Regulations: The Intrusive State at Work* (Vancouver: Fraser Institute, 1998), and Keith Acheson and Christopher Maule, "Canadian Content Rules: A Time for Reconsideration," (1990) *Canadian Public Policy* 16(3), at pp. 284–297. The Strachan quote at p. 195 is from Alex Strachan, "Eight Ways to Improve Canadian TV," *The Vancouver Sun,* October 21, 2002. For information on the South Korean cinema quota, noted at p. 196, see Hyungjin Kim, "The Audiovisual Sector in Another Part of the World," Speech to the WTO Audiovisual Industry Seminar, July 4, 2001, available from the WTO Web site: www.wto.org. The 1965 research paper on domestic TV Canadian content rules referred to at p. 198 was later updated and published in 1968: see Peter S. Grant, "The Regulation of Program Content in Canadian Television: An Introduction," (1968) 11 *Canadian Public Administration* 322. For the current CRTC Canadian content rules, see Peter S. Grant and Anthony Keenleyside, *Canadian Broadcasting Regulatory Handbook,* 6th ed. (Toronto: McCarthy Tétrault, 2002), at pp. 244–246 and 723–737. For the chronology of CTV's licensing and renewal decisions from 1961 to 2002, see Peter S. Grant et al., *Regulatory Guide to Canadian Television Programming Services* (Toronto: McCarthy Tétrault, 2002), at pp. 21–23. The Supreme Court of Canada decision referred to at pp. 201–202 is reported as *CTV Television Network v. CRTC,* [1982] 1 S.C.R. 530, 134 D.L.R. (3d) 193. For a journalist's recounting of the CRTC dispute with CTV, see Susan Gittins, *CTV: The Television Wars* (Toronto: Stoddart, 1999), at pp. 151–168.

For the Humphreys quotes at p. 204, see Humphreys, *Mass Media,* at p. 259. For the 2001 study referred to at p. 206, see *Study on the Provisions Existing Within the Member States and the European Economic Area to Implement Chapter III of the TWF Directive* (European Institute for the Media, May 2001). For the European survey noted at p. 207, see European Commission Press Release, November 8, 2002, at http://europa.eu.int. For the 2001 ABA report noted at p. 209, see "Review of the Australian Content Standard," issues paper, November 2001, at www.aba.gov.au/tv/content/ozcont/review_2001/index.htm. For the December 2002 ABA conclusion noted at p. 210, see *Australian Content Standard for Commercial Television,* December 19, 2002, at www.aba.gov.au.

For the 1960 FCC order referred to at p. 212, see *En Banc Programming Inquiry,* 44 F.C.C. 2303 (1960). For 1990 legislation referred to at p. 213, see *Children's Television Act of 1990,* Pub. L. No. 101–437, 104 Stat. 996 (codified at 47 U.S.C. ss. 303(a), (b), 394). For the FCC decision on children's educational programming referred to at p. 213, see Federal Communications Commission, *Report and Order, Policies and Rules Concerning Children's Television Programming,* FCC 96-335, adopted August 8, 1996, MM Docket No. 93-48. For the three-year review noted at p. 214, see Federal Communications Commission, "Staff Report on Three-Year Review of Broadcaster Implementation of the Children's Television Rules," January 18, 2001. For the mixed reviews referred to at p. 214, see "Children's TV Comes Up Short in Study by U.S. Researchers," *The Globe and Mail,* June 29, 1999, and Daniel McGinn, "Why TV Is Good for Kids," cover story in *Newsweek,* November 1, 2002. For the connection between the children's programming order and the award of digital spectrum, see Glen O. Robinson, "The Electronic First Amendment: An Essay for the New Age," (2000) 47 *Duke Law Journal* 899 at 917. For the "most sacred cow" quote at p. 215, see Robinson, "The Electronic First Amendment," at p. 938. For the critique referred to at p. 216, see William Stanbury, *Canadian Content Regulations: the Intrusive State at Work* (Vancouver: Fraser Institute, 1998), at p. 18. For the 1997 U.S. Supreme Court decision referred to at p. 217, see *Turner II,* (1997) 117 S. Ct. 1174. For a discussion of the application of First Amendment theories to government subsidies to the arts, see Kathleen M. Sullivan, "Artistic Freedom, Public Funding, and the Constitution," chapter 2 in Stephen Benedict, ed., *Public Money and the Muse* (New York: Norton, 1991), at pp. 80–95.

CHAPTER 10: SPENDING RULES

For a history of the British "quota quickies," see Linda Wood, "Low-budget British Films in the 1930s," chapter 6 in *The British Cinema Book,* 2nd ed. (London: BFI, 2001), at pp. 53–59. For the contemporary critic referred to at p. 222, see Lawrence Napper, "A Despicable Tradition? Quota-quickies in the 1930s," chapter 5 in *The British Cinema Book,* 2nd ed. (London: BFI, 2001), at pp. 45–52. Article 5 of the "Television Without Frontiers" directive, referred to at p. 224, excludes from the calculation transmission time devoted to news, sports events, games, advertising, teletext services and teleshopping. The French requirement referred to at p. 224 specifies that to make an independent production, the broadcaster cannot own the producer, finance the production, or buy the rights to its program for more than four years. For further material on the European and Australian expenditure requirements noted at pp. 224–225, see Carole Tongue, "Public Service Broadcasting: A Study of 8 OECD Countries," in Philip Collins, ed., *Culture or Anarchy? The Future of Public Service Broadcasting* (London: Social Market Foundation, 2002), at pp. 107–142.

For the chronology of CRTC licensing and its current expenditure requirements, see, generally, Peter S. Grant et al., *Regulatory Guide to Canadian Television Programming Services* (Toronto: McCarthy Tétrault, 2002). For the CRTC clarification of what qualifies as an expenditure, referred to at p. 231, see Public Notice CRTC 1993–93, June 22, 1993, available at www.crtc.gc.ca. It is worth noting that the rules did not preclude a licensee from counting a loan or equity investment towards its expenditure requirement, provided that the money is not recouped. If it is recouped, the effect is to return that sum to the pool of funds that must still be spent, not to the broadcaster's general revenue. For the U.K. example noted at p. 231, see Richard Collins, *Television: Policy and Culture* (London: Unwin Hyman, 1990), at pp. 111–112. For the history of the expenditure rules on Canadian free-to-air television services, referred to at p. 232, see Canadian Coalition of Audio-Visual Unions, *The Crisis in Canadian English-Language Drama* (March 2003), at pp. 7–13. For the Tongue quotation at p. 233, see Tongue, "Public Service Broadcasting," at p. 117. For the statistics at pp. 233–234, see Peter S. Grant et al., *Regulatory Guide to*

Canadian Television Programming Services (Toronto: McCarthy Tétrault, 2002), updated with 2002 numbers from the CRTC financial statistics for pay and specialty programming services, available at www.crtc.gc.ca.

CHAPTER 11: NATIONAL OWNERSHIP

For the quotations referred to at p. 237, see Tina W. Chao, Comment, "GATT's Cultural Exemption of Audiovisual Trade: The United States May Have Lost the Battle But Not the War," 17 *University of Pennsylvania Journal of International Economic Law* 1127 (Winter 1996), and Ian M. Rose, Note, "Barring Foreigners from Our Airwaves: An Anachronistic Pothole on the Global Information Highway," 95 *Columbia Law Review* 1188, at 1190 (1995). For a general discussion of the problems of foreign ownership noted at p. 240, see Isaiah A. Litvak, "The Marginalization of Corporate Canada," *Behind the Headlines,* Canadian Institute for International Affairs, vol. 58, no. 2. For the report of the British committee referred to at p. 240, see "Puttnam Warns of Creeping Americanisation in UK TV," *The Guardian,* July 31, 2002. For the MacMillan quotation at p. 241, see Testimony Before the Standing Committee on Canadian Heritage, December 4, 2002. For a further discussion of the reinvestment point made at p. 241, from which these arguments are taken, see *The Business of Culture: The Report of the Advisory Committee on a Cultural Industries Sectoral Strategy* (Toronto: Government of Ontario, 1994), at p. 60.

For a comprehensive review of the CRTC policies on foreign ownership, which includes references to the TSN cases discussed at pp. 243–245, see Grant Buchanan, Monique Lafontaine and Lorne P. Salzman, "Canadian Ownership and Control of Canadian Communications Companies," paper presented at *New Developments in Communications Law and Policy* (Ottawa: Law Society of Upper Canada, Continuing Legal Education, April 26–27, 2002). The Australian decisions relating to CanWest referred to at pp. 245–247 can be found on the website of the Australian Broadcasting Authority, www.aba.gov.au. For additional background on the Rupert Murdoch decisions, see Neil Chenowith, *Rupert Murdoch: The Untold Story of the World's Greatest Media Wizard* (New York: Crown Business, 2001); the Chenowith quotation at p. 248 can be found at p. 61 of his book. In April 1996, the ABA concluded that News Corp. did not control the Seven Network in Australia. For the CRTC decision approving a licence for History Television, referred to at p. 252, see Decision CRTC 96-599, September 4, 1996. For the CRTC decision approving a Category 1 digital licence for Connect, referred to at p. 253, see Decision CRTC 2000-462, December 14, 2000. (Category 1 licences entitled the licensee to niche protection as well as mandatory access to all digital cable and satellite distribution systems.) For the 2003 decision relating to MTV Canada referred to at p. 253, see Decision CRTC 2003-65, February 21, 2003. The Allan Gregg quotations at pp. 255–256 are from an author interview in August 2002. The Richard Green quotation at p. 256 is from an author interview in March 2003. The Canadian publishing data at p. 256 is from Statistics Canada, Culture, Tourism and the Centre for Education Statistics. See also *The Challenge of Change: A Consideration of the Canadian Book Industry,* report of the Standing Committee on Canadian Heritage, April 26, 2002. The Pearson quote at p. 257 is from Patricia Pearson, "Very Tired, Very Tall, But Very, Very Happy," *The National Post,* July 15, 2000.

For a further discussion of the incentives for program selection by foreign owners, noted at p. 258, and the advantages of vertical integration for the companies, see Richard E. Caves, *Creative Industries: Contracts Between Art and Commerce* (Cambridge, MA: Harvard University Press, 2000), at pp. 296 and 324–325. Caves notes that keeping gatekeepers independent of program suppliers enhances choice from the standpoint of consumers. It also clearly enhances diversity of sources of cultural expression. For the Oliver Sacks quotation at p. 259, see Oliver Sacks, *Oaxaca Journal* (Washington: National Geographic, 2002), at p. 3. For the concerns of U.K. producers noted at p. 260, see Darren Waters, "British TV 'Safe from Revolution,'" *BBC Online,* November 13, 2002. The ITC report noted at p. 260 may be found at ITC, "Report on New Communications Bill," November 26, 2002, available from www.itc.org.uk. For further information on the story of Harlequin, noted at p. 261, see Paul Grescoe, *The Merchants of Venus: Inside Harlequin and the Empire of Romance* (Vancouver: Raincoast, 1996).

CHAPTER 12: COMPETITION POLICY

For the story of MCA, see Connie Bruck, *When Hollywood Had a King: The Reign of Lew Wasserman, Who Leveraged Talent into Power and Influence* (New York: Random House, 2003). The quotation at pp. 263–264 is at pp. 15–16. The Flew quotation at p. 265 may be found in Terry Flew, "Broadcasting and the Social Contract," in Marc Raboy, ed., *Global Media Policy in the New Millennium* (Luton: University of Luton Press, 2002). For the Barnett quotation at p. 270, see Steven Barnett, "One Man, One Media?" *The Guardian,* May 8, 2002. For the Irving decision and its aftermath, referred to at p. 271, see *Re New Brunswick Broadcasting Co. and CRTC* (1984), 13 D.L.R. (4th) 77, [1984] 2 F.C. 410, summarized in Peter S. Grant, *Canadian Communications Law and Policy* (Toronto: Law Society of Upper Canada, 1988), at p. 901. For the CRTC decisions approving the licence renewals referred to at pp. 272–273, see Decision CRTC 2001-457, August 2, 2001 (CTV) and Decision CRTC 2001–458, August 2, 2001 (CanWest Global), at Appendix I. For the Jan Ravensbergen quotations at p. 273, see Proceedings of the Standing Committee on Canadian Heritage, December 4, 2002. Ravensbergen gave evidence on behalf of the Newspaper Guild of Canada. For the history of the studio anti-trust cases noted at p. 276, see Barry R. Litman, *The Motion Picture Mega-Industry* (Boston: Allyn and Bacon, 1998), at pp. 2–21 and 61–73. For the 2003 brief noted at p. 277, see "Joint Comments of WGA et al. to the Federal Communications Commission, Washington, D.C.," January 2, 2003. For a review of the European rules on independent production referred to at pp. 277–279, see Carole Tongue, "Public Service Broadcasting: A Study of 8 OECD Countries," in Philip Collins, ed., *Culture or Anarchy? The Future of Public Service Broadcasting* (London: Social Market Foundation, 2002), at pp. 107–142. For the Canadian rules noted at pp. 280–281, see Peter S. Grant et al., *Regulatory Guide to Canadian Television Programming Services* (Toronto: McCarthy Tétrault, 2002).

For the U.S. survey noted at p. 283, see Tasneem Chipty, "Vertical Integration, Market Foreclosure and Consumer Welfare in the Cable Television Industry," *The American Economic Review*, vol. 91, no. 3 (June 2001). For the statistics on the six entities noted at p. 283, see Joint Comments of WGA et al. to FCC, January 2, 2003. For the OFT decision on BSkyB noted at p. 285, see U.K. Office of Fair Trading, "BSkyB: The Outcome of the OFT's Competition Act Investigation," December 2002, at www.oft.gov.uk.

For the change in the CRTC policy on cross-ownership of cable companies and program services, see Public Notice CRTC 2001-66-1, August 24, 2001. For the regulation prohibiting undue preference noted at p. 287, see section 9 of the *Broadcasting Distribution Regulations*, set out in Peter S. Grant et al., *Canadian Broadcasting Regulatory Handbook*, 6th ed. (Toronto: McCarthy Tétrault, 2002), at p. 165. In the 2000 round, the CRTC added a new concept, namely, the issuance of licences for new services (Category 2 digital services) that would enjoy neither niche protection nor guaranteed carriage by cable or satellite distributors. However, as a safeguard against potential discrimination arising from cross-ownership, it ruled that cable or satellite distributors must carry at least five unaffiliated Category 2 digital services for each affiliated service. Hundreds of these licences were granted. Only a few dozen managed to negotiate their way onto cable or satellite systems. Several of those subsequently ran into financial difficulty. For a discussion of the U.K. Net Book Agreement, referred to at p. 288, see Caves, *Creative Industries*, at pp. 149–150. See also "Book Pricing Pact in Britain Near Collapse," *The New York Times*, September 29, 1995, p. D4, noted in Caves, *Creative Industries*. For the Canadian regulation noted at p. 289, see *Book Importation Regulations*, SOR/99-324. For the quotation noted at pp. 290–291, see Petros Iosifidis, "The Limits of Competition Policy," *Intermedia*, April 2002, vol. 30, no. 2, pp. 22–25. The statement of the commissioner of competition noted at p. 291 was made to the Standing Committee on Canadian Heritage on May 7, 2002.

CHAPTER 13: SUBSIDIES

For further background on the New Zealand subsidy of the Rings episodes, noted at pp. 292–293, see "Lord of the Rings: The Money Magic Behind NZ's $675 Million Epic," *New Zealand Listener*, October 21–27, 2000. For the Maule quotation at p. 294, see Christopher Maule, *Overview of Trade and Cultural Conference*, November 28, 2001, Centre for Trade Policy and Law, Ottawa, available at www.carleton.ca/ctpl/. For the Stanbury quotation at p. 294, see William Stanbury, *Canadian Content Regulations: The Intrusive State at Work* (Vancouver: Fraser Institute, 1998). For the Dale quote at p. 295, see Martin Dale, *The Movie Game*, at p. 117. For a recent summary of film subsidies in Europe, from which the material at pp. 298–304 was derived, see Tim Dams and Colin Brown, "The United States of Cinema," *Screen Digest*, December 23, 2002. On the French subsidy system, see also the report of the Centre national de la cinématographie, *Results 2001*, no. 283, May 2002. For the New Zealand information noted at p. 300, see the Film New Zealand Web site at www.filmnz.com. For the Kim quotation at p. 304, see Hyungjin

Kim, "The Audiovisual Sector in Another Part of the World," speech to the WTO Audiovisual Industry Seminar, July 4, 2001, available from the WTO Web site: www.wto.org. For the Macerola quote at p. 307, see Doug Saunders, "Chaos in the Culture Industry," *The Globe and Mail*, April 25, 1998. For the Fansten and Figgis quotes at p. 309, see Dale, *The Movie Game*, at pp. 116 and 117. For the Dale quote at p. 309, see Martin Dale, *The Movie Game*, at p. 128. For the *Screen Digest* comment at p. 311, see Tom Clark, "Soft Money—Germany," *Screen Digest*, December 23, 2002. For the Walker quote at p. 311, see Alexander Walker, "In the Grip of the Money Men," *The Evening Standard*, July 8, 2002. The Hancock and Clarkson quotes at p. 311 are based on author interviews in August and October 2002. The del Toro quote at p. 312 is from Xan Brooks, "First Steps in Latin," *The Guardian*, July 19, 2002. The Finland example at p. 312 was based on an interview with Kimmo Aulake in March 2003. Also see Jacob Neiiendam, "Nordic Films Fight Off Hollywood Releases," *Screendaily.com*, April 9, 2003. For the Platt and Martin quotes at p. 313, see Sandra Martin, "Bringing Home the Gold," *The Globe and Mail*, November 29, 2000.

CHAPTER 14: THE TOOL KIT AT WORK

For the David Suzuki quote at p. 315, see Steven Shrybman, *The World Trade Organization: A Citizen's Guide* (Toronto: James Lorimer, 2001), at p. 40. For the Tyler Cowen books referred to at p. 317, see *In Praise of Commercial Culture* (Cambridge, MA: Harvard University Press, 1998), and *Creative Destruction: How Globalization Is Changing the World's Cultures* (Princeton: Princeton University Press, 2002). For his critique of French film policy, noted at p. 318, see Tyler Cowen, "French Kiss-Off: How Protectionism Has Hurt French Films," *Reason Online*, July 1998, available at www.reason.com/9807/fe.cowen.html. For critical reviews of Cowen's books, see Clifford Geertz, "Off the Menu," *The New Republic*, February 17, 2003, at pp. 27–30; and Jacob Weisberg, "Art Heaven." *Slate Magazine*, December 13, 1998. For the 2000 production and box-office numbers relating to French films noted at p. 319, see Screen Digest, "Top 20 Countries Ranked by Production Investment in Feature Films, 1999, 2000," available at www.afc.gov.au/GTP/acompinvestment.html, and Centre nationale de cinématographie, *Results 2001*, No. 283, May 2002. See also "Amélie Sparks French Movie Export Boom," *Toronto Star*, December 24, 2002. Led by France's performance, 2001 was also an exceptional year for European cinema generally, with U.S. films dropping to only a 66 per cent market share across Europe. See European Audiovisual Observatory, Press Release, March 22, 2002, available at www.obs.coe.int. For the Stanbury critique at p. 320, see William Stanbury, *Canadian Content Regulations: The Intrusive State at Work* (Vancouver: Fraser Institute, 1998). The Vogel quote at p. 320 is from Harold L. Vogel, *Entertainment Industry Economics: A Guide for Financial Analysis*, 5th ed. (Cambridge: Cambridge University Press, 2001). For a recent analysis of the problems of Canadian drama, from which some of the points at p. 322 are drawn, see Canadian Coalition of Audio-Visual Unions, *The Crisis in Canadian Drama*, March 17, 2003, at pp. 22–24. For the quotation on French-language drama at p. 322, see Guy Fournier, "What About Tomorrow? A Report on French-language Drama," May 2003, at p. 1, available from the

CRTC Web site at www.crtc.gc.ca. For the parliamentary committee quotation at p. 324, see the Report of the Standing Committee on Canadian Heritage, *Our Cultural Sovereignty: The Second Century of Canadian Broadcasting* (Ottawa: House of Commons, Canada, 2003), at p. 274. For the critic referred to at p. 324, see Christopher Maule, *Overview of Trade and Cultural Conference*, November 28, 2001, Centre for Trade Policy and Law, Ottawa, p. 16, available at www.carleton.ca/ctpl/culture_issues.htm. For drama ratings in Europe, see European Audiovisual Observatory, Press Release, October 9, 2001, at www.obs.coe.int.

CHAPTER 15: TECHNOLOGY

For the Corcoran quote at p. 330, see Terence Corcoran, "Free Markets in Broadcasting," *The Globe and Mail,* November 23, 1996. For the Kimsey quote at p. 330, see James Kimsey, "AOL Founder: Censor the Net? Ha!" *Wired* (online), April 24, 2000. For the Scott and Elder quote at p. 330, see Sheridan Scott and David Elder, "Changing Communications Regulation in the Information Age," *Internet and E-Commerce Law in Canada,* vol. 2, no. 8 (October 2001). For the Maule quote at p. 331, see Christopher Maule, *Overview of Trade and Cultural Conference*, November 28, 2001, Centre for Trade Policy and Law, Ottawa, p. 5, available at www.carleton.ca/ctpl/culture_issues.htm. For the Fagan quote at p. 331, see Drew Fagan, "Canada's Cultural Protections Are Bound to Come Tumbling Down," *The Globe and Mail,* April 30, 2002. For the Guehenno quote at p. 331, see Jean-Marie Guehenno, "The Topology of Sovereignty," transcript of a presentation at the 1997 Virtual Diplomacy Conference, April 1, 1997. For the 2003 BSkyB numbers, see the SKY factbook 2003 at www.media.corporate-ir.net/media_files/lse/bsy.uk/reports/SKY_FULL.pdf. and the ITC Web site at www.itc.org.uk/latest_news/press_releases/release.asp?release_id=630. For the CRTC decision awarding a DTH licence to *Power DirecTV,* referred to at p. 333, see Decision CRTC 95–902, December 20, 1995. For the 1993 statement by the CRTC noted at p. 334, see *Structural Public Hearing,* Public Notice CRTC 1993–74, June 3, 1993, reproduced in Peter S. Grant et al., *Canadian Broadcasting Regulatory Handbook,* 6th ed. (Toronto: McCarthy Tétrault, 2002), at p. 487. For the critic referred to at p. 337, see Colin Sparks, "Is There a Global Public Sphere?" chapter 6 in Daya Kishan Thussu, ed., *Electronic Empires: Global Media and Local Resistance* (London: Arnold, 1998), pp. 108–124, at p. 113. For the Marsden quote at p. 337, see Christopher T. Marsden, "Pluralism in the Multi-Channel Market: Suggestions for Regulatory Scrutiny," 4 *International Journal of Communications Law and Policy* (Winter 1999/2000), at p. 23, available at www.ijclp.org. For the critic referred to and the Thussu quote at p. 337, see Colin Sparks, "Is There a Global Public Sphere?" For the DTH penetration numbers at p. 338, see Pacome Revillon and Karine Gallula, "Satellite TV and Video Services, World Survey and Prospects to 2010, A New Media Is Born," Euroconsult Research Report, 2002. For the audience share of out-of-country signals in Europe, see European Audiovisual Observatory, *TV Audience Market Share of Foreign Channels (2001),* Table T.8.4.

For the Magaziner quote at p. 340, see John Geddes, "Cultural Resistance Futile, Clinton Adviser Says," *Financial Post,* July 24, 1997. For the CRTC internet exemption order referred to at p. 342, see Broadcasting Public Notice CRTC 1999-84, May 17, 1999. The exemption order itself was issued in Public Notice CRTC 1999-197, December 17, 1999. For the amendment to the act referred to at p. 344, see Bill c-11, formerly Bill c-48, received royal assent on December 17, 2002, proclaimed in force March 21, 2003. For the CRTC report referred to at p. 344, see *Internet Retransmission; Report to the Governor General in Council Pursuant to Order in Council P.C. 2002-1043,* Broadcasting Public Notice CRTC 2003-3, January 17, 2003. For the ineffectiveness of border controls, see ibid., at Appendix D. For the quotation on p. 345, see *The Economist,* August 11, 2001, at p. 9. For the RIAA numbers at p. 347, see Dennis K. Berman and Anna Wilde Mathews, "Is the Record Industry About to Bust Your Teenager?" *The Wall Street Journal,* January 28, 2003. For the Anders and Bart quotes at p. 348, see the tapes and transcripts of the PBS *Frontline* program, "The Monster That Ate Hollywood," which first aired on PBS stations in the United States on November 2, 2001. The complete transcripts of the interviews made for this program can be accessed from www.pbs.org/wgbh/pages/frontline/shows/hollywood. For a further discussion of the pattern of traffic on "blogs," noted at p. 349, see Clay Shirky, "Power Laws, Weblogs, and Inequality," www.shirky.com, February 8, 2003. As noted there, a small set of Webloggers account for a majority of the traffic in the Weblog world. Instead of being governed by a bell curve distribution, Web site page views appear to be governed by a "power law distribution" where the value for the Nth position will be 1/N. For the CRTC licensing of video-on-demand services, referred to at p. 350, see Peter S. Grant et al., *Regulatory Guide to Canadian Television Programming Services* (Toronto, McCarthy Tétrault, 2002), at pp. 863–864. For the Degrassi use of new technology referred to at p. 351, see Kevin Marron, "Degrassi Encore Takes TV to the Next Generation," *The Globe and Mail,* March 13, 2002.

CHAPTER 16: TRADE WARS

For the Puttnam quote at p. 353, see David Puttnam with Neil Watson, *The Undeclared War: The Struggle for Control of the World's Film Industry* (London: Harper-Collins, 1997), at p. 357. For further background on the evolution of GATT and the theory of comparative advantage, discussed at pp. 356–357, see Michael J. Trebilcock and Robert Howse, *The Regulation of International Trade,* 2nd ed. (London: Routledge, 1999), at pp. 3–5, and Alan O. Sykes, "Comparative Advantage and the Normative Economics of International Trade Policy," (1998) 1 *Journal of International Economic Law* 49–82. See also Colin Hoskins et al., *Global Television and Film: An Introduction to the Economics of the Business* (Oxford: Oxford University Press, 1997), for a discussion of the economic factors relating to film and television programs that have led to the U.S. dominance in audiovisual trade. For a discussion of the 1960s submission referred to at p. 357, see W. Ming Shao, "Is There No Business Like Show Business?" (1995) 20 *Yale Journal of International Law* 105 at 112–113. For the Mitterand quotation at p. 358, see David Puttnam, *The Undeclared War,* at p. 7. For the Jack Valenti quote at p. 359, see official statement issued by the MPAA, quoted in Puttnam, ibid., at p. 343. For a study by the European parliament on the MAI, noted at p. 360, see *Report of the Culture Committee on the OECD Multilateral Agreement on*

Investment (MAI), adopted by the European parliament, spring 1998, Document A4-0073/98. For the Supreme Court of Canada case noted at p. 361, see *Capital Cities Communications Inc. et al. v. CRTC*, [1978] 2 S.C.R. 141, 81 D.L.R. (3d) 609. For an example of the criticism referred to at p. 362, see Steven Shrybman, *The World Trade Organization: A Citizen's Guide* (Toronto: James Lorimer, 2001), at pp. 32–33.

For further background on the periodicals dispute described at pp. 362–368, see Glenn A. Gottselig, "Canada and Culture: Can Current Cultural Policies be Sustained in a Global Trade Regime?" 5 *International Journal of Communications Law and Policy* (Summer 2000), available at www.ijclp. org, and Keith Acheson and Christopher Maule, *Much Ado About Culture: North American Trade Disputes* (Ann Arbor: University of Michigan Press, 1999), at pp. 186–205. For the Quill quotation at p. 366, see Greg Quill, "Protecting Canada's Magazines," *Toronto Star,* August 13, 1998, p. A23. For the WTO decision referred to at p. 366, see WTO Appellate Body Decision on Periodicals, Document WT/DS31/AB/R, available from the WTO Web site at www.wto.org. The arch-critic referred to at p. 368 was Maude Barlow, chairwoman of the fiercely isolationist Council of Canadians. For the quotation from Michael Elliot, noted at p. 368, see Simon Houpt, "New Time Canada Editor Faces Steep Learning Curve," *The Globe and Mail,* February 26, 2003, at p. B12.

For the Rawlco–Maclean Hunter decision referred to at p. 369, see Decision CRTC 94-284, June 6, 1994. For the CMT deletion order referred to at p. 369, see Public Notice CRTC 94-61, June 6, 1994. In 1997, the CRTC changed its deletion policy, indicating that it would no longer drop any foreign service from the Eligible List unless that service changed its program format to become competitive with an existing Canadian service. See Public Notice CRTC 1997-96, July 22, 1997, at para. 29. For further details on the history of country music in Canada, described at p. 370, see Rick Jackson, *Encylopedia of Canadian Country Music* (Kingston: Quarry Press, 1996). The country-music television dispute is also described in Keith Acheson and Christopher Maule, *Much Ado About Culture: North American Trade Disputes* (Ann Arbor: University of Michigan Press, 1999), at pp. 206–219. At p. 215, the authors argue that Canadian policy permitting Country Music Television (Canada) is inconsistent with the Canadian policy prohibiting split-run magazines. However, they base this on a misapprehension of how the channel operates. Unlike split-run magazines, the Canadian channel is controlled by Canadians and the entire content—both foreign music videos and Canadian music videos—is selected by Canadian management. No material is provided by the U.S. minority interest other than branding interstitials; all the music videos are obtained directly from the record companies.

For the USTR December 2000 proposal referred to at p. 372, see the USTR Web site at www.ustr.gov. For the analysts noted at p. 373, see Glenn A. Gottselig, "Canada and Culture: Can Current Cultural Policies be Sustained in a Global Trade Regime?" 5 *International Journal of Communications Law and Policy* (Summer 2000), available at www.ijclp.org, and Christopher Maule, *Overview of Trade and Cultural Conference,* November 28, 2001, Centre for Trade Policy and Law, Ottawa, available at www.carleton.ca/ctpl/culture_issues.htm. For the EBU commentary noted at p. 374, see European Broadcasting Union, *Audiovisual services and GATS: EBU Comments on US negotiating proposals of December 2000,* April 12, 2001, available at www.ebu.ch. For the quotation by Valenti noted at p. 375, see "Statement by Jack Valenti on the Free Trade Agreement between the U.S. and Chile, December 11, 2002," available at www.mpaa.org. For an analysis of the Chile and Singapore agreements, see Ivan Bernier, "A Comparative Analysis of the Chile–U.S. and Singapore–U.S. Free Trade Agreements with particular reference to their impact in the Cultural Sector," April 2003, available at www.mcc.gouv.qc.ca/international/diversite-culturelle/chronique.htm. The proposed agreements also provide that duties on the importation of cultural goods would be measured on the value of the media not the intellectual property. The Chile agreement also stipulates that no compulsory copyright licence will apply to retransmission on the Internet, an MPAA goal following the iCraveTV dispute in Canada. For the quotation by the MPAA noted on p. 375, see "Statement by Jack Valenti on the U.S.–Singapore Free Trade Agreement, January 17, 2003," available at www.mpaa.org. The press releases of the EIC referred to at p. 376 can also be found on the MPAA Web site. For the Flew quotation at p. 377, see Terry Flew, "Broadcasting and the Social Contract," in Marc Raboy, ed., *Global Media Policy in the New Millennium* (Luton: University of Luton Press, 2002). For the Puttnam quotation at p. 377, see David Puttnam, *The Undeclared War,* at p. 357.

CHAPTER 17: A NEW DIRECTION

The Paddington quotations at p. 378 are from an author interview in October 2002. The acronym TIDCO, referred to at p. 378, stands for the Tourism and Industrial Development Company of Trinidad and Tobago Limited. For the Merkin quotation at p. 379, see William Merkin, "United States Trade Policy and Culture: Future Strategies," *World Culture Report 2000, Cultural Diversity, Conflict and Pluralism* (Paris: UNESCO, 2000), at p. 68. For the Elie Cohen quotation at p. 380, see Elie Cohen, "Globalization and Cultural Diversity," pp. 66–91. For the UNESCO quotation at p. 381, see Mexico City Declaration on Cultural Policies, World Conference on Cultural Policies Mexico City; 1982, Articles 4, 10, 6 and 8. For the SAGIT brief referred to at p. 384, see *New Strategies for Culture and Trade: Canadian Culture in a Global World,* Cultural Industries Sectoral Advisory Group on International Trade, February, 1999, available at www.infoexport.gc.ca/trade-culture. For the civil-society quotation at p. 388, see INCD Closing Statement, Lucerne, September 23, 2001. For the UNESCO Declaration referred to at p. 388, see www.unesco.org/confgen/press_rel/021101_clt_diversity.shtml. The UNESCO text also drew force from an earlier statement adopted in the fall of 1999 by all fifteen of the European Union culture ministers, directing EU trade negotiator Pascal Lamy that all countries must retain the sovereignty to enact cultural policies. For the Throsby quotation at p. 390, see David Throsby, *Economics and Culture* (Cambridge: Cambridge University Press, 2001), at p. 133. For the Bernier quotations at pp. 391–392, see "A New International Instrument on Cultural Diversity: Questions and Answers," *Culturelink* 35, 2001. For the MPAA comment referred to at p. 395, see the Web site of the Valencia conference, at www.audiovisual-forum.net/backgroundmaterials/articleoo.htm. For the Dymond and Hart quotation at p. 395, see William A. Dymond and Michael M. Hart, *Abundant Paradox: The Trade and Culture Debate*, November 28, 2001, Centre for Trade Policy and Law, Ottawa, available at www.carleton.ca/ctpl/. The impact of the so-called "necessity test," referred to at p. 396, on other service sectors has been described by an investigative reporter who disclosed a confidential WTO document on the matter in 2001. See Greg Palast, "GATS Got His Tongue," in *The Best Democracy Money Can Buy* (London: Pluto Press, 2002), at pp. 67–72. The WTO document is available at www.corpwatch.org. For the Francophonie statement quoted at p. 397, see *Declaration de Bayreuth;* October 20, 2002: "nous sommes en conséquence décidés à contribuer activement à l'adoption par l'UNESCO d'une convention internationale sur la diversité culturelle, consacrant le droit des Etats et des gouvernements à maintenir, établir et développer des politiques de soutien à la culture et à la diversité culturelle. Son objet doit être de définir un droit applicable en matière de diversité culturelle. Cette convention doit aussi souligner l'ouverture aux autres cultures et à leurs expressions." For the Dymond and Hart quotation at p. 398, see Dymond and Hart, *Abundant Paradox.* For the Maule quotation at p. 398, see Christopher Maule, *Overview of Trade and Culture Conference,* November 28, 2001, Centre for Trade Policy and Law, Ottawa, available at www.carleton.ca/ctpl/. For the Kagan quotation at p. 399, see Robert Kagan, "Power and Weakness," *Policy Review* No. 113, June 2002. For the "bully on the block" quotation at p. 399, see U.S. House Armed Services Committee, quoted in David Armstrong, "Dick Cheney's Song of America," *Harper's,* October 2002, p. 78. For the McCaskill and Herman quotations at p. 400, see Heather Scoffield, "Ottawa Seeks Global Deal to End Cultural Trade Wars," *The Globe and Mail,* October 20, 1999. For the INCP research paper quoted at p. 404, see Special Policy Research Team on the Governance Issues of an International Instrument on Cultural Diversity, *Options and Issues for the Implementation of an Instrument: Depositary, Mechanism and Strategy* (INCP, July 2002), at p. 14.

CHAPTER 18: ROOM TO GROW
For the Jain quotation at p. 408, see Ajit Jain, "What Does It Profit a Nation," *The Globe and Mail,* February 28, 2001, p. A13. For the quotation at p. 410, see Robert W. McChesney and John Nichols, *Our Media Not Theirs: The Democratic Struggle Against Corporate Media* (New York: Seven Stories Press, 2002), at p. 49. For the Stone quotation at p. 412, see Philip Stone, "The Canadian Approach to Audiovisual Services: Domestic Policies and International Trade," Background Paper for UNCTAD Experts Conference on Audiovisual Services, November 13–15, 2002. For the Gwyn quotation at p. 416, see Richard Gwyn, "No Apologies Owed for Nurturing Culture," *Toronto Star,* February 12, 1997. For a discussion of the greater profit potential of drama compared with reality shows, see David Blum, "Why Reality Won't Rule the Fall," *The New York Times,* May 4, 2003.

ACKNOWLEDGEMENTS

A S A CANADIAN LAWYER working in the trenches of cultural and communications policy for many years, I have had an opportunity to meet some very creative people and to act for dozens of clients in virtually every sector of the cultural industries. This book is based in large part on that experience, coupled with further interviews and research carried out with the help of my co-author, Chris Wood. Accordingly, we have many people to thank.

First and foremost are my partners at McCarthy Tétrault, who gave me a five-month sabbatical in 2002 to work on this book and who have supported my continued work on it since then. I particularly want to thank my partners Grant Buchanan, Tom Heintzman, Hank Intven and Lorne Salzman, each of whom was involved with me in one or more of the cases referred to in the book. I also owe a debt to a number of clients for whom I have acted in particular matters over the years and who have enlarged my understanding of the cultural industries. They include Alliance Atlantis Communications Inc., Astral Media Inc., the Association of Canadian Publishers, Bell ExpressVu, the British Broadcasting Corporation, the Canadian Magazine Publishers Association, the Canadian Retransmission Collective, Craig Media Inc., the CRTC, the Directors Guild of Canada, RAI Corporation, the Government of Sri Lanka, Standard Radio Inc., Telesat Canada and many others.

For a number of years, I have been a member of the Cultural Industries Sectoral Advisory Group on International Trade (SAGIT), which advises the Canadian minister of international trade on cultural policy and trade issues. I would like to thank my fellow members on the SAGIT for their interest and support, as well as the officials at the Department of Canadian Heritage and the Department of Foreign Affairs and International Trade who have ably assisted the SAGIT over the years. In that regard, I want to acknowledge the particular support of the following present or former SAGIT members: Ivan Bernier, André Bureau, Michael MacMillan, Elizabeth McDonald, Scott McIntyre, Ron Osborne, Robert Pilon, Ken Stein and Richard Stursberg, and the following present or former government officials: Jean-Pierre Blais, Cathy Dickson, John Drummond, David Dubinski, Serge Frechette, John Gero, Louis Hamel, Janette Mark, Anne McCaskill, Barbara Motzney, Philip Stone and John Weekes.

Among the persons interviewed for this book were the following: Kimmo Aulake, Jacques Behanzin, Adheera Bodasing, Wayne Clarkson, Mike Dearham, Steve DeNure, James Early, Megan Elliott, Richard Green, Allan Gregg, David Hancock, Elizabeth Le Hot, Ellis Jacob, Avril Joffe, Al Litvak, Victor Loewy, Japan Mthembu, Bruce Paddington, Jeff Sackman, Linda Schuyler, Rafael Segovia, Stephen Stohn, Peter Sussman, Yvon Thiec and Carole Tongue. To each of them we express our thanks.

Finally, we wish to thank our families for their forbearance and support. On my side, I want to thank my wife, Grace Westcott, and our four children, Kristin, Tom, Rory and Robbie, for their constant encouragement. And for his part, Chris Wood wishes to thank his wife, Beverley Wood, for her understanding, patience and enthusiasm.

Needless to say, the views expressed by the authors in this book are entirely our own and do not necessarily reflect those of McCarthy Tétrault, its clients, or any other individuals or organizations referred to.

PETER S. GRANT

INDEX

ABOUT
THE
AUTHORS

PETER S. GRANT is a senior partner at McCarthy Tétrault, Canada's largest law firm, and the head of its communications and entertainment law group in Toronto. A prize-winning graduate of the Faculty of Law, University of Toronto, Mr. Grant was called to the Ontario bar in 1969. He is the author of numerous articles and publications, including standard references in the broadcasting field. Mr. Grant has pioneered the field of communications law in Canada, and over the years has acted for numerous radio and television broadcasters, pay and specialty programming services, cable and satellite distribution undertakings, and producers and creators of film and television programs. He has also acted for numerous firms and associations in the publishing and music industries, and has led a number of cultural industry task forces. Mr. Grant is an expert on international communications law and cultural policy, and has been a speaker or rapporteur at a number of international conferences on the issue of culture, trade law and globalization. Mr. Grant lives in Toronto with his wife, Grace Westcott, and four children.

CHRIS WOOD is a writer and broadcaster living in Vancouver, Canada. A native of Hamilton, Ontario, his career began in private radio in 1972. Since then he has written continuously for private and public radio, newspapers, television, magazines and the Internet as well as several books. For many years, Mr. Wood held a series of senior positions at *Maclean's*, Canada's national newsmagazine, including National Editor and Business Editor. He has won awards for his radio documentaries, investigative journalism and, with his wife Beverley Wood, the young adult novel *DogStar*. At different times he has lived in Central America, Japan and the United States, as well as on both the east and west coasts of Canada and in its media and cultural capital, Toronto. After repatriating from Texas to Canada's west coast in 1993, he and his wife lived for eight years aboard a motor trawler before moving ashore. The two now share adjoining work spaces at their media development company, White Dog Creative Inc., housed in a Vancouver loft. Recent projects include seminars, sequels to the best-selling *DogStar* and a new work of public policy scholarship for popular audiences, *America for Aliens*.